From Terrorism to World Peace

From Terrorism to World Peace

by

Charles W. Meister, Ph.D.

NEW FALCON PUBLICATIONS
TEMPE, ARIZONA, U.S.A.

International Standard Book Number: 1-56184-168-4
Library of Congress Catalog Card Number: 2002105421

First Edition 2002

Cover by Amanda Fisher

The paper used in this publication meets the minimum requirements of the American National Standard for Permanence of Paper for Printed Library Materials Z39.48-1984

Address all inquiries to:
NEW FALCON PUBLICATIONS
1739 East Broadway Road #1-277
Tempe, AZ 85282 U.S.A.
(or)
320 East Charleston Blvd. #204-286
Las Vegas, NV 89104 U.S.A.
website: http://www.newfalcon.com
email: info@newfalcon.com

TABLE OF CONTENTS

CHAPTER I

TERRORISM & DIVISIVE RELIGION: JUSTIFYING KILLING HUMANS

The destruction of the World Trade Center towers on 9/11 (September 11, 2001) shows at once the cause and the solution of the main dilemma of modern existence. Divisive religion—best seen today in terrorism—says that if you harm or kill innocent people, you will somehow thereby please God. Unitive religion—best seen today in the courageous actions of hundreds of firefighters, police, and volunteers who gave their lives to save other lives—states that your love of God is best seen when you help fellow human beings, considering all humans as God's children. This book describes how we can make giant strides towards achieving world peace by replacing divisive religion with unitive religion.

Osama bin Laden had no idea how quickly he would unify the United States in its defense. Crisis bring out deep values. Suddenly America's heroes were not athletes or movie stars but those intrepid volunteers on 9/11. America's loss was genuine. We all felt as if we had lost our own family members. And indeed we had. The common bond uniting us as one family proved to be far deeper than our petty social, political, or religious differences. What we prized now was the sanctity of all human life. Now we know that we are all members of one family, the family of God.

This recognition is a tribute to America's religious leaders, teachers, and families—the forces which mold an entire culture. For example, prisoners in Louisiana, working at 40 cents an hour, raised $11,000 in three weeks to help the families of those lost in the 9/11 attacks. Pop music stars and professional athletes modestly played down their popularity in comparison with recognition for America's newly designated heroes. Jesus said, "Greater love has no one than this, to give up your life for your neighbor." Our newest wake-up call can inspire us to use terrorist attacks to show us how to structure a world order of peace and justice.

What is Terrorism?

The word "terror" comes from the Latin *terrere,* "to cause to tremble." Fear is employed as an even more potent weapon than bullets or bombs. A good example is the anthrax scare in the United States in 2001. Few lives were lost, but millions of Americans were confused and frightened. Whatever his evil nature, Osama bin Laden can be called "a master of fear."

Attacks upon airports, bombs exploding on civilian flights, and the taking of civilians as hostages have become regular features of modern life. Since the terrorism is international in scope, measures to combat it must also be international, to be effective.

Goals of Terrorism

What are the terrorist's goals? To spread confusion and fear, to seize power, or to acquire a soapbox for expressing an opinion on a controversial issue. A major hostage event is a huge television production. Persons sidetracked by life suddenly see themselves on giant screens. One goal is to provoke the opposition into violent reaction, engendering sympathy and providing an excuse for further terrorism. Some goals seem minor, but are still serious. These include disrupting normal life, inconveniencing large numbers of people, or destroying a people's confidence in their government.

Mark Juergensmeyer, an authority on terrorism, says that radical religious movements in *all* world religions share certain common features: They reject compromises with more tolerant approaches to religion. They refuse to respect the boundaries which secular laws have placed on religion. They reject any growths or changes upon what they perceive to be their religion's original intent. And they feel that the decline of modern morality shows that in the eternal cosmic struggle between the forces of Evil and Good, they alone represent the Good.[1]

Terrorism acts are puzzling to those outside the movement, but wholly understandable to those within the movement. Terrorists prefer war to peace because war justifies the use of violence, and "violence, in turn, offers the illusion of power."[2]

Sometimes terrorism is a response to humiliation. When a group feels frustrated, it often tends to aggress. In Japan the members of Aum Shinrikyo released the nerve gas sarin into Tokyo subways when they felt that the police were closing in on them. The Muslim terrorist group Hamas broke out in terrorist acts after Yitzhak Rabin and Yasir Arafat signed a peace accord.

The Psychology of a Terrorist

Most terrorists are persons notably unsuccessful in life. The "fifteen minutes of glory" due to TV publicity is a type of widespread recognition (and sometimes awe) that this person never contemplated receiving. Knowing that his cause would be defeated in normal combat, he adopts the technique of guerrilla warfare. But by employing blind, irrational acts against a vastly more powerful adversary, he often gets the adversary's own type of violence: war. Terrorism hardly ever achieves its ultimate goal. In fact, it frequently results in further distancing the user of terrorism from his goal. Thus, a terrorist may be presumed to be unintelligent as well as immoral.

But, as 9/11 indicates, he can still do a lot of damage to people and property.

Why is the United States Hated So Much?

Juergensmeyer shows the ways in which many Muslims regard the United States:

1. The U.S. supports reactionary regimes, like Kuwait and Saudi Arabia, in order to get oil.
2. Television portrays a "Hollywood culture" of a nation of sex and violence.
3. American international corporations wield great economic power worldwide.

4. The U.S. supports free trade and globalization, which they feel harm third world economies.
5. As the world's only remaining superpower, the U.S. is envied, hated, and feared.[3]

Especially in nations which feel insecure, hatred builds up into "satanization," demonizing America as a scapegoat for a nation's own weakness. In psychology this is called projection–the extreme dislike in others that which one cannot stand to admit having in oneself. If one cannot fire weapons at a perceived adversary, one fires words, trying to assert that the possible opponent is not a real human bring. This makes it easier to kill others in the misguided notion that one is thereby pleasing a deity.

Arab Economic Depression

There is great economic depression throughout the Arab world. Despair breeds hopelessness, which feeds fanatical terrorism. Between 1985 and 1998 average per capita income declined in most Arab nations, but rose 30% in Israel, 50% in Uruguay, 90% in Chile, and more than doubled in China, South Korea, and Thailand. The only Muslim nations which thrived were those permitting free trade: Indonesia, Malaysia, Turkey, and several Gulf nations.

Most Arab nations do not belong to the World Trade Organization, which promotes international commerce. Also, most of them have very few exports and relatively little foreign investment, due to their political instability. The majority of them have most of their population under the age of 25, a time at which they have little economic productivity. These countries pay a huge price for considering globalization to be an ungodly tendency.

"The Arab-Israeli conflict was not widely regarded as a sacred battle until the late 1980s. Then the process of sacralization overtook the conflict and transformed it, in the eyes of religious activists on both sides, into cosmic war. When a struggle becomes sacralized, minor skirmishes are elevated to monumental proportions. The use of violence becomes legitimized, and the slightest provocation can lead to terrorist assaults."[4]

Religious Justification for Killing

The Egyptian writer Sayyid Qutb felt that modern life was so amoral and immoral that a spiritual revolution was needed. Although he was hanged for his radical views by Gamal Abdel Nasser in 1966, he has been a big influence on such modern terrorist groups as Hamas, the Islamic Salvation Front, the Muslim Brotherhood, and Sheik Omar Abdel Rahman, the designer of the World Trade Center bombing in 1993.

To Qutb, *jahiliyya* (spiritual malaise) leads people astray until they adopt a political system which places man above God. Since modern life allegedly does this, "opposing it grants Islamic militants the right to commit acts of terror anywhere against anyone, Arab or Western, Jew or Christian, or insufficiently Muslim." This book describes a set of international values that are a much sturdier foundation for world peace than Qutb's parochial outlook.

Another Egyptian writer, Abd al-Salam Faraj, also advocated violence against "infidels," even Muslims, whose interpretation of religion differed from his. He also recommended the use of trickery and deceit to help bolster his views. He was executed in 1982 for his part in the assassination of Egyptian President Anwar Sadat.

Warfare in the Unholy Land

On a plot of 35 acres, which you can walk across in ten minutes, the once Holy Land is starting to look more like the Unholy Land. As if to deliberately disturb the peace process, Israeli leader Ariel Sharon walked on ground considered sacred by the Muslim Palestinians. Muslims believe that it was from here that Mohammed made his midnight ascent to the seven heavens. The ground is also sacred to the Jewish people as the site of their great temples. Christians revere the area as the site of the Church of the Holy Sepulchre, allegedly the place where Jesus died.

Unitive religion would inspire one religious group to show respect for what was considered holy by another religious group. Divisive religion intentionally deprecates all other expressions of religious preference. It is the form of religion most often found today in the Unholy Land.

When Palestinians destroyed Joseph's tomb in Nablus in 2000, they were desecrating a memorial to a person who was not only a Jewish hero but also a man greatly honored in Islamic scripture and literature. Mobs are not noted for scholarship. Divisive religion employs violence rather than prayerful study. Violence begets violence. Israeli troops bulldoze Palestinian home sites in revenge for Palestinian stoning and shooting.

Dr. Baruch Goldstein

Dr. Baruch Goldstein became a hero to Israeli extremists when, in February 1994, he fired an assault rifle at Muslim worshippers in a mosque in Hebron. He killed over 30 worshippers and injured scores more. One supporter justified the slaughter, saying "All Arabs who live here are a danger to us." Rabbi Meir Kahane explained that it was permissible to kill innocent Muslim bystanders on the ground that in a spiritual war, everyone, including civilians, is a soldier.

Hamas

Hamas means "zeal" and is an acronym for "Islamic Resistance Movement." Hamas is a Muslim anti-Israeli terrorist organization in Lebanon supported by Syria. A founder of Hamas, Dr. Aboul Aziz Rantisi, says his followers kill civilian Jews because Jews have killed innocent Muslims at the al-Aqsa mosque in 1990, and Dr. Goldstein slaughtered Muslims in 1994. Dr. Rantisi says that five of his relatives have been killed while protesting Israeli takeovers of their land. "We are not aggressors, we are victims," Rantisi insists.[5]

Hamas leader Jaffar describes his ambush of Jewish soldiers. "Your cousin is coming to visit you," he is informed on his cell phone. He describes his feelings. "Before I start shooting, I concentrate on reading verses from the Koran. In the past two weeks I have wounded three Israeli soldiers. When I finish my job, I feel comfort and strength. This land belongs to the Muslims. I don't think in terms of happiness when I kill an Israeli or wound him. I think in terms of carrying out my religious obligations. I am asked by my God to fight the enemies until the last spot of blood."[6]

Yoel Lerner says there is a biblical requirement for Jews to possess and live on biblical land. Dr. Rantisi feels the same way about Muslims. Neither has any patience with members of their own side who are willing to make any compromise for peace. Some Muslims who do not actively support Hamas feel it is needed to keep Palestinian leader Yasir Arafat truly "Islamic."

World Trade Center Bombing—1993

Mahmud Abouhalima, convicted in the 1993 World Trade Center bombing, applauded Timothy McVeigh for his bombing of a federal building in Oklahoma City. The point was made: the American government is the enemy. Thus, Abouhalima said, there is no moral evil in the killing of innocent people, including babies.

Christian Identity Movement

Followers of this American movement assert that God created only Christian white people, but Satan created Jews and all people of color. "In this movement's view of the world," says Juergensmeyer, "the struggle is a secret war between evil forces allied with the United Nations, the United States, and other government powers, and a small band of the enlightened few who recognize these invisible enemies for what they are—satanic powers—and are sufficiently courageous to battle them."[7]

A leader in this cult, Richard Butler, left the Presbyterian ministry to help form this divisive religion of white supremacy. Butler states that 10% of U.S. territory, such as the states of Montana and Idaho, should be dedicated for the exclusive use of white Christians. Butler reported that his "greatest thrill was the knowledge that war had been going on for over six thousand years between the sons of Cain and the sons of God."[8]

Christian Identity leaders call Jews and people of color "mud people," since they were allegedly created by Satan. They seem not to know that Jesus was a Jew. One leader said that he had never known a Jew personally, but that he still believed that Jews were responsible for most of the world's current problems. Another leader, Bob Matthews, after being implicated in the killing of a Jewish radio talk show host, hid on an island north of Seattle, declaring that he and his comrades were in a "full and unrelenting state of war" against the United States government. Another Christian Identity member described the Bible as "a book of war, a book of hate."[9]

A somewhat similar approach is seen in the views of Matthew Hale, who formed the World Church of the Creator, claiming that all Christian churches are really part of a Jewish conspiracy.

Abortion Terrorism

Rev. Michael Bray is a leader of the Army of God, a group using violence against abortion clinics and doctors who perform abortions. He was convicted of arson against seven abortion clinics, causing over a million dollars in damages. Bray defended his friend, Rev. Paul Hill, who killed Dr. John Britton and his volunteer escort James Barrett on 29 July 1994, as they drove to an abortion clinic in Pensacola, Florida. Bray's defense is that these killings are pleasing to God, since they will deter others from "destroying life" in the wombs of the mothers. Paul Hill quoted approval from the Bible, quoting Psalm 91: "You will not be afraid of the terror by night, or of the arrow by day."[10]

Osama bin Laden's Terrorism

Coming from Saudi Arabia, Osama is a Wahhabite Muslim. This sect feels that it is the only "true" Muslim group. Osama hates moderate Muslim nations like Jordan and Turkey as much as he hates the United States. He quotes that part of the Koran that advocates killing all "infidels," or non-believers. Here is a partial list of his terrorist acts against the United States:

1993: Muslim soldiers trained by him killed 18 U.S. soldiers in Somalia.

1995: A car bomb in Riyadh, Saudi Arabia, killed 5 U.S. soldiers.

1996: A truck bomb in Dharan, Saudi Arabia, killed 19 U.S. soldiers.

1998: U.S. embassies in Kenya and Tanzania were bombed, with over 200 casualties; Al-Qaeda issued a *fatwa* (religious order) stating that "to kill Americans and their allies both civil and military is an individual duty of every Muslim who is able, in any country where this is possible."

2000: U.S. Destroyer Cole is bombed in Aden harbor in Yemen; 17 U.S. sailors killed.

2001: Four U.S. planes hijacked and crashed on 9/11, with over 2,800 casualties.

Terrorist Links

Osama's al-Qaeda ("The Base") learned how to make car bombs from Hezbollah, the Iranian-backed terrorist group in Lebanon, where al-Qaeda operates an anti-Israeli terrorist group, Asbat al Ansar. Al-Qaeda also trains members of Hamas.

Taliban Atrocities

In November 2001 the White House issued a report on Taliban atrocities. It said that when the Taliban captured Kabul in 1996, they castrated the country's president, and tortured his brother. In 1998 they massacred 600 Uzbek villagers, and captured the city of Mazar-e-Sharif, "which included, according to Human Rights Watch, the execution of scores of men and boys, and the rape of women and girls; and a 2001 massacre in Yakaolang, executing at least 170 men. Recently eight boys were killed because they laughed at soldiers, an entire family was burned alive, and 100 Afghan Taliban members were slain by foreign Taliban, and their bodies were hung from lamp posts, because 'they were not pure enough.'"[11]

The Sunni Taliban detest the Shiite Hazara Muslims. When Mazar-e-Sharif fell to the Taliban, Human Rights Watch reports that the Taliban governor told the Hazaras: "Hazaras are not Muslims. You are Shiites, and thus infidels. If you do not show your loyalty, we will burn your houses and we will kill you. Either accept to be Muslims or leave Afghanistan."

Taliban soldiers went door to door, demanding Sunni prayers from the Hazaras. Those who refused, over 6000, were killed. Their bodies remained on the street as a warning to other Hazaras. Even the Taliban admitted that U.S. bombing by November 2001 had killed only 1000 Afghan civilians. Muslims all over the world need to know that the Taliban killed far more Afghan civilians than did U.S. bombs.[12]

Women as Second-Class Citizens

The Taliban has established new lows in their treatment of women. Here are excerpts from the Taliban penal code: "Women are not allowed to go to public baths. A woman who is arrested for washing something in public will be punished. Speaking is forbidden between a female doctor and a male nurse, or between a female nurse and a male doctor. Female doctors must wear old clothes and no accessories to the hospital. Female nurses are not allowed to go to the rooms of male patients. Women should not be heard singing or dancing at a wedding or a celebration. A cab driver with an unescorted woman as a fare will be punished. If a woman is seen leaving home with a naked face, the woman will be threatened on the spot."[13] Some Afghan women have been killed because they have been seen with bare ankles or elbows.

Unfortunately, it is not only in Afghanistan where women are deprived of basic human rights. An official for the Human Rights Commission of Pakistan asserts that Hindu women are frequently raped by their Pakistani masters. So-called "honor killings" still take place in many countries, especially in Muslim nations. "Thousands of times each year, a woman is murdered somewhere in the world by her father or brothers for acts that are seen as besmirching the family's honor, including committing adultery, defying a parental order to marry, being seen in public with a man, or becoming the victim of rape." Pakistan had 1000 such killings in 1999, and Yemen had 700 in 1997. Jordan has been the country most opposed to a strong United Nations resolution outlawing such killing.[14]

Even in the United States, of the Fortune 500 top executive officers, 497 are men. Slowly, ever so slowly, women are being appointed to the U.S. Supreme Court. No one so far has the bravery to give serious consideration to a woman as a candidate for president of the United States, although over fifty world nations have elected women as their chief executives.

Outlawing Joy

The Taliban have been a far more joyless regime than the Puritans of England and America. Their penal code reflects this attack on joy: "Those who insist on flying kites will be deprived of education and their homes will be searched. No pictures are allowed in shops, cars, hotels, and other public places. Whoever has drunk wine will be tried before a court. Whoever flies pigeons will be jailed as long as the pigeons disappear from his home. Some clerics and corrupt people wear turbans that cause dissent. A person who wears his hair in an un-Islamic style—

Beatle-like—will be arrested and his head will be shaved. Equipment that produces joyful music (such as pianos, drums, and harmonicas) is banned, as well as TVs, satellite dishes, VCRs, computers, cassette tapes, film projectors, neckties, and necktie pins."[15]

Religious Strife in Asia

In India, Hindu militants recently killed a Roman Catholic priest, burned to death an Australian Christian missionary and his two sons, and bombed four Christian churches. Kashmir remains the classical tinder box. Most Kashmiris are Muslims, but the state is ruled by Hindu India. Since 1989 Muslim Kashmiris have been revolting, wishing to join neighboring Pakistan. "Atrocities—real and concocted—are employed as necessary skullduggery. The death toll has been tabulated at more than 34,000 by the Indian government. Others insist the count is double that." In March 2000 a group of 35 Sikhs were massacred by militant Muslims clad in Hindu army uniforms. Malik, an 18-year-old gunman, said he considered it his religious duty to kill persons identified as enemies by the leader of his terrorist group.

Tamils are Hindus seeking to secede from Buddhist-controlled Sri Lanka. Both side use violence, the weapon of divisive religion. "Since it began in 1983, the war has claimed 62,000 lives and has displaced a million people."[16] The president of Sri Lanka, Chandrika Kumaratubga, lost both her husband and her father to assassin's bullets. A female suicide bomber from the Tamil Tigers nearly killed Chandrika in December 1999. One piece of shrapnel blinded her right eye, another came within a quarter inch of her brain. Now she has vowed a war of vengeance against the Hindu Tamils.

Indonesia, the world's fourth largest country, now has armed Muslim militants roaming the streets of Jakarta looking for Jews to kill. "If we find any Israelis, we will first try to persuade them to leave, but if they refuse, we will slaughter them," said Zain-uddin, a spokesman for the radical group called the Islamic Defenders Front. "Israelis are not welcome in Indonesia because their illegal colonization has killed thousands of Muslim people," he said. "We are ready to go war, a holy war, to defend Islam."[17]

Defense Against Biological Weapons

On 7 December 2001 the United States blocked efforts to establish an agency to inspect all nations that have the facilities for building lethal germ weapons. Physicians for Social Responsibility (PFSR) reports that 143 countries, including every U.S. ally, resented American blockage of this projected agency. The American position was that some nations would cheat. If so, is it not advisable to have regular international inspection teams looking for cheaters? Princeton Research Services reported that 79% of Americans support mandatory inspections of bio-weapon capability facilities, and 71% support creation of an international agency with enforcement powers. PFSR warns: "America must not be blind-sided by a future bio-terrorist attack from an enemy we deliberately chose to learn nothing about."[18]

Nuclear Terrorism

Terrorists in a number of nations are trying to gain access to nuclear weapons. Stephen Dolley, research director of the Nuclear Control Institute, says that al-Qaeda might get atom bomb materials from Russia or the former Soviet republics, but even more likely from "the growing British, French, and Japanese plutonium industries and from a new German research reactor to be run on bomb-grade uranium. Controls against losses and thefts of these materials remain weak." Alan J. Kuperman adds that Germany's reactor, with fuel enough for 16 Hiroshima style bombs, will be in a relatively unprotected university site. Also, "most of the world's medical-isotope producers still employ bomb-grade uranium at commercial facilities less secure than Russia's weapons sites."

Larry D. Johnson, former legal advisor to the International Atomic Energy Commission, says urgent action is needed on two matters. First, we should support the IAE's new initiatives on ways to prevent terrorism involving nuclear materials. Second, the Legal Committee of the U.N. General Assembly has a draft, prepared in 1998, of a convention suppressing acts of nuclear terrorism. Besides outlawing such acts, "it also deals with the use of other radioactive material that could be used with a conventional device ('dirty bomb') to terrorize and spread radiation."[19]

How on Earth Are We Going to Survive?

Without world law there will continue to be world lawlessness. International anarchy in a nuclear age, when terrorists show great ingenuity, courage, and inhumanity, is a condition inviting catastrophe. A terrorist holding New York City or some other great metropolis hostage with a nuclear bomb will awaken us to the need for international machinery to maintain peace and order. A nuclear device exploded in a large metropolitan area could produce as many as twenty million casualties.

We need a world of law and order, based on justice. Terrorism defeats this goal. Working within an international framework we need to define what constitutes unlawful acts, how violators are to be apprehended and tried, what audience is to be given grievance procedures, and what penalties are appropriate. Every orderly community needs the machinery of policing and justice. The world must become an orderly community if our species is to survive.

The nations of the world, Mikhail Gorbachev reminds us, are like "a pack of mountaineers tied together by a climbing rope. Security is indivisible. It is equal security for all or none at all. Adversaries must become partners and start looking jointly for a way to achieve universal security."[20]

In the Bible, Paul explains to the Galatians the responsibility entailed by freedom—that without love, freedom can be deadly: "The whole law is summed up in one commandment: 'love your neighbor as yourself.' But if you act like animals, hurting each other, then watch out, or you will completely destroy one another."

Much modern aggression has not evoked an international response. For example, China conquered Tibet, the Soviet Union invaded Afghanistan, the United States invaded Grenada and Panama, Turkey took over northern Cyprus, Israel overran the West Bank, the Gaza Strip, and the Golan Heights, and many African countries fight constantly over disputed borders.

Winning the Peace

A Muslim journalist reminds us that winning a war does not necessarily ensure winning the peace. Saad Mehio says that the only way to win the current war against terrorism is by winning hearts and minds. "This can be achieved," he says, "only by correcting the historical mistakes made by the West, including the United States, in undercutting the modernizing forces of pan-Arabism, and by correcting the spectacularly misguided choices made by Arab elites in their use of power and of politicized Islam as a way to keep it."[21]

Secretary of State Colin Powell shows what is involved in winning the peace. Muslim nations listened closely to Powell's speech on 19 November 2001. Powell described a Middle East "in which all people have jobs that let them put bread on their tables and a roof over their head and offer a decent education to their children. We have a vision of a region where all people worship God in a spirit of tolerance and understanding, where respect for the sanctity of the individual, the rule of law, and the politics of participation grow stronger and stronger."[22]

The terrorist attack on 9/11/01 may force the United States to do what it should have done all along: be an honest and fair peace-broker between Palestinians and Israelis in their dispute for territory in the Holy Land. Even concerning the one big error—constantly aiding Israel with never a concern for Palestinians—a number of American presidents, from Jimmy Carter to Bill Clinton, have worked hard to try to bring peace to the bellicose adversaries. The Bush administration has also promised to assist in setting up a peaceful and just relationship between the two countries.

When governments respond with violence to terrorist attacks (although in some cases it is necessary), they provide the terrorists with some seeming justification for the terrorists' original charges. President George W. Bush has made a number of moves designed to avoid this trap. First, he has made repeated public statements that most Muslims are not terrorists but are excellent citizens, and that there should be no ethnic profiling that causes *all* Muslims to be suspect. Second, he has provided for hundreds of thousands of food packages to be dropped for the Afghani poor and refugees. This is one of the few times in history when one side in a war goes out of its way to tend to the needs of people on the other side. Third, Bush has assured everyone that the United States wants to turn over the organization and administration of the new Afghan government to the United Nations, giving the assurance that there will be broad representation of all ethnic groups, as well as women, in constituting the new government. Nominal Taliban members should be given a chance to see if they can live in accordance with the **unitive** teachings in the Koran, where each *sura* begins with the dedicatory phrase, "In the name of Allah, the Merciful, the Compassionate."

To counter Taliban propaganda, the United States must publicize its generous aid to many Muslim nations, such as Egypt, Jordan, Pakistan, and Turkey. Publicity must also be given to the times when the United States took vigorous action on behalf of Muslims, such as Bosnians and Kosovars, against persecution by Orthodox Christian Serbians.

Summary

In summary, the devastating and deadly terrorist attack on America on 9/11/2001 can already be seen to have had several salutary effects. It has united Americans in defense of their homeland in a manner not seen since World War II. It has forced us to take security measures to assure that our citizens will not have to fear repeated terrorist attacks. There will always be law-breakers and innocent victims in this imperfect world. But from now on terrorists, as well as individuals and nations which aid or shelter them, will pay a dear price for their crimes. Terrorism and all divisive religion can cause a lot of human suffering, but by their base inhumanity and lack of concern for everyone's civil rights, they are losing games. Osama bin Laden and other terrorists will be shown to be discredited, as world leaders strive to build a world free from international terrorism and violence.

The succeeding chapters of this book will emphasize the dire need for world law and order, and demonstrate that by replacing divisive religion with unitive religion, we can indeed have a world of peace and justice for all.

References

1   Mark Juergensmeyer, *Terror in the Mind of God: The Global Rise of Religious Violence,* updated edition (University of California Press, 2001), pp. 221–224.
2   Ibid., pp. 149, 153, 154.
3   Ibid., pp. 180–182.

[4] Ibid., p. 163.

[5] Ibid., pp. 74, 75.

[6] *Time*, 23 October 2000, p. 55.

[7] Juergensmeyer, p. 35.

[8] Ibid., p. 155.

[9] Ibid., p. 146.

[10] Ibid., pp. 21, 24, 154.

[11] *Payson Roundup*, 23 November 2001, p. 4A.

[12] Peter Beinart, *The New Republic*, 19 November 2001, p. 6.

[13] Amy Waldman, *New York Times*, 2 December 2001, 4:7.

[14] *New York Times*, 12 November 2000, 4:14.

[15] Waldman, loc. cit.

[16] Somini Sengupt, *New York Times*, 16 July 2000, p. 3.

[17] Calvin Sims, *New York Times*, 15 October 2000, p. 11.

[18] *New York Times*, 9 December 2001, 4:13.

[19] Ibid., 25 November 2001, 4:10.

[20] Mikhail Gorbachev, *Perestroika* (Harper & Row, 1987), p. 142.

[21] Saad Mehio, *New York Times*, 2 December 2001, 4:15.

[22] Ibid.

CHAPTER II

THE GOOD NEWS OF DAMNATION

On December 2, 1942, underneath the stands of Stagg Field at the University of Chicago, the first controlled self-sustaining nuclear chain reaction was accomplished. The careful work of many scientists, engineers, and technicians had led to this precise and precarious goal.

On August 6, 1945, the first atomic bomb ever used in warfare was detonated by the United States upon Hiroshima. Pandora's box of possible complete extinction of the human species was thus opened.

Shortly after the Hiroshima bomb was dropped, Chancellor Robert Maynard Hutchins of the University of Chicago preached a sermon at the university chapel. His topic was "The Good News of Damnation." How could damnation of the human race be good news? Hutchins's reply was that now that our destructive potential had reached such perilous perfection, our one remaining chance for survival is for us to love one another. There is no other way out. The great religious teachers had told us this from the beginning, but there seemed to be no urgent need to agree with them or at least to obey them. Now to fail to carry out their precepts meant the suicide of our species.

The most shrewd and selfish egotist now has the same means to his goal as Buddha, Christ, and Gandhi. The wisdom of the ancients has been corroborated by the most modern science.

Love It or Leave It

The biggest casualty of the atomic age is war itself. Because of the monstrous inhumanity of nuclear weapons, war is no longer a viable option in the civilized community of humankind. Our only choices are peace or annihilation.

We must update our thinking. Newtonian politics will not suffice in an Einsteinian world. Modern physics not only makes materialism obsolete but also points towards a oneness of the universe that was previously believed in only by the religious. For millions of years earth's landmasses had been assembled in one supercontinent called Pangea, Greek for "all lands." Now the unitary view was being restored.

The ecosystem of our planet is unitary, held in delicate balance by many natural phenomena. Tampering with one part of the environment, as with atomic testing, upsets the balance, causing potential harm to the ecosystem. Nations cannot pass laws outlawing the drift of radioactive clouds. No nation's sovereignty includes the right to pollute our common atmosphere. In the global village the good citizen identifies with every other citizen, partly to preserve his own existence. Enlightened selfishness is now altruism.

We can neither blow up our fellow man nor defile the atmosphere if we love our neighbor and ourselves. If we reject altruistic love, we ultimately die of the weapons or poisons used upon fellow humans. Thus love is the only logical answer to the question of what is best for ourselves. Now I love my neighbor because I love myself, and I cannot survive alone.

Common problems create community. Humanity's common problem of survival makes our planet a village. The theologian Paul Tillich says that our job is to transform the community of fear of the ultimate holocaust into a community of love and acceptance.

All communities need law and order if they are to survive. Fear and terror are impossible foundations for world peace and order. Any policeman will tell you that respect for the law and for the networks of belief underlying the law are factors that produce an orderly community. These factors are much easier to develop when community members have a high regard for one another.

Gershom Gorenberg's book *The End of Days* shows how the Temple Mount in Jerusalem could be the ultimate powder keg. Gorenberg says there are fundamentalist Christians who think the end of the world is coming, as predicted in the book of Revelation. The Jews have returned to Jerusalem. Now if they rebuild their temple and restore animal sacrifice, get ready for the end, say the fundamentalists. Reviewer John Dorfman states that some of the devout Jews "are not averse to being manipulated by their Christian counterparts. Add to the mix angry Zionists who want to dynamite the Dome of the Rock, and Arab nationalists who see a Jewish presence on the Mount as the first step of the disfranchisement of Islam, and you have a recipe for a war of apocalyptic proportions."[1]

Playing the Game of War

Palestinian youths daily risk their lives in the *intifada*. They are glad to die for God, they say. Feeling that they are being deprived of land that was originally theirs, and that peace negotiations can stumble along for further decades, they are desperate. Nearly every day another Palestinian dies as a martyr to their cause. The mother of Ahmed, a 15-year-old boy killed recently, said of his death: "I am proud. Thanks be to God. I will give all my children (she has eight more), if that's what it takes to get our homeland back. All of them can become martyrs. It will be a dignity to me."[2]

The United States now has in operation 18 Class Ohio submarines, each carrying the nuclear destructive power of 4000 Hiroshima A-bombs. This is but a fraction of our entire nuclear capability. Some hawks say we need more weapons. An accident, a false warning, terrorists seizing hostages—what might trigger a nuclear holocaust?

Iran is now working with outlaw nuclear powers like China to develop delivery systems for biological and chemical weapons. Saddam Hussein, with no United Nations inspections since 1998, has enough anthrax and other biochemical weapons to kill all human life on our planet. Can we trust Saddam to be responsible?

The Death of Idols

The idol of nationalism is starting to crumble as it becomes increasingly clear that no nation can now achieve its first purpose: guarantee security against terrorist attack and great destruction.

Scientism, meaning the worship of the scientific method as humanity's one great absolute, died for good at Hiroshima, although its intellectual underpinnings had already been weakened by Clerk Maxwell's discoveries in electricity, the Curies' discovery of radium, Einstein's time-space cosmogony, and developments in modern quantum physics.

The idol of technology also died at Hiroshima. Since their machines can be used in such inhuman fashion, technologists are no longer sacred cows. Many of them admit being disillusioned with the anti-social uses to which their work has been applied.

Of these three idols, nationalism is the one most likely to lead to war. Broader sovereignty outlaws the pettiness of disputes leading to war. California and Arizona may quarrel over use of Colorado River water, but resort to arms to settle the dispute would be unthinkable, not to mention illegal. In the United States, the broader sovereignty intervenes with parliamentary machinery to settle disputes in a nonviolent manner. Now, in a world with both incredible destructive power and widespread terrorism, the broader sovereignty must be recognized, for survival reasons. The sovereignty we must work toward is that of the entire globe, particularly in matters concerning warfare or pollution of our ecosystem.

Loyalty to the human race does not mean that we forfeit love of our country. As a matter of fact, to preserve our country we must embrace all of humanity. But except for matters of survival, local and national governments will always be necessary.

Like Socrates and Benjamin Franklin, we must now declare ourselves to be citizens of the world. In their call for a nuclear freeze, the Roman Catholic bishops in America said that "the virtue of patriotism means that as citizens we respect and honor our country, but our very love and loyalty make us examine carefully its role in world affairs, asking that it live up to its full potential as an agent of peace with justice for all people."[3]

A Peaceful World Community

British historian Arnold Toynbee sees the decline of nationalism coming in the light of the shrinking distance between countries, the economic interdependence of modern society, and the dreadful increased destructiveness of nuclear weaponry. He cautions that we should not try to build a world state, lest we have an even greater potential idol of misused power. Jefferson's principle is not outmoded—that government is best which governs least. Unfortunately, as man's control over nature increases, the need for his control over human nature also increases, lest great destructive power be unleashed. To keep such power under control, some of our former liberty needs to be sacrificed. Heavy traffic on a crowded road demands more traffic signals. In our more crowded world, what was once liberty easily degenerates into license, and harm to others' liberty. The terrorists of 9/11 used American liberties and education to try to undo America.

A coalition of sovereign states, united in opposition to war and nuclear proliferation, is what the world now needs. With the codification of world law which effectively outlaws violence in the settlement of disputes, and supported by the policing power needed by every orderly community, nations will be free from crippling munitions expenditures, taxes could be reduced, and each nation could devote more of its resources to consumer goods and services. The only sovereignties that member nations would surrender are those they should no longer have: the right to wage aggressive war and to pollute our single ecosystem.

Out of love of my country of course I want my country preserved. But now my country can be preserved only if other countries are also preserved. The most fundamental purpose of any government is to safeguard the lives, values, and property of its citizens. No national government on earth can now guarantee this. To this extent, many powers of earth's nations are obsolete or obsolescent. We are in the process of building supranational structures to achieve some of the fundamental goals of government.

Mature Religion

William E. Hocking, in *The Coming World Civilization,* says that only a mature religion will serve humanity's needs now.

Such a religion incorporates the insights of science, is grounded in human dignity and human survival, and recognizes the validity of other religions similarly constituted.

Thomas Matus, a Christian monk, says that "the Second Vatican Council puts an official seal of approval on the search for a new theological paradigm, and provides a common ground for the new paradigm." Another Christian monk, David Steindl-Rast, adds that "the communal aspect of salvation is almost impossible to appreciate except in terms of global community."[4]

Carl Jung put his faith in persons adopting the transpersonal perspective, through what he called raising the level of human consciousness. Whereas some persons seem to be destroyed by problems, others find a wider or higher horizon, a perspective from which the apparently insoluble problem seems relatively tiny or insignificant.

Edwin Markham wrote:

> He drew a circle to keep me out,
> Heretic, rebel, a thing to flout—
> But love and I had the wit to win,
> We drew a circle to keep him in.

In 1975 a group of spiritual leaders read this statement to a United Nations body:

> The crises of our time are challenging the world religions to release a new spiritual force transcending religious, cultural, and national boundaries into a new consciousness of the oneness of the human community, and so putting into effect a spiritual dynamic towards the solutions of the world's problems. We affirm a new spirituality divested of insularity and directed towards planetary consciousness.[5]

Sociologist Peter Berger explains the three options concerning modern religion. The deductive option is to assume that there is no contemporary crisis. The reductive option reduces religion to a secular experience, such as a political program. The inductive option, the one preferred by Berger, is one in which a person turns from external authority to seek within his psyche those truths and values which are to that person most relevant. Since others will make other choices, such a person will necessarily be called a heretic.

What is more, all religions, being aware of other world religions, are faced with this heretical choice, since honesty demands seeing the validity of other religions in addition to one's own. This, says Berger, "has given all world religions a commonality of condition that must have an effect upon their self-understanding and an effect upon their relations with each other."[6]

Erich Fromm foresees the coming of Messianic time, a term used in the Torah to refer to the rule of God in the coming age, or simply the Kingdom of God. Only by going through alienation and atonement can humanity achieve this oneness with God, Fromm believed. Human choices, he feels, are to destroy ourselves through selfish narcissism or to advance towards the realization of the new harmony. Messianism is the alternative to human self-destruction.

Fromm explains the alienation of the Israelites as being due to an incestuous love of the soil of their country. "The concept of Messianic time," Fromm concluded, "is that of the complete victory over incestuous ties, and the full establishment of the spiritual reality of moral and intellectual conscience, not only among the Jews, but among all peoples of the earth."[7]

When will the Messiah come? Fromm says that the Talmud gives two views: He will come either as a result of continuous improvement of humanity, or else when evil and suffering have reached such an intolerable degree that humans will repent and thus be ready for Him.

God's Role in Survival

Chuang Tzu, a Taoist writer, describes a drunken man who falls from a cart but is not hurt. The drunk's escape from reality gave him a protective relaxation. "If such security is to be gotten from wine," says Chuang, "how much more it is to be got from God!"

The early Christians believed that the end of the world was coming soon, and so they strove to know God personally through prayer and a good life. Whether or not a nuclear holocaust is imminent, one thing is certain—for each of us the end of our life on earth is a certainty, and so concentration upon our relationship to our Creator is a good investment of our time.

Richard K. Taylor has applied the Biblical concept of shalom to resolve many enigmas of modern life. "Shalom," says Taylor, "means not just peace, but unity, partnership, health, wholeness, community, and justice." It involves proper relations with God, one's fellow humans, and our entire ecosphere. "Our collective greeds destroy our basic sources of life," he feels. "Our collective injustice creates intolerable balance between rich and poor. Envy and fear can unleash the nuclear holocaust. At last, our facts and our morals have come together to tell us how we must live."[8]

Churches are increasingly asserting that it is God's will that persons love and nurture one another rather than focus on building weapons of mass destruction. When America's Roman Catholic bishops in 1983 called for an end to the nuclear arms race, they drew instant support from many other denominations. The National Council of Churches, representing over forty million Americans, also spoke for a nuclear freeze. Evangelicals for Social Action, representing conservative Protestantism, has taken strong stands supporting social issues, including the outlawing of wars except in cases of legitimate self-defense. The Union of American Hebrew Congregations and the conservative Rabbinical Council of America took a strong stand in defense of a bilateral weapons freeze.

Globalization

As we enter the global village, parochial views will have to give way to broader concepts of good and evil. Kofi Annan has received much deserved praise for his evenhanded search for peace in his role as Secretary General of the United Nations. Respect for "the fundamental sovereignty, territorial integrity, and political independence of states," Annan said in 1999, "will remain a cornerstone of the international system. Nevertheless, the principle of sovereignty cannot provide excuses for the inexcusable," such as the massacre in Rwanda in 1994. The protection of human rights, Annan feels, must "take precedence over concerns of state sovereignty." He stated that under his leadership, "the United Nations will always place human beings at the center of everything we do."[9]

"Globalization is really defining our era," Annan said, explaining why he forged alliances with multinational corporations to improve labor and environmental standards, as well as to bridge cyberspace gaps between the industrial and the developing nations. When citizens of a country are abused, Annan said, the rulers have no right to tell others to stay out of their affairs. "The world around us is changing," Annan stated, "and we change with it or we will be left behind."

Globalization was the topic of a Millennium Summit of over 150 world leaders in New York City in September 2000. Sponsored by the United Nations, the conference began with a meeting of world religious leaders. The conference pledged to make progress in improving living conditions, especially among the poor in the world. Areas designated for emphasis included wages, clean water, educational opportunity, and reducing infectious diseases.

The Search for Universal Values

The Roman emperor Marcus Aurelius said that our common reason leads humans to a common law, growing out of our condition as members of one species. Napoleon declared that in war the moral factors outweigh the material factors by a ratio of three to one. Faith Bandler, a leading Australian black writer, said: "They say we blacks are a part of the Third World, but to me there's no such thing. There's only one world."[10]

The common sense of Homo sapiens now realizes that in a world so interconnected by communication, economics, transportation, and a common ecosphere, each nation, for its own self-interest, must learn to be a good neighbor. Interdependence and the need for survival bind us into an ever closer unity.

"For the first time in history," states Mikhail Gorbachev, "basing international politics on moral and ethical norms that are common to all humankind has become a vital requirement. Philosophers and theologians throughout history have dealt with the ideas of 'eternal' values. Then these were 'scholastic speculations' doomed to be a utopian dream. Now mankind should acknowledge the vital necessity of human values."

In 1986 India and the Soviet Union adopted the Delhi Declaration, which "recognizes the priority of universal human values in this nuclear age. Enriched by the Indian political tradition and the specifics of Indian philosophy and culture," the two nations called for building a non-violent world, free from nuclear and other mass weapons. They stated: "In the nuclear age, humanity must evolve a new mode of political thought, a new concept of the world that will provide reliable guarantees for humanity's survival. People want to live in a safer and more just world. Humanity deserves a better fate than being a hostage to nuclear terror and despair. We must build a nuclear-weapon-free world, free of violence and hatred, fear and suspicion." "In our relations," stated Gorbachev, "we see a budding world order in which peaceful coexistence and mutually beneficial cooperation based on goodwill will be universal norms."[11]

Professor Paul Kennedy is optimistic about a better world order if we concentrate on our planet's four chief issues: reduce the population explosion; cut back on nuclear proliferation; reduce the gap between the wealthy North and the impoverished South (North Americans and Europeans, 10% of the globe's people, cannot be islands of prosperity in a sea of poverty); and all persons must be educated for world citizenship.

The New World Order

President George H. Bush, in his State of the Union address in 1991, said: "This is a defining hour. We are part of something larger than ourselves: a new world order, where many nations are united to achieve the universal aspirations of mankind—peace, freedom, security, and the rule of law. We seek a Persian Gulf where conflict is no longer the rule. The community of nations will not stand for aggression. This victory in Kuwait is for world peace and justice. The world community will have sent a warning to any dictator who performs aggression.

The world is a community of conscience. We all yearn for a world where we will never have to fight again. With few exceptions, the world now stands as one. The leadership of the United Nations is now confirming its founders' vision. We need to build a new world order, based not on an armament race but on shared principles and the rule of law. We find meaning by serving some higher purpose than ourselves. We selflessly confront evil for the sake of good. Freedom works. Let us all do the hard work of freedom."

Ronald Reagan, in a speech at Oxford University in 1992, said that what the world needs is "nothing less than a human velvet glove backed by a steel fist." He endorsed the change in

United Nations food policy which now permits relief agencies to operate without the consent of the host government. He said that the success of the Somalian intervention suggests that perhaps it should be repeated on a larger scale in sub-Saharan Africa. American intervention in Somalia, Reagan stated, is "only the beginning of what must be done. We must work toward a standing United Nations force—an army of conscience—that is fully prepared to carve out human sanctuaries through force if necessary."[12]

The Sacredness of Life

The current wave of religious terrorism, coupled with the nuclear peril described above, demands not only that we must not kill our neighbors but we must also permit them to be born in some future time. The way to international peace begins by searching within, says Sri Aurobindo Ghose. "Only when man has developed not merely a fellow feeling with all men, but a dominant sense of unity and commonality, only when he is aware of them not merely as brothers but as parts of himself—only when he has learned to live, not in his separate ego-sense, but in a large universal consciousness, can the phenomenon of war pass out of his life."[13]

The anthropologist Ruth Benedict pointed out the superiority of a high synergy culture over a low synergy one. In the high synergy culture members cooperate not merely because of their unselfishness but also because society's customs are such as to make cooperation worthwhile. Thus, by serving oneself one is also serving the group. The Hopi Indian, praying for rain, is praying for everyone, including himself.

In the low synergy culture the individual advances only at someone else's cost. In this society the rich get richer and the poor get poorer. There is not even a mechanism for working off one's humiliation, as there is in the high synergy culture. The accumulated frustrations in the low synergy culture can lead readily to the hatred level necessary for carrying out a war.

A high synergy culture with a well developed survival ethos is the Balinese society. As Erich Jantsch observes, "the inhabitants of Bali do not view themselves as possessors of the island, but as guests on the 'island of the gods.' This spirited feeling of being the guests of the gods never fades. It is the never depleted source of a happiness which manifests in continuous gratitude, in sacrifices to all gifts of life—water, fire, food, everything."[14] Needless to say, the Balinese are a very peaceful people; they would much rather dance than make war!

Survival Through Spirituality

Physical survival is an immediate important necessity for our species. Satisfying our survival drive in mental and spiritual ways is another. Eternal life of the spirit is no doubt the best recompense to our survival drive, since it is beyond physical decay. Albert Einstein found a unity of music and mathematics in a realm of universal principles beyond the pale of time. Combining mathematics with mysticism, he sought to unravel the mystery of the underlying unity of life.

The ultimate expression of the survival drive is spiritual in nature. Examples are the Christian heaven, the Hindu nirvana, and the timeless truths of Spinoza and Einstein. When a person lives in what she feels is an imperishable reality, her survival drive can be said to have reached its fullest expression. This kind of atonement (at-one-ment) comes not only to the believer, the artist, or the scientist. Persons can live on in the lives of people whose lives were touched by them. By identifying with eternal principles of goodness and truth, one can gain a type of immortality.

Persons with poor satisfaction of their survival drives are easy prey to anxiety, crime, immorality, and personality disintegration. The high incidence of these conditions testifies to the poor spiritual and mental health of modern humanity. Terrorists commit criminal acts in desperation, feeling that life is not worth living under modern conditions. War, with its accompanying hatred, is a handy release valve to low synergy people, for then all persons, including the "good" people, are expected to hate. An ultimate triumph of terrorism would be to reduce the human race to its very lowest moral dimension.

"War is unthinkable," says Marilyn Ferguson, "in a society of autonomous people who have discovered the connectedness of all humanity, who are unafraid of alien ideas and alien cultures, who know that all revolutions begin within and that you cannot impose your brand of enlightenment on anyone else."[15]

A series of paradoxes underlies the good news of physical damnation. Spiritual salvation is the only thing that can save us from physical damnation. Thus, ultimate physicality leads to ultimate spirituality. Overstress on the physical leads to proper stress on the previously neglected spiritual. The only way the physical can survive is through spiritual means.

The only way for humanity to survive is to follow God's way. This is the good news of damnation. Avoiding God, man got into this mess. Returning to God, humans can get out of it.

Arnold Toynbee gives an inevitable sign of the decline of a civilization: the vulgarity and barbarism of its everyday life. Professional wrestling certainly fits the paradigm of a dying culture. So do many of the mass media, in which sex and violence seem to be certain box office winners. Dignity, politeness, nobility, and respect for each human being as a child of God seem remote from popular culture in our time. Often those who live by vulgarity die by vulgarity. Vulgarity and barbarism in religion are earmarks of divisive religion.

Unfortunately, world scriptures contain both unitive and divisive ways to God. Terrorists invariably quote the divisive passages. Before the onset of world community, divisive religion was limited in its antisocial effects. World community makes divisive religion not only obsolete, but a part of the problem rather than a part of the solution. This book enables the reader to distinguish between those aspects of religion which lead toward war and possible human extinction, and those that lead toward world cooperation and peace.

REFERENCES

[1] *New York Times Book Review*, 7 January 2001, p. 19.

[2] Michael Finkel, *New York Times Magazine*, 24 December 2000, p. 50.

[3] *St. Anthony Messenger*, July 1983, p. 57.

[4] Fritjof Capra and David Steindl-Rast, *Belonging to the Universe* (HarperSanFrancisco, 1991), pp. 52, 57.

[5] Marilyn Ferguson, *The Aquarian Conspiracy* (Tarcher, 1980), p. 369.

[6] Peter L. Berger, *The Heretical Imperative* (Anchor, 1979), p. 31.

[7] Erich Fromm, *The Sane Society* (Fawcett, 1967), 55.

[8] *St. Anthony Messenger*, February 1977, pp. 59, 60.

[9] Judith Miller, *New York Times*, 18 April 1999, 4:4.

[10] *National Geographic*, February 1988, p. 203.

[11] Gorbachev, pp. 141, 144.

[12] *Arizona Republic*, 20 December 1992, p. C3.

[13] Aurobindo Ghose, *The Human Cycle; The Ideal of Human Unity; War and Self-Determination* (Pondicherry, India: Sri Aurobindo Ashram, 1971), p. 587.

[14] Erich Jantsch, *The Self-Organizing Universe* (Pergamon, 1980), p. 274.

[15] Ferguson, p. 411.

Chapter III

Divisive Religion: Barriers to Peace

We have seen how the deadly phrase "There is no God but mine" has brought great suffering and even killing, allegedly in the name of God. This chapter will show many current examples of divisive religion, all of them roadblocks as we seek to achieve lasting world peace.

The Six Blind Men and the Elephant

We all recall the ancient Hindu fable of the six blind men and the elephant. Each man had hold of a part of the elephant—and immediately concluded that he grasped the entire animal.

"An elephant is like a rope," said the man holding the tail.

"No, he's like a snake," replied the one handling the trunk.

"By no means," answered the one touching the vast side. "Clearly he is like a wall."

"How can you say that?" asked the man grasping a leg. "He is like a great tree."

"A tree?" shrieked the one holding an ear. "I can prove that he is like a great fan."

"Ridiculous!" responded the man holding onto a tusk. "He is like a huge spear."

Of course, all six were partly right and partly wrong. Like all of us who believe in God, we tend to believe that our particular pathway to God is the only valid one. What does the fable teach us?

First, that God, being infinite, cannot be fully comprehended by any finite person.

Second, that no one experience of God can be said to exclude all others.

Third, if you want to experience God at all, the biggest error is to cease holding onto the grasp that you have of God's reality.

Recent Divisive Religion in Asia

It is paradoxical that India, the spiritual cradle of Asia, with Hinduism generally tolerant of other world faiths, is the site of much modern divisive religion. In 1947, when India was partitioned into Muslim Pakistan and Hindu India, hundreds of thousands of people were killed as Hindus migrated to the new India and Muslims moved to Pakistan.

In 1992 a group of Hindu militants tore down a mosque in the city of Ayodhya. In the ensuing riot between Hindus and Muslims, over one thousand persons were killed. Recently the Indian government opened old wounds by deciding to build a temple on the site of the mosque.

When the Bharatya Janata Party was elected in 1997, religious fanaticism grew. Christian missionaries were killed, Bibles were burned, and churches destroyed. When Pope John Paul II visited India in 1999, special protection had to be given him because of Hindu fundamentalists. In 1999 scores of persons were hacked to death in caste rivalries. Violence in the 1999 elections, fueled primarily by religious differences, led to a number of deaths in the state of Bihar.

In China the government seeks to limit religious practices to certain approved organizations. When the Falun Gong spiritual movement held an unauthorized demonstration in 1999, its leaders received prison sentences ranging from 7 to 18 years. The group declares that 50,000 of its members were detained by the government from July 1999 to January 2001. Spokesmen say that at least 3000 of their members have been given psychiatric treatment simply for having made statements opposing governmental policies. Also, Tibetan Buddhists have long been persecuted by the Chinese government, and the Dalai Lama is forced to live abroad.

Japan has witnessed the growth of a lay Buddhist sect, Soka Gakkai, with some uneasiness. "Members of the group have used arson and a bomb threat against temples of rival Buddhist groups."[1] Also, members have been known to break into homes in order to smash relics of other faiths. The Aum Shinrikyo cult released sarin nerve gas in a Tokyo subway system in 1995, killing eleven and injuring several thousand people.

In 1996 in Indonesia 27 Christian churches and a Buddhist temple were destroyed by religious rioters. A Protestant minister, his wife and child, and a church worker were burned to death. The village of Benteng Karang, population 1360, is gone now, destroyed by violence between Christians and Muslims. "Several thousand Muslims stormed through the village, hacking to death at least fifteen people, and setting homes and a church on fire." Two German travelers saw "the bodies of two elderly Muslims lying outside their hotel, battered and stabbed to death. One victim was decapitated."[2]

In Sri Lanka Buddhist Sinhalese and Hindu Tamils clashed. "By 1991 Amnesty International had reported thousands of disappearances, largely the result of state terrorism. Atrocities have been committed on both sides: torture, suicide bombings, executions, and the massacre of whole villages."[3] Here is divisive religion in its purest form.

Osama bin Laden, whose wealth is estimated at $300 million, operated his terrorist organization from Afghanistan. It is believed that his main terrorist group, Al Qaeda, may have followers in as many as fifty nations. His television interviews make clear that he is delighted to have followers who have killed thousands of innocent American civilians. He felt that the 9/11 terrorists were carrying out the 1998 *fatwa*: "It is the individual duty of Muslims to kill Americans, including civilians, anywhere possible."[4] The Great Buddhas of Bamiyan were destroyed by the Taliban in March 2001. Taliban leader Muhammad Omar declared that "these idols have been the Gods of the infidels."[5]

Divisive Religion in Europe

As a continent, Europe can claim the distinction of harboring the most divisive religion throughout history. The Crusades, the Inquisition, witch hunts, Protestant-Catholic wars, constant anti-Semitism, and the unspeakable Nazi Holocaust are shameful indications of unprecedented and cruel bigotry. During the Crusades, many Christian zealots would kill all Jews in their home town, on their way to killing all the Muslims they could find in the so-called Holy Land. Where in the teachings of Jesus did they find justification for such terrorist behavior?

At the Fourth Lateran Council of 1215, the Roman Catholic Church passed laws excluding Jews from public office, curtailing Jewish financial transactions, limiting Jewish interaction with Christians, and mandating Jewish dress requirements. In 1492 Ferdinand and Isabella gave Jews in Spain three choices: convert to Christianity, leave Spain, or be killed. Anabaptist leaders, repulsed after seizing control of the city of Münster, were tortured to death by the bishop's soldiers in 1534. For questioning the concept of the Holy Trinity, Michael Servetus was burned at the stake in 1553, with the approval of John Calvin.

German Anti-Semitism

In 1543 Martin Luther published a pamphlet called "Concerning the Jews and Their Lies." Here "Luther suggested sanctions for Jews who would not embrace Christianity: burn their places of worship, destroy their homes, seize their prayer books and Talmudic writings, and expel them from Europe."[6] In this work Luther said that the Jews' age-old suffering proved that God hated them, that the Talmud recommended robbery and murder of Christians, and that Jews poisoned water sources and killed Christian children to use their blood in Jewish rituals! This attack "influenced the Electors of Saxony and Brandenburg to expel the Jews from their territories, and set the tone in Germany for centuries, preparing its people for genocidal holocausts."[7]

"After 1918, the campaign literature of the German National People's Party was indistinguishable from that of the Nazis. In 1919 the former Kaiser called for the gassing of the Jews. In 1920 Orgesch, whose leaders often called publicly for death to the Jews, had some 300,000 members, 2.5 million rifles, 100,000 machine guns, 3000 artillery pieces, and 30 planes."[8] Knowing Adolf Hitler's stand against the Jews, German leaders gave him absolute power in 1933.

Alfred Rosenberg, ideologue of the Nazi Party, in *The Myth of the 20th Century,* said that the Nordic race, particularly the Germans, because of their innate superiority, were entitled to rule Europe, against their enemies, "the Russian Tatars and

Semites." Here Semites included not only Jews but also all Latin peoples and all Christians.

In 1935 the Nuremberg Laws virtually made outcasts of German Jews. They could not marry or have sexual relations with German non-Jews. Jews could not employ female non-Jews below the age of 45 in their homes. Jews were not allowed to fly the German flag but they could display "Jewish colors." A climate of hatred was being nourished that led to the monstrous cruelties of the Nazi Holocaust. For centuries, Germans are going to have to undergo rigorous self-examination to explain how their country arrived at this nadir of human existence.

Hannah Arendt pointed out that several other countries were also extremely anti-Semitic. Romanian soldiers killed 300,000 Jews, "mostly without any German help." Jews were executed "on the spot" in Serbia, despite German orders to transport Jews to concentration camps.

England

Protestant-Catholic hatred in England goes back at least to Henry VIII, who confiscated the monasteries when he succeeded the Pope as the religious authority in England. Oliver Cromwell, as governor of Ireland, massacred the garrisons of Drogheda and Wexford as examples of how Catholic Ireland would be treated unless it submitted to Protestant English rule. Ever since then, Irish soil has been stained with the blood of Catholic rebels and Protestant soldiers. Absentee landlordism accentuated the exploitation of Ireland by England.

Here is an example of modern religious terrorism in Ireland. Though Catholic, Chrissie Quinn sent her three sons to a Protestant school in Northern Ireland, since their father was Protestant. But her Catholic background was presumed to be a stain, and so Protestant arsonists threw a gasoline bomb into the Quinn home, burning the three boys to death. "All it takes is a trace of one religious background to make someone an enemy in the murderous minds of people from the other side."[9]

Leonard McCreery saw a Protestant paramilitary leader who had helped kill his brother. Leonard stabbed the leader, not fatally, confessed, and was imprisoned. Leonard's 17-year-old son Leon was ambushed, stabbed, and beaten with a bat. Leon survived, but needed 63 stitches to repair his wounds. Leon and his mother were forced to move to England to escape further violence. Robert Hamill, a Catholic, was killed in 1999 by Protestant militants. The lawyer appointed to represent him was killed when she turned on the ignition of her car.

David Trimble, the Northern Ireland Protestant leader who won the Nobel Peace Prize for his efforts to find common ground with the Irish Republican Party, won reelection by a small majority in March 2000. All 120 members of the Orange Order who are on the Ulster Party Council opposed Trimble. "I think he's finished," said Timothy Johnston, one of the delegates.[10]

Religious Persecution in Russia

Although the war between Russia and Chechnya is primarily over secession, there are many religious overtones to this struggle that has claimed tens of thousands of lives. Chechnya is Muslim, and wants to be ruled by its version of *sharia*, the Muslim code of conduct, which bans both alcohol and adultery. For example, adultery with a virgin can be grounds for being stoned to death. One thing uniting all Chechnyans is hatred of Russians. Recently Ramzan Idigov, 18, a Chechnyan soldier fighting the Russians, said: "When the war is over, I want to slaughter all Russians, women, children, old men. It makes no difference. In all wars, Muslims must win. It is written in the Koran that the year 2000 is the year of Muslims."[11]

Russia has a long history of having the church dominated by the state. Although the Russian Orthodox Church has always been a powerful force affecting all Russians, it kept silent during anti-Semitic pogroms and other instances of religious persecution. When the Soviet Union was dissolved, many Christian missionaries appeared in Russia and in other former Soviet republics. The Russian mafia sometimes kidnaps American missionaries and holds them for ransom. In one case, after holding the missionary in secret for many months, the mafia cut off his right index finger and mailed it to the missionary's parents to prove his identity. Steven Lee Myers reports that "during 1996 and 1997, the Russian Orthodox Church used its political influence to promote actions that discriminate against other religious groups."[12]

Religious Hatred in the Balkans

The Balkans are a textbook example of divisive religion. Ever since the Muslims won the battle of Kosovo in 1349, the Serbs have been trying to recapture that area for Orthodox Christianity. An Albanian writer, Fatos Lubunja, said: "We have a long history of manipulation. All those politicians, historians, and teachers who have created and nourished dangerous myths have manipulated history and in the end, created those close-minded horrible human beings who are ready to kill the others."[13]

Hatred among Croatian Catholics, Serbian Orthodox Christians, and Bosnian Muslims produced eight wars and two million deaths in the 20th century. During World War II the Croatian government conducted an especially vicious campaign against the Serbians and the Jews. A fascist group of Croatians called the Ustase killed as many as 100,00 Serbians and Jews. Recent Serbian leader Slobodan Milosevic, being tried for crimes against humanity, kept telling his people that all Croats are fascist killers, ignoring what his troops were doing to Muslim Bosnians. The Serbian Orthodox Church, though at times critical of Milosevic, has consistently sponsored Serbian nationalism. "The Orthodox Church is both bound by and responsible for the notion that wherever Serbs live and bury their dead should be a part of Serbia. The warlord Zeljko Raznjatovic, indicted as a war criminal, said his supreme commander was Patriarch Pavle."[14] Metropolitan Nikolaj, the highest ranking Serbian Orthodox official in Bosnia, dismissed the Roman Catholic Church as a "political organization," and Islam as "probably not a religion at all, but a weird mixture of Judaism and Christianity."[15]

In 2001 the United Nations war crimes tribunal in The Hague heard the testimonies of many Bosnian women who reported having been raped repeatedly by Serbian soldiers. Serbian barracks sometimes kept Bosnian women as sexual slaves: "at times, they rented or sold them for cash."[16] For the first time in history, an effort is being made to have a war crimes tribunal recognize sexual slavery as a crime against humanity. In March 2001 a judge from Zambia convicted three Bosnian Serbian soldiers of rape and sexual enslavement, a landmark case.

Divisive Religion in Africa

Recent African history depicts the end of European colonization, the rise of unfamiliar nationalism, and an accompanying lack of civil, political, and religious tolerance.

Algeria, the second largest country in Africa, has huge oil and gas reserves. Its proximity to France, Italy, and Spain makes it a geographical bridge between Africa and Europe. In 1992 army generals called off an election in Algeria, fearing a victory for the fundamentalist Islamic Salvation Front (ISF). A militant splinter from the ISF called the Armed Islamic Group (AIG) told its soldiers that "the triumph of Islam justifies the killing of anybody who does not actively support them."[17] More than 100,000 people have been killed in clashes between the AIG and government forces. The U.S. State Department lists the AIG among the top ten terrorist groups in the world.

In December 1999 an Algerian, Ahmed Rissan, was arrested for attempting to smuggle bomb-making materials into the United States. In 2000 Yasmina Khadra's book *In the Name of God* described current religious violence in Algeria.

In December 1988 Pan-American Flight #103 crashed over Lockerbie, Scotland, killing 270 people. Wreckage traced evidence to two Libyan intelligence officers, who were finally tried by a court in the Netherlands.

Recently violence has broken out between the mostly Christian Igbo and the predominantly Muslim Hausa in Nigeria. Thousands of lives have been lost, and numerous homes, churches, and mosques have been destroyed. The Yoruba, almost equally divided between Muslim and Christian, seem to be able to get along reasonably well with both sides.

The Slaughter in Rwanda

One of the worst recent cases of genocide occurred in Rwanda in 1994. The Hutu president demonized Tutsis as uncontrollable rebels. When he died in an airplane crash that year, a terrible wave of killings ensued. "The government of Rwanda called on everyone in the Hutu majority to murder everyone in the Tutsi minority. In 100 days 800,000 persons were killed, most of them individually cut down with knives. The daily killing rate exceeded that of the Nazi Holocaust and the deed was done mostly by neighbors, coworkers, even family members."[18]

The Hutu militia believes in the divine mission of wiping out the Tutsis. One Hutu, a leading citizen in his village, was bawled out by a Hutu government official for being lax in carrying out his mission. The citizen asked if the policy applied to those with 50% Tutsi blood. Assured that it did, the citizen beheaded his wife in the village square. Then the citizen asked if the policy applied to those with 25% Tutsi blood. Told that it did, he seized his machete, brought his four sons to the square, and one by one decapitated them. Thus did this Hutu citizen show his loyalty to the "divine" mission![19] Hutu raiders, called the *interahamwe*, have attacked refugee camps near the border of Rwanda and Congo. One Hutu engineer stated that "they used to lie to the population that God sent the *interahamwe* to help the Hutu in Rwanda."[20]

Sudan

A Harvard law professor, Mary Ann Glendon, says that "Sudan's National Islamic Front has been conducting a genocidal campaign, increasingly driven by religious radicals, against rebels in the predominantly Christian and animist southern part of the country that has already claimed more victims than the conflicts in Rwanda, Bosnia, and Kosovo combined. The overwhelming majority of the casualties are not rebels but civilians who do not share the regime's radical Islamic ideology."[21] Some persons have been beaten and forced into unpaid labor. Some have been given Arabic names and been forced to convert to Islam. Government planes have repeatedly bombed humanitarian targets, such as hospitals and food distribution centers.

Egypt

An Egyptian religious leader, Sheik Omar Abdel-Rahman, was the mastermind behind the bombing of the World Trade Center in New York City in 1993, a terrorist act which killed six people and wounded more than a thousand others. Calling the United States "a den of evil and fornication," Abdel-Rahman said that "Muslims must kill the enemies of Allah, in every way and everywhere, in order to liberate themselves from the grandchildren of the pigs and apes who are educated at the table of

Zionists, communists, and imperialists."[22] Once again we see divisive religion at work, killing people allegedly in the name of God.

Divisive Religion in the Middle East

All scriptures contain both unitive and divisive elements. While Yahweh was still conceived of as a God of war, the Torah brings out some of Yahweh's divisive commands.

For example, in I Samuel 15:3, Yahweh tells Samuel to "slay man and woman, infant and suckling Amalekite." When some children made fun of Elisha's baldness, "Elisha cursed them in the name of the Lord, and two she-bears came out of the woods and tore 42 of the boys" (II Kings 2:24). When Jehu was chosen by Yahweh to succeed Ahab as King of Israel, he had Ahab's 70 children killed and beheaded, with their heads put on display at the city gates (II Kings 10:7–8). The prophet Isaiah tells what will happen to the Babylonians: "Their infants will be dashed in pieces before their eyes, and their wives ravished" (Isaiah 13:16).

It is ironic that the region called the Holy Land has been throughout history the site of the greatest intolerance, violence, and unholy conduct among the various religious groups located there. It has been the site of Jewish, Christian, and Muslim terrorism for centuries.

In 1947 the United Nations adopted resolutions establishing homelands in Palestine for two emigrant peoples, the Muslim Palestinians and the Jewish Israelis. Immediately each group refused to acknowledge the U.N. resolution providing for the other's homeland On 14 May 1948, the day the independent nation of Israel was established, armies from the Arab League attacked Israel. In 1949 armistices were reached between Israel and member nations of the Arab League.

Israel

During the Suez Crisis of 1956 Israel invaded Egypt's Sinai peninsula, and when forced back by the United Nations, retained control of the Gaza Strip. In 1967 Egypt recaptured the Gaza Strip and blocked the Gulf of Aqaba to Israeli ships. Israeli troops won the Six-Day War, however, and so once again Israel controlled the Gaza Strip, the Sinai peninsula, the West Bank of the Jordan River, and the Golan Heights.

Israel repeatedly invaded southern Lebanon to destroy hostile bases, and launched a full-scale invasion of Lebanon in 1982 in an effort to destroy the Palestine Liberation Organization. Israel collaborated with Lebanese Christian militia to enter Palestinian refugee camps at Sabra and Satila, where hundreds of civilians were massacred.

Meron Benvenisti, former deputy mayor of Jerusalem, resented that Israeli forces took all of the extensive Palestinian archives upon entering Beirut. "This was not only to destroy them as a military power, but also to take from them their history, not to allow them to be a respectable movement. If you are at war, you dehumanize your enemy, otherwise you are a murderer."[23]

Anthony Lewis said in 1989 that at his family's seder table at Passover, the Palestinians were like "Banquo's ghost," for Prime Minister Yitzhak Shamir said that Israel's army would crush them "like grasshoppers." Lewis listed Israel's violations of the spirit of Passover: "122 Palestinians shot or beaten to death; mass detention without trial; isolating resistant populations; and banning the press. At the heart of the choice is a simple question: 'Are Jews ready to accept Palestinians as a people with their own claim to nationhood?'"[24]

When Jewish settlers on the West Bank expelled Palestinians from their homes in the middle of the night and danced in exultation, Israeli scholar Clinton Bailey said that "the humane Judaism of our fathers" seemed to be quickly turned into arrogance and oppression. "Where," asked Bailey, "is the Biblical teaching, 'deal justly with the stranger in thy gates?'"[25]

Iran

Iran is a huge country, larger than Alaska (population 70 million), the only non-Arabic Islamic country in the Middle East. It is 89% Shiite and 10% Sunni Muslim. "The core of the Shiite faith is that the earthly community should be led by a charismatic semi-divine leader, the imam, who acts as the mediator between the human and the divine, while the Sunni belief is that the individual stands directly face to face with God, with no need for an intercessor."[26]

Shah Pahlavi, supported by Britain and the United States, was overthrown by a revolution led by the Ayatollah Khomeini in

1978. Violence resulted from the widespread religious protests that year. Thousands of persons were killed by religious militia forces in 1979. Khomeini replaced the civil code of the 1906 constitution with the Islamic *sharia*, under which the mullahs served as prosecutors, judge, and jury. The Family Protection Act of 1975 was nullified. Khomeini declared, "There can be only one party in Iran, the Party of God." Opponents were to be considered as God's enemies and thus subject to execution.

Khomeini's view was that the United States, by supporting Israel, was keeping the Muslims from Jerusalem, their third holiest shrine (after Mecca and Medina). Thus the United States was "the country of Satan." Elementary schoolchildren chanted, "Death to America!"

Muslim militants seized the American embassy in Tehran on 4 November 1979, and held 62 Americans hostage until President Ronald Reagan was inaugurated on 21 January 1981. The next day Iran's elected president, Abolhassan Bani-Sadr, was removed from office and Khomeini took over all executive powers. Another wave of executions then took place, chiefly of political moderates and non-Islamic persons.

In September 1980 Saddam Hussein sent his Iraqi troops into Iran in an effort to overthrow the Khomeini regime. Hussein wanted to capture the oil-rich border province of Khuzistan, as well as gain control of both sides of the Shatt-al-Arab waterway, the confluence of the Tigris and the Euphrates Rivers. Also, Hussein was reacting against his own Shiite majority, which Iranian Shiites were exhorting to overthrow Hussein's Sunni minority.

Hussein underestimated Khomeini's charismatic hold on Iran's army, particularly the youth. Tens of thousands of Iranian young men cast themselves on barbed wire, or marched into mine fields under machine-gun fire, willingly dying for their faith. Many of them wore red headbands with the phrase "Warrior of God" and with small metal keys showing that they would go directly to heaven if killed in the holy war declared by Khomeini. Across their backs was often stenciled the slogan: "I have the special permission of the Imam to enter heaven."[27]

The holy war between Iran and Iraq raged on for eight years, with over one million persons killed on each side. The Reagan administration secretly sold weapons to Iran in exchange for release of hostages being held in Lebanon.

Khomeini died in 1989. His successor as president, Ali-Akbar Rafsanjani, continued the practice of religious terrorism. In 1993 James Woolsey, director of the U.S. Central Intelligence Agency, testified before Congress that more assassinations of Iranians living outside Iran had been done in the 3-year regime of Rafsanjani than in the 10-year rule of Khomeini.

In 1997 a new president, Mohammed Khatami, was elected by a huge majority. His friend and yet adversary, the Ayatollah Ali Khamenei, remains the religious leader of Iran. Khatami clearly wants better relations with the United States and other Western nations, but Khamenei fears that such relations would weaken Islam in Iran.

Despite continuing violence in Iran, Khatami seems to be making a genuine effort to lead his country away from divisive religion and towards a democracy that respects human rights. History will record whether a long period of religious terrorism is finally reaching a well deserved end.

Iraq

Iraq, a nation of 25 million people (roughly 2/3 Shiite and 1/3 Sunni), is on the site of ancient Mesopotamia, the fertile land between the Tigris and Euphrates Rivers. Sumer was an early civilization here, followed by Babylon. First the Assyrians, then the Persians, and finally the Ottoman Turks conquered the land and ruled it for centuries.

After World War I Great Britain governed Iraq under a League of Nations mandate. British influence, protecting huge oil interests, remained predominant until World War II. Iraq was part of the Arab League that had attacked Israel at its inception. Following that conflict, most of Iraq's 85,000 Jews emigrated to Israel.

A revolution in Iraq in 1958 overthrew the monarchy and set up a republic. Oil holdings and other industries were nationalized. In 1968 a branch of the international Ba'ath Socialist Party took over the government. Iran aided Kurdish rebels in northern Iraq, leading to the destruction of numerous Kurdish villages by Iraqi bombers.

While the Ayatollah Khomeini lived in exile in Iraq in the 1970's, he saw Saddam Hussein's harsh treatment of Iraq's Shiites. He constantly urged this majority group to get rid of Saddam's "godless" regime. In 1986 the May 15 Organization, a terrorist group supported by Iraq, exploded a bomb on an American plane flying from Rome to Athens. Four American passengers were killed. In 1988 Iraq used chemical weapons against Iranian and Kurdish forces in northern Iraq. The United Nations called this action an atrocity.

In 1990 the *Washington Post* reported that "over the past five years, the United States approved for sale to Iraq $1.5 billion worth of computers, electronic equipment, and machine tools that could be used to develop nuclear weapons, missiles, and poison gas." Anthony Lewis stated in the *New York Times* that the Reagan administration "lobbied against and blocked Congressional efforts to impose sanctions on Iraq in 1988 for its use of poison gas against its Kurdish citizens."[28]

When President George H. Bush mounted a successful international coalition to drive Iraq out of Kuwait, Saddam's battle cry was the superiority of the Muslims over "the infidels, a confrontation of justice against evil, of faith against infidelity, of the rights of the supreme Allah against the devil's desire."[29] During the Gulf War Iraq bombed civilian targets in Israel. "By God," said Saddam, "the fire will eat up half of Israel if it tries anything against Iraq."

Following the Gulf War, United Nations inspectors found installations in Iraq where outlawed chemical weapons were being made or stored. Saddam kept blocking inspectors from access to certain areas. Kurds and Shiites in Iraq wonder how Saddam's dictatorship there can have the gall to call itself a "republic."

Jordan

Modern Jordan corresponds to the Biblical lands of Edom, Gilead, and Moab. It is 92% Sunni and 8% Christian. In 1948 Jordan joined the Arab League in fighting Israel. Jordanian troops occupied the West Bank and the Old City of Jerusalem, which was annexed in 1950. Israel recaptured these areas in the Six-Day War of 1967, after which many Palestinians fled to Jordan.

Jordan's location places it in a frontline position opposing Israel. This gives it support from a number of Muslim nations. But King Hussein's moderate stance also gave it support from the United States. Initially King Hussein recognized the Palestinian Liberation Organization, but when he found the PLO guilty of political subversion, he forced the PLO out of Jordan.

In the Gulf War, King Hussein actively supported Iraq, feeling that his small army could not protect its border from stronger Iraqi forces. But he constantly sought for peace in the Middle East. In 1994 he signed a peace accord with Yitzhak Rabin and the Israelis. King Hussein was one of the most prominent Middle East leaders trying to substitute unitive religion for divisive religion. It is hoped that other Middle East leaders will duplicate his passion for peace.

A striking example of divisive religion in Jordan, however, occurred in 1999, when a 22-year-old Jordanian, Wafik Abu Abseh, bashed his sister with a paving stone, killing her when he found her with a man. "We do not consider this murder," he said. "It was like cutting off a finger." He added that he was simply carrying out God's law. His brother stated, "We are Muslims, and in our religion she had to be executed."[30] Many Muslims would not agree with this interpretation of the Koran.

Often the killing takes place on rumor alone, and autopsy reveals that the girl is still a virgin. Even if the girl is pregnant due to rape, she and the baby must die. In one case a 17-year-old Jordanian girl, raped by a friend of her father, was shot eight times by the father and the brother. Jail sentences are minimal in such cases, frequently no more than two months.

Divisive religion has no difficulty in taking lives, even asserting that God is pleased with the murder. Humanity needs a worldwide code of spiritual rights, not only to protect human beings, but also to keep God from being used as a shield for human error, sin, and cruelty.

Lebanon

Modern Lebanon made an interesting experiment with unitive religion. For a while, its governmental structure reflected its religious diversity. The custom was for the president to be Maronite Christian, the prime minister to be Sunni, and the president of the legislature to be Shiite. Unfortunately, in time divisive religion dissolved this bold effort.

In 1975 religious strife turned violent. Palestinians and fundamentalist Muslims fought Maronites and the Christian Phalange Party. Over 60,000 deaths occurred, with billions of dollars of property damage. Syrian troops tried to bring peace, even battling Palestinians.

Then, in 1981, fighting broke out between Syrian troops and Christian militia. As the war spread, Israel bombed Beirut, killing many civilians. Israeli and Syrian soldiers fought in the Bekaa Valley in 1982. President Bashir Gemayel, a Maronite, was assassinated. In response, Israeli forces occupied the Muslim quarters of West Beirut. Christian militia, with Israeli approval, invaded two refugee camps and killed hundreds of Palestinian civilians.

Western nations stationed troops in Beirut in an effort to keep peace. The U.S. embassy in Beirut was bombed in April 1983, resulting in 50 deaths. In October the U.S. marine barracks was bombed, killing 241 Americans and 58 French soldiers. The bombs were attributed to the Lebanese Party of God (Hezbollah), a terrorist group supported by Syria and Iran.

Religious terrorism now included hijacking of airplanes and kidnapping of innocent civilians. The Party of God hijacked TWA Flight 847 in June 1985. An American marine's body was dumped on the tarmac at Beirut airport. In 1987 President Rashad Karabi of Lebanon was killed.

Two American journalists, Joseph Cicippio and Terry Anderson, were kidnapped and held hostage in Lebanon. When interviewed, the captor of Cicippio said that his children had been burned by napalm dropped by an American plane piloted by an Israeli. "The hostage holder of Terry Anderson found his village shelled by the U.S. battleship New Jersey, during which he lost his entire family, including his wife, children, aunts, uncles, and grandparents."[31] Violence begets violence, especially when God's name is used by both sides.

In 1988 the Party of God kidnapped and killed American Lt. Col. William R. Higgins, a member of the U.N. peacekeeping force. The government led by Christian prime minister Omar Karami was ousted in 1992 after a series of riots. In 1994 Lebanon banned the Christian political party Lebanese Forces and arrested its leader. This bloody record of religious violence helps demonstrate the fact that without world law, there will be world lawlessness. In 1987 Mikhail Gorbachev pleaded for an international tribunal capable of outlawing terrorism. At present, the World Court can handle cases against nations but not against individuals. A bill of spiritual rights is needed to protect all human beings from the use of violence in adjudicating disputes. Such a code will need United Nations approval and follow-up to prevent it from being merely words that do not deter terrorists.

Palestinians

Palestinians like to point out that the United States and other Western countries are quick to support all United Nations resolutions favoring Israel, but deaf to such resolutions on behalf of their cause. Simple fairness and evenhanded justice have been woefully lacking in the Western powers' approach to Middle Eastern problems. There religion, which should be a unifying force, has been not only divisive but deadly. Without justice, vengeance and hatred mount daily, and peace seems a forlorn and distant prospect.

When Israel successfully defended itself in 1948, Jews from all over the world began to migrate to Israel. Many Palestinians left for refugee camps in Jordan, Lebanon, and Syria. In many ways the Palestinians are now like the Jews of history—a people without a homeland. Of the nearly six million Palestinians in 1992, 15% are outside the Middle East but the remainder are near to their original home—from 32% in Jordan down to 5% in Syria.

The effort to reunite the Palestinians has been fruitless. In 1970 King Hussein evicted the PLO from Jordan, stating that it was trying to undermine his government. Syria expelled Yasir Arafat in the 1980's for failure to agree with Syrian foreign policy. When Arafat supported Iraq during the Gulf War, Saudi Arabia switched from its link with the PLO and instead made friendly overtures to the rival group Hamas.

The Palestinians are badly split among themselves, mostly over how much violence should be used in an effort to secure land. Leaving behind his early days as a terrorist, Arafat takes a more moderate stand than most other of their leaders. Supporting him are El Fatah, the Popular Front for the Liberation of Palestine (PFLP), the Democratic Front for the Liberation of Palestine, the Palestine Liberation Front, and the Arab Liberation Front. Most of these groups are quite small. Active in opposition to Arafat are the PFLP-General Command (which condones hijacking and attacks on all Israelis and some other civilians), El Fatah Uprising, El Fatah Revolutionary Council (which wants to destroy Israel, and has used terrorist attacks in Europe), and the Popular Struggle Front.[32]

In 1987 Palestinians in Gaza and the West Bank began the stone-throwing protests called the *intifada.* By 1991 hundreds of demonstrators had been killed by Israeli police. In one retaliation ten Israelis were stabbed to death. To get even, the Shamir government in Israel set up a curfew and travel bans for Palestinians, resulting in the loss of jobs for most of the 120,000 Palestinians from Gaza and the West Bank who worked in Israel.

Referring to Arafat's support of Iraq in the Gulf War, Israeli professor Avishai Margalit said, "The Palestinians made a mistake, but we mortally ambushed them. Their daily lives had become so rotten—with humiliations, harassment, arrests, detentions, beatings, and torture—that I understand, but not accept, why they acted as they did. In a sense, the Palestinians were entitled to their irrationality. Our occupation is tragically emulating South African apartheid."[33]

In 1992 Israel deported 400 Palestinians to Lebanon as terrorists. When the Palestinians resumed the *intifada,* Israel attacked suspected terrorist bases in Lebanon, killing many Palestinians. In 1996 the terrorist group Hamas took responsibility for a series of suicide bombs which killed 60 Israelis. In 2000 the *intifada* intensified, resulting in many deaths on both sides. Divisive religion keeps Semitic peoples engaged in a violent civil war, ignoring the teachings about peace contained in the Torah and the Koran.

Saudi Arabia

Saudi Arabia is a Muslim monarchy based on the *sharia.* King Ibn-Saud, an ardent anti-Zionist, contributed troops to oppose the new Israel in 1948. His son, King Faisal, sent soldiers to fight in the Arab-Israeli war in 1973. Saudi Arabia not only opposed the Camp David Accords, but even tried to get Egypt ostracized by Muslim countries for working for peace with

Israel. In 1987, when Iranian pilgrims rioted in Mecca, Saudi troops fired on them, killing 275 Iranians and 127 other persons. An American military training center in Riyadh was bombed in 1995, killing seven people. Four anti-royal Saudi dissenters were convicted and beheaded. In 1996 an American barracks in Dhahran was bombed, killing 19 American airmen and wounding over 300 other persons.

Syria

Syria was established as an independent republic in 1941. It took part in the Muslim coalition against Israel in 1948. When the Ba'ath Party took control in 1963, all other political parties were banned. The Golan Heights, from which Syria had long shelled Israel, was lost to Israel in the 1967 war. In 1973 Syria and Egypt attacked Israel in the Yom Kippur War

The Muslim Brotherhood attempted a military coup in 1982. It was put down by the Syrian army, but only after each side had suffered over 5000 casualties. Called a rogue nation by some, Syria has been implicated in a number of acts of international terrorism in support of Iranian, Libyan, and Palestinian causes.

However, Syria supported the coalition against Iraq in the Gulf War. Bombings by the militant Hamas led to cessation of peace talks with Israel in 1995. Despite peace overtures by the Israeli government of Ehud Barak, hostilities continue to occur in Lebanon between Syria and Israel. When the Party of God killed seven Israeli soldiers, Israel retaliated by bombing electrical generating plants in Lebanon. When Barak said that rightist elements in Israel were trying to derail the peace movement, a high Syrian official replied, "We could also get 100,000 people on the street to protest against the peace."[34]

Turkey

At one time the Muslim Ottoman Empire controlled not only Turkey but also Arabia, Bulgaria, Egypt, Iran, Serbia, and most of the Middle East. Large numbers of Christian Armenians were killed or driven from Turkey from 1875 to 1925. For collaborating with Germany and its allies in World War I, the Ottoman Empire was dissolved after the war. In 1923 the Republic of Turkey was established. The Kurds, a large Muslim minority in southeastern Turkey, were pressured to abandon their ethnic identity.

General Mustafa Kemal Ataturk was elected first president of the republic. During a civil crisis in 1924 he condemned to death some of his former colleagues. Fearing the influence of the mullahs on the government, he got the assembly to abolish the caliphate and dervish sects, making Turkey a secular republic. Its strategic location makes Turkey a natural cultural bridge between Asia and Europe. Although it served as the site of historic clashes between Muslims and Christians, Turkey has managed to insulate itself quite well from fundamentalist militants on both sides. Because of its tolerant treatment of Jews, Turkey was often a refuge for them when no other country seemed hospitable to Jews.

Cyprus has long been contested between Christian Greeks and Muslim Turks. In 1974 Turkey invaded Cyprus and established a state among Turkish residents. Clashes between the two religious groups occur sporadically, especially in border areas.

Violence has also been seen as Turkey puts down extremist Muslim sects or Kurdish efforts at separation. "Prior to September 12, 1980, there were some 20 political murders every day," reported Ali Kocman, head of a Turkish business association. A Turkish Party of God is suspected of killing thousands of Kurdish separatists in the late 1980's. Occasionally Turkish warplanes bomb Kurdish bases in Iraq and southeastern Turkey. In March 1995 Turkey sent 50,000 troops into Iraq to try to stop Kurdish guerrilla raids. Turkey regularly receives American financial support because of its determined effort to avoid Muslim fundamentalism.

Historic American Religious Intolerance

An authority on American Puritans, Perry Miller described their innate intolerance: "New England Congregationalists had come to the wilderness assuming, as the wisdom of several centuries had assumed, that the notion of a state's permitting different religions to exist side by side was unthinkable." Massachusetts Puritans exiled Roger Williams because of his different religious beliefs, feeling assured that his colony would end in savage anarchy. "The New Englanders were in no sense pioneers of religious liberty," Miller stated. "They resolved to stand resolutely for absolute uniformity, for a rigorous suppression of all dissent, by capital punishment if necessary."[35]

Puritan leader John Cotton said, "I do not conceive that God did ever ordain democracy as a fit government for either church or commonwealth. Theocracy is directed by scripture as the best form of government in both areas." When John Winthrop governed Massachusetts, as chief magistrate he was responsible to see that people obeyed the laws outlined in the Bible. "As steward entrusted with a divine stewardship, he exercised absolute legislative and judicial powers. In his council the ministers were summoned to participate, but no others."[36]

The Puritan preacher Nathaniel Ward said that "God does nowhere in His word ask Christian states to give toleration to such adversaries of His truth as Anabaptists, Antinomians, and other enthusiasts. He that is willing tolerate any religion besides his own either doubts his own or is not sincere in it."[37] Early America had its share of divisive religion.

In his popular poem "The Day of Doom," Michael Wigglesworth in 1662 explained that when unbaptized babies died, God showed them His mercy by allowing them to live in "the easiest room in Hell." Quakers suffered because of their religious beliefs. Between 1659 and 1661, for example, four Quakers were hanged for being dissenters.

Roman Catholics were not welcome in early America. Even in Maryland Catholics could not vote or hold public office. In Virginia Catholic priests were given five days to leave the colony or be punished. In Pennsylvania in 1757 Catholics were forbidden to bear arms. New York finally repealed its anti-priest law in 1784. North Carolina did not allow Catholics to vote until 1835.

In 1844 an angry mob stormed the jail in Carthage, Illinois, and murdered Mormon leaders Joseph and Hyrum Smith because of their religious views. Disqualification of Jews from holding public office was finally removed in Maryland in 1826, and in North Carolina in 1868. Jews were granted the right to vote in New Hampshire as recently as 1877. America had a hard time accepting Jefferson's grand statement that "all men are created equal, and endowed by their Creator with certain inalienable rights."

Anti-Catholic Feelings

Samuel Adams said that there is "much more to be feared from the growth of Popery in America than from the Stamp Act." John Jay, the first Chief Justice of the Supreme Court, said that Catholics should be denied the right to vote. Harvard sponsored a series of lectures, one of which was dedicated to "exposing the idolatry, errors, and superstitions of the Romish church."[38]

Anti-Catholic sentiments grew more intense as more Irish people came to America. Robert Baird in his book *Religion in America* (1841) said that "of all the forms of error in the United States, Romanism is by far the most formidable." Catholics were attacked for having their own private schools, for having large and opulent churches, and for supporting big city political bosses. In 1834 Reverend Lyman Beecher warned that "the Catholic Church holds now in darkness and bondage nearly half the civilized world." Orestes Brownson, a convert to Catholicism, confessed: "I do not like in general our Irish population. They have no clear understanding of their religion."[39] In big cities job notices often read: NO IRISH NEED APPLY.

Soon violence began to be used to express religious preferences. The Ursuline nunnery in Charlestown, Massachusetts, was pillaged and burned in 1844. That year an anti-Catholic riot in Philadelphia burned 30 Irish homes and an Irish fire station. A clash at a Catholic church led to 14 people killed and 50 injured. In 1854 Father John Bapst was tarred and feathered over a quarrel about whether the Bible should be read in schools. In 1855 in Louisville more than 20 were killed and hundreds wounded in an anti-Catholic riot.

The *Atlantic Monthly* joined the bandwagon in 1870, stating that "devotion to a constitution, to a flag, respect for law, regard for others' rights—all these true republican characteristics are most rarely to be found in an Irishman." "Prestigious journals like *Harper's Weekly* and the *Atlantic Monthly* regularly featured anti-Catholic articles and cartoons" in the 1880's. When candidate James G. Blaine campaigned for president in 1884, he called the Democrats the party of "rum, Romanism, and rebellion."[40] In 1887 Henry F. Bowers founded the American Protective Association, whose members promised "to never vote for a

Catholic, never to hire one when a Protestant was available, and never join Catholics in a strike."[41]

The Ku Klux Klan always had Catholics at or near the top of the list of people to hate. When Al Smith ran for president in 1928, smear politics were used against him because of his religion. With this sort of seamy background, we can appreciate what a milestone was reached when John F. Kennedy was elected president in 1960.

Recent American Divisive Religion

In 1985 Louis Farrakhan spoke to an audience of 25,000 people in Madison Square Garden in New York City. Bob Herbert said that "he ranted and raved about white people in general and Jews in particular." Farrakhan even suggested that Afro-American leaders who opposed him should "pay a price. Do you think the leader should sell you out and then live? We should make examples of the leaders."[42]

In the late 1980's an Operation Rescue movement in Atlanta claimed Biblical justification for killing abortion providers. Rev. David Trosch, a Catholic priest in Mobile, called the murder of Dr. David Gunn, an abortion provider, "justifiable homicide." Trosch commended four bombings of abortion clinics, declaring that "all of the bombings were against people highly offensive to God."[43]

Eric Rudolph is being sought in connection with the bombing at the 1996 Olympic Games in Atlanta. The anti-Semitic Christian Identity Movement resents such games as representing One Worldism and racial integration. Rudolph is also suspected of involvement in the 1998 bombing of an abortion clinic in Birmingham, in which a security policeman was killed. Notes left at the scene were signed by agents of the so-called Army of God.

Chevie Kehoe, a member of the Christian Identity sect, killed 8-year-old Sarah and her parents Nancy and William Mueller in 1996 in Idaho. The Christian Identity group believe that Jews are not white people, and are descendants of Satan. Kehoe said, "If they're not white, they have no right to exist." Kehoe sent a robber, Faron Lovelace, into a grocery store owned by Jewish people. Lovelace said, "Jews are easy to kill if they resist the robbery."[44] Divisive religion could scarcely be better stated than this insulting nonsense.

A group calling itself Arizona Patriots was arrested in 1996. The members had plans to blow up hydroelectric dams, abortion clinics, and synagogues. One wonders what type of patriotism they had in mind. Then again, people who have killed at abortion clinics justify their actions by saying they are pro-life.

Benjamin Smith, of the World Church of the Creator, killed two persons and wounded a number of other people before committing suicide in 1999. Letters from the group sent to Afro-American colleges in eight states quote the church's mission: "The total destruction of your race is our mission in life."[45] Some of the letters were also sent to the American Jewish Community Center in Atlanta. Benjamin Williams, an admitted white supremacist, confessed to setting arson fires at three synagogues in San Francisco in June 1999, causing a million dollars in damages.

Often Christians are the victims of hate group killings. In 1997 three Christian students were killed at a prayer meeting in West Paducah, Kentucky. At the Littleton massacre in 1998 Eric Harris killed Cassie Bernall because she said that she believed in God. In Fort Worth Larry Gene Ashbrook attacked a group of teenagers at Wedgewood Baptist Church in 1999. His guns and pipe bombs left seven persons dead and seven more wounded. "It's all bull what you believe,"[46] he said in explanation of his actions. Divisive religion respects no belief but its own.

Buford Furrow Jr. entered a Jewish daycare center in Los Angeles in 1999 and started shooting children and adults. Five people died. Later he killed a Filipino-American postal worker. A member of the Aryan nation, Furrow says that he hates Jews and people of color. An editorial analyzing Furrow's crime said that "racism and supremacism are the legacy of a violent history from which we have only recently begun to think of absolving ourselves. One only needs to know that any argument that ends in division, exclusion, and hatred is by its nature evil."[47]

Some girls in Utah are being forced into polygamy against their will. One teenager, badly bruised, called police from a truck stop. She said that her father had forced her into becoming the fifteenth wife of her uncle. When she tried to escape, her father whipped her. Lillian Bowles is one of forty children in a family where her mother is one of eight wives. "We were always taught to hide," she said. "We were taught early on that we were God's chosen people, and everyone else was condemned to hell. If you left, you were condemned too."[48] In cases like these, the state of Utah has decided not to press polygamy charges. Most men in plural marriages have only one marriage certificate; the others are sealed in church records, leaving no paper trail.

Bob Jones University, which until recently banned interracial dating among its students, issued an Internet statement explaining its policies. Citing the Tower of Babel account in Genesis 10 and 11 as evidence of God's opposition to racial mingling, the statement confessed: "If there are those who charge us with being opposed to the doctrines and theology of the Catholic church, we plead guilty. All religion, including Catholicism, which teaches that salvation is by religious works or church dogma is false. We love the practicing Catholic and earnestly desire him to accept the Christ of the Cross, leave the false system that has enslaved his soul, and enjoy the freedoms of sins forgiven that is available for any of us in Christ only."[49] This would have given Mother Teresa a chuckle as she bathed the sores of the lepers in Calcutta.

Divisive religion, which negates all faiths other than one's own, continues to be one of the most powerful barriers to world peace, and one of the main causes of religious terrorism. It obviously must be replaced by unitive religion if we are ever to achieve lasting world peace.

REFERENCES

[1] Howard W. French, *New York Times,* 14 November 1999, p. 3.

[2] *New York Times*, 31 January 1999, p. 10.

[3] Jacqueline Cary, *New York Times Book Review*, 17 January 1999, p. 17.

[4] *New York Times*, 25 October 1998, 4:9; 14 January 2001, p. 13.

[5] Barry Bearak, *New York Times*, 4 March 2001, p. 6.

[6] Michael Marissen, *New York Times*, 2 April 2000, 2:38.

[7] Will Durant, *The Reformation* (Simon & Schuster, 1957), p. 727.

[8] John Weiss, *New York Times Book Review*, 28 February 1999, p. 4.

[9] Warren Hoge, *New York Times*, 19 July 1998, 4:4.

[10] Ibid., 26 March 2000, p. 4.

[11] *New York Times Magazine*, 27 February 2000, p. 51.

[12] *New York Times*, 27 July 1997, 4:7.

[13] Ibid., 11 April 2000, 4:5.

[14] Blaine Harden and Carlotta Gall, *New York Times*, 4 July 1999, pp. 1, 4.

[15] Chris Hedges, *New York Times*, 16 March 1997, p. 6.

[16] Marlise Simons, *New York Times*, 18 February 2001, p. 4.

[17] John F. Burns, *New York Times*, 2 January 2000, 4:4.

[18] *New York Times Book Review*, 6 December 1998, p. 98.

[19] Wole Soyinka, *New York Times Book Review*, 4 October 1998, p. 11.

[20] *Maryknoll*, April 1999, p. 42.

[21] Steven Emerson, *Arizona Republic*, 11 July 1993, p. C1.

[22] Ian Fisher, *New York Times*, 27 December 1998, p. 8.

[23] David K. Shipler, *New York Times*, 20 February 1983, p. E4.

[24] Anthony Lewis, *New York Times*, 3 April 1988, 4:17.

[25] Ibid., 2 February 1992, 4:17.

[26] G.H. Jansen, *New York Times Magazine,* 6 January 1980, p. 45.

[27] Terence Smith, ibid., 12 February 1984, p. 21.

[28] *The Washington Spectator*, 1 January 1991, p. 1.

[29] *Christian Science Monitor*, as quoted in *The Washington Spectator*, 15 November 1990, p.2.

[30] Douglas Jehl, *New York Times*, 20 June 1999, p. 9.

[31] M.T. Mehdi, *New York Times*, 27 August 1989, 4:18.

[32] *New York Times,* 20 March 1988, 4:3.

[33] Judith Miller, *New York Times Magazine*, 21 July 1991, p. 32.

[34] Susan Sachs, *New York Times*, 13 February 2000, 4:6.

[35] Perry Miller, *The American Puritans* (Doubleday, 1956), p. 94.

[36] Vernon L. Parrington, *Main Currents in American Thought* (Harcourt Brace, 1930), vol. 1, pp. 31, 42.

[37] Perry Miller, pp. 97, 100.

[38] James Hennesey, *American Catholics* (Oxford University Press, 1981), p. 56.

[39] Ibid., p. 119.

[40] Ibid., pp. 164, 182.

[41] Ibid., p. 182.

[42] Bob Herbert, *New York Times*, 29 August 1999, 4:15.

[43] John Kifner, ibid., 6 December 1998, 4:13.

44 Jo Thomas, ibid., 12 December 1999, p. 22.

45 *New York Times*, 9 January 2000, p. 17.

46 David Van Biema, *Time*, 27 September, p. 42.

47 *New York Times*, 15 August 1999, 4:14.

48 Timothy Egan, *New York Times Magazine*, 28 February 1999, pp. 51 ff.

49 *New York Times,* 5 March 2000, 4:5.

CHAPTER IV

UNITIVE RELIGION: PATHS TO PEACE

Divisive religion, as we have seen, involves exclusiveness and discrimination, and often leads to hatred, terrorism, and war. Unitive religion, on the other hand, involves acceptance of persons and viewpoints unlike one's own. In the process, broad bridges of understanding and awareness are built across chasms of religious, racial, gender, and nationality difference. Here then is humanity's best hope for laying the foundations of world peace. Fortunately, there is much unitive religion in the modern world.

Recent Unitive Judaism

Shortly after he resigned as Israeli Foreign Minister in 1979, Moshe Dayan said, "You have to know the Arabs to like them. And I like them." He admitted he was surprised to see "how some of the toughest Israeli officers, when they became governor of occupied territory, within a short time spoke for the Arabs."[1]

In 1985 Dina Charnin, director of the program Interns for Peace, described how she, a Jew, lived in a Muslim town for two years, helping develop cooperative community programs. "Our rewards were great," she said, "as we witnessed the positive effects of interaction on the attitude of Jews and Arabs toward each other."[2]

Yehezkel Landau is executive director of *Oz veShalom-Netivot Shalom*, an organization which asserts that peace between Israelis and Palestinians can come only through mutual sacrifice. This is how he describes his position: "Our struggle is not essentially a political one. It is primarily a spiritual struggle to sanctify God's Holy Name in God's Holy Land. Our sacred Torah has become a prisoner of war. We are engaged in a mission to rescue our life-affirming tradition from those who have warped its teachings and turned them into weapons in an unholy war. This spiritual pollution keeps us all enslaved to fear, anger, and grief, when we could be, with God's help, agents of trust building, reconciling forgiveness, and inclusive compassion." Landau points out that, like the Jews, the Palestinians are also an exiled people. "May our joint strivings," he says, "help us to share the promise of the Abrahamic blessing, 'that through you, *all* the families of the earth shall be blessed.'"[3]

The Oslo Agreement

In 1992 Terje Rod Larsen, head of a Norwegian research institute, told Israeli leader Yossi Beilin that he could arrange for Beilin to discuss peace negotiations with some top Palestinian officials. This started a lengthy dialogue between Israeli and Palestinian leaders, culminating in the famous handshake on the White House lawn between Yasir Arafat, PLO leader, and Prime Minister Yitzhak Rabin of Israel. The crux of the agreement was that Palestinians were to be granted virtual autonomy in the Gaza Strip and on the West Bank, in exchange for a guarantee to stop the *intifada* stone-throwing resistance, and to withdraw all Palestinian support for violence by any Muslim terrorist groups. Rabin, who had been the Israeli military leader in the 1967 war, said, "Long enough have we made war on each other. Now is the time for peace."

When an American Jew, Baruch Goldstein, murdered many Palestinians in a Hebron mosque in 1994, *Tikkun*, an American Jewish periodical, printed an open letter of protest signed by more than 200 American Jewish leaders. It said, "We are as much outraged by this violence as by the outrageous Hamas attack at Afala. We support the demand of the Israeli peace movement calling for the dismantling of the Jewish settlements at Hebron, Kiryat, Arba, and in the Gaza Strip, and their call for an acceleration of the peace process aimed at achieving Palestinian self-rule, as well as security for Israelis and Palestinians."[4]

Assassination of Rabin

In November 1995 a young Israeli terrorist Yigal Amir killed Yitzhak Rabin, shouting, "God told me to do it!" Amir resented Rabin's courageous efforts to bring peace to the Holy Land. Numerous persons lauded Rabin as a peace maker, some saying that "pursuing peace is risky, but not pursuing it is unthinkable." Journalists recalled how Rabin had supported President Clinton's effort to get Congress to bolster Jordan's economy by forgiving the Jordanian debt to the United States. Rabin had said, "We seek not revenge but peace." To deny Palestinian self-rule would be alien to the democratic tradition of Judaism, Rabin averred. "We must learn to live together on the same soil," he stated, "to open a new chapter of mutual recognition, of good neighborliness, of mutual respect, of understanding. We must put an end to hostilities so that our children's children will no longer experience the painful cost of war."[5] It is hard to overestimate the profound influence of this soldier-turned-statesman on subsequent Israeli peace efforts.

A hallmark of Judaism has been its tolerance of divergent views. For example, there were two Talmuds, one created by rabbis while in Babylonian captivity, and another by rabbis in Jerusalem. The great rabbis Hillel and Shamai debated issues with firmness but with love. Thus, Judaism will be stronger if its diverse streams—Orthodox, Conservative, and Reform—can show traditional love and respect towards diverse viewpoints.

The Israeli economy benefits from peace efforts. International capital wants to flow where it is assured it will not be confiscated or endangered by war. Jacob Frenkel, governor of the Central Bank, states that business is always better when progress is being made towards peace. With security more likely and military expenditures cut, Israel can serve as the hub of a Middle Eastern free trade area. "Israel's economy is now far larger than that of all of its contiguous neighbors—Lebanon, Syria, Jordan, and Egypt—combined. Per capita gross domestic product stands at $17,000, well within European norms, and twenty times greater than Jordan's or Egypt's average incomes."[6]

In 1998 three important American Jewish groups (American Jewish Committee, American Jewish Congress, and Anti-Defamation League) issued a joint statement of congratulations to the Republic of Turkey, celebrating its 75th anniversary.

Turkey was praised for its values, its close ties to the United States, "its ever deepening relations with Israel, and its historic tradition as a haven for Jews fleeing persecution."[7]

Also in 1998 Prime Minister Benjamin Netanyahu and his Likud Party ended the efforts towards a "Greater Israel," that is, a land devoid of Palestinians, and agreed to place Hebron and parts of the West Bank under Palestinian jurisdiction. Even Ariel Sharon, a longtime hard-liner for Israel sovereignty, reluctantly agreed that peace was worth the cost of the land exchange.

The American Jewish Committee in 1999 praised the peace efforts of King Abdullah of Jordan and Prime Minister Ehud Barak of Israel. The committee cited cooperation on tourism, trade, foreign investment, and development of water resources. It called upon other regional powers to work together similarly.

In the year 2000 Israel withdrew its troops from southern Lebanon. This not only reduced casualties in the area but also gave Israel a trump card in negotiating with Syria. Syria has always used the Israeli presence in Lebanon as a reason for its own troops there. Now, in negotiations with Syria, Israel has removed one more source of discontent.

Likewise in 2000 the American Anti-Defamation League applauded Pope John Paul II's apology for his church's centuries-long anti-Semitism. "We share his commitment to enhancing Catholic-Jewish relations," the League said. "He has called upon Christian scholars to avoid any anti-Jewish interpretation of the Christian scriptures, further demonstrating his belief that the Jewish people are 'our dearly loved brothers.' The Anti-Defamation League shares his goal of making the world a better place to live for people of all religions and races."[8]

Recent Christian Unitiveness

Pope John Paul II has been building upon the historic search for reconciliation begun by his great predecessor Pope John XXIII, whose Vatican II Council was one of the most important moves towards peace and unity made by any church in the past 500 years. Angelo Roncalli (1881–1963) was installed as Pope John XXIII in 1958. At the age of 77 he was a compromise choice, with the College of Cardinals feeling that they would be able to make a more permanent choice within several years. But this short chubby pope changed Christianity as few have done.

During World War II, when he was Papal Nuncio to France, Roncalli pleaded for humane treatment of the 260,000 German POW's in France. He also sponsored a program for priests to work in factories in order to learn what a laborer's life is like. He worked hard to prevent Greece from deporting all of its Jews. In his first speech as pope, he said, "We tell the rulers of all nations to stop making arms and to start making peace with justice." He defined his credo: "Always respect the dignity of those you are with, and above all, the freedom of every human being. God Himself does so!"

Vatican II Council

In 1959 Pope John XXIII announced the Vatican II Council, to renew the vitality of the Church and to work towards eventual Christian reunion. Previous church councils had tried to protect the Church from external enemies, but Vatican II made an effort to change enemies into friends. This Council deplored narrowness and legalism, and sought for unitive service to the entire human race. Church leaders confessed previous Roman Catholic errors, admitting the need for reform. The Council curtailed the pope's authority somewhat, in order to give greater weight to collegiality between the College of Cardinals and the Pope.

Greater freedom was also granted to the laity. The mass could now be conducted in the people's vernacular, and not necessarily in Latin. Deacons were restored to a rank in the church hierarchy, and were permitted to be married. Discrimination of many sorts was attacked. Every church was seen to be a congregation of faith, equal in importance to every other church. Each church could trust the Holy Spirit to guide it in making decisions, without waiting for every dictate from higher authority.

Richard McBrien, chairman of the theology department at Notre Dame University, said:

"Now when we say Church, we mean all Christian churches. Moreover, although the Church is a universal agent of salvation, God is engaged in the same process in other religions, and even outside the religious communities. Salvation is universally available. There will come a day when women will not only be priests but bishops, and there will be a woman pope some day."[9]

In 1962 Pope John XXIII helped mediate the Cuban missile crisis involving the United States and the Soviet Union. The following year he issued his *Pacem in Terris* decree, showing how a person achieves peace within oneself, in the family, in the community, and in the world. Peace means respecting other persons' rights, he said. We must observe justice at home and abroad. People should live according to the universal laws of peace inscribed in their hearts, the pope advised. We need to show special love and mercy toward the weak and the weary.

Pope John XXIII said that a main task of the Council would be "to consolidate the path toward the unity of mankind." Peace had the highest priority. "More and more people," he said, "are becoming more deeply convinced of the paramount dignity of the human person and his perfection, as well as the duties that these imply. Even more important, experience has taught us that violence inflicted on others, the might of arms, and political domination are of no assistance in finding a happy solution to the serious problems that afflict mankind."[10]

Pope Paul VI

Pope Paul VI, the successor to Pope John XXIII, continued in the spirit of his predecessor. He convened Vatican II Council, and made statements of reconciliation and mutual understanding. In November 1964 he issued the Council's Decree on Ecumenism, which called for the ultimate reunion of all disunited Christianity. It states that the world is not interested in petty theological disputes, but wants a church to be magnanimous enough to permit a wide variety of viewpoints, as long as the central meaning of the church is not lost. Since the gospel of Christ is a gospel of love, one can easily see which advocate in a split shows the most love to the other.

Like his Biblical namesake, Pope Paul VI traveled widely in an effort to build church unity. In a meeting with the Orthodox Patriarch Athenagoras in Istanbul, the two high leaders declared the ages-old schism between their confessions to be at an end. Since 1054 there had been this major split in Christianity. Although not all differences between the two churches were reconciled, there was a spirit of brotherhood which made it seem as if unitive religion might finally triumph. Pope Paul VI promulgated the Vatican II Decree on the Church in the Modern World, which called for church reforms to better serve the needs of a rapidly changing world.

Pope Paul VI signed an agreement with a Muslim state, Tunisia, concerning the transfer of property owned by the Church. He appointed many cardinals from Africa, Asia, and Polynesia, making the College of Cardinals a mixture of races, colors, and tradition that was finally truly catholic. He surprised many people when he received the feminist leader Betty Friedan in an audience, telling her, "We wish to thank you and congratulate you on your work."[11] He also broke the Italian hold on the papacy, which eventually led to the selection of Karol Wojtyla as Pope John Paul II, the first non-Italian pope in centuries.

Karl Rahner

The German Roman Catholic Karl Rahner (1904–1984) was, along with Paul Tillich, the most influential theologian of the twentieth century. He stressed that Christians need a new understanding of how Christianity functions in a global civilization which has many important non-Christian elements. Church dogma, he said, must be in a constant state of flux, lest it be outmoded, superfluous, or downright wrong. He coined the phrase "anonymous Christian" to describe a person who obeys the inner teaching of conscience, though the person might be a non-Christian or perhaps even no believer at all.

"Must the marital morality of a Masai in East Africa be that of a Western Christian?" he asked. "Or could the chieftain there, even if he is a Christian, live in the style of the patriarch Abraham?"[12] He even stated that he felt that most people in the world will be saved apart from any contact with church dogma. A missionary, he said, should concentrate on helping the people develop the implications of their own original faith. Here is unitive religion, pure and simple.

Rahner believed that in time the Roman Catholic Church would permit priests to be married, and would ordain women as priests. Since he thought that all life is the subject matter for theological reflection, he wrote meditations on such ordinary actions as sleeping or eating. He even wrote an essay on the Beatles, saying that a theologian who wishes to understand the modern world should listen to popular music. "There is missing today," Rahner felt, "a spirituality which is deep and which speaks to normal human beings."[13]

To illustrate his point, Rahner said he understood how Latin America could ask the Church to develop a "theology of liberation," in view of the long servitude role played by the majority of its citizens. Rahner also defended theologian Hans Küng, with whom he frequently differed, when Küng was threatened with a Vatican investigation on charges of heresy. "Rahner is a man who observes the world not to indict it like a wrathful prophet but to understand it like a wise old therapist," said Eugene Kennedy. Rahner summarized the role of a theologian this way:

"He is concerned about a person as a subject with freedom and responsibility before the mystery of God."

The Christophers

In 1945 Father James Keller, a Maryknoll priest, founded an organization designed to further the cause of peace and justice in the world. The name Christophers comes from the Greek word for Christ-bearers. Their goal is to motivate individuals to do peaceful things. For example,

"A Chicago muralist founded a peace museum; an American who had been held hostage in Iran left his career in the diplomatic service to be the director of a peace institute in a New York church; and a nuclear engineer decided he could not continue in a job in which he made weapons with a first-strike potential."[14]

The movement reaches out to non-Christians and even to secular humanists who are compassionate and concerned about justice. Jewish and Muslim guests often appear on television programs run by the Christophers, and many letters from non-Christians thank this group for messages of faith, hope, and peace. Joan Ganz Cooney, the creator of TV's "Sesame Street," helps raise funds for the Christophers, saying, "No cause is closer to my heart. The Christophers led me to the road that led to "Sesame Street.""[15]

Raoul Wallenberg

Raoul Wallenberg was a Swedish Lutheran who repeatedly risked his life to save Hungarian Jews from death in Nazi concentration camps. In 1944 Jewish leaders asked President Franklin Roosevelt for assistance in saving Jews headed for cruel extinction. Roosevelt created the War Refuge Board, which asked the Swedish government to provide someone to visit Hungary backed by American dollars.

Wallenberg was selected for the mission. He packed a knapsack with dollars and with sets of spurious identification papers. He gave Jews in Budapest "protective" Swedish passports, and he ran a series of safe houses, apartment houses displaying Swedish flags, in which Jews with these passports were hidden. He often pulled Jewish people out of death trains, flashing documents that he brazenly asserted were authentic. His sense of authority often was accepted by local police. It is estimated that he saved nearly 100,000 Jewish people from death.

In January 1945 Russian troops captured Budapest. Wallenberg was taken under military guard to Moscow. After years of duplicity, Russian officials finally admitted that Wallenberg was executed at the Lubyanka prison in Moscow in 1947. In 1981 Wallenberg was declared to be an honorary American citizen, only the second person so honored (after Winston Churchill).

World Council of Churches

In 1998 the 8th Assembly of the World Council of Churches was held in Zimbabwe. At its founding in 1948 the Council had 147 member denominations. Now the Council has 339 Protestant and Orthodox Christian member denominations. The Council exists to promote international understanding and cooperative church endeavors, such as coordination of missionary efforts, consolidation of emergency assistance during catastrophes, and encouraging fellowship among all churches in Christendom.

The growth of Christianity in Africa is attributed largely to the decline of narrow sectarianism, the opening of churches to aid in solving economic, educational, and medical problems, and the churches' tolerance of native African types of worship, such as tribal forms of music and dance. At some point in the early 21st century, said the Reverend Konrad Raiser, the Council's general secretary, "Africa may have the largest Christian population of any continent."[16]

Peace in Ireland

After three decades of terrorist violence that cost 3600 lives and injured thousands more, Northern Ireland in 1999 installed for the first time a governing body equitably apportioned between Catholic and Protestant constituents. An outstanding peacemaker was George Mitchell, former U.S. senator, who patiently got religious leaders on both sides to listen to each other, and to suggest mutual compromises. Major progress was made when Mitchell convinced the leaders to set up an independent international body, headed by Canadian General John de Chastelain, to decide how disarmament would be achieved.

Credit also goes to Northern Ireland's leaders. John Hume, head of the largest Catholic group, persuaded the Irish Republican Army to stop using violence. Gerry Adams, leader of the I.R.A.'s political arm, Sinn Fein, encouraged his organization to lay down their arms. David Trimble, the Protestant leader, finally got his colleagues to agree to share power with Catholics.

A signal figurehead was Martin McGuiness, who had long been active as an I.R.A. troublemaker. In his new role as education minister, McGuiness said, "My job is to press on, to show politics can work, and then help create circumstances that will allow armed groups to destroy their weapons."[17] In May 2000 the I.R.A. made a historic decision, that it would put all of its weapons "beyond use." This meant that neutral inspectors from the International Crisis Group could periodically inspect the secret stores of the I.R.A. arsenal to ensure that no weapons were being used. Everyone seemed content with this decision, including Prime Ministers Tony Blair of Britain and Bertie Ahern of Ireland.

Pope John Paul II

Pope John Paul II, by opposing the priesthood of women and marriage of priests, has often been considered a supporter of divisive religion. There have been, however, many unitive actions made by this Polish pontiff. In 1982 he traveled to London to embrace the Archbishop of Canterbury, as a symbol of a determined effort to restore unity between the Roman Catholic and the Anglican churches. They asked all Christians to pray for a resolution of their remaining differences. "We wish to serve the cause of peace, of human freedom and human dignity," they said, "so that God may indeed be glorified in all his creatures. We greet in the name of God all persons of good will, both those who believe in God and those who are still searching for God."[18]

In his Easter message in 1994, the pope continued his prayers for unity among all Christians, and referred to Jews as "elder brothers in the faith." He also attended, with Jewish leaders, a solemn concert at the Vatican commemorating victims of the Holocaust. In 1998 he appointed a commission to investigate the Inquisition conducted by his church from 1231 until 1834. He deplored the "acquiescence given, especially in certain centuries, to intolerance and even the use of violence in the service of truth."[19]

The Pope Apologizes for His Church

"More than any pope in history," writes Celestine Bohlen, "Pope John Paul II has asked forgiveness for the sins, crimes, and errors committed in the name of his faith. He has apologized for the persecution of Protestants and for the crimes of the Crusaders. He has asked forgiveness for the abuses of Europe's colonial-era proselytizing around the world. He has voiced regret at the Church's repression of Galileo, and condemned its silence regarding Italy's own Mafia."[20]

In this spirit a group of 2500 Christians in 1999 retraced the route of those engaged in the First Crusade in 1095, turning it into a repentance journey. When they arrived in Jerusalem, they gave a formal apology to Chief Rabbi Yisrael Lau, Greek Orthodox Patriarch Diordoros, and Muslim Mufti Ekrem Sabri. "Better late than never," said Rabbi Lau. "Let us hope that your visit signals the end of what started with the Crusades. We must all live in brotherhood."[21]

In his Christmas message in 1999, the pope said that the millennium year of 2000 would be a Jubilee Year, during which he would lead his church in repentance for the wrongs it had committed through the years. "At times," he said, "people have refused to respect and to love their brothers of a different faith or race. They have denied fundamental rights to individuals and nations."[22] Other Christian groups have been in a similar repentant mood. "In the mid-1990's, for example, three American Protestant denominations issued statements of repentance—the Southern Baptists for supporting slavery and segregation, the Evangelical Lutheran Church in America for anti-Jewish writings of Martin Luther, and the United Methodists for the brutality of a lay preacher who led a Civil War era Indian massacre in Colorado."[23]

In 1998 Pope John Paul II issued "a call to repentance" on behalf of Catholics who did not speak against the Nazi Holocaust. "We deeply regret the errors and failures of those sons and daughters of the church," he said. In his various statements of repentance, the pope was carrying out the philosophy of the Declaration of Religious Freedom from Vatican II Council, which asserted that religious pluralism is needed now in a shrinking global society.

Pilgrimage to the Holy Land

In March 2000 the pope made the first official visit of a pope to Israel. The six-day trip included visits to both a Holocaust memorial and a Palestinian refugee camp. In Nazareth the pope visited the Basilica of the Annunciation, where Christians believe that the angel Gabriel visited the virgin Mary to tell her that she was to bear Jesus. The pope's reception in Nazareth was like that of a rock music star. Muslims waved yellow Vatican flags, and children wearing papal baseball caps hoisted placards reading "Benvenito Papa Carissmo" (Welcome Dear Pope). Israeli security forces wore lapel stickers stating "Mivtza Yedid Vatk" (Operation Old Friend). Orthodox Christians greeted the pope with enthusiasm, feeling that his visit reasserted their belonging in the city of their Lord Jesus. Unitive religion was playing its vital role as a path to understanding, love, and peace. A *Time* reporter wrote that "it would not be surprising, a few years down the road, to hear from an Arafat, a Barak, a Clinton, or even an Assad that one of the things that had kept them on the track in the fateful spring and summer of 2000 had been a bent old man who dropped by the neighborhood and suggested, by word and deed, what strong will, good faith, and leadership are all about."[24]

Recent Islamic Unitiveness

The death by cancer of Jordan's King Hussein in 1999 led to widespread encomium of his role as a peacemaker for decades. As a young man in 1951, Hussein had seen his grandfather King Abdullah assassinated by a Palestinian in Jerusalem. He vowed to continue his grandfather's search for peace with the Israelis.

Encouraged by President Clinton, King Hussein met repeatedly with Prime Minister Rabin to work out compromises acceptable to both sides. Unitive religion showed its best side, as these two broadminded leaders found common ground. In his eulogy at King Hussein's death, Clinton summarized Hussein's achievement: "We remember him piloting his plane, traveling wherever his cause took him. He lived his life on a higher plane, with the aviator's gift of seeing beyond the low-flying obstacles of hatred and mistrust that heartbreak and loss place in all our paths. He had seen in one panorama at sunset the lights of Amman and Tel Aviv and Damascus shining in the sky—that in the relationship among peoples who share this small sacred corner of earth, one thing and only one thing is predestined: all are bound to be neighbors. The question is not whether they will live side by side, but how soon, God willing, all will see what he saw and preached. There can be no peace, no dignity, no security for any of Abraham's children until there is peace, dignity, and security for all of them."[25]

King Hussein's son, King Abdullah II, openly declares that his goal is to bring further democracy to Jordan. Aided by his wife Rania (who worked in the marketing departments of both Citibank and Apple Computer in Amman), Abdullah II says, "The message has changed. We have peace and we want others to enjoy it. We need to shift from politics to the economy. My priority is to bring prosperity."[26]

When Syrian President Hafez al-Assad died in June 2000, he was replaced by his son, Dr. Bashar al-Assad, an ophthalmologist, who had been groomed as his successor by his iron-willed father. Like his father, Bashar is a member of the Muslim Alawite sect, an offshoot from Shiite Islam. He is determined to modernize Syria by permitting satellite television stations and by eliminating business bribes, in order to attract foreign capital. Although he wants to return the Golan Heights to Syria, he seems open to peace negotiations with Israel on the matter.

A Peace Greeting

The Kingdom of Saudi Arabia extended a peaceful holiday greeting to the American people on 4 January 1981. Part of it read as follows: "We share with you this great religion of Abraham. We share Abraham's belief in The One God. We share our beliefs in the Holy Prophecies of Moses and Jesus. We revere the Virgin Birth of Jesus, and we honor His Blessed Mother Mary. This is the guidance of God for the good of all mankind. The Koran quotes Jesus as saying, 'Peace is on Me the day I was born, the day that I die, and the day that I shall be raised up to life again.'"[27]

Syncretism in Africa

Native tribal religions survive even in African countries where Islam or Christianity is practiced widely. For example, "among the Yoruba, it is common to find Muslims and Christians in the same family." Some Yoruba even practice both religions, with a touch of traditional Yoruba beliefs. "Half the cars in Lagos may have bumper stickers professing the driver's love of Jesus, but polygamy is still practiced among Nigerian and African Christians."[28] Haruna Salihi, a Muslim scholar, credits this syncretism with the absence of Islamic terrorism in Nigeria. "Here you find various combinations of Muslims, Christians, and traditional beliefs, and it is a restrictive factor against the kind of eruption you find in the Arab world."[29]

A Modern Sufi

Sufis are Muslim mystics who believe that God loves all of his creation. M.R. Bawa Muhaiyaddeen, a Sufi who died in 1986, wrote much to try to bring peace and unity to the followers of all world religions. In troubled Sri Lanka Buddhists, Hindus, and Muslims would hear his teaching that all of God's children should love one another. In 1971 he visited the United States and found sympathetic audiences among Caucasian and Afro-American citizens, in Jewish and Christian groups. "According to one's background, Bawa would strengthen the listener's faith in God by illuminating the inner meaning of each religion. He had the unique ability to reveal the essential truth of each religion: the oneness of God."[30] In his book *Islam and World Peace*, Bawa showed that the Koranic intent of the term *jihad* was not traditional warfare but rather the internal battle against selfishness and impurity that each of us wages in our own hearts.

Arafat Celebrates Christmas

In 1999 Yasir Arafat welcomed visitors to Manger Square in Bethlehem as he celebrated the beginning of the new millennium: "From the heart of this holy city, the city of Jesus, the city where it all began, in the name of God, in the name of Palestine, I declare open the celebrations of the third millennium," read his message. After a five minute reading from the Koran, there were choral hallelujahs, tolling church bells, and the lighting of a Christmas tree in front of the Church of the Nativity. "We wish you a Merry Christmas" came in Arab-accented English from a bullhorn. A police band stood in front of the newly opened Peace Center, which until 1995 was the site of an Israeli police station surrounded by barbed wire. Arafat clapped his hands in glee to applaud a local girls' choir, and again when praise was offered to Pope John Paul II, due to visit there soon. "This kind of ecumenical business doesn't happen every day in the Christian world," said the Reverend Eugene Kamar, a Franciscan priest, "so thanks be to President Arafat."[31]

The Dalai Lama

The Dalai Lama (whose name means "Ocean of Wisdom") was expelled from Tibet by the Chinese Communist government in 1959. He now runs a Tibetan government-in-exile in India. The purity of his vision and conduct has led to his being considered one of the world's foremost spiritual leaders. His support of peace without bloodshed led to his winning the Nobel Peace Prize in 1989. His spiritual leadership was shown at a meeting with ten prominent Jewish people in 1990. The Jews shared ideas from the Kabala on meditation, and the Dalai Lame quoted similar views from Tibetan Buddhist scripture. Many of the Jews felt that they has a deeper understanding of their own faith as a result of this spiritual dialogue.

In his book *Ethics for the New Millennium*, the Dalai Lama said that the West's overemphasis on the importance of material goals produces great stress, anxiety, and unhappiness. Both oneself and the world can be transformed, he believes, if instead we cultivate such qualities as compassion, forgiveness, love, patience, tolerance, a sense of harmony, and a sense of responsibility. The Dalai Lama was one of the leaders of the Second

Parliament of World Religions, held in 1993 in Chicago, where the first one was also held. An unprecedented declaration of global ethical values was signed by representatives from 125 various religious groups. The primary author of the document was the well-known Catholic theologian Hans Küng. The declaration exhorts religions in whose names wars and atrocities have been committed to rid themselves of arrogance, hostility, mistrust, and prejudice. It also enjoin all humans, whether religious or not, "to live by a rule that respects all life, individuality, and diversity, so that every person is treated humanely. It condemns sexual discrimination and limitless exploitation of the environment, and forsakes violence as a means of settling differences."[32]

Early American Unitiveness

Although New England Puritans were generally intolerant of religious faiths other than their own, their Congregational Church made an important contribution to the development of democracy in America, by permitting church members to select their own leaders. Soon New Englanders thought, if we have the right to select our own church leaders, why should we not have the right to select our governmental leaders?

V.L. Parrington praised New England Unitarians for their spiritual integrity. He summarized their position in this way: "With ebbing faith men may deny their own divine nature, but the divinity is not destroyed. The music of the indwelling Godhead murmurs in the shell till the tide returns to flood it again. The one great miracle is the daily rebirth of God in the individual soul."[33] Ralph Waldo Emerson explained that self-reliance ultimately meant reliance upon your greater Self, or God. William Ellery Channing persuaded Unitarianism to abandon the major Calvinist beliefs—total depravity, predestination, and a God of wrath—for a God of love, with human beings considered as God's children.

Catholic Unitiveness in America

Alarmed alike by the discovery and use of nuclear weapons and the growing secularism in America, the Roman Catholic bishops in the United States in 1953 issued a joint statement on "The Dignity of Man." They declared three sources of human dignity: our origin in God, our role as members of society, and our destiny in helping bring forth the Kingdom of God on earth. Since human souls come from God, the statement said, no government has any authority to transcend certain fundamental human rights. The bishops reaffirmed that "people must be governed by God or they will be ruled by tyrants." Their statement concluded with the words of a contemporary historian: "Unless we find a way to restore the contact between the life of society and the life of the spirit, our civilization will be destroyed by forces which it has the knowledge to create but not the wisdom to control."[34]

The ecumenism of Pope John XXIII was warmly supported by Americans of many faiths. His death in 1963 led to many eulogies and summaries of his leadership in breaking down religious barriers. That year the Third Order Secular of St. Francis awarded its Peace Medal to Martin Luther King, Jr., for his non-violent crusade for racial justice. The newly selected Pope Paul VI announced a pilgrimage to the Holy Land in search for peace among all peoples.

A lifelong bridge of understanding between Christians and Jews was Monsignor John Oesterreicher. An Austrian Jew who converted to Roman Catholicism at the age of 19, he was a priest who spoke so openly against Hitler and the Holocaust that he had to flee from the Gestapo and find a haven in New York City. Here he set up the Institute for Judeo-Christian Studies at Seton Hall University. His successor as chairman of this program, Rabbi Asher Finkel called him "the spirit of the movement to renew the links between Judaism and Christianity." Oesterreicher was also a prime contributor to the Vatican II declaration on religious unity, particularly on the Roman Catholic attitude towards Judaism. "Some have called me the architect of the statement," he said. "I am not. Maybe I was the midwife."[35] Rabbi Finkel said of him, "He comes from a Jewish background, so he recognizes what the world has done to the Jews. There's a sense of urgency in him."

Further Catholic Unitiveness

When Afro-American Bishop Emerson Moore was arrested in 1984 in a peaceful protest against apartheid in South Africa, he had the full support of Archbishop (later Cardinal) John J.

O'Connor. "It was not all capricious," O'Connor said. "It was very symbolic and effective."[36]

Sister Mary Joy Yokoyama, of the Franciscan Congregation of the Sisters of St. Felix, is full-time manager of St. Clare's Home for Babies with AIDS in Elizabeth, New Jersey. These babies have continual pain, delayed motor skills, respiratory problems, and neurological impairment. Sister Mary feels she is doing what St. Francis would do if he were alive today. St. Francis, she said, viewed handicapped people as beloved *minores* (people of lower rank, in society's eyes), and thus in need of special attention. Whatever their ages, said Sister Mary, they are "our brothers and sisters in God."[37]

Father George Clements in 1980 in Chicago started a program called One Church-One Child. He urged each Roman Catholic parish to adopt a homeless child. Then he started a similar program called One Church-One Addict. Now hundreds of churches have programs to fight alcohol and drug abuse. "If Jesus was here today, he'd be working in the area of substance abuse," Clements said. "Jesus lived on the cutting edge, helping others. We must do the same."[38]

The death of Mother Teresa in Calcutta in 1997 evoked millions of eulogies throughout the world. The tiny Albanian Roman Catholic nun was esteemed for her Christlike sacrificial living in a foreign land, specializing in helping the poor, the outcasts, and the terminally ill. She was an inspiration to all who believe in the power of unitive religion to transform the world.

Father Doug Lorig, a priest in Gilbert, Arizona, wanted to show teenagers that religious love should work towards unity. Thus he developed programs in which Catholic and Mormon students worked side by side on common projects. They worked on food banks, mural art, and construction of a local park. "The kids from both communities have been awesome," said Father Lorig. "It's harder to throw stones at people you know. It's no longer 'them' and 'us.'"[39]

In recognition of the Jewish High Holy Days in 1999, Cardinal John J. O'Connor of New York City published an open letter, a part of which said that he greeted his friends as they entered a new year. He said, "God, who gives all humanity the dignity of being made in his image, has chosen Israel as his particular people that they may be an example of faithfulness for all the nations of the earth. Working in our own ways, but also working together, let us both remain committed to the fulfillment of God's reign. I ask this Yom Kippur that you understand my own abject sorrow for any member of the Catholic Church, including myself, who may have harmed you or your forbears in any way. Be assured of my prayers and friendship."[40] Unitive religion can scarcely ever be better expressed than in these great phrases.

When Cardinal O'Connor died in 2000, former governor Mario Cuomo said, "He courageously visited AIDS patients, sought to comfort them and even changed bedpans. His archdiocese has educated, housed, and cared for hundreds of thousands of Catholics and non-Catholics. He advanced ecumenism, particularly with the Jewish community. He was an extraordinary prince of the church."[41]

American reaction to Pope John Paul II's apology to the Jewish community for all the sins and crimes committed by present and past Roman Catholics has been very positive. Letters to the editor of *Time* magazine included such statements as:

"His presence and timing helped change history."

"He is apologizing for the frailty of mankind."

"By taking a major leap forward to help bring Christians, Jews, and Muslims together in a bond of peace, he should be named Diplomat of the Millennium."

"His courage, moral integrity, and indomitable spirit set him apart from other world leaders." "He is a man of peace for people of all nationalities and faiths."[42]

Religious Apologies

Lance Morrow, in an editorial in *Time*, placed the pope's apology within the context of current similar apologies. Not only had the Baptists apologized for slavery and segregation, he said, but "the Japanese Prime Minister apologized for Japan's behavior in World War II, and the Canadian government lamented its programs injuring native peoples." Was the pope's apology mere words, as some critics asserted? Morrow thinks not. He says that although an apology certainly must be made with a sincere heart, it must also be received with a sincere heart. "Only such reciprocity can set in motion the dynamic of apology and forgiveness and transcendence: a powerful liberating force for all concerned."[43]Unitive religion works best when it is returned with unitive religion.

Maryknoll missionaries in Guatemala respect native customs and beliefs. Instead of shaking hands with female parishioners (considered too intimate by Q'eqchi Indians), Father John Ruessman pats them on the shoulder. The incense used during mass is *pom*, the incense sacred to the Mayan people. After holy communion, congregation members drink *Mayehak*, a sacred cocoa which symbolizes the unity and togetherness of all community members. "The Q'eqchi have a great understanding of human dependence on God," says Father William Mullan. "Everything they do—growing crops, praying for rain, raising children—draws them back to an awareness of their connection to God."[44]

The canonization of an American heiress in 2000 reminded Americans of the faith and dedication of Katherine Drexel, who used her $7 million inheritance to create a congregation of missionary nuns established to educate Native Americans and Afro-Americans. She thereby predated the American civil rights movement by about seventy years. Asked what most impressed them about her, a nun who remembered her said it was Katherine's humanity and humility. "She patched her stockings in the evening alongside of us," said the sister.[45]

Recent American Unitive Protestantism

When President John F. Kennedy was assassinated in 1963, many Protestant leaders mourned his death, affirming that the nation's first Roman Catholic president had been an inspirational executive. Ecumenism was in the air. Numerous Protestant bodies sought to merge with others. The Reverend E. Stanley Jones, longtime Methodist missionary to India, conducted Christian ashrams, or retreats, bringing Hindu spirituality into Christian services as a vital force.

Mary Steenhoek, a Presbyterian laywoman, works with WHEAT (World Hunger Ecumenical Arizona Task Force) to raise conservation awareness. "I'm interested in ecojustice," she says. She feels that following the Flood, God mandated in Genesis 9:9–10 a partnership between human beings and the environment. In Mary's view, "our planet needs a better understanding of where we fit in. Any relationship based on domination or exploitation, whether with a person or the environment, is not satisfactory."[46]

The call to worship used by one Protestant church reflects a constantly widening ethos:

Leader: Our world is filled with conflict among nations and between one another.
People: The promise of God is peace.
Leader: Oppression takes place in our communities and our relationships.
People: The promise of God is justice.
Leader: We want to control others without mercy; we imprison ourselves in hopelessness.
People: The promise of God is freedom.
Leader: Neglecting the poor, we blame them for their problems.
People: The promise of God is healing.
Leader: Our hearts lack room for all in need.
People: The promise of God is love.
All: Strengthen us, O God, to be your peacemakers, justice bearers, freedom givers, healers, and lovers of all people.[47]

This church, a fairly typical one, sponsors 27 separate projects aimed at helping people. Some of the projects assist their own members, such as programs for youth, shut-ins, or the aged. Other projects have community outreach: medical loan equipment, food bank, time-out shelter, and Habitat for Humanity. Still others have a worldwide impact: missionaries in Russia and Alaska, heifer projects, and food programs for Mexico. Some churches adopt churches in other lands, often providing help with building programs, food, clothing, and medical supplies. Peace here is defined as sharing one's substance with those who are less fortunate.

In recent years North Korea has been plagued by floods, typhoons, and famines. Southern Baptists in Texas have provided outstanding relief to afflicted North Koreans. A project "Coats for Christmas" sent 180,000 coats to needy Korean children. In early 1996 Texas Baptists sent several semitrailer loads of food to flood victims. Baptists volunteers also went to North Korea to remove salt from farms flooded by sea water. Dr. John La Nove, a Baptist leader, said that even though governments find it hard to overcome barriers, "God opens doors. Some people don't realize that God is still at work in the world."[48]

A number of American churches engage in pulpit exchanges, not only within their own denominations but in some cases with rabbis and imams. Nearly always the widening of spirituality is experienced as a growing awareness of God's presence and love. One Lutheran church devoted its entire series of Lenten services to a fuller understanding of Judaism. Worship themes included these Feasts: Rosh Hashanah, Yom Kippur, Sukkoth, Pesach, and Chanukah. For more profound effect, Jewish music, Hebrew prayers, and the sounding of the *shofar* (ram's horn) was used.

Ecumenism

The nation's largest Lutheran church, the Evangelical Lutheran Church in America, resulted from a merger of three smaller church groups in 1988. Then these Lutherans voted for full communion with three other Protestant churches: The Presbyterian Church (U.S.A.), the Reformed Church in America, and the United Church of Christ. Full communion means not only accepting each other's rituals but even sharing a common pastor in rural or financially deprived areas. There is also full cooperation on social service work and in the mission field. In 1999 the Evangelical Lutheran Church in America reached a similar agreement for full communion with the Episcopal Church. Quoted by many people was Jesus's wish in John 17:11 that all his followers "may be one."

Recent American Jewish Unitiveness

Rabbi Albert Plotkin of Phoenix in 1994 published a book *The Ethics of World Religions.* In it he showed the commonality of belief among all of the leading religions in the world. "The most challenging part of our life today is ethics," Plotkin said. "The growth of crime, drugs, and juvenile delinquency has much to do with not bringing out basic ethics and morals." Ethics also plays an important role in the search for peace, he believes. He cites as examples the Holy Land, where their scriptures could help overcome differences between Israelis and Palestinians, and Bosnia, where Christian Serbians and Muslin Bosnians could find unifying factors in their respective scriptural pronouncements on ethics. Rabbi Plotkin cites the Golden Rule as a standard of conduct found in all major religions.

"We are all people, not just one world," Plotkin says. "We just have varying traditions. People get so involved with the trivialities of their own religion that they fail to see the important things such as basic ethics. I want people to broaden their horizons. If people don't know about other religions, they become provincial and build barriers of indifference."[49] As he says, ethical living is a universal prerequisite for us to have any hope for having a world of peace and justice.

The Anti-Defamation League is a Jewish watchdog agency which fights against bigotry, discrimination, and hatred. Periodically it publishes lists of telephone numbers for people to call if they feel they have been victims of discrimination or harmful hatred. Professional help is available to such persons. The ADL says, "We are dedicated to the protection of traditional American values of pluralism and tolerance."

Jewish tradition says that if a would-be convert knocks on the door of the synagogue, the rabbi should turn the person away not one, but three times, to test the seriousness of intention on the part of the inquirer. This stance may bother some Jewish people, but it is much more in line with unitive religion than is the zealous boast that "everyone should be in my church."

In 2000 Nathan D. Baxter, Dean of Washington National Cathedral, explained the symbolic art used in the clerestory windows of the cathedral. They all exhibit instances of faith taken from the Torah. The mayor of Jerusalem, Ehud Olmert, sent a piece of rock from the oldest section of Jerusalem, where the Wailing Wall stands. Mayor Olmert said that this piece of rock symbolizes the hope for peace shared by all three Abrahamic faiths. Later Muslim and Christian artifacts will also be inserted in the window. Despite the current violence in the Holy Land, Dean Baxter feels that "as people of faith, we also find hope in the knowledge that God is a God of compassion and justice. Jerusalem is a symbol of hope, not only for the three Abrahamic faiths, but for many other peoples as well."[50]

Random Acts of Kindness

College professor Charles Wall heard a news report of "another act of senseless violence." It got him thinking, Why not have random acts of sensible kindness? He told his students to perform an act of sensible kindness, and report it to the class. One student handed out blankets to the homeless. Another paid his mother's utility bills. Still another began a weekly practice of hospital visitation. Soon writers began writing books on the topic. They include Anne Herbert, Meladee and Hanoch McCarty, Dawna Markova, and Gavin Whitsett. In Connecticut a man reported selling over 15,000 car bumper stickers reading "Practice Random Acts of Kindness."

Devorah Halberstam went beyond kindness to forgiveness. Her son Ari, a 16-year-old Hasidic Jewish student, was shot to death by a man who said he hated Jews. Devorah urged Mayor Giuliani and Governor Cuomo to promote legislation encouraging all schools to have students perform acts of kindness for at least one hour each week. "Some people have bitterness," Devorah said, "but our teaching is to turn and do everything for the good. I don't see anger or hatred. Ari's death is beyond my understanding, but I believe there was a purpose. People are doing kindness in his name around the world."[51]

Reducing Prejudice

Radio star Casey Kasem recently received a special peace award for his efforts to promote non-violent conflict resolution among Arabs, Jews, and other American ethnic groups. Kasem, whose background is Lebanese, points out how American mass media tend to perpetuate stereotypes of persons with Arab blood as violent and hateful terrorists. Kasem showed that Americans with Arab heritage have contributed much to the nation. He cited Dr. Michael DeBakey, the pioneer heart surgeon; Professor Elias Corey, who won the 1990 Nobel Prize for chemistry; and Farouk El-Baz, who worked on Apollo missions 8 through 17, and who pioneered in the use of space photography to locate desert water and oil deposits. Other prominent Arab-Americans mentioned by Kasem are former senators George Mitchell and James Abourekh, actors Danny and Marlo Thomas, White House correspondent Helen Thomas, and Candice Lightner, the founder of Mothers Against Drunk Driving.

In 1998 the U.S. Congress passed the International Religious Freedom Act. This act requires the State Department to submit an annual report on religious persecution. The president is empowered to take appropriate action, ranging from diplomatic protest to economic sanctions, against countries where citizens are persecuted on religious grounds. Consular officers are trained to enable them to identify religious persecution when it occurs.

The state of Idaho is taking steps to reverse its image as a haven for white-supremacy zealots. Greg Carr in 2000 spearheaded a movement to build the Anne Frank Human Rights Memorial along the Boise River. It will be a 175-foot wall of granite panels with quotations and images of human rights leaders, such as Nelson Mandela, Margaret Mead, and Martin Luther King, Jr.

A court trial in Coeur d'Alene is threatening to divest Richard Butler, head of the Aryan Nations movement, of his property. Butler, seated amid his heroic pictures of Adolf Hitler and white-robed Klansmen, says that "Jews run the government" and that "Jewish conspirators" are trying to destroy him. The lawsuit, supported by Morris Dees and the Southern Poverty Law Center, alleges that Butler's security guards assaulted a 44-year-old berry picker and her 21-year-old son. Dees and his support group have won over $40 million in damages from nine Ku Klux Klan and other hate groups. He won a $12.5 million judgment against the White Aryan Resistance in 1990. Many Idahoans feel ashamed of their state's image as a haven for hate groups, and are hoping for another victory for Dees.[52]

German Aid to Israel

A large number of Germans, including many born after the Holocaust, have feelings of guilt and shame over what their country did to Jews in World War II. Some of the Germans go to Israel to help survivors of the Holocaust, or to work with handicapped or terminally ill Israelis. Germany has paid over $50 billion in reparations to individual Israelis and to the state of Israel. Germany is now Israel's second most important military and trading partner. Germany and Israel work very closely on matters of military intelligence. One report stated that "German support is central to Israel's security."[53] The Holocaust can never be forgiven, but it is encouraging that many Germans are trying to show an attitude of unitive religion to heal some of the wounds.

As the United States enters the new millennium, the nation continues to have a strong religious base for its value systems. This chapter depicts a worldwide movement away from divisive religion and towards the unitive belief that the God of love, as creator of the entire human family, desires for all human beings to be treated with dignity and respect. It is incumbent upon the United States, as one of the leading nations of the world, to concentrate upon building its spiritual strength to match its leadership role in military and political spheres.

REFERENCES

[1] *New York Times*, 28 October 1979, 4:3.

[2] Ibid., 28 July 1985, 4:22.

[3] *Harvard Divinity School Bulletin*, Summer 1990, pp. 2, 18.

[4] *New York Times*, 17 April 1994, 4:18.

[5] Ibid., 5 November 1995, p. 18.

[6] William A. Orme, Jr., *New York Times*, 18 October 1998, 4:3.

[7] *New York Times*, 8 November 1998, 4:15.

[8] Ibid., 19 March 2000, 4:15.

[9] *St. Anthony Messenger*, November 1984, pp. 20, 22.

[10] Ibid., vol. 93, p. 19.

[11] Eugene Kennedy, *The Now and Future Church* (Doubleday, 1984), p. 109.

[12] Eugene Kennedy, *New York Times Magazine*, 23 September 1979, p. 64.

[13] Ibid., p. 72.

[14] Liz O'Connor, *St. Anthony Messenger*, November 1985, p. 13.

[15] Ibid., p. 18.

[16] *New York Times*, 13 December 1998, p. 16.

[17] Ibid., 5 December 1999, 4:3.

[18] Ibid., 30 May 1982, p. 12.

[19] *Arizona Republic*, 1 November 1998, p. A26.

[20] *New York Times*, 30 November 1997, 4:1.

[21] *Time,* 6 September 1999, p. 24.

[22] *New York Times*, 26 December 1999, p. 6.

[23] Gustav Niebuhr, *New York Times*, 12 March 2000, 4:3.

24 David Van Biema, *Time*, 3 April 2000, p. 36.

25 *New York Times*, 14 February 1999, p. 21.

26 *Time*, 14 February 2000, p. 58.

27 *New York Times*, 4 January 1981, p. 11.

28 Ibid., 9 January 2000, 4:20.

29 Ibid.

30 *Treasures of Wisdom from the Fellowship Press,* n.p.

31 Deborah Sontag, *New York Times*, 5 December 1999, p. 6.

32 *Arizona Republic*, 5 September 1993, p. A2.

33 V.L. Parrington, *Main Currents in American Thought* (Harcourt Brace, 1930), vol. 2, p. 382.

34 *New York Times*, 22 November 1953, p. 84.

35 *Arizona Republic*, 23 March 1985, p. F3.

36 *St. Anthony Messenger*, June 1986, p. 10.

37 Ibid., November 1990, p. 8.

38 *Parade Magazine*, 26 November 1995, p. 8.

39 *Arizona Republic*, 27 December 1997, p. R4.

40 *New York Times*, 19 September 1999, p. 23.

41 *Time*, 15 May 2000, p. 35.

42 Ibid., 24 April 2000, Letters to the Editor.

43 Ibid., 27 March 2000, p.64.

44 *Maryknoll*, April 2000, p. 18.

45 *New York Times*, 19 March 2000, p. 16.

46 *Arizona Republic*, 17 November 1991, p. C2.

47 Payson (Arizona) United Methodist Church, Order of Worship, 29 November 1998.

48 *Arizona Republic*, 3 January 1998, p. R4.

49 Ibid., 22 January 1994, p. D7.

50 *Cathedral Age* (Washington National Cathedral), Fall 2000, p. 19.

51 *Arizona Republic*, 24 April 1994, p. F2.

52 *Time*, 4 September 2000, p. 33.

53 Roger Cohen, *New York Times*, 4 March 2001, p. 10.

CHAPTER V

THE THEOLOGY OF PARTICLE PHYSICS

Those who led us astray are now getting us back onto the right course. Ignored during the Middle Ages, science began asserting itself during the Renaissance as a more precise mode of approaching reality than the religious mode. Because of its substantial accomplishments, science soon began to be worshipped as a god in itself, replacing the God of history.

Scientism developed when first scientists and then the public began to invalidate every approach to knowledge but the scientific one. If something could not be perceived by the five senses, it was said not to exist. The fundamental building block of the universe was supposed to be a small hard piece of matter called an atom.

Philosophers felt that they were deserting the truth unless they built their metaphysics upon a materialistic base. John Locke, David Hume, and Karl Marx all assumed that one need not speculate about things that sensory experience could not validate, since such things did not exist.

The findings of particle physics have destroyed materialism as a legitimate basis for a philosophy. Bernard d'Espagnat, an expert on quantum mechanics, says that the term "scientific materialism" is now but a meaningless association of words. Physicists now believe that at the subatomic level, matter does not exist with certainty at definite places. Dr. Henry Stapp of the Berkeley Lawrence Laboratory says that "an elementary particle is not an independently existing entity. It is, in essence, a set of relationships that reach outward to other things. There definitely is not a substantive physical world."[1]

There is great rejoicing in Heaven by such writers as Plato, Plotinus, and the early Christian mystics, as well as countless Hindus, Buddhists, and Taoists at seeing their views corroborated by modem science.

Particle physicists sound increasingly like religious mystics. The time-honored search to reconcile science and religion has ended.

The Tragic Split

T.S. Eliot describe the "dissociation of sensibility" or the split between thought and feeling that occurred during the Renaissance. Henceforward feeling was considered to be inferior to and subordinate to thought. Such a split in human personality produces mental illness, but society itself was organized so as to encourage this cleavage.

This fragmentary view of human personality produced a society whose parts made no coherent whole. Spurred by specialization and professionalization, science divorced itself from ethics, in an effort to be more "objective." Especially as cultural relativism crept into ethics, science wanted no part of something lacking an absolute universal at its base.

Recent developments have led to the re-marriage of science and ethics. Interdisciplinary scientific study was one factor. Biology and physiology contribute to a study of how the mind works and thus get involved with ethics. Bioethics raises questions about scientific research on human subjects. Scientific processes are heavily laden with value questions.

The reintegration of knowledge bodes well for human survival. Instead of running at cross purposes, knowledge is getting ready to serve humanity in new and creative ways. While watching a sunset in a Budapest park, Nicola Tesla was reflecting on a passage from Goethe's Faust. In a sudden flash of insight, Tesla had a vision depicting the principle of alternating current polyphase power, which forms the basis of modern electrical systems. Poetry and engineering can unite to serve humanity's basic needs.

Time, Space, and Relativity

A childlike wonderment led Albert Einstein to proclaim that "the most beautiful thing we can experience is the mysterious." The pure-chance aspect of quantum mechanics bothered him. "Quantum mechanics is very impressive," he said, "but I am convinced that God does not play dice."

Einstein thus perceived a kind of divine order even in a relativistic universe. His famous equation $E = mc^2$ states that energy and matter are convertible into forms of each other. He believed that physical concepts are not uniquely determined by the external world but are partly reactions of the human mind.

His theory of relativity led to the acceptance of the idea that space and time are mental constructs, dependent upon each other as well as upon the observer's position in the universe. He was thus led to postulate a fourth dimension, space-time, to be used in trying to establish the coordinates of any thing. Professor Heinz Bechert says that "Buddhist cosmology is characterized by its knowledge of the enormous dimensions of time and space."

The early Church Fathers also wrote about the relational concepts of space and time. Later Meister Eckhart, who died in 1327, said that the religious seeker would have to free himself from the limits of space and time. Eckhart said that "Heaven is pure and without spot, touching neither time nor space. Corporeal things have no place in it. It is not inside of time; its orbit is compassed with speed beyond belief. The course of heaven is outside time, and yet time comes from its movements. Nothing hinders the soul's knowledge of God as much as time and space, for they are fragments, whereas God is one."[2]

Mircea Eliade reminds us that many religions postulate a sacred time, encompassing past, present, and future into one matrix, and being a state as well as a period. In sacred time the creation occurred and is occurring. All religions, Eliade says, yearn for the return of sacred time, when once again all forms in the universe will be fluid, as they were in the beginning.

Black holes are old stars that have collapsed in upon themselves, so that they have enormous gravitational pull. "If the black hole is not rotating," says Gary Zukav, "the object will be pulled directly to the center of the black hole to a point called singularity. There it literally will be squeezed out of existence. At singularity all of the laws of physics break down completely, and even space and time disappear. It is speculated that everything that is sucked into a black hole is spilled out again on 'the other side'—the 'other side' being another universe!"[3]

Ken Wilber shows how we measure space and time at different levels. We slow down or speed up psychological time, to savor the moment or forget the past. Sometimes current time is replaced by historical time, as when we identify with a person from past history. One's psychological space can include one's family, friends, and treasured parts of one's environment. A person's mental space might include the creations of his imagination and dreams.

Wilber describes how complex the spiritual measurement of time and space becomes. "At the spiritual level," he says, "space-time has become so subtle that we can either say that time and space cease to exist, or that all time and space exist now in what the mystics call the eternal moment."[4]

Mysticism in Science

David Fowler, a scientific consultant, asserts that all of the great recent theoretical physicists tell of having received mystical revelations. This includes Albert Einstein with his theories of relativity, Niels Bohr with the complementarity principle, Max Planck with the quantum theory, Werner Heisenberg and the uncertainty principle, Erwin Schrödinger and wave-mechanics, Louis-Victor de Broglie with the matter-wave equivalence theory, and Wolfgang Pauli and the exclusion principle. Foster says that "all of the major developments in the 20th century have been of mystical origin, with the outcome generally being some new mathematical formula."[5]

Einstein's theory of special relativity proved that "any object moving with the speed of light would have infinite energy and infinite weight." His theory of general relativity says that "masses distort space-time so that it curves in such a way that the track of a particle will be exactly the same as though it were attracted by gravitational action at a distance." Max Planck in the quantum theory showed that radiation (such as heat or light) is not continuous, but is emitted in exact and unvarying packets (quanta) of energy. Erwin Schrödinger's wave-mechanics showed that "solid" matter had waves—the electron microscope demonstrated that electrons behaved like light waves.

Schrödinger concluded that the universe has only one Self or Mind.[6]

The modern Sufi Inayat Khan sees all of creation in terms of vibrations, not only physical phenomena but also thoughts and feelings. Schrödinger too envisioned each electron as a segment of vibrations. Current superstring theory says that the fundamental building blocks of the universe are "superstrings," tiny vibrations one hundred billion times smaller than a proton. The speeds with which electrons move in their orbits is the very same ratio as the vibrations in the most harmonious musical chords.[7]

Astronomer Arthur Eddington stated that "the stuff of the world is mind-stuff. Religion first became possible for a reasonable man of science about the year 1927. The idea of a Universal Mind or Logos would be a fairly plausible inference from the present state of scientific theory."[8]

Ludwig von Bertalanffy developed General Systems Theory, which states that you cannot understand something isolated from its context. A single thing is both cause and effect: it had forerunners, and it will have successors. The world, he says, is not a blind play of haphazard atoms but rather a meticulously planned design of organization. Kabalist Moses de Leon in his *Zohar* (Book of Splendor) stated that "everything in the cosmos is in constant interplay, with an irreducible order underlying all."

The Honesty of Science

Science can teach religion much about honesty. Werner Heisenberg, for example, formulated the uncertainty principle, which states that it is impossible to determine simultaneously both the position and the velocity of a subatomic particle. The more accurate one measurement, the less accurate the other. We cannot observe a particle without changing it, for the beam of light focused on it alters it.

Kurt Gödel has a theorem stating that it is impossible to prove that a branch of logic or mathematics is internally consistent. With no guarantee that the laws of logic and mathematics are free from contradiction, one accepts them largely as a matter of faith.

The nature of light puzzled scientists for decades. Sometimes it behaved as if it were a wave, sometimes as if a string of particles. Niels Bohr's explanation was the most satisfactory one. His theory of complementarity says that light can be experienced as a wave or a particle but never as both at the same time. Chinese sages represented this complementarity of opposites as yin and yang. Bohr was so impressed with the yin/yang concept that he used it as his coat-of-arms.

Bohr's theory tells us that we never really experience external reality but only our reaction with it. The world consists not so much of things as of interactions. Dogmatic and divisive religion, cock sure that everything is false but its view, is rendered untenable by modern science.

John Hick derives a religious teaching from the dual nature of light. Early theologians, he says, found a continuity between a source of illumination and its light. So too Hick finds that the relationship between Christ and God is no more an external relation between distinct entities than is the relationship between a source of light and the light itself.

Heisenberg, discussing their mutual findings with Bohr, asked: "Can nature possibly be so absurd as it seemed to us in these atomic experiments?" Absurdist playwrights ask a related question: "Can human beings be so absurd as to misuse the power found in these atomic experiments?"

In 1927 a group of physicists evolved what was called the Copenhagen Interpretation of quantum mechanics. It maintained that the collapse of the lightwave packet was purely random, not to be calculated with predictability. But randomness is not science's forte! Scientists were admitting that a complete understanding of reality was beyond rational thought. Now they were starting to sound like theologians. Schrödinger even quoted with approval the words of the Persian mystic Aziz Nasafi: "The spiritual world is one single Spirit who stands like a light behind the bodily world."[9]

The Cosmic Dance of Particles

We realize that subatomic particles, such as pions, neutrons, and muons, cannot be directly observed by any of our senses. Quantum theory states that only the fields are real; particles are momentary manifestations of interacting fields. What is more, particles seem to be constantly making decisions, sometimes in reaction to events as far away as another galaxy.

How does this information get transmitted instantly, faster than light or electricity? Physicist E.H. Walker speculated that photons may be conscious. Carl Jung might explain it by synchronicity, an acausal connecting principle. Einstein thought that photons might be "ghost waves," mathematical constructs that had no actual existence.

In a sense, then, quantum mechanics is psychedelic. By deciding whether to measure the position or the momentum of a particle, *we* give reality to that aspect which we wish to measure. Scientific objectivity is a myth. Physics becomes a branch of psychology.

In the Hindu creation story Brahman makes all things out of minute particles of himself, with the particles containing great power within themselves. Krishna, the Hindu savior God, says: "With me as overseer, material nature brings forth the world of beings; by this motive force the world goes around. All beings pass into My material nature at the end of a world con; them again I send forth at the beginning of a new world eon."[10]

The deeper we penetrate to isolate a particle, the more interdependence we find. All things are related in the seamless web of the universe. Reality has no boundaries.

Particles are a creation of the fields of force surrounding them. These force fields exist always and everywhere. The Chinese sage Chang Tsai remarked that "when one knows that the Great Void is full of *ch'i* (energy), one realizes that there is no such thing as nothingness."

The Void is an important concept in Oriental thought. The Hindu word *sunya*, often translated as "the Void," might better be rendered as "the Relative," since it implies interrelationship.

The Void can be described as that which is void of all boundaries. In other words, God is no respecter of persons. If everything in the universe is interrelated, how can I harm my neighbor without harming myself and God, who created my neighbor?

Previously, science used analysis to separate the thing being studied from its environment.

Now, in the systems approach, study is being made of the interrelationships that exist among entities.

Stress is now upon synthesis, upon the search for meaningful wholes. The dead end in the search for the tiniest particle of matter has reversed the direction of the search itself.

Human beings exist as a part of an ecosystem. If we ignore what is happening to animal life, plant life, and the atmosphere, we are headed for extinction as a part of that ecosystem.

Wolfgang Pauli, Nobel prize physicist, says that the mythos of our time is to unite opposites, to synthesize rationality with the mystical experience of unity. Particle physics reconciles opposites.

Particles are both destructible and indestructible. Energy and matter are different aspects of the same thing. Space and time are unified in relativistic physics. All apparent opposites are seen to be a part of dynamic unity.

Zen Buddhism reconciles opposites. Distinctions like good/bad, beautiful/ugly, and life/death are seen to be false dichotomies, since one cannot exist without the other. Zen Buddhists use the *koan*, a paradoxical puzzle without a definite answer, to show how we can alter our perceptions in the light of the ambiguity of the universe. "Is it a coincidence," asks Gary Zukav, "that Buddhists exploring 'inner' reality a millennium ago and physicists exploring 'external' reality a millennium later both discovered that 'understanding' involves passing the barrier of paradox?"[11]

Christ's whole life was a paradox. He who was despised and rejected by men came to be worshipped as God. He who would gain his life must first lose it, Christ taught. The meek shall inherit the earth. He who would be greatest among you must be your servant. Full of paradox, religion is once again relevant in a world that has rediscovered the value of paradox in pursuing truth.

In his book *The World of Elementary Particles* Kenneth Ford shows how particles go through a continual dance of creation and destruction. All matter is engaged in a perpetual cosmic dance.

In Hinduism Shiva, the destroyer and recreator God, is depicted in a cosmic dance. Shiva represents the life cycle of birth and death, illusion and reality, suffering and ecstasy. Once again early religion has anticipated and been affirmed by the latest science.

Beginnings and Endings

Like the field of particle physics, astronomy is starting to sound scriptural. Sir James Jeans said that modern discoveries make the universe look less like a great machine and more like a great thought. Astronomer Fred Hoyle sees great interrelation among all the parts of the huge cosmos. He states that "our everyday experience even down to the smallest details seems to be so closely integrated to the grand-scale features of the universe that it is well-nigh impossible to contemplate the two being separated."[12]

Robert Jastrow, former director of NASA's Goddard Institute for Space Studies, believes that "the astronomical evidence leads to the biblical view of the origin of the world. The chain of events leading to man commenced suddenly and sharply at a definite moment in time, in a flash of light and energy. The scientist's pursuit of the past ends in a moment of creation. It appears that there was only one beginning, and there will be only one end. The scientist has scaled the mountains of ignorance; he is about to conquer the highest peak. As he pulls himself over the final rock, he is greeted by a band of theologians who have been sitting there for centuries."[13]

The English mathematician Roger Penrose has established that the astronomical universe must either have originated in a singularity, end in one, or both. Most scientists believe that the known universe began with a big explosion. Physicist Alan Guth says that there was an inflationary period from 10^{-35} to 10^{-32} seconds after the Big Bang. Essentially all the matter and energy in our universe was created during this brief period.

Another physicist, Michael Turner, says that "to get a universe that has expanded as long as ours has without collapsing or having its matter coast away would have required extraordinary fine-tuning." The odds on doing this "without an early homogenizing inflation would be the same as throwing an imaginary microscopic dart across the universe to the most distant quasar and hitting a bull's-eye one millimeter in diameter."[14]

It is generally assumed that there are four basic physical forces in the universe: gravity, electromagnetism, the weak force of radioactivity, and the strong force that binds atomic nuclei together. Many scientists now feel that in the newborn universe these four forces were part of an underlying field which manifested itself in an unbroken symmetrical form. As the universe cooled, the four forces separated out and thus broke the symmetry. Recent discoveries of the W boson and the Z-zero boson particles further support the theory of the unification of the weak and the electromagnetic forces.

Symmetry, an esthetic and religious term, proves useful in particle physics, especially in dealing with quarks, elementary entities that have so far eluded direct observation. Quarks get their name from a random phrase in James Joyce's *Finnegans Wake*.

Astronomers speculate on how not only the earth but the entire universe may end. Allan Sandage of Mount Wilson Observatory poses some ultimate questions on the fate of the universe:

"Will it expand forever? Will all energy dissipate and the cold descend? Or will the universe one day collapse on itself in big crunch? Will, as St. Peter described, 'the heavens being on fire be dissolved and the elements melt with the fervent heat?'"[15]

Freedom Leads to Order

The second law of thermodynamics states that the universe is running down, shooting itself away in non-retrievable energy loss. This condition is known as entropy. But Albert Szent-Gyorgi, who discovered Vitamin C, finds that syntropy, the opposite of entropy, is also a fundamental principle of nature. This means that living things have an inherent drive to perfect themselves. How does this drive work? Perhaps, says Szent-Gyorgi, the periphery of a cell can feed back information to the DNA at its nucleus, thereby altering the genetic code of instructions. As living things, human beings can also feed back information which can help them adapt to such an environmental threat as the danger of a nuclear war.

A Belgian chemist, Ilya Prigogine, won the Nobel Prize for chemistry in 1977 for his theory of dissipative structures. A dissipative structure is any system in nature which takes in energy, transforms it, and returns it to the environment. All living things are dissipative structures.

Inner tension and instability are key requisites for the transformation, and thus improvement, in this energy exchange. A stable system is a dying one. Life is a continuous adjustment of internal to external forces. A dissipative structure is always open toward newness and the unexpected.

Human parallels abound. The very bewildering chaos of modern life may give us opportunities for upward transformation of a spectacular kind. Disequilibrium need not be a threat to survival. As Erich Jantsch sees it, "Globally viewed, mankind gets further away from equilibrium and seems to urge a new structure which may be reached only after a major instability. There is no lack of fluctuations (oil crisis, recession) or escalation of tensions. But it is precisely the preparation of a huge arsenal of nuclear weapons and strategies of mutual strikes which may also act in a strongly inhibiting way."[16]

Oneness of the Universe

Ernst Mach, German physicist and philosopher, put forth the principle that the inertia of an object is a measure of its interaction with all the rest of the universe. If the stars were to disappear, the inertia would likewise vanish.

Physicist J.S. Bell propounded a theorem stating that if paired particles that are identical in polarity separate, and the polarity of one particle is changed by an experimenter, the polarity of the other particle changes instantaneously, even if the particles are galaxies apart. They somehow remain mysteriously connected.

Physicist Nick Herbert sees this as proof of the mystics' unitary vision: "we are all one." David Bohm, professor of physics in the University of London, finds an implicate order underlying the explicate order of sensory perception. This new order is the non-Newtonian structure process which the equations of quantum mechanics describe. It is like a vast sea of quantum potential energy. To Bohm, the implicate order suggests a holy Being beyond the proofs of reason. It indicates the wholeness and holiness of humanity. It postulates that man's chief problem is confusion of the apparent explicate order with the inner ultimate implicate order. To get the peace that passes human understanding, one engages in meditation which quiets the mind so that it can decode the implicate frequency patterns, and then one experiences a state of unitive consciousness with the universe.

In biofeedback, people can learn, through meditation, to alter their heart rates or to control or affect motor responses, even, in some cases, to "fire" a single motor nerve cell. Thus, one's will can alter one's physiology, and religious faith can manufacture endorphins.

The Holographic Universe

Holography is another modern field of study supporting the oneness of the universe. Dennis Gabor invented the principle of the hologram in 1947, but development of a hologram had to await the invention of the laser. A laser is the purest form of light, since all of its waves are of one frequency. When two laser beams intersect, they produce an interference pattern that can be recorded on a photographic plate. If one of the beams is reflected off an object, the resulting pattern is a hologram of the object. What seems to be a meaningless swirl on a photographic plate can be restored by a laser beam to produce a three-dimensional likeness of the object.

The striking thing about a hologram is that if it is broken, any piece of it will reconstruct the entire image. Brain surgeon Karl Pribram discovered that removal of parts of the brain where memory was supposedly located did not always destroy memory. Memory was seen to be a function of the whole brain rather than of a localized part of it.

Pribram was led to perceive the possibility of the universe as one huge hologram. He found Bohm to be describing a holographic universe. "In a nutshell," says Marilyn Ferguson, "our brains mathematically construct 'hard' reality by interpreting frequencies from a dimension transcending time and space. The brain is a hologram, interpreting a holographic universe."[17]

The holographic model synthesizes science and spirit. It might even provide the explanation for psychic phenomena such as extrasensory perception, faith healing, and the meaningful coincidence of synchronicity.

Religious mystics and many modern physicists tend to agree on the essential unity of all things in the universe, and that humans and their consciousness are an integral part of this unity. Beneath this unity lies much dynamic diversity. But underlying the universal flux of the universe, reality consists of the interconnectedness of all things in a magnificent whole.

Anyone who perceives this whole and his/her intrinsic part of it cannot engage in warfare or even hatred of the "enemy." Indeed, there can be no real enemy, for to love this universe is to love each part of it. In this way one loves one's enemies, and forgives them for actions done in ignorance.

In his book *The Holographic Universe* Michael Talbot shows how the paradoxes of the quantum theory support a unitary view of physical reality. Talbot says that quanta appear as particles only when we look at them. All particles are part of a deeper cosmic unity. Dreams try to unify and preserve humanity. A dream may be a visit to a parallel universe.

Athletes good at imaging are the kind who become champions. Mentally retarded people have a very low cancer rate because they do not understand the concept. People with hostility and aggression are seven times as liable to heart attack as those lacking such qualities.

Life is a vibrational pattern consisting of interacting and resonating frequencies. Our consciousness may be contained in a plasmic holographic energy field that both surrounds and permeates the physical body. Near-death experiences are a visit to an entirely different plane of reality, and parallel the afterlife scenes of the major world religions. Psychologist Kenneth Ring says that death may be simply the shifting of a person's consciousness from one level of the hologram of reality to another level.

Jesus and the Sufis teach that the kingdom of heaven is within us. It may be what Bohm calls the implicate order underlying physical reality. Leo Schaya, a Swiss expert on the Kabala, states that "the entire creation is an illusory projection of the transcendental aspects of God."[18]

By now it can be seen that modern science has overcome the tragic division of thought and feeling, of reason and religion, that occurred in the Renaissance. Overcoming this fragmentation leads moderns back to the unity of the world as perceived by early Greek, Christian, and Oriental thinkers. Increasingly scientists are joining mystics in being aware of the unity of the cosmos and the interrelationship of all things in it.

Science and Religion Reunited

Buckminster Fuller, inventor of the geodesic dome, defined God as follows:

God, to me, it seems, is a verb not a noun;
Is the articulation not the art;
Is loving, not the abstraction of love.
Yes, God is a verb,
The most active, connoting the vast harmonic
Reordering the universe from unleashed chaos of energy.

Einstein said that the cosmic religious experience is the noblest mainspring of scientific research, that the sensation of the mystical is the sower of all true science. To know the answer to the meaning of human life is to be religious, he felt. The true value of a human being, in his opinion, lay in the degree to which he attained liberation from the self. Moreover, only intuition can arrive at elementary cosmic laws concerning the structure of the universe.

Einstein showed the similarity of science and religion. "The scientist's religious feeling," he said, "takes the form of a rapturous amazement at the harmony of natural law, which reveals an intelligence of such superiority that, compared with it, all the systematic thinking and acting of human beings is utterly insignificant reflection. This feeling is the guiding principle of his life and work. It is beyond question closely akin to that which has possessed the religious geniuses of all ages."[19]

Johannes Kepler, the Christian astronomer, first observed nature carefully, then turned inward, said Wolfgang Pauli. Kepler sought to bring to light "the archetypal images used in the creation of our scientific concepts." Having an "abstract spherical picture of the Trinity as primary," Kepler came up with general planetary laws by adhering to the heliocentric pattern with religious fervor. "In Kepler," Pauli felt, "the symbolical precedes the conscious formulation of a natural law."[20]

Jonathan Schell welcomes the return of feeling into reason as a safeguard against mutual mass destruction. Only cold reason could ever possibly contemplate the thought of self-extinction, he feels. But united with emotion, reason can sit at the knee of instinct and learn reverence for the miraculous fact of creation.

Ken Wilber describes all conflict between science and religion as a category error. If each remains itself, there can be no conflict, he avers. The problem arises when science tries to be religion or religion tries to be science. He cites as an example the virgin birth of Christ: "The virgin birth as an empirical fact means that a person was born without a biological father. As a mental symbol it might signify the birth of one whose Father is in Heaven (thus, one who realizes the transpersonal Self). As a contemplative insight it might be a direct realization that one's true Self is virgin-born moment to moment. Now the virgin birth as an empiric fact is probably quite wrong; as a symbol and a realization, it is probably quite valid."[21]

Fritjof Capra avoids the category error described by Wilber, as he explains the relationship between science and mysticism: "Science does not need mysticism and mysticism does not need science, but humans need both. Mystical experience is necessary to understand the deepest nature of things, and science is essential for modern life. What we need, therefore, is not a synthesis but a dynamic interplay between mystical intuition and scientific analysis."[22] Such an interplay can have an important bearing on humanity's ability to survive on planet earth.

The Physics of Immortality

Frank J. Tipler, professor of mathematical physics at Tulane University, has an astounding viewpoint in his book *The Physics of Immortality*. Calling theology a branch of physics, Tipler asserts that physicists can calculate and prove both God's existence and human resurrection. He believes that all great theologians accept the current science-religion entente, and that modern physics requires the God principle. "The afterlife predicted by modern physics," says Tipler, "is the same as that hoped for in the world's religions."[23]

Tipler goes on to say that in 1979 Freeman Dyson established the field of physical theology by writing an article in which he calculated, in a rigorous way using the known laws of physics, what life must do in order to survive forever. In his own book, Tipler has a 123-page appendix of mathematical formulas supporting his religious conclusions.

The Omega Point

The Omega Point, first used by the paleontologist and priest Teilhard de Chardin, is a key term in Tipler's approach. He states that the entire space-time is a single past lightcone; thus, there is only one point in the final singularity, and that is the Omega Point. Omega Point theory can be the foundation of all religions,

Tipler believes, for it proves two things: God is a personal God, and there is an afterlife for human beings. Tipler says that perhaps the early Church Father Origen was correct in believing in universal salvation.

The Omega Point, says Tipler, is Being itself, that is, God. At the Omega Point everyone will be perfected. Tipler states that the Omega Point theodicy is the first one to absolve God from the responsibility for evil.[24]

Tipler states that "the universal wave function is the unique field which gives being to all other fields—the electroweak fields, the gluon fields, the quark fields, indeed all the usual physical fields. With the Omega Point Boundary Condition, this all-determining field becomes ultimately personal. Furthermore, the universal wave function is not restricted to living things, but it is everywhere. It has the power of self-transcendence."

"Self-transcendence is a power that continuously raises the organism beyond its limitations and thereby grants it its life," according to theologian Wolfhart Pannenberg. He adds, "in biblical traditions, the life-giving power is seen as an agent that influences the organism from the outside."

The Holy Spirit: The Universal Wave Function

"In the biblical traditions," says Tipler, "this life-giving power is the Holy Spirit. I am thus in effect proposing that we identify the universal wave function constrained by the Omega Point Boundary Condition with the Holy Spirit. The universal wave function constrained by the Omega Point Boundary Condition is an omnipresent invisible field, guiding and creating all being, and ultimately Personal—these are the traditional defining properties of the Holy Spirit."[25]

Strangely, Nicholas of Cusa, the cardinal who tried to bring peace and unity to the divided medieval Church, had a very similar view: "Things owe their origin to motion. Motion descends by degrees from the universal to the particular. This movement or spirit descends from the divine Spirit, who moves all things by this motion. God, who is Spirit, is the one from whom all motion descends."[26]

Hinduism speaks of The Cosmic Sea. This is the ocean of life-substance, the sea of eternal life in its primal state. The ocean stands for universal consciousness, and resembles Tipler's description of the Holy Spirit as the universal wave function.

Tipler says that there are many universes. Some are so small that they recollapse into a final singularity before life has a chance to evolve. On the other hand, some universes have a radius so large that by the time they reach their maximum expansion, life has already died out. But universes of the optimum size have life in them all the way to the Omega Point—these are ones constrained by the Omega Point Boundary Condition. Tipler feels that we humans fortunately are in such a universe.

God, says Tipler, is the completion and perfection of human destiny. "It is necessarily true," he states emphatically, "that we cannot forever be cut off from God. The universe emanates from God. All reality proceeds outward and downward from God until all possibilities connecting God with a given creature have been realized. All humans will be resurrected to immortal life because God, the Omega Point, loves us."[27]

Modern science proves what world religions have long asserted, according to Tipler. "It can be said that humans resemble God in His/Her essence, something that cannot be said of any other living being on Earth. This assertion of the uniqueness of *Homo sapiens* among life forms created to date is basically the same as the claim of human importance made in the Jewish, Christian, Islamic, Mayan, Zuni, Iroquois, ancient Egyptian, ancient Chinese, and Bantu religions," Tipler asserts.[28]

The Cosmic Blueprint

Paul Davies, professor of theoretical physics at the University of Newcastle upon Tyne, says that much of Charles Darwin's theory of evolution is now obsolete. The universe is creative, Davies believes, showing that behind all of life is an impressive design. Life did not originate spontaneously through random shuffling of molecules. Matter and energy are arranged in the universe in a most unrandom way. Consciousness transcends the mechanistic principles in human beings. All particles that have ever interacted belong to a single universal wave function. "There is a cosmic blueprint," Davies states. "The present nature of things, including the existence of human beings, and maybe even each particular human being, is part of a preconceived plan by an all-powerful deity."[29]

The New World View

Thomas S. Kuhn in his influential book *The Structure of Scientific Revolutions* details the tension that appears when scientific breakthroughs are so novel that existing structures of thought require radical alteration. The resulting shift in the prevailing paradigm or world view is like a new Reformation, calling for profound restructuring of the way we think. Lawrence Beynam believes that contemporary physics has provided nothing less than a comprehensive model for the nature of mystical religious experience.

The new world view calls upon us to rethink many of our long-held beliefs, says Gary Zukav. Now there is no tangible matter at the base of things. "The search for the ultimate stuff of the universe ends with the discovery that there *isn't any.* At the subatomic level there no longer is a clear distinction between what is and what happens, between the actor and the action. The dancer and the dance are one."[30]

The world of particles is one of energy forever taking shape as matter and then dissolving in a constant dance of creation and destruction, like the dance of Shiva. Reality is transient, just as religious mystics East and West have always described it. Even as Newtonian physics led to pluralism, so now modern physics leads to unity.

The extreme fragmentation of church and society, says Thomas Torrance, is "now being undermined, not simply by the concept of the world as a global unity which rises through the universal spread of technology facilitating worldwide communication, travel, and interdependence, but by the concept of the world as an organic unity in which visible and invisible structures cohere and operate indivisibly together." Under pressure from modern science, ecumenism must press forward, Torrance believes, "towards its God-given goal of a single comprehensive community of faith and love in which all of humanity is brought to share."

Torrance perceives how the emerging world view will affect modern religion. Elimination of the false dualism of matter and spirit will help heal the breach between liberals and conservatives within the church, he says, and return the church to its historical position rooted in its Hebraic foundation and in line with the thinking of the great Greek Church Fathers. "This will have the effect," he says, "of giving Eastern Orthodox Churches a place of crucial significance in the reunion of the church, and also of including within the ecumenical activity serious dialogue with Israel, which could produce the all-important catalytic ingredient needed for the reconciliation and unification of the whole people of God."[31]

Thus Orthodox churches, like the Russian Orthodox Church, never having been seduced by the dualism of a physical/spiritual split, may play a critical role in providing a metaphysical foundation of the coming world view. Modern science has made atheistic Russia intellectually obsolete, but has given Christian Russia a prominent role to serve in providing a foundation for the value system of the coming world community.

The newest science returns us to the oldest religion. Both approaches see a unitary cosmos characterized by interdependence, with the separate parts playing organic functions as necessary entities in a synchronized whole.

Torrance sees a type of spiritual evolution at work through the activity of the Holy Spirit as "interlevel coordination and synthesis by means of which the forms of created being are opened to higher levels which endow them with their meaning."[32]

Frozen at the physical level, meaningful patterns are hard to detect. Seeing physical events in their broader metaphysical context, one can indeed divine the Eternal Voice at work, calling us to live as privileged children in the family of God. Let us now examine more closely what is involved in spiritual evolution.

REFERENCES

1 Gary Zukav, *The Dancing Wu Li Masters* (Bantam, 1980), pp. 71, 82.

2 Raymond Blakney, *Meister Eckhart* (Harper, 1941), pp. 130, 131, 213.

3 Zukav, p. 185.

4 Ken Wilber, *Eye to Eye* (Anchor, 1983), pp. 78, 79.

5 David Foster, *The Philosophical Scientists* (Dorset Press, 1985), p. 147.

6 Ibid., pp. 4, 5, 16, 138.

[7] H.J. Witteveen, *Universal Sufism* (Element Books, 1997), pp. 55, 59, 128.

[8] Foster, pp. 32, 169.

[9] Ferguson, p. 173.

[10] Mercia Eliade, *From Primitives to Zen* (Harper & Row, 1967), p. 592.

[11] Zukav, p. 205.

[12] Quoted in Fritjof Capra, *The Tao of Physics* (Bantam, 1977), p. 196.

[13] *New York Times Magazine*, 25 June 1978, p. 29.

[14] *National Geographic*, June 1983, pp. 743, 744.

[15] Ibid., p. 745.

[16] Jantsch, p. 73.

[17] Ferguson, p. 182.

[18] Michael Talbot, *The Holographic Universe* (HarperPerennial, 1992), *passim.*

[19] *New York Times Magazine*, 24 April 1955, p. 17.

[20] Ira Progoff, *Depth Psychology and Modern Man* (McGraw-Hill, 1973), pp. 235, 236.

[21] Wilber, *Eye to Eye*, p. 35.

[22] Capra, *The Tao of Physics*, p. 297.

[23] Frank J. Tipler, *The Physics of Immortality* (Doubleday, 1994), p. 269.

[24] Ibid., pp. 12, 143, 248, 254, 264, 327, 338.

[25] Ibid., pp. 183, 184, 185.

[26] *Nicholas of Cusa: Selected Spiritual Writings*, translated by H. Lawrence Bond (Paulist Press, 1997), p. 156.

[27] Tipler, pp. 184, 214, 215, 247.

[28] Ibid., p. 250.

[29] Paul Davies, *The Cosmic Blueprint* (Simon & Schuster, 1989), pp. 108, 118, 121, 177, 194, 202, 203.

[30] Zukav, p. 193.

[31] Thomas F. Torrance, *Theology in Reconciliation* (Eerdmans, 1976), pp. 74–76.

[32] Ibid., pp. 291, 292.

Chapter VI

Spiritual Evolution

Discussing Darwin's theory of evolution, Arthur Clutton-Brock said that "science told a lot of little truths in the interest of a big lie" whereas "orthodox Christianity told a lot of little lies in the interest of a big truth."[1] In other words, science tried to use fossil remains and other evidence to show that humans were purely animals. Shocked Christianity responded by trying to deny obvious evidence from geology and paleontology in an effort to establish the spiritual nature of human beings.

Fortunately neither side need lie any longer. Nowadays a religionist can look scientific facts squarely in the eye, and a scientist frequently pioneers in validating the reality of the unseen. The two might come close to accepting each other's concept of spiritual evolution.

Teilhard de Chardin was a front-runner in discussing spiritual evolution. He traced much of modern man's pessimism to ignorance concerning the outcome of human evolution. He asserted that humans are playing a critical role in achieving a crowning summit of the evolutionary processes.

In describing planet earth, Teilhard called its central metallic core the barysphere. Then, in order, comes the rocky lithosphere, the fluid hydrosphere, and the gaseous atmosphere. More recently humans have identified the biosphere as a living membrane composed of the earth's plants and animals. Second only to the origin of the universe and its life patterns, Teilhard said, is the birth of human thought, which provided this planet with a "thinking layer" that he called the noosphere.

Once thinkers had been let loose on this planet the entire panorama of life changed. Sharing secrets with God, humanity now has the potential for working toward the achievement of the finest of heavens or the direst of hells. We need to be careful to fulfill our role in the generally upward evolution of human thought, feeling, and institutional development.

Like particle physicists, Teilhard found an interrelatedness of all of life. "The least molecule is a function of the whole sidereal process, and the smallest of the protozoa is structurally so knit into the web of life that its existence cannot be annihilated without *ipso facto* undoing the whole network of the biosphere,"[2] Teilhard said.

Teilhard believed in orthogenesis, that the rudiments needed to produce all evolutionary development are present in even the most elementary particles of primordial life. The geneticist Theodosius Dobzhansky has stated that both survival (or generativity) and play (or advance) as dimensions of the evolutionary process are synthesized in Teilhard's mystical philosophy. Although he thinks that Teilhard has played down the important elements of chance and random mutation, Dobzhansky grants Teilhard's point that evolution has an overall upward orientation. Other viewpoints supporting Teilhard are Alfred North Whitehead's philosophy of organism and the psychologist Erik Erikson's stress upon generativity.

Cells show a hunger for wholeness. Thus, a number of living molecules decide to form a cooperative, the single-celled amoeba. Then more cells form a higher cooperative, a specialized organ with a specific function. A number of these organs, in turn, cooperate to form a whole individual. The community prospers in all of its parts because it can cooperate. Cooperation may be more important to survival than competitive struggle to determine who is fittest.

Are there not downward reversions in the evolutionary process? Of course. Erich Jantsch says that if a dissipative structure is forced to retreat in its evolutionary pattern, it does so along the same path as it has come. This implies, says Jantsch, a primitive holistic memory system. The system is thus capable of *re-ligio*, or linking backward to its origin so as to restore the broken symmetry and unity. This holistic knowledge of the system's own history can be called intuition, which literally means learning from within. During a time of rapid change, intuition may be the only factor guiding the direction of the system.

Jantsch finds an application to human social structures. To him *re-ligio* provides the possibility of seeing evolution at work at its origin and it also makes morality effective. Human ethics needs to concern itself with responsibilities as well as with rights. It is fine to speak about my rights, but what about my neighbor's? To stress rights is to take a purely defensive stance, whereas to stress responsibilities implies creative participation in the design of the human world.

Wrinkles in Time

George Smoot, who led the team working on NASA's Cosmic Background Explorer, discovered background radiation from the Big Bang explosion that started the universe. Smoot called this radiation "wrinkles in time." "There is an underlying unity," said Smoot, "to the sea of matter and stars and galaxies that surround us." He referred to the 1993 annual meeting of the American Association for the Advancement of Science, where a session called "The Theological Significance of Big Bang Cosmology" spoke of a parallel between Big Bang science and the Judeo-Christian story of creation.

In 1951 Pope Pius XII supported Big Bang theory, saying that "scientists are beginning to find the fingers of God in the creation of the universe." Smoot states that as science matures, we will probably see scientific societies having theologians to advise them about the spiritual world, just as the Vatican now uses astronomers and other scientists to advise it about the physical world.[3]

Evolution Beyond the Physical

Fred Hoyle, former head of the Royal Astronomical Society, has challenged both Darwin's concept of gradual evolution of different life forms from a common origin, and that the first living cells developed by random processes in a primordial ooze. Instead, according to Hoyle, life came from micro-genetic fragments from outer space. "We received life with the fundamental problems already solved," say Hoyle and co-author Chandra

Wickramasinghe in their book *Evolution from Space.* "The requisite information," they say, "came from an 'intelligence,' calling it a series of question marks, or God. The new evidence points clearly to a cosmic origin of life."[4]

The Age of the Universe

Paul Davies estimates that the amount of time it would take for an *accidental* creation of the universe would be $10^{10^{80}}$ years. But the universe is merely five billion years old, or 10^{18} seconds old. Davies adds that "the spontaneous generation of life by random shuffling is a ludicrously improbable event." He calls it less probable than the chances of flipping only heads continuously on a coin six million times in a row!

Hoyle and Wickramasinghe demonstrate Darwin's error: a complex structure like DNA (deoxyribonucleic acid), necessary for coding living organisms, could not have evolved by chance, because the universe is not old enough for that to have happened. Hoyle says that the age of the universe "does not allow enough time for the evolution of nucleic acid codes for each of the 2000 genes controlling life processes in higher animals." The likelihood of such life evolving *accidentally* on earth, says Hoyle, is like the probability that a tornado hitting a junkyard could assemble a Boeing 747.

The DNA codes for all the proteins of a creature by arranging the order of molecular sequences. Every DNA molecule has the immense information required for all bodily functions. Some DNA, as a computer printout, would be 10,000 miles long, in the opinion of David Foster.[5]

There are 574 amino acids in the hemoglobin chain, making all kinds of combinations possible. To get the precise combination used for oxygen-carrying blood chemistry by *accident,* the chances are 1 out of 10^{650}, Foster states. Even a tiny creature like the T4 phage (which preys upon bacteria) has its very specific DNA code. For its DNA code to have evolved accidentally, there is 1 chance in $10^{78,000}$! Foster concludes, "Put simply, God exists. We are virtually back to something like Genesis."[6]

Foster believes that the DNA code was programmed by the Programmer, the Logos, God. John's Gospel is correct, says Foster: In the beginning was the Logos (the Word). Since the Logos operates through the mental aspects of human DNA, at moments of mystical insight we are unified with the Logos (God), in a way compatible with Erwin Schrödinger's one Mind synthesis. When a scientist has a creative flash of insight, his mind has tapped the Universal Mind.[7]

Scientific Proofs of God's Existence

In his book, *God and the New Physics*, Paul Davies lists five reasons why one can no longer assume that our universe is the result of an accidental combination of elements. First, "if the initial state were chosen at random, it seems exceedingly probable that the Big Bang would have coughed up black holes rather than dispersed gases. The present arrangement of matter and energy, with matter spread thinly, would only result from a very special choice of initial conditions. Roger Penrose has computed the odds against the observed universe appearing by accident as $10^{10^{30}}$ to 1!"

Second, the universe exists in precarious balance between gravity and expansion. A little more gravity, and the cosmos would collapse in a big crunch. A little less gravity, and there could have been no concentration into galaxies. A difference, in the beginning, of 1 part in 10^{60} would have doomed creation—one way or the other.

Third, there is extraordinary uniformity in the distribution of matter and the rate of expansion. If they are causally disconnected, why are galaxies so similar in structure and behavior? At Planck time (10^{-43} seconds), the earliest moment at which time and space have meaning, the entire observable universe was separated into at least 10^{80} causally disconnected regions. "How is it possible to explain this cooperation without communication?" Davies asks.

Fourth, there is an extreme degree of cosmic isotropy. "Careful measurements of the relic cosmic background heat radiation shows that the incoming flux is accurately matched on all sides to better than one part in a thousand. Had the Big Bang been a random event, such exceptional uniformity would be almost impossibly unlikely."

Five, the fundamental constants of nature provide the most convincing evidence of a grand design. For example, an atom of hydrogen has a proton 1836 times as heavy as its electron, alike on a distant star or on planet Earth. Also, the strong (nuclear) force is just right. Had it been a little weaker, matter could not exist. Had it been a little stronger, there would be virtually no hydrogen, and thus no stars like our sun (so we could not exist), and no water (again, we could not exist). A remarkable "coincidence" exists among the fundamental constants of nature. "An alteration in the strength of the gravitational force by a mere 1 part in 10^{40} would be sufficient to throw out this numerical coincidence," and our type of universe could not exist.[8]

The Anthropic Cosmological Principle

English physicist Brandon Carter in 1974 stated the Anthropic Cosmological Principle: "If the physical parameters were any different, life would not be possible; hence, the universe must have been organized to support life."

John D. Barrow (professor of astronomy at the University of Sussex) and Frank J. Tipler developed this thesis in some detail. They say that the cosmological argument in theology states that since the universe exists, there must be some reason for its existence. Charles Partin, they point out, described the set of remarkable structural coincidences in the universe that has produced the human species. As Freeman Dyson states, all these remarkable coincidences tell us that the Universe must have known that we humans were coming.

Barrow and Tipler explain that the Strong Anthropic Principle says the Universe must be such as to create observers of it, and that observers play a key role in evolution. The Final Anthropic Principle avers that intelligent information processing must come into existence and then can never die out.[9]

Barrow and Tipler feel that we humans are probably the only communicating civilization in our galaxy. Also, that human evolution is such a rare event that it probably has not happened anywhere else in the visible universe. A species like ours, they say, will evolve on earthlike planets from 10^{400} to 10^{800} light years apart!

The odds against assembling the human genome spontaneously, they believe, are so great as to make it virtually impossible. Further, to have a universe created, it must be nearly flat, that is, have matter evolving just fast enough to fill the expansion of space. An open universe would have space expanding too rapidly, and a closed universe would have matter expanding too rapidly.

Teleology, or design in nature, is an essential ingredient in modern mathematical physics, according to Barrow and Tipler. They also state that teleology is found in such diverse cultures as the Bantu, Chinese, Egyptian, Indian, and Islamic cultures.

They declare that the Anthropic Principle implies a melioristic evolving cosmos, one constantly getting better. Life, they say, could encompass the entire universe and regulate all matter in it.[10]

What is the future of the universe? Barrow and Tipler feel that it will ultimately converge to a single point, called the Omega Point. "At the instant the Omega Point is reached, life will have gained control of *all* matter and forces, not only in a single universe but in all universes whose existence is logically possible. Life will have spread into all spatial regions in all universes which could logically exist, and will have stored an infinite amount of information, including all bits of knowledge which it is logically possible to know. And this is the end."[11]

The Great Chain of Being

Sir Julian Huxley feels that Teilhard has achieved a threefold synthesis: of matter with the mind and spirit, of the past with the future, and of variety with unity, or the many with the one. Because he prized human personality so highly, Teilhard believed that the highly developed individual achieved the conscious integration not only of the separate parts of his own self but of the self with nature and the selves of other people. Unlike those who inveigh against the sinful outer world, Teilhard found no distinction between that which is human and that which is godlike as long as the unitive energy of agape love motivates human actions.

To Teilhard, spiritual energy is not anti-material or extra-material but rather trans-material, passing though matter. Thus, instead of repudiating the flesh as sinful, one transcends the material, always in the direction of the spiritual.

Ken Wilber likewise finds the spiritual transcending the material. In the following chart on the Great Chain of Being, Wilber explains the hierarchy of relationships: *"Prana* is implicate to matter but explicate to mind; mind is implicate to *prana* but explicate to soul; soul is implicate to mind but explicate to spirit; spirit is the source of the entire sequence. I am using implicate to mean the larger ground out of which the explicate emerges."[12]

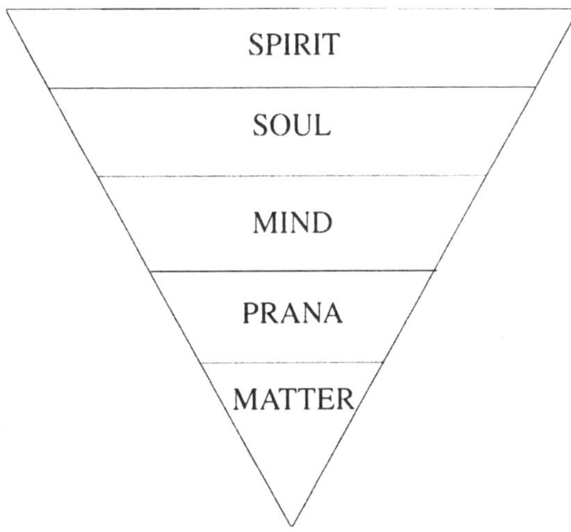

In the above chart, *prana* is used to mean bioenergy or libido or *elan vital*. Mind, says Wilber, creates *prana* which in turn creates matter. Spiritual evolution thus does not repudiate matter but transfigures it, as well as all the other categories below the spiritual. The soul is the divine as seen in the individual; the spirit is the divine as seen in Ultimate Reality or God.

In evolution, short-range specialization is a blind alley. Many animals are stronger, faster, and better endowed in many ways than we but lack the overall general capacity to adapt and control an environment. Aldous Huxley points out that only by remaining precariously generalized can an organism on the one hand employ rational intellect to gain worldly success, and on the other hand advance towards spirituality and a return, through unitive knowledge and religion, to the divine Ground of its origin.

Erich Jantsch sees evolution taking place at all levels, including the spiritual. Life then becomes a process of total self-realization. In true mysticism, he says, the God-idea is found in the unfolding and self-realization of evolution.

To Teilhard, humans have a sacred torch to bear not only in survival but also in evolving spiritually. "The fibers of cosmogenesis demand their prolongation in us in a way that goes far deeper than flesh and blood," he says. "Evolution is now gaining the psychic zones of the world." The cosmic stuff of creation is now part of our spirit, and we dare not let creation down.

It is a great moment for persons, says Teilhard, "when they discover that they are not isolated units lost in cosmic solitudes, and realize that a universal will to live converges in them. In such a vision a person is seen not as a static center of the world, as the person long believed himself to be, but as the axis and leading shoot of evolution, which is something much finer."[13]

Teilhard's concept of evolution involves development of higher powers of knowing, feeling, and willing. As a result, we find better cooperation in all phases of human life—work, play, family life, political life, and religion. Sir Julian Huxley praises Teilhard for pointing out the necessary conditions for advance: global unity of human noetic organization or system of awareness, but retaining variety within the unity; personal integration and internal harmony; and constant dedication to increased stores of love and knowledge.

A good example of a person whose love and knowledge had matured in a glorious unity was Dr. Thomas Dooley. Although he knew he had terminal cancer, Dr. Dooley spent his last years providing free medical services to the needy in Southeast Asia. One day the male relatives of a woman he had treated knocked him down and kicked him. They assumed he had harmed her, since the medication caused redness and swelling. Dr. Dooley refused to fight back. Several days later the woman was completely cured. Now the relatives were apologetic, and several of them volunteered to work at Dooley's clinic to atone for their rash action.

Planetization

One aspect of Ilya Prigogine's theory of dissipative structures is that social structures which are highly unstable have a great capacity for change, especially upward change. The more complex the structure, the more interconnections and thus the more instability. But this instability is the key to change. As fluctuations mount up, they perturb and shake up the system. The parts reorder themselves into a new whole. The system escapes upward, into a higher order.

Prigogine connected this "science of becoming" with Oriental and Western mysticism. Since science is no longer confined to a linear concept of time, he says, it can deal not only with quantities but also with qualities, a sort of "human physics." The rich pluralism of this outlook has been well expressed, he felt, in poets like Tagore and Pasternak and by philosophers like Whitehead and Bergson.

Teilhard agreed that evolution moves toward ever greater diversity and complexity of forms. But because of humanity's increased ability to think and to communicate, a new stage of evolution has been attained, one of increasing unification. Teilhard calls this new phase "planetization."

Teilhard describes this process in this way. First comes the symmetrical grouping of thousands of atoms into molecules of carbon compounds. Then the cell uses thousands of molecules linked in a complicated pattern. Next come the metazoa containing countless cells in a new unity. Later the metazoa make myriad efforts to enter into symbiosis and raise themselves to a higher biological state. Finally comes the thinking layer, "a germination of planetary dimensions," which "intertwines its fibers to reinforce them in the living unity of a single tissue. I see no way of grouping this immense succession of facts," Teilhard states, "but as a gigantic psychobiological operation, the 'super-arrangement' to which all the thinking elements of the earth find themselves individually and collectively subject."[14]

Teilhard said that it would be easier to stop the earth from turning than to halt the totalization of mankind. Sir Julian Huxley said that the development of mankind into a world community has given the evolutionary process a rudimentary head. We and our posterity must organize the global system more perfectly, fleshing out the details of political and economic organization in line with this global unification.

The Omega Point

The Foundation for Integrated Education, which published the journal *Main Currents in Modern Thought,* was led by such persons as Kirtley Mather and Harlow Shapley of Harvard and Edmund Sinnott and F.S.C. Northrop of Yale. The Foundation sought unifying concepts to integrate the sciences and the humanities. A main goal was to overcome the fragmentation and the loss of shared cultural values and moral purposes in modern society. It found three main conditions.

First, the universe is orderly. Whether viewed in atomic patterns or galactic structures, natural law governs the universe.

Next, the universe is esthetic. All the building blocks of the universe, such as energy waves, molecules, crystals, and planetary orbits are recognized artistic patterns.

Finally, the universe is just. Even as there is natural law, so there is spiritual law. In either sphere, to understand and to obey the law is to lead the rational, happy, rewarding life.

The Russian philosopher Vladimir Solovyov cited many examples from science and logic to buttress his belief that all history moves towards a single preconceived destination. To Solovyov ultimate reality consists of the interplay of three factors: the Divine Principle, nature, and human individuality.

Each part of the world, said Solovyov, consists not only of itself but of its relationship in a complex web to the cosmic Whole, whose absolute principle is agape or divine love. Even humans are real only to the extent that they seek this unifying Principle in nature. Cut off from God, a human is mere feeling. But human beings have a divine role to play, for they are God's instruments for revealing His/Her existence.

Solovyov believed that the job of humans is to assist nature in revealing the Divine Principle. Stated in Jungian terms, the collective unconscious is striving to express itself as the collective conscious. Hence, many moderns stress the necessity of raising consciousness levels if humanity is to survive.

If a person is a miniature cosmos, that person can learn something about his/her own nature by studying the cosmos. Conversely, by probing deeper into oneself, one can better comprehend the nature of the universe. The better one understands oneself, the better one understands the cosmos of which one is a part.

To Teilhard, evolution is purposive. It moves from the Alpha state of elementary particles to the Omega Point of reconciliation with the Creator. Several factors are working together to produce this unification of the noosphere, or the world of thought. One factor is our increasing knowledge about the universe. Another is the roundness of the globe—the limits to territorial expansion and the accompanying increase in psychosocial pressure on our planet. Where can we go to get away from people and their (and our) problems?

Another factor is what Teilhard called "the cosmic convergence of mind." As cultures converge, ideas and institutions interact, with a resulting survival of the fittest. Unlike Gresham's Law, which states that bad money drives out good money, Teilhard's Law states that in the competition of ideas for moral excellence, the inferior must give way to the better. Synthesis of ideas from a variety of sources leads to constant improvement in values and customs. In time a consensus develops as to which ideas are the best for the whole society.

The cycle runs as follows: Evolution produces specialization and complexity, but these factors require organization and thus unity. In this way the particular leads back to the universal. Aristotle said that when all potential has been realized, the result is God.

Planetization serves an important survival function. Aurobindo Ghose says that the force behind our evolutionary drive leads us toward the Oversoul, or God. To Hegel, history is the process of the Spirit self-actualizing in three stages: the prepersonal, the personal, and the superpersonal.

Ken Wilber describes the movement towards Omega Point: "Evolution is moving through the links in the Great Chain of Being—starting with matter, moving to biological structures, then to mind, then to subtle and causal realms, and finally to supermind or Omega Point. The Absolute existed all along, but could only be realized when consciousness itself evolved to its highest estate. Once we get out of the cave we see there is and always has been only light."[15]

The highest evolved humans show a remarkable humility. Albert Schweitzer worked as a carpenter and mason in helping construct his medical compound at Lambaréné. One day, as he was dragging a heavy timber, he asked a nearby African to help him. "I can't," replied the African. "You see, I am an intellectual." He was sadly not intellectual enough to realize he was talking to a man with four earned doctorates—a man whose agape was so consuming that he worked unceasingly to help the unfortunate of the world.

Christ as Cosmic Love

Without love, humanity's hope for survival is indeed dim. For Teilhard, love of the universe was the basis of religion. In order for evolution to be purposive, it needs a center of attraction, an Omega Point toward which all creation drives. Only love can purify the soul from slavery to one's selfish self. Paradoxically, self-seeking leads to a reduction of self, while self-sacrifice leads to self-fulfillment in union with the "other." All types of love are related, but only agape, the redemptive love best shown by Christ, can synthesize all loves in line with evolution's purpose.

The Jewish philosopher Leo Baeck said that Judaism was a horizontal stress on ethical conduct toward one's neighbor, whereas Christianity has a vertical stress on human beings achieving a oneness with God. Teilhard saw the agape of Christ as combining both tendencies, thus providing the kind of divine love that can save the world.

Teilhard believed that Christ played a vital function in evolution. "In St. Paul and St. John we read that to create, fulfill, and purify the world is, for God, to unify it organically with Himself. How does He unify it? By partially immersing Himself in things, and then assuming control of evolution. Christ, principle of universal vitality, aggregates to Himself the total psychism of the earth. When He has gathered together and transformed everything, He will rejoin the divine focus He has never left. Then, as St. Paul tells us, 'God shall be all in all.'"

This, again, is the Omega Point of evolution. Teilhard says that the Christian, after initially being frightened by evolution, now realizes that "what it offers him or her is nothing but a magnificent means of feeling more at one with God and of giving oneself more to God. In a spiritually converging world this Christic energy acquires an urgency and intensity. It is in no way metaphorical to say that one finds oneself capable of experiencing one's God in the whole length, breadth, and depth of the world. To be able to say literally to God that one loves Him, not only with all one's body, heart, and soul, but with every fiber of the unifying universe—that is a prayer that can only be made in space-time."[16]

The daughter of an Albanian grocer, Teresa Boyaxhiu went to Calcutta to share the poverty conditions with the neglected and the dying. She set up a home for the terminally ill, saying that they needed the sight of a loving face to ease their anguish. To Mother Teresa, each individual she nursed or comforted represented Christ. Her mass, she said, was to break bread with lepers, prostitutes, and outcasts. A great tribute to the lasting spiritual force of Christ is this humble woman whose life loomed larger than that of kings and presidents.

Teilhard saw Christianity as humanity's best hope for world peace, partly because it best promised to preserve the personal in the final embrace with God, he felt. "We can hope for no progress on earth," he said, "without the primacy of the personal at the summit. At the present moment Christianity is the unique current of thought sufficiently audacious and sufficiently progressive to lay hold of the world in an embrace where faith and hope reach their fulfillment in love."[17] The following chapters will probe this assertion in greater depth, showing the many contributions to world peace available from within the framework of the world's great religions.

REFERENCES

[1] Reinhold Niebuhr, *The Self and the Dramas of History* (Scribners, 1955), pp. 109, 110.

[2] Pierre Teilhard de Chardin, *The Phenomenon of Man* (Harper & Row, 1965), p. 218.

[3] George Smoot and Keay Davidson, *Wrinkles in Time* (William Morrow, 1993), pp. 17, 23, 296.

[4] *Arizona Republic*, 11 December 1982, p. G1.

[5] Foster, p. 77.

[6] Ibid., pp. 82, 171, 173.

[7] Ibid., p. 151.

[8] Paul Davies, *God and the New Physics* (Simon & Schuster, 1983), pp. 178–181, 187, 188.

[9] John D. Barrow and Frank J. Tipler, *The Anthropic Cosmological Principle* (Oxford University Press, 1996), pp. 6, 23, 28, 103, 250, 318.

[10] Ibid., pp. 133, 565, 588.

[11] Ibid., pp. 93, 565, 675, 676, 677.

[12] Wilber, *Eye to Eye,* pp. 197, 198.

[13] Teilhard, p. 36.

[14] Quoted in Don S. Browning, *Generative Man* (Westminster, 1973), p. 227.

[15] Wilber, *Eye to Eye*, p. 160.

[16] Teilhard, pp. 293, 294, 297.

[17] Ibid., pp. 297, 298.

CHAPTER VII

WORLD RELIGIONS & WORLD PEACE

"Our century has witnessed the largest massacres recorded in history."[1] Thus, we have to ask ourselves, what conditions are required for human survival? We need to understand one another's faith, and accept each person's right of conscience. Live and let live must become the byword of humanity. Enlightened self-interest demands that we have a tolerant awareness of the major religious beliefs held on this planet. "Today the Bhagavad-Gita, the Dhammapada, the Analects, the Tao Te Ching, the Talmud, and the Qur'an have become the property of all people, as does the New Testament."[2] Despite the atomic bombs, "the worst, most destructive explosives are the crassly egoistic evil human passions: lust, hate, greed, pride, fear, jealousy. It is these which manufacture all the secondary material explosives."[3]

Paul Tillich, however, assures us that "the philosophical idea of God is inborn in every human being." Aristotle said that God drives all finite beings towards Him by means of love. The Charter of the United Nations says that "since wars begin in the minds of men, it is in the minds of men that we must sow the seeds of peace." Every heart warms during the opening and closing ceremonies of the Olympic Games, when men and women athletes of every country in the world clasp hands and hug the athletes of all the other countries. Finally, the human race is recognizing its identity: it is the family of God.

Arthur Schopenhauer said that all religions reveal only one truly existent Being, present and ever the same in all. This Being, he said, "is found in the Vedas, the Upanishads, Pythagoras, the Neoplatonists, the Sufis, the Christian mystics, Kant, and Schelling. The metaphysical ground of ethics is simply this: that one individual should recognize in another himself in his own true being." In Sanskrit it is stated, "Thou art That."

In 1993, at the Parliament of World Religions held in Chicago, representatives of almost all the world religions signed a Declaration of a Global Ethic, which called for an end to all religiously inspired violence. It also condemned environmental pollution, sexual discrimination, and extreme inequities in the world economy.

Bhagavan Das states that all religions depict human beings as emerging from God, then wandering around confused for a long time before finally deciding to return and go home to God. "Has the same God created all the races, past and present?" asks Das. "If the same, then must not the same truths about Himself, and the same commands for mutual good will and peace, be embodied in all the religions of the past and the present?"[4]

Religion as a Unifier

Just as the word "religion" means "to bind back," so does "dharma" mean to "bind together." The Sanskrit word for man "arya" means "the person to whom others go for help." The Arabic-Persian term for man "insan" means "the friend of all, the lover of his kind." "Islam" denotes "surrender oneself to God." Christianity says, "Not my will but Thy will be done." Differences between religions, says Das, "are differences only of words, languages, or of superficial forms, and sometimes emphasis on this aspect of the Truth rather than another—never of essential ideas."[5]

Das finds five chief virtues common to all religions: compassion, honesty, respect for life, self-control, and spiritual love. To Plato, the four main virtues were courage, justice, temperance, and wisdom. Denise and John Carmody note that all Eastern faiths stress contemplation of the Divine: "Hindu yoga, Buddhist meditation, Taoist reflection, and Confucian study were so many variations on the same theme: set your mind and heart on the Source, the creative Mystery."[6]

Major General Kermit D. Johnson preached a sermon at the Washington National Cathedral in June 2000 at the Interfaith Service for Peace. His topic was Micah 4:3–4: "The Lord shall judge between many peoples, and shall arbitrate between strong nations. They shall beat their swords into plowshares, and their spears into pruning hooks. Neither shall they learn war any more."

General Johnson spoke for all Abrahamic religions (Judaism, Christianity and Islam), saying, "We all stand under the searchlight of God's presence. We have not always been faithful to the transcendent God of creation. Too often we have been seduced by earthbound loyalties that have prevented us from seeing the world as God sees it, as one humankind. Too often the innocent have disappeared, been tortured, assassinated, incinerated, or starved without anyone coming to their defense."

General Johnson quoted from a speech given in 1957 by General of the Army Omar Bradley, who said, "Missiles will bring anti-missiles, anti-missiles will bring anti-anti-missiles. But inevitably this whole electronic house of cards will reach a point where it can be constructed no higher. Our plight is critical and with each effort to relieve it by further scientific advance, we have succeeded only in aggravating our peril." General Johnson thus called for reduction and ultimate destruction of all nuclear weapons.[7]

Speak truth to power, said the Jewish prophets, whose courage in asserting God's will against political forces are an inspiration to all who sincerely desire and work towards world peace.

"When the oversoul of a whole people falls sick," Das reminds us, "it requires, as history shows, a fresh influx of the Divine Spirit, a new advent of a new Son of God, an Avatara, a Messiah, a Rasul, to cure it." All religions recommend conquering hatred through love, and commend the Golden Rule as a universal guide. One corollary of the Golden Rule is to refrain from faultfinding, ill-natured criticism, and scandal mongering. Lies about enemies are used to build "national unity" at home.

"If the followers of different religions quarrel with one another," each alleging that his way is the only true way, "they are not sincere devotees but arrogant egoists," declares Das. "None of them really follows the great Master whom he pretends to honor, but each really loves his own narrow and conceited little self."[8]

Peace in Hinduism

The cure to the illness of narrow egoism is found in the scriptures of the world's religions. The Hindu Mahabarata says: "Self-denial, sense control, forgiveness, gentleness, charity, chastity, truthfulness, purity of heart, and knowledge that the Self is All in All—bathe in these sacred waters." The Purana Bhagavata adds, "In varying ways the sages have described the same unvarying truth. There is no real conflict twixt them all— the knowers know the way to reconcile."

The Bhagavad-Gita describes the road to peace:

> They who have cast aside all pride and fear,
> Conquered lust of the flesh, its loves and hates,
> And tied their hearts to Me, the Self of all,
> They come to Me, the Universal Self,
> And enter into My eternal Peace.[9]

The most peaceful man I ever met was a chaplain of the First Infantry Division in World War II. I asked him how he could do such a wonderful job consoling and counseling shell-shocked infantrymen as they emerged from combat. His smile was beatific as he quoted his inspiration from Isaiah 26:3: "Thou wilt keep him in perfect peace, whose mind is stayed on Thee." Psalm 51:17 adds: "A broken and a contrite heart, O God, Thou wilt not despise."

In Galatians 5:22–23 Paul describes the fruit of the Holy Spirit as love, joy, peace, goodness, gentleness, kindness, patience, self-control, and faithfulness. And in Romans 3:30 Paul states that "God is one, and He will put the Jews right with Him-self on the basis of their faith, and the Gentiles right through their faith." In Acts 10:34–35 Peter says that "God treats all alike. In every nation whoever fears Him and does what is right is acceptable to Him."

The Carmodys tell of an ancient Christian song which declared "where there is charity and love, there is God." They further state that "realizing peace and justice among human beings would be tantamount to realizing the Reign of God."[10]

A Muslim *Hadith* (saying of Mohammed) states that "there are as many ways to God as souls, as many as the breaths of Adam's sons." Another *Hadith* avers religious unity:

> All creatures are the family of God;
> And he is the most beloved of God
> Who does most good unto His family.

In the Koran we read: "The poor, the orphan, and the captive, feed them for the love of God alone, desiring no reward, not even thanks." Also, "The noblest religion is this, that others may feel safe from thee; the loftiest Islam, that all may feel safe from the tongue and hands."

The Sufi poet Rumi wrote:

> By loving wisdom doth the soul know life;
> What has it got to due with senseless strife
> Of Hindu, Muslim, Christian, Arab, Turk?

Islam asserts unity in the words of the Koran: "The Holy Koran is to be found within the ancient seers' writing too, for Teachers have been sent to every race. Disagreement there is none betwixt these Prophets. All have been sent one truth to proclaim: 'I verily am the One, am God, the universal All-pervading Self.' Teachers are sent to each race that they may teach it in its own tongue, so that there may be no doubt as to the meaning. Let us all ascend and meet together on the common ground of those high truths and principles which we all hold. Verily, all who faithfully believe in God and the Day of Judgment, and do good, whosoever they be—Jews, Christians, Sabians—they shall have their reward from the Lord God."[11] Muslim terrorists: consult your scriptures!

Early Efforts Towards Peace

Often in a primitive society a more humane method of adjudicating tribal disputes was used than is generally employed by nations in the modern world. Each tribe selected its greatest warrior and the two men fought. Whoever won the individual contest also won a victory for his tribe. Scores or hundreds of lives were saved by using a method of adjudication probably as just as that of the clash of modern gigantic military forces.

The Carmodys tell how Confucianism works towards peace: "One has to trust that education, social service, peacemaking, and trying to right wrong relations are factors in what is finally a trustable whole. Keeping at these factors even through the dark days when human perversity says that they are useless, is tantamount to trusting in the goodness, the meaningfulness of the entire cosmic venture."[12] Mo-Tzu (470–391 B.C.E.) said that the Will of Heaven, the absolute norm for all persons, is the doctrine of universal love.

Erwin Rousselle described a discussion he had with some Confucian and Taoist masters. "These masters," he said, "made me swear to walk in the paths of Christ, understood in a very profound and ultimate sense." The urging was to soar to that lofty level at which all religions are one.

Rousselle says that a Taoist master has "the conviction that the mystical core of all religions is the same, and constitutes what is deepest in them. Therefore experience this deepest element in oneself, but otherwise stand firmly within that historical religion, whatever it may be, which lives in one's own consciousness." Taoists teach that by letting go of one's selfish self, every man will be a gentle man, "inwardly a saint, outwardly a sovereign," and "the world of the great community will be achieved."[13]

Hinduism is by its very nature unitive. Many a Hindu will say that you are a good Hindu if you faithfully observe all of the teachings of your own religion. The assumption is that underlying superficial ritualistic differences lies a common core of universally held spiritual truths, such as *bhakti* (agape love) and *ahimsa* (non-violence), both wonderful instruments of peace.

Mahatma Gandhi said that everything we do must be motivated by love. He combined his three basic values (truth, non-violence, and self-suffering) into his main teaching, which was *satyagraha* (peaceful civil disobedience). It was so powerful a weapon that the great British Empire could do nothing but grant Gandhi's goal—independence for India. By conquering himself, Gandhi showed how strong spiritual power can be.

The paramount Buddhist virtue is compassion. One Buddhist teaching says that "as fields are damaged by weeds, so mankind is damaged by hatred. A gift bestowed on those who do not hate brings great reward." A Buddhist trinity consists of Gautama

Buddha, *dharma* (the law), and *sangha* (the monastic order). It teaches us to "overcome anger by non-anger, overcome evil by good."

The Buddhist 8-fold path to virtue consists of right action, right effort, right speech, right views, right concentration (meditation), right intention (wisdom), right livelihood (morality), and right mindfulness (mental discipline). One can easily see that these qualities work well to produce peace.

Nagarjuna, an Indian living in the second century C.E., founded Mahayana (large vehicle) Buddhism. His key term is emptiness, speaking not of a cosmic void, but that a person must empty oneself from self-essence, the mistaken assumption that we are real apart from our existence in the One, the Whole. Wonhyo (617–686), a Korean Buddhist, wrote a treatise containing ten approaches on how to reconcile doctrinal differences. He said that all religions have some validity, as manifestations of the One Mind. Zen Buddhism employs both humor and paradox to awaken flashes of insight into a condition of blissful unity known as satori.

Judaism and World Peace

Judaism, although not numerically as large as the other major world religions, has enormous contributions to make towards world peace. Shalom implies not only peace but wholeness, health, and security. It can be inner peace of heart, as the psalmists describe it. It can mean freedom from war, to be achieved permanently only through reconciliation of person to person and nation to nation. It can mean the peace of God, involving the reconciliation of the person to God, and thereby an experience of God's grace. Finally, it can be Messianic peace, when nations will finally beat their swords into ploughshares. Isaiah 32:17 says that "the effect of righteousness shall be peace." Psalm 37:37 observes that we should "mark the perfect man and behold the upright, for the goal of that man is peace."

The Jews quote the Torah in saying that they are God's chosen people. But the prophet Amos said they were His chosen only if they showed responsibility and not elitism. The prophets were courageous monitors of human behavior, even challenging kings whose conduct was improper. Some modern rabbis declare it was not so much that God chose the Jews as that the Jews chose God.

Since a Jew finds all of his life linked to God, he automatically carries a great responsibility to live in accordance with God's teachings. A pervading sense of justice underlies all Jewish actions. A rabbi disqualified himself as a judge when he found out that the man who had helped him across a bridge was the plaintiff.

The great teacher Hillel summarized the Torah while standing on one foot: "What is hateful to yourself do not do to your fellow man." Engaged in dialogue, Hillel always gave equal time to views opposed to his own. The Carmodys encapsulate Hillel's teaching as "We ought to enter into other people's suffering with the expectation that what is afflicting them would also afflict us."[14] The Torah reminds Jews to share in the suffering of the Palestinians.

The Talmud tells the story of Elijah, in the marketplace, asked if anyone there had a share in the world to come. "No," replied Elijah, "but here come two men who will." Asked their vocation, the two men replied, "We are merrymakers. When we see men troubled in mind, we cheer them up, and when we see two men quarreling, we make peace between them." The Carmodys conclude that "from God's perspective we are all simpletons, people far too inclined to take ourselves seriously."[15]

Three treasures, say the Carmodys, shaped medieval Judaism: the Torah, marriage, and good deeds. "In Jewish perspective, life is something people should enjoy. God did make it good, beautiful, and satisfying." For Jews, "charity has been a foundation of the entire covenant," for God is "a Lord compassionate and merciful, slow to anger and abounding in steadfast Love. Were the nations to make charity something habitual, many of the world's claims of injustice and ventures into war would be undercut at a stroke."

"The prophets called Israel to stress mercy rather than animal sacrifice, to let justice roll down like a mighty stream. When tempted to wars of vengeance, the people ought to think about beating their swords into ploughshares. When irritated with one another, they ought to heed God's invitation and sit down and reason together." Since God Himself had shown them tolerance, forgiveness, and generosity, they should imitate His actions and do likewise. God has shown them the way to peace and justice. "To date," conclude the Carmodys, "we have been hit or miss about translating religious wisdom into foreign policy," and have not learned how to treat our poor or ameliorate cutthroat competition."[16]

In the Talmud one finds that "a man should always be soft as a reed and not hard like a cedar."[17] Forgiveness is recommended. If, for example, you have slightly wronged someone, consider it a grave offense. This might deter you from further similar action. But if someone wrongs you, minimize the offense. Keep this act from alienating you from a possible friend. Forgiveness, like charity, is preferable to strict justice, just as you want mercy when you have sinned. It is quite clear that this kind of behavior fosters international understanding and peace.

The Kabala

The Kabala is the collection of esoteric Jewish wisdom, much of which was transmitted orally for centuries. The word Kabala comes from the Hebrew *kabeil* (to receive), and thus it means "revelation" or "tradition." Its two chief books are The Book of Creation (*Sefer Yetzirah*) from the 8th century C.E., and The Book of Splendor (*Zohar*) from the 13th century C.E. These books contain occult and metaphysical speculation on God, the universe, and science.

Kabalists say that major Biblical figures like Abraham and Moses had advanced psychic abilities, enabling them to commune more readily with God. The light of creation was so intense that ordinary humans could not stand it, so instead each of us contains merely sparks of that divine light. Spiritual masters incorporate more of that light, but all of us can grow spiritually through good deeds.

Each of us, says the Kabala, is born with a *neshamah*, a transcendent Self that strives to rise above our petty wants and desires. We also need to sponsor *devekuth* (cleaving to the Divine), for it brings relief from inner tension and anxiety, replacing these with inner peace. As Rabbi Luzzatto said, "If one sanctifies himself, even his physical actions have Holiness."[18]

During the founding of modern Israel, Chief Rabbi Abraham Isaac Kook preached about the unity among one's physical, emotional, and spiritual selves. Many doctors now prescribe classical meditation to combat such diseases as cancer and heart trouble. For emotional growth we need to focus relentlessly on objectionable traits like anger or fear, until such traits no longer have power to move us. Clinical psychologist Edward Hoffman says that a midnight study or prayer vigil enhances one's spiritual life. After sundown there are more negative ions in the air, and they help increase one's creativity, Hoffman states.

The Kabala tells Jews that their Diaspora is for the purpose of their helping save the world through faithful adherence to the Torah. Isaac Luria (1534–1572) taught that such action could restore the holy shards of creation to enable them to harbor the intensity of God's sacred light. To keep it from seeming that God was unjust, Luria preached a doctrine of reincarnation. Thus, through rebirth at a higher level, one might atone for a seemingly unjust reward in this life. His disciples said that Luria could perceive auras around people, enabling him to tell them details of their past lives.

Most Kabalists believe in an afterlife, that "death is a gateway to other realms of awareness." As one approaches death, one should be serene, hopeful, and confident. To some Kabalists, heaven is a "celestial academy," where prophets like Elijah explain the mysteries of the universe. Here, they say, is finally a state of supernal joy, without enmity or strife. "For the Kabalists, the union between man and woman—encompassing physical, emotional, and spiritual dimensions—is a key pathway to the Divine."[19]

The Baal Shem Tov (1698–1760) taught that we each must liberate the fallen divine sparks, to help redeem the cosmos from its current condition of darkness and alienation. He said that "all paths lie open to the presence of the Divine." His Hasidic movement stressed pleasure as a necessary companion to prayer.[20]

Hasidism finds the whole world full of God's presence. Also, good stewardship of God's creation implies a concern for ecology. Some modern Jewish theologians, such as Martin Buber, Hans Jonas, and Richard Rubenstein, feel that Luria's Kabalistic assumptions help them explain the paradoxes and conflicts found in the modern world.

Christianity and World Peace

Despite the many wars involving Christian nations, Christianity in its essence has many important contributions to make towards world peace. At the birth of Jesus, a chorus of angels sang, "Glory to God in the highest, and on earth peace and goodwill to men" (Luke 2:14). In his sermon on the mount, Jesus said, "Blessed are the peacemakers, for they shall be called the children of God" (Matt. 5:9). The bothersome phrase attributed to Jesus: "I came not to bring peace but a sword" (Matt. 10:34), he explained in the subsequent verses: If your family members reject his gospel of love, select his way over that of family members. Also, Jesus said he gave not worldly peace (which never lasts long and is often unjust), but rather the peace of God, which passes human understanding, and is based upon replacing our wills with God's will.

The apostle Paul said, "The peace that Christ gives us is to be the judge in your hearts, for to this peace God has called you together in one body" (Col. 3:15). This peace, says Paul, "makes the Jews and the Gentiles one people" (Eph. 2:14). Paul adds, "God, through Christ, changed us from enemies into friends, and gave us the task of making others his friends also" (II Cor. 5:18). Paul describes what a peaceful life is like: "Lead a life worthy of the calling you have been chosen to, with all humility and gentleness, with patience, bearing with one another in love, making every effort to maintain the unity of the Spirit in the bond of peace. There is one God and Father of all, who is above all and through all and in all" (Eph. 4:1–3, 6).

Paul warns what happens when peace is lost. "If you act like animals, hurting and harming each other, then watch out, or you will completely destroy one another" (Gal. 5:15). Rather, "we must always aim at those things that bring peace, and that help strengthen one another" (Rom. 14:19). Paul told the Hebrews, "Try to be at peace with all men, and try to live a holy life, for no one will see the Lord without it" (Heb. 12:14).

In the New Testament, James combines peace with good deeds: "The wisdom from above is pure, first of all. It is also peaceful, gentle, and friendly. It is full of compassion and produces a harvest of good deeds. It is free from prejudice and hypocrisy. And righteousness is the harvest that is produced from the seeds the peacemakers planted" (James 3:17–18).

There is no evidence of Christians serving in the Roman army until the year 173. Especially after Constantine made Christianity the official Roman religion, many Christians took part in Roman wars. St. Ambrose said that a just war was a war of defense, or of protection of innocent people, or to avenge wrongs. Vengeance was not what Jesus recommended. He said, "Love your enemies and pray for those who persecute you, that you may be children of your heavenly Father" (Luke 6:35). St. Augustine called a war just when waged against an aggressor, when carried on under the authority of a ruler, and when conducted in a humane manner.

Some popes served as peace negotiators, including Innocent I, Leo I, and Gregory I. The abbot of Cluny declared the Peace of God, stating that non-combatants, defenseless people, and the clergy should not be attacked. In the eleventh century the Truce of God prohibited warfare at certain seasons of the year and stated times of the day.[21]

Both Justin Martyr in the second century and Paul Tillich in the twentieth century believed that the Word of God, the Logos, extended beyond the Christian church, "making it possible for people in all religions and cultures to have a partial grasp of the truth, a love of beauty, and a moral sensitivity."[22]

St. Francis, said Tillich, began the Renaissance by opening up nature to religion. St. Francis was strongly influenced by Celtic Christian practices and beliefs. Celtic and Irish missionaries evangelized much of northern Europe, even working as far south as central Italy. Edward Armstrong characterized Celtic Christianity as having "complete dedication to Christ, blithe acceptance of poverty, loose organization, adventurous missionary enterprise, and love of nature."[23]

The Dominican friar Johannes Eckhart, called Meister Eckhart, wrote tellingly of Christian mysticism. A great deal of his message hinges on his assurance that all human beings are God's children. How does he know this? He quotes I John 4:16–17: "God is love, and anyone who lives in love lives in God, and God lives in him." "Love will come to its perfection in us when we can face the Day of Judgment without fear, because even in the world we have become as He is." We can never love God adequately, Eckhart states, unless we are aware of being God's children. "See what love the Father has given us," Eckhart quotes I John 3:1, "that we should be called the children of

God." Eckhart liked Paul's summary in Romans 8:14, 16–17: "All who are led by the Spirit of God are children of God. God's Spirit joins Himself to our spirits to declare that we are God's children. And if children, then heirs—heirs of God, and joint heirs with Christ, so that if we suffer with him, we may also be glorified with him."

You cannot be a child of God if you have sin or sorrow in your heart, Eckhart asserts. Sin separates you from God, and sorrow is a sign that you are apart from God, since oneness with God is pure joy, unalloyed by sorrow. Also, as members of one family, the family of God, we should be good family members and love all of our siblings, the entire human race. Peace grows out of this relationship.

As God's children we, like God, can be creative and compassionate. To Eckhart, compassion means awareness of the interdependence of all human beings. Eckhart said, "God is in us and we are in God." Matthew Fox felt that for Eckhart, "the purpose of living is not to flee the earth or run from its pleasures but to return the blessings one has received by blessing others." We should let go of our material concerns and let creation be the blessing that it is. Fox says "that which most prevents our rejoicing and our celebrating with creation is our tendency to grab, control, dictate, possess, and cling."[24] In other words, we must let go of our greed, and let God be God in us.

Eckhart has a penetrating but endearing honesty. "God is at home in us," he says, "but we are abroad. Humanity is dearer to me than the human being I carry about in myself." What a great connotation for peace! The more we go out of ourselves, the more we enter our true selves, Eckhart taught. Blessed are the pure in heart, he says, for they see unity. Sin is a way of looking at the world devoid of unity. "Unity," he says, "is the negation of negation."

Eckhart tells of the man who found 100 marks, then lost 60 marks, and complained of his bad fortune. So we too, with all of life's riches, complain because we also get life's sorrows. Like Buddha, Eckhart says, Let go of your suffering. Let go and let God bear your concerns. Let go of what separates us from God, and then we also let go of what separates us from other people, and even from our most intimate Self. We are, in God, a unity, so that the happiness of one is the happiness of all, when we bathe in the ocean of God.

Salvation means wholeness. In Eckhart's words, "The soul cannot be purged unless it returns to its original integrity and wholeness, as it was created by God. If we are united to Him, we become 'new' again."[25]

Nicholas of Cusa

Nicholas of Cusa (1401–1464) was a church leader and scholar who was an ardent spokesperson for peace. He strove hard to reunite Eastern and Western Christianity, and to reform the Christian church at a time when the papacy was a hotbed of controversy. Nicholas brought healing to a fragmented and dissident age, a time not unlike the present. He stressed ecumenism, pluralism, tolerance, and reconciliation.

Nicholas coined the term "learned ignorance." By this he meant that we, as finite beings, cannot possibly fully comprehend infinite God, but since we are all alike in this "ignorance," we can humbly build a community of faith. He described a God so immense that He jostles us out of our parochialism. As we seek God we find ourselves. God's oneness unites all humanity.

"He wrote about the peace of faith in heaven, where there is an assembly in which it is taught that the Logos, the divine Word, is present in every religion—in accordance with the interpretation of Paul—and that therefore the struggle between religions in unnecessary.[26]

Nicholas said that not all unity is good. For example, some unity is achieved by one side destroying or threatening to destroy the other side. Also, unity might be achieved through lying or injustice. In adjudicating a dispute, the method Nicholas used was to pursue a disagreement to its radical roots, and then see if some common ground, acceptable to both sides, could be found. Honesty and mutual trust, plus a sincere desire for a peaceable outcome, were nourished wherever possible seeds of reconciliation could be discerned.

Nicholas is noted for his "coincidence of opposites." It meant that since all things originate in God, all things (including seemingly apparent opposites) have a common origin, and thus must have some commonality. If both sides believe in God, the chasm must be able to be crossed. Recognizing our limitations and stating them may encourage the opponent to confess his limitations, and the atmosphere of peace is furthered. Respect for an alternate route to God is the basis for finding God's unity. God teaches us that otherness does not exist, Nicholas said.[27]

Erasmus

Desiderius Erasmus (1466–1536), Dutch clergyman and humanist, was the greatest figure of the northern Renaissance in Europe. As the angry tides of the Reformation swirled around him, Erasmus patiently searched for a calm atmosphere to reduce the verbal war between Roman Catholics and Protestants. His understanding, fairness, and sympathy with both sides made him an admirable umpire in the dispute between the warring theological factions.

Erasmus realized that a corrupt church needed reform. He bravely attacked anyone, including the pope, when he felt that the church had lost sight of Christ's vision of love and peace. As a pacifist, he could not stand idly by when Pope Julian II personally led armies of conquest. Erasmus wrote, "War is so monstrous a thing that it befits beasts and not men, so violently insane that poets represent it as an evil visitation of the Furies, so pestilential that it causes a general corruption of character, so criminal that it is best waged by the worst men, and so impious that it has no relation to Christ. Nevertheless, our popes neglect everything else to devote themselves to war."[28]

Erasmus said that he wanted the popes to be warriors, "but against the true enemies of the Church: ambition, anger, irreligion, lust, pride, and simony." He even went so far as to say that "an unjust peace is far preferable to a just war." We cannot convert Muslims to Christianity, he declared, until we first become Christians ourselves.

As kings prepared to attack each other, Erasmus wrote *The Complaint of Peace,* a passionate plea for the settlement of international disputes through arbitration. He opposed not only traditional warfare but even family quarrels and scholarly disputes. Among his recommendations were: limit nationalistic ardor; stabilize national borders; do not give the ruler the power to declare war; organize arbitration bodies; and mobilize everyone for peace, through schools, churches, and public media.

As Christians prepared to war against Turkey, Erasmus wrote that "the most effective way of overcoming the Turks would be if they beheld that which Christ taught and exemplified shining forth in our own lives." Rather than see how many of the enemy we can kill, said Erasmus, Christ asks us to see how many of them we can save.

When open hostility broke out between Roman Catholic and Protestant Christians, Erasmus protested, "How will there be peace in the whole church if everyone closes his eyes to the virtues of the other fellow and magnifies his blemishes? The particular source of this turmoil is the irreligious moral habits of men. Since we have all aroused the wrath of God, it behooves us altogether to be converted to Him with sincere hearts."[29]

Mystical Activism

Contemplation of God did not necessarily lead a person into an ascetic life. On the contrary, Friedrich Heiler says that "all the great contemplative souls (St. Augustine, St. Benedict, St. Bernard, Gregory the Great, Meister Eckhart, St. John of the Cross, St. Hildegard of Bingen, St. Catherine of Genoa, St. Catherine of Siena, and St. Teresa of Avila) were also great in their active lives."[30] Contemplation led them into a love of God, but they immediately gave themselves to service to their neighbor.

Martin Luther and some other Protestant leaders did not like the way some sects isolated themselves, "claiming that they were the true church and that their members were the elect." Ignoring John Calvin, Paul Tillich said that "such a thing was unthinkable for the Reformers.[31] The Swiss reformer Huldreich Zwingli did assert that the Holy Spirit was present in all persons.

The conflict between Catholics and Protestants culminated in the Thirty Years' War, in which one-third of the population of Germany and Austria were slaughtered. "If intolerance had been continued," said Tillich, "all Europe would have been destroyed by the religious wars." Bigotry, he added, was the process of cutting God down to one's own size. It took Voltaire and the Enlightenment to restore a sane balance between faith and reason.

One product of the Enlightenment, John Wesley, wrote: "In their trouble they cry unto the Lord, and He opens the Kingdom of Heaven in their hearts: righteousness, peace, and joy in the Holy Spirit. One may be disordered in the body, while the soul is calmly stayed on God, and remains in perfect peace." Wesley spoke for pacifism and abolition of slavery, and his church, now called the United Methodist Church, is notable for its many programs of social action, including pacifism.

Another church with a long record in favor of pacifism and abolition of slavery is the Society of Friends, also known as the Quakers. They believe that the Holy Spirit will enter any congregation which sincerely prepares itself to receive the Inner Light. They accept the Bible as a Word of God, but not necessarily as God's only Word. They avoid written credal statements, respecting each individual's right to his/her personal communication with God. War is opposed not only for its obvious inhumanity, but also for its providing a barrier to one's achieving inner peace with God.

In modern times, Pope Leo XIII was sought as a mediator of European conflicts. In 1905, Pius X attacked jingoistic nationalism and the concept that might makes right. Benedict XV tried unsuccessfully to end World War I. Pius XI issued an encyclical calling all humans members of one family, who should recognize other nations as having legitimate rights to freedom and economic prosperity.

During World War II Pius XII spoke against wars of aggression. In his 1948 Christmas message he said that "the commandment of peace is a matter of divine law." In 1953 he added that "every war should be punished on the international plane unless it be demanded by the absolute necessity of self-defense against a very grave injustice affecting the whole community which cannot be prevented by other means." Recently, however, Pius XII has come under severe criticism for his failure to speak out against the Holocaust in World War II.

In his encyclical *Pacem in Terris* in 1963, Pope John XXIII made two main points: relations between nations should be conducted in truth and justice, and the modern arms race destroys both truth and justice. Paul VI in 1967 confirmed that the use of violence, even to redress a wrong, causes additional wrongs and therefore should be avoided. His plea to the United Nations in 1978 was "no more war, war never again!"

The activist monk Thomas Merton said that modern weapons are so heinous that there no longer is such a thing as a just war. Peace, he stated, "demands greater heroism than war. It demands greater fidelity to the truth and a much more perfect purity of conscience."[32]

Gordon Zahn feels that the modern Christian church should return to its original New Testament position of pacifism and non-violence. Archbishop John R. Quinn of San Francisco explains why there can be no just war in a world where the United States alone in the 1980's had a stockpile of nuclear weapons equal to 650,000 times the explosive force of the nuclear bomb dropped on Hiroshima.

Islam and World Peace

Like the other great world religions, Islam has much to offer in helping the people of the world achieve a just and lasting peace. The Koran calls Mohammed the last of the prophets but the previous ones, such as Abraham, Moses, and Jesus, are accepted as authentic. The Islamic view of Allah is that He is compassionate and merciful, and desires justice for all human beings. Orphaned at an early age, and later married to a widow, Mohammed stresses giving aid to all who need it, especially widows and orphans. Similar statements are found in the Torah and the New Testament.

Sometimes, as in the Torah, the Koran describes God in plural terms. For example, in both scriptures the plural form is used to describe the God of creation. The Koran states that all persons who did good deeds will be rewarded on Judgment Day, including Jews and Christians. Jesus will return at that time, and we shall hear on all sides only the greeting, "Peace, Peace."

Akbar (1542–1605), the great Mogul emperor of India, respected all religious faiths. He insisted that "no one should be interfered with on account of religion, and anyone is to be allowed to go over to the religion that pleases him." Akbar set up conferences involving not only Muslim and Hindu spokespersons, but also those representing Jews, Christians, Parsees, and Jains. He even tried, albeit unsuccessfully, to launch a new religion combining the best elements of all of these faiths.

Abulfazl Allami (1551–1602) said universal peace would come when a broadminded ruler like Akbar made bigotry impossible, since the Islamic concept of "surrender to God" can be achieved in any faith. The Arabic term *muruwah* (communal sense) resembles that of the Russian *sobornost* (togetherness), both terms suggesting a strong feeling of human unity.

Some Muslim sects, like the Alawis and the Druzes, are influenced by modern science. "Muslim mystics," said Karen Armstrong, "had often used mathematics and science as an aid to contemplation." The Sufi Sheikh Darwish even went so far as to say that science and philosophy were the most secure paths to the knowledge of God.

Sufism

The most important Muslim mystics are the Sufis, named for the *suf*, or simple wool robe, they wear. Their basic tenet is the mutual love of God and humans. They are clearly a powerful force for peace in the modern world.

Cyprian Rice, a Roman Catholic, says that the future purpose of Sufism will be "to make possible a welding of religious thought between East and West." Al-Hallaj, who was greatly influenced by Jesus, said that since all religion stems from a simple principle, God, we should not try to make a person change his or her religious preference. Ibn 'Arabi said, "I accept all religions. I practice the religion of Love."

Some Sufis refer to Jesus as "Our Lord Jesus," and point out that in the Koran Jesus is often called the Spirit of God. More bridges between Islam and Christianity will be discussed in the next chapter.

The story is told of a Christian who became a Muslim. But his mother, seeing him drunk, said, "My son, acting in this way you have spurned Jesus, and you have also failed to please Mohammed. Stay in the belief which is yours."[33]

Sufis describe how the soul matures. First it may be biased towards evil, then it becomes aware that it is in the wrong, and finally it overcomes evil and achieves eternal peace. Sufis are critical of empty ritual in religion, saying ritual is good only when it leads to a greater love of God and people. The true Mosque, they say, is built in a pure and lowly heart.

The great Muslim theologian al-Ghazali, who synthesized Sufism and orthodox Islam, said that a human being is not being human when he engages in self-indulgence, temper, covetousness, and attacks on other people. One Sufi group, the followers of Haji Bektash, were considered immoral by conservative Muslims because they permitted women to attend their meetings. "Nobody could, or would, understand that it was necessary to redress the social balance of a society based upon male supremacy."[34]

Sufis say that we progress successively from fear to knowledge to love. God is the mirror in which you see yourself as you really are. Another Sufi triad is the progress from faith to spiritual beauty to absorption in the Divine Will. As Platonists, Sufis believe in archetypes which derive from Divine Omniscience. They know the *Sakina* as Divine Peace, analogous to the Hebrew concept of the *Shekhinah* as Divine Glory. Religion, Sufis say, is like recognition of a debt. The soul soars when it praises God for all of His blessings. Angels are rays of Universal Intelligence which connect humans to God. One prominent Sufi order, the Bektashis, have a girdle liturgy, in which a 7-pointed star hangs from a girdle or belt. The liturgy states:

> I tie up anger and unbind meekness.
> I tie up avarice and unbind piety.
> I tie up greed and unbind generosity.
> I tie up hunger and unbind contentment.
> I tie up ignorance and unbind the fear of God.
> I tie up passion and unbind the love of God.
> I tie up the power of Satan and unbind divineness.[35]

A Sufi master said, "The true way to hurt the enemy is to be occupied with the love of the Friend (God). On the other hand, if you engage in war with the enemy, he will obtain what he wanted from you and at the same time you will have lost the opportunity of loving the Friend." If someone is hostile towards you, and you fight back, you fight alone. Instead, "do what your Lord has commanded." Let Him do the fighting for you. Remember, "God has power over all things."[36]

Like the Quakers, Sufis place great stress on the achievement of inner peace. Recognizing the spark of divinity in all persons, they say, we can never wish to harm our neighbor or our enemy. What disturbs peace is evil, but what fosters peace is good, in the Sufi vocabulary. Here is a Sufi teaching on how to achieve inner peace: Since physical life is ephemeral, seek the eternal life of the soul. Since earthly knowledge is limited, seek the knowledge of God. Since earthly power is limited, seek the power of God. Since earthly happiness is limited, seek the happiness of the soul.[37]

One Sufi tells of the role of mysticism in religion, saying, "The great teachers and inspirers of humanity in all ages were mystics. One has only to study their lives. All the destruction which has been caused by wars, by humans fighting one another, this is all caused by a lack of mystical understanding. What the world needs today is to see the whole of humanity as one, the single Being.

The essence of spirituality is readiness to serve the person who is next to us. As one evolves spiritually one rises above intolerance, and so one unites oneself with the other person in God. Tolerance is the sign of an evolved soul. A soul gives a proof of its evolution in the degree of tolerance it shows. The knower of truth will find truth in the symbols of the Roman Catholic Church, and will also find truth in the absence of symbols in the Protestant Church."[38]

Baha'i

The Baha'i faith, which grew out of a branch of Shiite Islam, is one of the most all-inclusive of all world religions. The founder, Baha-u-llah (1817–1892), felt that most religions are one in purpose, even as they pursue their separate pathways to God. "Let not a man glory in this," said Baha-u-llah, "that he loves his country; let him rather glory in this, that he loves his kind."[39] The Baha'i faith is almost unique in accepting all the scriptures of the major world religions as sacred.

Baha-u-llah states that if your religion does not bring you closer to your neighbor, discard it and seek a more authentic approach. He felt that as God's children, women deserve equal treatment with men. He also recommended universal disarmament, and a world parliament and court to work under the jurisdiction of a world federation of sovereign nations.

The Great Peace

Kang Youwei (1858–1927) was a Chinese utopian philosopher. Humanity, he said, had three stages: The Age of Disorder, The Age of the Small Peace, and The Age of the Great Peace.

When human agape love becomes universal, he predicted, the earth will have the latter peace, which will also be The Age of Great Unity. Then, he felt, we will have one world with universal peace and harmony. Nations will no longer have war-making powers, and wisdom and love will reinforce human dignity.

To those who feel the search for universal peace is a chimera, a lofty dream of religious idealists that can never be achieved in a "real" world, I conclude with what General Douglas MacArthur said in his book *Revitalizing a Nation*: "You cannot control war; you can only abolish it. Those who shrug this off as idealistic are the real enemies of peace—the real warmongers. Those who lack the enterprise, vision, and courage to try a new approach when no others have succeeded, fail completely the most simple test of leadership. Let us regain some of the courage and faith of the architects who charted the course to our real greatness."

REFERENCES

[1] Denise L. Carmody and John T. Carmody, *Peace and Justice in the Scriptures of the World Religions* (Paulist Press, 1988), p. 7.

[2] Ibid., p. 11.

[3] Bhagavan Das, *The Essential Unity of All Religions* (Theosophical Press, 1966), p. xx.

[4] Ibid., p. 151.

[5] Ibid., p. 66.

[6] Carmody, p. 184.

[7] *Cathedral Age* (Washington National Cathedral), Fall 2000, pp. 22–23.

[8] Das, pp. 409, 507.

[9] Ibid., pp. 41, 66, 533, 534.

[10] Carmody, p. 5.

[11] Quoted in Das, pp. 62–64, 149, 294, 527, 546.

[12] Carmody, p. 90.

[13] Joseph Campbell, ed., *Spiritual Disciplines* (Princeton University Press, 1985), vol. 4, pp. 64, 90, 92.

[14] Carmody, p. 136.

[15] Ibid., pp. 138, 140.

16 Ibid., pp. 125, 128, 129, 132, 133.

17 Ibid., p. 130.

18 Edward Hoffman, *The Way of Splendor* (Shambhala, 1981), pp. 93, 94, 126.

19 Ibid., pp. 173, 190, 191, 196, 199.

20 Ibid., p. 29.

21 Thomas A. Shannon, *What Are They Saying About Peace and War?* (Paulist Press, 1983), pp. 10, 12, 13, 18

22 Paul Tillich, *A History of Christian Thought* (Simon & Schuster, 1972), p. xix.

23 Matthew Fox, ed., *Breakthrough: Meister Eckhart's Creation Spirituality in New Translation* (Doubleday, 1980), p. 33.

24 Ibid., pp. 44, 45.

25 Ibid., pp. 61, 141, 190, 196, 233, 234, 236, 271.

26 Tillich, p. 375.

27 *Nicholas of Cusa: Selected Spiritual Writings.* Tr. and intro. by H. Lawrence Bond (Paulist Press, 1997), pp. 18, 27, 28, 176, 261.

28 John C. Olin, ed., *Christian Humanism and the Reformation* (Fordham University Press, 1975), rev. ed., p. 14.

29 Raymond Himelick, ed. and tr., *Erasmus and the Seamless Coat of Jesus* (Purdue University Studies, 1971), pp. 83, 85.

30 Joseph Campbell, *Spiritual Discoveries*, p. 237.

31 Tillich, p. 241.

32 Shannon, pp. 24, 28, 29, 31, 36, 66.

33 Idries Shah, *The Way of the Sufi* (Dutton, 1970), p. 71.

34 Ibid., p. 30.

35 Kenneth Cragg, *The Wisdom of the Sufis* (New Directions, 1976), p. 17.

36 Ibid., pp. 48, 49.

37 Witteveen, p. 79.

38 Ibid., pp. 186, 223, 236, 237, 250, 254.

39 J.E. Esslemont, *Baha-u-llah and the New Era* (Baha'i Publishing Committee, 1948), p. 50.

CHAPTER VIII

CREATIVE INTERFACE
AMONG WORLD RELIGIONS

The mandala, or circle, is a design employed in Hinduism and Buddhism to represent the oneness of the universe, and often the One creator of that unity. Likewise, it is a basic form used in the art and religion of Native Americans. They used the circular design in their dances, their lodgings, and even in their prayer staffs. To them it is a symbol "that everything is connected to everything else. All people and nature and the Maker, and no matter where you go and who you become you are still part of it all. And that cannot be ignored. Never."[1]

A Test of Religion

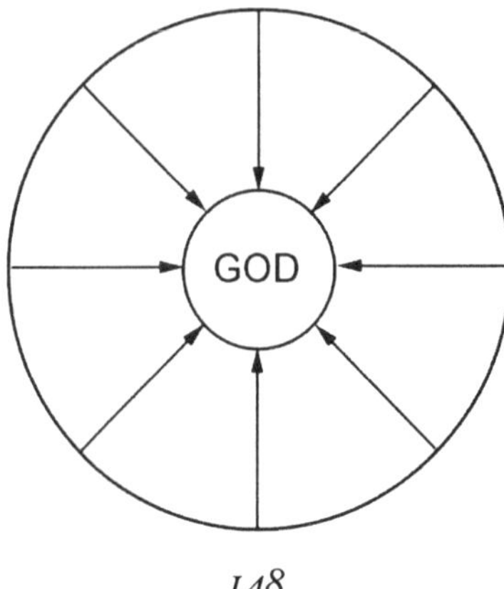

This mandala might be called the wheel of God. It depicts how we all start from different beginnings in our common journey towards God. Necessarily, we thus can be traveling in quite different directions toward our common goal.

A wheel cannot function without a hub. Moreover, each spoke helps support all the other spokes. Because of the dynamics of a wheel, spokes opposite to you are more important in having a strong wheel than those alongside you.

Above all, the wheel of God contains a test, to tell you whether you are traveling in the right direction. The clue is in whether you feel closer all the time to the other spokes, the closer you get to God. If you feel you are increasingly alienated from your fellow searchers, you probably are also getting more distant from God.

The Syncretism of Pico della Mirandola

Although he died at the early age of 31, Giovanni Pico della Mirandola was the greatest mind of the Renaissance. He mastered not only Greek, Latin, and Hebrew, but also Arabic and even Chaldean. Pico followed the *prisca theologia*, the ancient syncretist theology which foreshadowed Christianity. It states that since God is One, all sincere search for Him is essentially the same. Each culture adorns its particular search with some of its peculiar trappings, but the mystic perceives the fundamental unity underlying the search.

Pico offered to debate in public on his defense of a broadened Christianity, contained in his collection of 900 theses. His introduction to the proposed debate was called "Oration on Human Dignity." Pico called on humans to live up to their highest, their spiritual nature. Human freedom is extolled as each person's legacy as a child of God, albeit accompanied by its sister attribute, responsibility.

Since Pico felt that God is One, he found validity in not only Christianity but also in Plato, Aristotle, the Muslim thinker Averroes, the Jewish Kabala, and every other sincere search. Humans achieve the peace that passes understanding, Pico said, when they expand their consciousness to engulf all of God's creation. Pico quoted the Christian theologian Origen on the idea that there could not be eternal punishment, for that would be infinite retribution for finite error, something that a God of love could not countenance.

Pope Innocent VIII appointed a commission to investigate possible heresy in Pico's position. Of his 99 theses, the commission condemned 7 as heretical and 6 more as suspect. The condemnation was based on Averroistic statements and Kabalist doctrines which deviated from Roman Catholic dogma.

In his defense Pico pointed out that church fathers like Eusebius, Origen, Jerome, and Augustine had all quoted parts of the Kabala approvingly, and so had Moses Maimonides, Raymond Lull, and Arnold of Villanova. Pope Sixtus IV had even ordered several parts of the Kabala to be translated.

Seeing Christianity in his day in its corrupt form, with simony, immorality, and worldliness even invading the papacy, Pico viewed his syncretism as a needed step towards universal religious reform and ultimate religious union. Pico would enthusiastically endorse current movements toward ecumenism and peace among world faiths.

"By universalizing all religious knowledge," said David Ruderman, "Pico (and his friend Marcilio Ficino) fashioned a more tolerant theology of Christianity. They came to appreciate the centrality of Hebrew culture in western civilization." With the guidance of the Kabala, Pico believed, all controversies between Jews and Christians can be resolved.

"For the first time in the history of western thought," said Ruderman, "postbiblical Judaism as conceived by Christians was neither negative, irrelevant, or peripheral to their culture. On the contrary, Judaism had intrinsic worth and represented a significant dimension of the human experience."

Pico's approach showed the Jews the chasm between their own national aspirations and their desire to belong to a larger family of humankind. Pico argued that if the walls of separation between Jew and Christian could be removed, the essence of Jewish culture would be shared by the entire human family. Not only Pico's Christian Kabala but humanism in general threatened to seriously alter the exclusivity of Jewish culture. Syncretism was one way by which enlightened persons in the Renaissance sought to bring peace among intolerant warring religious factions.

The Divine Ground

A Hindu has no trouble accepting Jesus as one of the avatars or reincarnations of the Savior God. Swami Prabhavananda reminded us that Jesus said, "Before giving your gift on the altar, first be reconciled with your brother." The swami added, "There is only one way to feel sincerely reconciled, and that is to try to see God in all beings, and to love him in all. It is taught in Buddhism and in Vedanta that it is a person's duty to pray for others before one prays for oneself. The desire to argue and quarrel is a sign of ego."[2]

Aldous Huxley found in all world religions a common core, the Divine Ground. He said: "In Hinduism it is Brahman, with its creative, sustaining, and transforming aspects manifested in the Hindu trinity, the Trimurti. In Mahayana Buddhism the Divine Ground is called Mind or the Pure Light of the Void; the place of the High Gods is taken by the Dhyani-Buddhas."

Huxley also found the Divine Ground in Christianity. "For Eckhart and Ruysbroeck there is an Abyss of Godhead underlying the Trinity." Henry Suso shows how a person can ascend beyond the Trinity to the ultimate Unity of the Divine Ground. In Islam, "some Sufis conceive of *al-Haqq*, the Real, as being the Divine Ground or the Unity of Allah."[3]

Huxley continues: "In regards to man's final end, all the higher religions are in complete agreement. The purpose of human life is the discovery of Truth, the unitive knowledge of the Godhead. The practice of mysticism makes good Christians, good Hindus, good Buddhists, good Taoists, good Moslems, and good Jews. For the Buddhist, the right livelihood was incompatible with the making of deadly weapons or of intoxicants; for the medieval Christian, with the taking of interest and various monopolistic practices."[4]

The Unity Way

Marcus Bach states that the Unity School of Christianity stresses "a God of peace, a Son of Love, and a Spirit of joy. All people are God's children, all faiths are a part of God's family. Above and beyond the things that separate various religions are Truths which unite them." Bach quotes St. Augustine, who said "that which is now called the Christian religion existed among the ancients, and never did it not exist from the beginning of the human race until Christ came in the flesh."

Bach says that "all roads that lead to God are good. Among the great religions, Zoroastrianism is the path of righteousness, Hinduism the path of identification, Buddhism the path of deliverance, Confucianism the path of harmony, Islam the path of submission, and Christianity the path of love.

God is so great that He can never express Himself fully in one exclusive sect. He is a prism through which the one light is refracted. He is the sea from which and into which the rivers of thought are flowing. He is Love Eternal, out of which love in its myriad forms expresses itself." Bach describes a group of Japanese religious leaders who toured the United States in the 1960's. They visited "the Mormon Temple in Salt Lake, the Baha'i Temple in Wilmette, Islamic centers, Jewish synagogues, Catholic and Protestant churches, and many universities. They said they found unity in diversity, and world peace through spiritual understanding."[5]

The Heretical Imperative

Sociologist Peter Berger states that as much as modern persons might wish to use reason as the fulcrum of their philosophy of life, we are all forced to use faith in making important life choices. This "heretical imperative" Berger found existing in all world religions. He quotes Pope Pius XI as saying, "Today we are all Protestants," with something to protest about—but also with something to declare. Ernst Troeltsch said that all religions work toward a common goal, a higher life, despite various paths used in the search. Berger quotes the Koran (35:24): "There is no nation that has not been warned by a disciple."[6]

A Wichita journalist described how spiritual quests unite seekers. Rabbi Abraham Heschel calls the spiritual "the direction of the Here toward the Beyond. It is the ecstatic force that stirs all our goals. When we perceive it, our mind glides for a while in an eternal current." A Sufi prayer states: "O God, break this shell of self, until Thy light is reflected in glory from the mirror at the foundation of my soul." Jack Kornfield provides a Buddhist perspective: "We all have, without exception, a very deep longing to give—to give to the Earth, to give to others, to work, to love, to care for this Earth. One of the worst human sufferings is not to find a way to love."[7]

The Intrareligious Dialogue

Raimon Panikkar, a professor of religion, provided ground rules for engaging in intrareligious dialogue. First comes the recognition that in the modern world, religious imperialism is obsolete. For example, it is an insult to God to assume that God would have any chosen people. "All religions are transformations of primordial experience. Religions do not stand side by side, but they are actually intertwined and inside each other." Examples are the confluence of Aryan and Dravidian cultures that produced Hinduism, and the synthesis of Hebrew and Greek beliefs that resulted in Christianity.

"Most of mankind's great religious geniuses," says Panikkar, "did not create or found new forms of religiousness out of nothing; rather they fused more than one religious stream, molding them with their own prophetic gifts." Before we can have effective interreligious dialogue, says Panikkar, we must first have intrareligious dialogue. We must be willing to challenge some of our fundamental assumptions, if we expect other members of the dialogue to do likewise. Once we understand the other, he or she is no longer "the other."

Religion can make us changed persons. "I cannot love my neighbor as myself until I take my place on the one bit of higher ground that will hold us both—in other words, unless I love God," Panikkar asserts. He believes that the common thread in all religions is the human desire for immortality. We really do not appreciate our own faith until we have a deep awareness and respect for at least one other religion. Syncretism enriches the merging faiths, providing a "mutual fecundation of religious traditions."[8]

Impact of Vatican II Council

The great Roman Catholic theologian Karl Rahner summarized how Vatican II Council changed his church permanently. He says that it is now a pluralistic world church, and thus its theology can no longer be an inner-church affair. In Rahner's view, Christians need a new understanding of how Christianity functions in a global civilization which includes important non-Christian elements.

Vatican II Council declared that not only a saving piety can be found outside the Church, but that probably most of the world will be saved without contact with Church dogma. Rahner called non-Christians who were true to their conscience "anonymous Christians." A prominent role of a modern Christian missionary, Rahner said, would be to help non-Christian people to develop the implications of their original faith. What the Roman Catholic Church needs to do, in Rahner's opinion, is reformulate its mystical theology, concentrating on central mysteries but dropping marginal issues. In all of this, he felt, the best Christian witness would be accomplished by a unified Christianity, rather than by the efforts of any one Christian church.

A recent editorial in the *New York Times* used a religious holy season to call for unitive rather than divisive religion. The writer pointed out the cruel irony in that the NATO bombing in Kosovo in 1999 occurred during a week when the observances of Easter, Passover, and the Muslim feast of sacrifice, *Id al-Adha*, all were being recognized. If there is any solace, the article said, "it is in the lesson of how much these religions have in common at a time when so many of their adherents are in conflict."

Passover, it was stated, celebrated the ancient Hebrews' escape from oppression in Egypt, clearing the way for them to receive a code of conduct from the one God. Now the holy day can be significant for any people suffering from alienation and expulsion, like the modern Kosovars.

Easter is a symbol of the promise of salvation after defeat, its vision showing that justice, in the end, can prevail against misused temporal power. The Muslim holiday of *Id al-Adha,* commemorating Mohammed's flight from Mecca to Medina, is very much in the minds of the Muslim Kosovars, expelled from their homes by belligerent Serbs. "Ruthless leaders persecute others in the name of religion, ignoring the genuine tradition of tolerance enshrined in Judaism, Christianity, and Islam, and articulated by the prophets, saints, and seers of each faith," the editorial stated. "Thus, it is especially important to remember the horrors of viewing others with different backgrounds as strangers, or even enemies, whether they live in Northern Ireland, the Middle East, Indonesia, or any other place of entrenched religious and ethnic conflict. Therefore this season's confluence of holidays and horrors can serve as a powerful reminder of that high yearning among peoples of all traditions."[9]

Meister Eckhart's Creation Spirituality

Matthew Fox, priest and professor, feels that Eckhart's spirituality is "uniquely suited for an age of the global village and of ecumenism of all world religions." Fox says that no other writer since Eckhart has "so profoundly integrated biblical theology and spirituality, prophecy and mysticism, faith and reason, and art and life." To show Eckhart's ecumenicity, "his works are heavily annotated with references to Greek, Arab, and Jewish philosophers as well as the Greek and Latin Church Fathers."

In Eckhart's cosmic vision, "all things are connected," like the Higgs field of modern particle physics. Fox summarizes Eckhart's teachings under four headings: we experience God in creation; we should let go of our materialism and let be (accept ourselves); by conquering our sinful self, we make a breakthrough, giving birth to our higher Self, the Spirit of God within us; and we must always show compassion for fellow human beings, and work for social justice in all human affairs.

Hindu scholar Ananda Coomaraswamy finds a similarity between Eckhart's position and Vedantist traditions. Dr. D.T. Suzuki speaks of the "closeness of Eckhart's way of thinking to that of Mahayana Buddhism, especially of Zen Buddhism." Professor S. Ueda of Kyoto believes that Eckhart breaks "the sound barrier of the normal intellectual world of Christianity and thereby enters the world of Zen." Eckhart has also received acclaim from Quakers, from Carl Jung, and from theologians like Josiah Royce and Rudolf Otto.[10]

Hans Küng on Christian Syncretism

Professor Hans Küng is a pioneer in working for cooperation among world faiths. He quotes the great Orientalist Louis Massignon as asking Christians for "a spiritual Copernican revolution," ending in "a reconciliation between the religion of hope (Judaism), the religion of love (Christianity), and the religion of faith (Islam)." Küng identifies unifying factors in these three Semitic religions: monotheism; the God of history; a personal God, one you can speak to; and the fact that God is gracious and merciful. Küng adds that "Christians can never honestly invoke Jesus of Nazareth to bless violence, hatred, killing, and war."

Küng says that the Bible states that even non-Christians can know God:

> 1. From Genesis to wisdom literature, from Romans to the prologue of John's Gospel, the Bible opens up universal perspectives.
> 2. According to the Old Testament, God is the creator and preserver of all men and women, his power reaches everywhere; he has entered into an alliance (through Noah) with all of humanity.
> 3. According to the New Testament, God is no respecter of persons, but seeks the salvation of all people.
> 4. Non-Christians, too, can be justified as doers of the Law. The book of Acts says that God has not left the pagans without witnesses to Himself, that He is close to every person.[11]

Küng continues: "Jesus questions no one about the true faith. He asks no one to profess his or her orthodoxy. People continually forget that Jesus was a Jew and looked more like a modern Palestinian Arab than a Greek, Roman, Italian, or German image of him. This Jewish Jesus had no more notion than a Muslim in our time would of weakening faith in the one God (breaking the First Commandment). He said, 'Why do you call me good? No one is good but God alone' (Mark 10:18)."

If we go back to our beginnings, we find unity, Küng asserts. "At our origins, all of us—Jews, Christians, and Muslims—are closer to one another." Heiki Raisanen, a New Testament scholar who studied the Koran, says that "some passages of the New Testament show a striking similarity to the Koran's portrait of Jesus." In Küng's view, "It was an unparalleled calamity for the developing Christian church to be almost completely cut off from its native Jewish soil." Paul Schwarzenau states that "it is the Jewish element of the Christian message which the Koran decisively accentuates." Küng adds, "Mohammed always spoke sympathetically of Jesus as the great messenger, indeed as the Messiah who brought the Gospel."[12]

Christian-Jewish Dialogue

The Crusaders, using a cross as a symbol, desecrated the memory of Christ by slaughtering thousands of Jews and Muslims in a most unchristian fashion. Here was divisive religion at its worst. Mary Boys says that "the symbol of the cross reminds Christians of our betrayal of Jesus, the Jew from Nazareth." Now the cross must "embody the power of reconciliation for which Jesus lived and died. Only then will Christians walk in the way of Christ."[13]

Jesus told his followers to "deny themselves and take up their cross and follow him" (Mark 8:34). This, says Boys, is a call to the Christian church "to be of service to humankind at the expense of prestige and power." The cross can be a symbol of Christ's stress upon the two most important commandments: the upward thrust is our striving towards God, and the lateral thrust is our oneness with all of God's creation.

Michael Lodahl feels that the Shekhinah, or the Holy Spirit, can be a unifying force between Jews and Christians. He believes that the Holocaust calls for a re-examination of Christian theology. The starting place is to recognize Christianity's deep roots in Judaism. Nearly all of the New Testament was written by Jews. Some persons believe that the historic Christian anti-Semitism paved the way for the Holocaust.

The Shekhinah, portrayed in the Old Testament and the Kabala as God's Presence or Holy Spirit, is a female counterpart of God. In fact, some Jews explain such great evil as the Holocaust as due to the exile of the Shekhinah, which occurred when the Temple was destroyed in Jerusalem in 70 C.E. The Kabala describes how evil comes when human sin is so great that it causes God's hand of justice (sefirah DIN) to overrule God's hand of mercy (sefirah HESED). Then it takes good deeds for the balance to be restored.

Tikkun, or restoration, is dependent upon human beings helping overcome the Shekhinah's exile. *Halakha* (study of the Torah) became the Shekhinah's dwelling place. Love causes the Shekhinah to draw near, but selfishness drives her away.

Rabbi David Hartman says that God's covenant extends to many persons besides the Jews. Joel 2:28 quotes God as saying, "I will pour out My Spirit on all humanity." In Acts 10:35 Peter states, "In every nation anyone who fears God and does what is right is acceptable to him."

In the Holocaust, all the evildoers were nominally Christian. Thus, the Holocaust is a greater challenge for Christians than for

Jews. Where was the Christian God? A Christian response to the Holocaust means Christianity must cleanse itself of assumptions of superiority, prejudice, and hatred of "other" peoples, cultures, and faiths, and possibly even accept the fact that the establishment of modern Israel may be a sign that God's ancient covenant with the Jews is being re-established.

Lodahl says that modern Christians need to do these things: eradicate anti-Semitism; accept God's covenant with the Jews as genuine; accept the Shekhinah (the Holy Spirit) as seen in Judaism; learn from Jewish scholars; and recognize the base of Christian theology as being grounded in the Jewish covenant.[14]

Christian Reaction to the Holocaust

Roman Catholic priest John Pawlikowski agrees that the Holocaust has changed the world forever. He says that it was an attempt to wipe out the divine image in human history. "For the Nazis God was dead as an effective force in governing the universe." The Holocaust was an effort to separate humanity from moral values, at the same time desacralizing God.

Elie Wiesel says that the Holocaust shows that God and humans need each other. Since God did not prevent it, humans must guarantee that such a dreadful thing never again occurs.

Pawlikowski says we must return to the I-Thou personal God first revealed in the Torah. "Without liturgy and prayer," he says, "there is no real way of overcoming self-centeredness, and the destructive use of power evidenced in the Holocaust." Pawlikowski even asserts that for Christians, "salvation can be achieved only in alliance with Jews within history."[15]

Mary Boys states that "our history would have been radically different if we could have seen that God's relationship with one tradition does not diminish the sacredness of the other's. The image of Jews and Christians as partners in witness and work is a new vision."[16]

Divisive religion was present in historical Christianity. St. Augustine said that "the Church avows the Jewish people to be cursed. After killing Christ, they continue in impiety and unbelief." Anti-Semitism continued in Christian circles up to the present. Boys states that "for Christians, it evokes deep shame that our ancestors in faith could have acted toward another tradition of faith with such insensitivity and harshness."[17] Slowly Christianity is beginning to resemble its founder.

The World Council of Churches, a Christian organization, has made many statements of regret for Christian silence during the Holocaust. Among churches which have made apologies for inaction are Baptists, Disciples of Christ, Evangelical Lutherans, Methodists, and Presbyterians.

Mary Boys says that the Advent season might be a good time for both Jews and Christians to "see anew that the Holy One requires us 'to do justice, love kindness, and walk humbly with your God' (Micah 6:8)." She hopes that the current dialogue can actually result in a deepening of faith for adherents of both traditions. She suggests a rephrasing of the great hymn "O Come Emmanuel." Where the verse now reads "ransom captive Israel that mourns in lowly exile here until the Son of God appear" as follows:

> Come, blest Dayspring, come and cheer
> Our spirits by your advent here;
> Bless every people, every race
> Embrace us, young and old, within your grace.

"There cannot be two Chosen People," said Adolf Hitler. "We are God's people. Two worlds face one another—the men of God and the men of Satan."[18]

If ever Satan had a first lieutenant, it must have been Hitler. John Pawlikowski said that "a lack of a theory of human rights significantly curtailed Catholic institutional response to Nazism."[19] Mary Boys points out that the first significant international reaction against the Holocaust came in 1947 in Switzerland, when the International Council of Christians and Jews stated:

1. One God speaks to us all through the Old and New Testaments.
2. Jesus was born of a Jewish mother of the seed of David.
3. The first disciples, apostles, and martyrs were Jews.
4. The fundamental commandments of Jesus, to love God and one's neighbor, were proclaimed in the Old Testament.
5. Avoid distorting Judaism with the object of extolling Christianity.

6. Avoid using the word Jews in the exclusive sense of the enemies of Jesus.
7. Avoid presenting the Passion so as to bring the odium of killing Jesus upon all Jews or upon Jews alone.
8. Avoid scriptural curses. Use the more weighty words, "Father, forgive them."
9. Avoid the superstitious notion that Jews are accursed or reserved for suffering.
10. Avoid speaking of the Jews as if the first Christians were not Jews.[20]

Mary Boys quotes the 1998 Vatican study which declared that when Jesus prayed to Abba, the Father, he was praying to the God of Abraham, Isaac, and Jacob, the God of the covenant with Israel. The study states that "One God is truly revealed in both the Jewish people and in the followers of Jesus. In Paul's metaphor, the church is a wild olive shoot grafted onto the root (Romans 11:17)."[21]

Roman Catholic Efforts at Reconciliation

In 1980 Pope John Paul II said that the Jewish-Christian dialogue is "the meeting between people of God of the Old Covenant never revoked by God." Roman Catholic documents state that "nowhere is the deep spiritual bond between Judaism and Christianity more apparent than in the liturgy. The very concepts of a liturgical cycle of feasts and of the lectionary are adopted from Jewish liturgical practice. Easter and Pentecost have historical roots in the Jewish feasts of Passover and Shavuot. The Catholic and Jewish liturgical cycles spiral around one another in a stately procession. Christianity is engrafted on and continues to draw sustenance from the common root, biblical Israel."

Catholic sources say that Jesus was observant of the Torah, and asked respect and obedience to it. "To the extent that Christians over the centuries made Jews the scapegoats for Christ's death, they drew themselves away from the paschal mystery. It is becoming familiar in many churches for persons to participate in a Passover Seder during Holy Week. This practice can have educational and spiritual value. Also encouraged are joint memorial services commemorating the victims of the Holocaust."[22]

In 1985 the Vatican published *Notes*, consisting of advice on how the Church should present Jews and Judaism. It said: "Attentive to the same God who has spoken, we witness to the same memory and common hope in Him who is the master of history. We must also accept our responsibility to prepare the world for the coming of the Messiah by working together for social justice, respect for the rights of persons and nations, and for social and national reconciliation. To this we are driven, Jews and Christians, by a common hope for the kingdom of God, and by the great heritage of the prophets."[23]

In 1998 the Vatican's Commission for Religious Relations with Jews published *We Remember: A Reflection on the Holocaust*. In an act of repentance, it expresses "deep sorrows" of the Roman Catholic Church for the "failures of some of her sons and daughters in every age." It states that reflecting on the Holocaust makes one conscious of a warning: "the spoiled seeds of anti-Judaism and anti-Semitism must never again be allowed to take root in any human heart." The Church admits that in the Christian world "erroneous and unjust interpretations of the New Testament regarding the Jewish people and their alleged culpability have circulated for too long, engendering feelings of hostility towards this people."[24]

The Jewish Response

Rabbi Irving Greenberg, inspired by the candid admission of sin and error by numerous Christians, shows how the two faiths can be partners in what he calls "the strategy of redemption." He says both faiths have one central message: the triumph of life. Human life grows constantly to be ever more like God. Human beings have God-like qualities: freedom, consciousness, relatedness, and power. The Torah tells us we are made in God's very image—a high calling, indeed.

God has thus chosen humans to manifest his will. When, however, the Christian concept of the incarnation of Jesus devalues Jews as inferiors, it also desacralizes humankind by playing down the preciousness of humans in the original covenant.

Because of recent Christian openness to a more balanced approach, Rabbi Greenberg now sees both Christianity and Judaism as authentic outgrowths of the original covenant. Both, however, must seek ways to limit their power. Christianity must not only eliminate anti-Semitism but also cease trying to prose-lytize Jews. Judaism must stop thinking of Christianity as merely a branch of itself, and must also cease considering other religions to be inferior to Judaism. Both faiths need to realize that it is possible to see models of faith and the Spirit of God at work in the other.

Greenberg goes so far as to say that he often feels that Christianity can be considered closer to biblical covenantal religion than is Judaism. Above all, he states, the world as a global village now needs to develop a positive theology of religious pluralism.[25]

Rabbi David Hartman believes that "Christianity and Islam, although claiming to supersede Judaism, are really God's instruments for universal messianic redemption through Judaism," because they are spreading a knowledge of the Bible and its backgrounds throughout the world. He states that to accept other faiths as valid is not a violation of the Jewish covenant, but rather "the very presence of a dignified other can create within the Judaic spiritual life an enhancement of our covenantal consciousness." Jews, he says, have a communal sense of identity. "Heresy in Judaism is imagining that the self alone is addressed by God." When the great Hillel taught, he made sure to present views contrary to his own with equal time and conviction. Fairness is at the core of the Jewish faith. "History," says Hartman, "is not the revelation of eternal truth, but God's ability to love us in our imperfection."[26]

Rabbi Pinchas Lapide, in his book *The Sermon on the Mount*, calls the sermon the world's best blueprint for a peaceful and just world community. Dr. Ellis Rivkin, a professor of Jewish history, is a bridge of understanding between Christians and Jews. Jesus modeled himself on prophets like Moses and Isaiah, Rivkin believes, adding that "Christianity is a treasure trove of spiritual insights into the nature and meaning of God." He explains that he is not speaking of that part of Christian dogma or practice which might be hurtful or hostile to any of God's creatures. Rabbi A. James Rudin, director of interreligious affairs at the American Jewish Committee, says that "more progress has been made in the last 25 years of Catholic-Jewish relations than in the preceding 1900."[27]

In September 2000, 168 Jewish rabbis and other spiritual leaders issued a joint statement *Dabru Emet* (Speak Truth), which acknowledged appreciation for the change in many Christians concerning the validity of Judaism. The document had eight brief statements on how Jews and Christians might relate to one another:

1. Jews and Christians worship the same God.
2. Jews and Christians seek authority from the same book, the Bible.
3. Christians can respect the Jewish claim upon the land of Israel.
4. Jews and Christians accept the moral principles of the Torah, including the "inalienable sanctity and dignity of every human being," since all are created in God's image.
5. Nazism was not a Christian phenomenon, even though many Christians should have done more to oppose its cruelty.
6. "The humanly irreconcilable differences between Jews and Christians will not be settled until God redeems the entire world as promised by scripture."
7. A new relationship between Jews and Christians will not weaken Jewish practice.
8. "Jews and Christians must work together for justice and peace. Our joint efforts, together with those of other faiths, will help bring the kingdom of God for which we hope and long."[28]

Rabbi Irving Greenberg, who is president of the Jewish Life Network and chairman of the U.S. Holocaust Memorial Council, said that Jewish leaders had finally gone on record recognizing the monumental shift in Christianity. "It's a response to the Christian repentance and self-correction, which is one of the greatest religious accomplishments ever," he said. "It took 1900 years, and I'm sorry it took the Holocaust to generate it, but it is still impressive."[29]

Christian-Muslim Dialogue

One of the measures of the greatness of Judaism is the fact that two of its offshoots, Christianity and Islam, now account for the religion of over half of the world's population. Christians are 33.7% and Muslims 19.4% of the world's people. Thus, if these two religious giants could cooperate in working for world peace, enormous strides toward that marvelous goal could be accomplished.

Most readers are familiar with the growth of Christianity, but how do we account for the rapid growth of Islam, especially considering that it is over 600 years younger than Christianity? Through deep faith and allied military skill, Islam became the home of the world's largest empire within its first 100 years. Moreover, Muslim culture flourished. At a time when Christianity was in its Dark Ages (roughly 550–1000 C.E.), Islam had the world's leading architects, artists, doctors, philosophers, and theologians. Manuscripts of classical Greek thinkers such as Aristotle were preserved by Islamic scholars. Crusaders were amazed to see the advanced stage of Muslim architecture, art, dress, medicine, and nutrition. European society flourished in the Middle Ages, partly because of its borrowings from its Muslim neighbors.

Islam made vast inroads into Africa, especially as a reaction against European colonialism in the 19th century. Because of its African colonies, in France Islam is now the second largest religious movement. The great majority of Muslims are not Arabs, but are found in Bangladesh, India, Indonesia, and Pakistan. The decline of western imperialism has sparked an increase in national pride among Muslim nations. Islam rejects western materialism, and feels its own stress on high moral standards contrasts favorably with the rise of immorality in western nations.

In the United States Islam is the fastest growing religion. Because of immigration and a high birth rate, Islam could be America's second largest religious community by 2020. There are now more Muslims than Episcopalians in the United States. Black Muslims in the United States feel that their faith has less racial prejudice than has Christianity.

Islamic Definitions

A Muslim (or "true believer") is one who follows Islam (meaning "submission" to Allah's will). Allah means "the Divine." Among the attributes ascribed to Allah in the Koran are the oft-cited phrases, "the Compassionate, the Merciful, the Oft-Forgiving." Koran signifies "recitation," and Muslims believe that the archangel Gabriel recited the Koran to Mohammed. The

Koran is for Muslims what Christ (not the Bible) is for Christianity. Mohammed said that he was the last in long line of prophets, including Adam, Abraham, Moses, and Jesus, among others.

All major world religions have suffered important splits. In Islam the split came over whether succession to Mohammed should go through the first four caliphs (this is the view of the majority, the Sunni, meaning "tradition"), or through solely the fourth caliph, Mohammed's son-in-law Ali (this view is held by the Shiites, meaning "partisans"). American Black Muslims tend to be Sunnites, and many have given up hatred of white people as being forbidden by the Koran.

Jesus in the Koran

Although the Koran denies that Jesus is the Son of God (since that could be viewed as polytheism), the Muslim scripture praises Jesus very highly. Maria Jaoudi finds agreement between Jesus and Mohammed on several important matters. Both state that how we journey towards God is as important as the journey itself. The two agree that a person needs to love God with that person's entire being. The Koran envisions Jesus as the only perfect human being, the giver of the Gospel. At one point (3:45) the Koran defines Jesus as "an intimate of God."

Geoffrey Parrinder, former professor of comparative religion at the University of London, made a careful study of how Jesus is depicted in the Koran. Parrinder feels that the Koran confirms and protects the Gospel of Jesus. Eleven times Jesus is called the Messiah in the Koran. Other names used for Jesus there are Example, Mercy, Messenger, Prophet, Servant, Son of Mary, Spirit of God, Witness, and the Word. Jesus is also called "a sign to all men." Always, says Parrinder, Jesus is spoken of with reverence in the Koran. The evidences in support of the role of Jesus are said to be his Gospel, his miracles, his prophecy, and his teachings.

Parrinder quotes many similarities in passages found in the Koran and in the New Testament. The Koran says that God made a covenant with those who follow Jesus, and God will reward them on the Day of Resurrection.

According to Parrinder, the Koran states that all People of the Book (Jews and Christians) will surely believe in Jesus. The

Koran states that all believers—including Jews, Christians, and Sabaeans—will be saved. Sabaeans are more commonly known as Shebans. The Koran advises all these people to follow their own scriptures. Imagine how adherence to this teaching could alleviate the tension in modern Jerusalem! The Sufi 'Arabi stated that just as Mohammed is "the seal of the Prophets," so is Jesus "the seal of the Saints." It can be seen that there is much to build on in seeking for peaceful relations between Christians and Muslims.

In 1919 a Roman Catholic priest, Miguel Asin y Palacios, showed the great extent to which Dante and his friends had been influenced by Muslim writers. One reviewer wrote that "the great epic of Christianity is enthroned in the world of Muslim mysticism." In *The Legacy of Islam* R.A. Nicholson said about Dante: "The infernal regions, the astronomical heavens, the circles of the mystic rose, the choirs of angels, the three circles symbolizing the Trinity—all are described by Dante exactly as Ibnu'l-'Arabi described them."

Sufism

The great early Sufi Rabi'a (717–801) has many Christian counterparts. She and St. Francis both loved animals, even considering them important parts of God's creation. Like St. Teresa of Avila, Rabi'a found healing love within her own heart. Both women universalized their personal spiritual experiences into paths to help guide others to God. The Christian mystic Jan van Ruysbroeck describes death as a dwelling in God eternally; Rabi'a says that death is a process of bringing friend and Friend together.

The poet and philosopher Rumi (1207–1273) found Christ in everyone. He said, "Christ is the population of the world. Why use bitter soup for healing when sweet water is everywhere?"[30] Rumi and St. John of the Cross agreed that the first step in spiritual growth is to purge oneself of all materialistic concerns. Rumi gave a poetic description of how all three religions had helped his soul to grow: Moses changed him from a dead piece of wood to a powerful dragon. Jesus gave him spiritual life through transformation. Mohammed's words caused him to shimmer like a tree in the wind.

"In Sufism and Christianity," says Maria Jaoudi, "the integrator is the Spirit." She quotes St. Bonaventure: "Every creature is by its nature a kind of likeness of eternal Wisdom." In the Koran Jaoudi found: "Truly there are signs in the whole of God's creation in the heavens and in the earth."[31]

The Muslim theologian Mahmoud Ayoub describes an "Islamic Christianity": "The free spirits of Islamic mysticism found in the man Jesus not only the example of piety, love, and asceticism, which they sought to emulate, but also the Christ, who exemplifies a humanity illumined by the light of God. In this concept of divine manifestation, the Christian and Muslim images of Jesus converge at many points." Ayoub hopes for "a true ecumenism that will accommodate Islam not as a heresy of true Christianity, but as an authentic expression of the divine truth."[32]

Christian Response

After pointing to some parallels between Islam and Christianity, Vatican II Council stated that "the Muslims adore one God, living and enduring, merciful and all-powerful, Maker of heaven and earth. They strive to submit wholeheartedly even to God's inscrutable decrees, just as did Abraham, with whom the Islamic faith is pleased to associate itself."

Like Roman Catholicism, Islam has an elaborate doctrine of the saints. Called friends of God, the saints can perform miracles and give intercessory prayers. Shiites venerate Fatima, Mohammed's daughter, as many Roman Catholics venerate the Virgin Mary. Both women are considered to be immaculate and sinless, and both are channels of grace from God to believers. Both faiths have savior-martyrs—Jesus and Husayn, son of Ali. Iranis felt that as a Shiite, the Ayatollah Khomenei rules as a surrogate for the 12th Imam (descendant of Ali), who is in occultation (hidden from view).

Vatican II stated that the Church rejects nothing that is holy and true in the major religions, saying they often "reflect a ray of the Truth that enlightens all persons." It further stated that all persons are God's people, and God is revealed everywhere in His creation. We are thus encouraged to not only tolerate but even accept those whose paths to God may deviate somewhat from our own.

There is a tendency in every religion to use the "ideal me and the real you" syndrome. A religion likes to view itself at its best, and rival religions at their worst. Pope John Paul II said that in the past, Christians and Muslims have not understood each other, but that "God is calling us today to change our old bad habits." Some Muslim scholars state that the Koran has some obscure verses which it admits only God understands, and so whoever says that he alone has the true meaning is causing unnecessary dissension.

John Renard, professor of Islamic studies at St. Louis University, feels that "the more we keep trying to make strides in inter-religious dialogue, the greater the possibility of our religious traditions really contributing to world peace." Renard admits "there is no justification in the Koran for terrorist activity, but there is justification for acting against aggression and injustice." He adds that the Koran says fighting must be stopped if the enemy wishes to stop, and that even in the midst of combat one must maintain a sense of justice.

Speaking in Muslim Indonesia in 1989, Pope John Paul II said: "We who follow Christ are inspired to work for peace and harmony among all people. The unity of the human family becomes more and more apparent. Together let us strive for mutual understanding and peace. Let us generously serve the will of God in a spirit of dialogue, respect, and cooperation."[33]

Recent Trends

Charles Kimball feels that rather than attempting to unsnarl theological and dogmatic differences between the two faiths, a good starting place might be to coordinate their activities in addressing social problems, such as hunger, medical conditions, environmental concerns, and aid during natural catastrophes.

Lucille Walsh, a nun in the order of the Sisters of St. Francis of Assisi, has been a bridge of understanding between the two faiths in Milwaukee. She has organized common prayer meetings and religious services in recognition of holy days in both faiths. She recalls how St. Francis visited the Sultan of Egypt, unarmed, in 1219. "In a spirit of brotherly love," she says, "he reversed the prevailing un-Christian crusade spirit of warfare, hatred, and suspicion. He opened the way to a relationship of goodwill and mutual respect between Christians and Muslims." Lucille recalls that when she was seriously ill, "a Muslim student of mine brought a plant with three white blossoms and said it was in honor of the Trinity." Perhaps as a response to her testimony of love and mutual understanding, the Archdiocese of Milwaukee contributed funds to help erect an Islamic Center there.[34]

Murad Hofmann, a German convert to Islam, is another person seeking a creative interface between his new faith and Christianity. "My mission is to build bridges," Hofmann said, "to do whatever I can to make sure that we don't come to a violent clash of civilizations." Hofmann has served as Germany's ambassador to Algeria and to Morocco, and also as a director of information at NATO. He understands Islam's protest against growing materialism and immorality in the Christian West, but he also laments the acts of violence performed by Muslim terrorists, which he says have no basis in the Koran. He likewise is critical of Muslim nations which deny basic human rights, and which treat women as if they are inferior to men. Above all, his very impartiality and fairness gain him listeners whenever he asks both faith traditions to be more tolerant and kind.

Recently the crescent-and-star symbol of the Muslim holy festival of Ramadan joined the gigantic Christmas tree and the large Hanukkah menorah in the common holiday season, as recognized in the park located between the White House and the Washington Monument. "This shows that Muslims are becoming more of a mainstream part of society," said Fahhim Abdulhadi, a spokesman for the American Muslim Council. Ramadan is a time of fasting and prayer, the month in which the Koran was revealed to the prophet Mohammed. Adherents of both faiths declared that the United States is growing in its effort to be a nation housing multiple religious traditions. "The crescent and star symbol is becoming visible," says Elsa Arnett, "on display now at the Empire State Building and in public libraries, courthouses, parks, and businesses around the country."[35]

Christian-Hindu Dialogue

Hans Küng asks, Cannot we have "a postmodern paradigm of society and religion on that basis of the one true faith which worships not the false god of progress but the one true God? Might not such a faith be common to Jews, Christians, Muslims, and

Hindus, because all of these religions share the same fundamental experience?"[36]

To illustrate his point, Küng shows how the different types of Hindu yoga have their Christian analogs: karma yoga is similar to Roman Catholic Christianity, jnana yoga to Greek Orthodox Christianity, and bhakti yoga to Protestant Christianity.

Professor Heinrich von Stietencron says that "almost every religious feature of popular Hinduism could be matched with an analogue from Catholicism." Perhaps, he states, both religions employ henotheism: "The believer venerates the one God and also renders quasi-divine veneration to the other figures." The Hindu finds his or her sacred center not in the temple but in the home. Why is Hinduism the most tolerant of all world religions? Professor von Stietencron replies because it has the greatest knowledge of the inner structure of the world and its creatures.

The Roman Catholic priest Raimon Panikkar has been an outstanding contributor to the Hindu-Christian dialogue. In his book *The Unknown Christ of Hinduism* he finds a parallel between Brahma (the Absolute) as related to Ishvara (the Creator) and the Christian God the Father (the Creator) as related to the Son (Christ, the Logos). Rammahan Roy "thought of the unity of Jesus with God the Father in the New Testament sense of a unity of will, intention, and obedience, not of being." Panikkar recalls Mahatma Gandhi saying that it was the Sermon on the Mount that endeared Jesus to him. Gandhi said that "Jesus would have lived and died in vain if he did not teach us to direct our lives according to the eternal law of love."

Panikkar believes that Christianity must be open to other religious systems. "It must be willing to listen to them, to learn from them, even to absorb all that they have to offer that will enrich or deepen the Christian interpretation."[37] As an example, John Hicks in *God and the Universe of Faiths* reconciles the Hindu view of reincarnation with Christian beliefs.

Panikkar feels that Christians who can accept *advaita* (non-dualism), the Hindu belief that all of creation relates to God, can be wholly Christian and wholly Hindu at the same time, since God is One. Hindus constantly ask, why cannot we all agree that we are *all* God's children? A Hindu can accept Christ as a divine model to emulate, but not as the *only* divine model.

By validating other religious approaches, Panikkar says, Christianity achieves an unselfish and honest pluralism. Jesus called the Supreme Being "my Father." But Panikkar sees no reason for not also calling that Being "my Mother."

He states that many strong Christians stressed Christianness instead of Christianity, meaning using Christ as a motivating symbol of one's personal life. Panikkar visions that the path to the future is shown to us by Meister Eckhart, Sri Aurobindo, and Pope John XXIII. It is a path of love, freedom, justice, and tolerance. To be truly tolerant requires one to be tolerant even of the intolerant.

Hans Küng believes that enculturation, or adaptation to the deep roots of another culture, is not only permitted but required by the recommendations of Vatican II Council. This would mean the following for Christianity in India:

1. Introduction of Indian forms of meditation, song, dance, and other liturgical elements.
2. "Traditional Indian incorporation of nature (flowers, light, sunrise, sunset) into Christian worship."
3. Liturgical reading of Indian sacred scriptures which attest to the transition of human beings to the transcendental dimension.[38]

"The last stanza of the *Rig-Veda*," Panikkar says, "is a song in praise of religious harmony." But our goal should never be the one true path to God, he warns. Because "Pilgrim, there is no path; you yourself are making it by walking." Jesus had no New Testament—his scripture was the Torah.

In the religious symphony of the world, we do not all play the tuba. Panikkar explains: "The *theanthropocosmic* view (which sees the unity of the divine, the human, and the cosmos) proposes a kind of trinitarian dynamic where everything is contained in everything else (each person represents the community, and each tradition reflects, corrects, complements, and challenges the other)."[39]

Christian-Buddhist Dialogue

Buddhism is finding a comfortable home in the United States. Hawaii is 46% Christian and 37% Buddhist, so there is much interfaith dialogue there. Among interfaith projects are many homes for the elderly. There are more than 150 Buddhist temples in southern California, and more than a half million Buddhists in the Los Angeles area.

Raimon Panikkar says that just as the Christic principle is present in every person, so is the Buddhist principle. "One talks about a universal spiritual church," he says, "one single God who can make sense also to Buddhists, and one law which does not exclude *nomos, dharma, karma, or li.* The ideal is a universal theology of religion, or in more scientific language, a universal field theory."[40] Frank Tipler, in Chapter 5 above, lends scientific support to this search.

Thomas Matus is a Camaldolese monk who helped open the door to Oriental religions. He found that interaction between Christianity and Buddhism can strengthen both faiths. Christianity can give Buddhism more stress on its social gospel, and Buddhism can provide Christianity with more emphasis on ecology and nature, particularly concern for animals.

David Steindl-Rast, a Benedictine monk, believes that the two faiths had similar origins. Buddhism built upon Hinduism but added Gautama's stress on enlightenment achieved through the Dhamma or Law. Christianity developed from Judaic roots, with Christ's concept of agape or divine Love being predominant. Steindl-Rast asserts that both traditions show a preference of works over faith. We need a new world faith, he says, and it is now emerging. Thus, "both science and theology will have to express themselves in new ways. If we belong to God, God belongs to us; we are in a relationship. Personhood arises not only in relation to others but also from relationship to self. We are challenged to be faithful to our innermost self. When Buddhists trace the compassion they receive back to its source—emptiness—they know what Christians mean when they say, 'God has loved us first.' Salvation is one's sense of belonging to the whole."[41]

Emptiness, in Buddhism, means emptying oneself of all selfish concerns in order to achieve nirvana, which is freedom from the tyranny of desire, and attainment of permanent truth and peace. One is then truly connected to the entire cosmos, which is the goal of all great religious traditions.

Asked if they have a term for God, Buddhists often do not reply. Buddhists also have many different interpretations of the term Ultimate Reality. Buddhists can always say that actions speak louder than words, for no other religion has the record for peace and gentleness that characterizes Buddhism.

Professor Leonard Swidler presents a series of guidelines for use in facilitating interreligious dialogue. Religion, he says, is "an explanation of the ultimate meaning of life, and how to live accordingly, based on some understanding of the Transcendent." Participants in dialogue must keep in mind that its primary purpose is for them to learn more from others, not to try to convert them. Here are Swidler's suggestions:

1. At the start, avoid the most difficult differences.
2. Each participant needs to show total honesty and sincerity.
3. Compare ideals with ideals and practices with practices.
4. Each participant has the right to define his/her position.
5. No participant should assume he/she fully understands the other participant's position.
6. "Only equals can engage in full authentic dialogue."
7. Each participant should remain self-critical towards his/her own position.
8. A fundamental assumption must be that each person can learn from others, and change accordingly.[42]

Parallels Between Jesus and Buddha

Professor Marcus Borg delineates a series of striking similarities in these two great religious figures. Both mystics, they each had a profound spiritual experience around the age of thirty. They each stressed compassion, and presented paths to wisdom. Each initiated a reform of an important religious tradition. Both were seen as incarnations: Jesus as the Word of God, and Gautama as the earthly manifestation of the heavenly Buddha. Both recommended radical change: one must die to old ways of doing things, and awaken to a new life. The promise is that followers will be new persons, full of compassion.[43]

Borg then lists parallel deeds of these two religious leaders:[44]

Jesus	Buddha
Born of the virgin Mary.	No sensual thought occurred to his mother.
A bright star shone at his birth.	Bright constellations shone at his birth.
The single boyhood story was of a wise boy lost in a temple.	The single boyhood story was of a lost boy deep in meditation under a jambu tree.
Tempted by the devil during a great fast, he turned his back on great promises.	Tempted by the devil during a great fast, he turned his back on great promises.
He was criticized for teaching sinners, prostitutes, and tax collectors.	He was criticized for teaching prostitutes, gamblers, and drunkards.
He made strict demands of his followers.	He made strict demands of his followers.
At his death there were earthquake and thunder.	At his death there were earthquake and thunder.

Buddhist monk Thich Nhat Hanh in 1995 wrote of these two great leaders: "I touch both of them as my spiritual ancestors." The Dalai Lama and other Buddhists made similar statements.

Roy Riegert has provided a list of parallel teachings of these two great leaders:[45]

Jesus	Buddha
Love your enemy; return good for evil.	Hatreds cease not by hating but by love.
He without sin cast the first stone.	Do not criticize the faults of others.
Blessed are the poor, for theirs is the kingdom of God.	Live happily, having nothing. Feed on joy, like the radiant gods.
The gate to life is narrow, and few take it.	There are few pleasant parks, and few people who will be reborn.

How, asks Professor Borg, can we account for so many striking similarities, in the absence of a direct cultural influence? He replies, by the fact that the two men had similar spiritual backgrounds. "I see each religion," Borg concludes, "as both a response to the experience of the sacred and a mediator of such experience. The striking parallels point to a shared religious experience of the most powerful kind."[46]

Christian Buddhism

Don Cupitt, Dean of Emanuel College at Cambridge University, has proposed the establishment of Christian Buddhism. Abbe Huc shows similar ceremonial practices in Buddhism and Roman Catholicity: celibacy, confession, crozier, holy water, mass, mitre, relics, rosary, and tonsure. The Thai monk Buddhadasa, in *Christianity and Buddhism*, analyzes "the parallel meaning and function of the eternal, universal, absolute *dharma* in Buddhism and of God in Christianity." *Dharma* has been defined as "the body of cosmic principles by which all things exist."

Leonard Swidler notes another parallel. Just as in Buddhism there was a shift from the religion of Buddha to the religion about Buddha, so in Christianity there was a similar change of emphasis from the religion of Christ to the religion about Christ. But there are also differences. Whereas Buddhism stresses the *process* of life's journey, Christianity puts emphasis upon *arrival* at the end of the journey. Swidler says that Buddhism sees ultimate reality as *sunyata* (emptiness), meaning not the absence of everything but rather the existence of the Ultimate Source of everything—a position akin to the Godhead, as described by Meister Eckhart.

Swidler elaborates on the three-fold body (*Trikaya*) of ultimate reality as seen in Mahayana (large vessel) Buddhism:

1. Nirmana-kaya—the manifestation body. Human manifestations include Gautama, Moses, Jesus, and Mohammed.
2. Sambhoga-kaya—the heavenly body. These are the personal Gods of the various traditions: Yahweh, the Holy Trinity, Allah, Ishvara (Hinduism), Amida (Pure Land Buddhism).
3. Dharma-kaya—boundless openness. Examples: the Godhead, the Ground, Infinity, Sophia. Swidler cites as an example of

this openness Judaism's definition of God as "I will be who I will be."

A Christian Buddhist

Seiichi Yagi underwent two conversion experiences: in Japan he embraced Christianity and in Germany he became a Buddhist. He is in an excellent position to compare the two faiths.

Yagi says that "the consequence of faith in both Christianity and Jodo-Buddhism is the giving up of the self-affirmation of the Ego." Jodo-Buddhism is also called Pure Land Buddhism, in which Amida is the God figure. Yagi quotes Paul (Gal. 2:20): "Now it is no longer I that lives, but Christ lives in me." The Pure Land Buddhist would say, "Amida lives in me." Yagi adds that both Christ and the Amida-Buddha "are eternal Life and light, the ground of the self-enlightening Life of the individual human being."[47]

Yagi proclaims that "the Front of the coming reign of God has broken into our history." How can the Kingdom of God come on earth? Yagi says there are only two ways: "either the earthly must be transformed into the heavenly (I Cor. 15:52), or everything must be created anew as the heavenly (Rev. 21:1)."[48]

Katsumi Takizawa (1909–1984) distinguished between primary and secondary contacts with God. Primary is the fact that the spirit of God dwells in all of us. Secondary is a deeper inspiration, showing others how to achieve oneness with God. Christ said, "The Kingdom of Heaven is within you." Mahayana Buddhism declares that everyone has the Buddha nature, but must be enlightened about the fact. "Our concept of the activated Self ("Christ in me") can well be compared with the concept of Buddhahood," Yagi concludes.[49]

Pure Land Buddhism

The founder of this school of Buddhism was Amida, a Chinese king who gave up his crown in order to achieve Buddhahood. Upon achieving his goal, he told his followers that they could achieve the Pure Land or heaven by merely thinking of him ten times. In gratitude for salvation, the follower would offer his own store of merit, achieved by good deeds to one's neighbors.

In Japan Pure Land Buddhism is now the largest religious body. Honen (1133–1212) simplified the doctrine until it now sounds like "salvation by faith" as promulgated by Martin Luther and other Protestant reformers. Honen stressed universal salvation, saying: "There shall be no distinction, no regard to male or female, good or bad, exalted or lowly. None shall fail to be in His Land of Purity after having called, with complete desire, on Amida."[50]

Zen Buddhism

Zen Buddhism is nearly the opposite of Pure Land Buddhism, for it postulates no god, nor does it give magic phrases to achieve salvation. The word Zen is a Japanese transliteration of Sanskrit *dhyana* (meditation). Christmas Humphreys says that the Zen process is "the breaking down of the bars of the intellect that the mind may be freed for the light of Enlightenment." There are over twenty different Zen sects in Japan. Many of them are merged with Shinto, or Confucianism, or other branches of Buddhism.

In 552 C.E. the Chinese emperor asked the Indian philosopher Bodhidharma who he was. "I have no idea," replied Bodhidharma. A pupil petitioned Bodhidharma, "Please pacify my mind." "Show me your mind," answered the teacher. "I cannot produce it," said the student. "See, now I have pacified your mind," Bodhidharma said.

Zen says that if a finger points at the moon, do not look at the finger. "What is the sound of one hand clapping?" This is a *koan*, a humorous riddle with no logical answer. It is designed to get a person out of linear single-dimension thinking. Laughter is used intuitively as a great cleansing agent, ridding the conscious mind of unnecessary baggage that clutters itself, blocking simple sincere experience of oneness. As literalness dissolves, you can experience *satori*, a sudden burst of enlightenment that gives you an ecstatic feeling of unity with the cosmos.

Zen master Nyogen Senzaki finds Zen in Meister Eckhart when he said, "The eye with which I see God is the eye with which He sees me." Senzaki says Zen is popular in the United States because Americans are informal, practical, capable of simplicity, lovers of nature, believers in universal brotherhood, and they ground their ethics in individual responsibility. Senzaki feels that Zen is the American pragmatism of William James and John Dewey in another form.

Another Zen master, Soyen Shaku, stated that "religion is not to go to God by forsaking the world, but to find Him in it. Our faith is to believe in our essential oneness with Him and not in our sensuous separateness. 'God is in us and we in Him' must be made the most fundamental faith of all religions."[51]

Nishida Kitaro (1870–1945) was a Japanese Zen master who fused Eastern and Western thought. He admired William James's pragmatism and Henri Bergson's logic. He said that the only way to improve society is to improve individuals. True selfhood is what Christians call conversion and Buddhists call enlightenment. By following the best in both Oriental and Occidental beliefs, Kitaro said, one arrives at the basic truth in all religions.

At a Zen center in California, two parents, both ordained Buddhist priests, had their baby baptized in a joint Christian-Buddhist ceremony, because both parents are also practicing Christians. They believe that these two faiths are completely compatible when rightly understood. Some Zen leaders go so far as to predict that "the great event of the 21st century will be the encounter and unity of Christianity and Buddhism."[52]

Thomas Merton

Thomas Merton was a Trappist monk who became a Cistercian priest. He tried to integrate, with the help of Christ, all valid religious insights within himself. He broke new ground in building bridges of understanding with Buddhism, particularly Zen. Buddhist monastic silence helped Merton explain his mystical understanding of the nature of reality. The Buddhist influence reinforced his feeling that western religion insufficiently attacked materialism and scientism, attachments which ultimately lead to suffering. He incorporated Buddhist prayer techniques into his Christian practice. Zen's meditative prayer ritual is called "the Great Death." Merton called it "dying and rising with Christ, both referring to the feeling of being 'born again.'"

Merton developed a new understanding of God as Being, of God's indwelling. He was one of the first persons to speak of God in terms recognizable to Zen Buddhists. Many of his books advanced the Christian-Buddhist dialogue. Among them are *The*

Asian Journal, Introductions East and West, Mystics and Zen Masters, and especially *Zen and the Birds of Appetite*.

Merton felt that by experiencing Zen, a Christian discovers her or his own roots. He defined true freedom as "being fully alive in Christ." He encouraged international travel, to help people build friendship and acceptance. He said that "the deepest level of communication is communion."[53] It is believed that Merton's insights were a salutary influence upon Vatican II Council.

Like Merton, Father Patrick Hawk also found common ground with Buddhists. Asked why he attended a Zen session, Hawk replied, "To be a better Christian!" As well as being a Roman Catholic priest, Hawk became a Zen master, "with the special responsibility of maintaining the perennial stream of no name and no sect where the Buddha and the Christ bathe together."[54]

Similar ecumenism is found in the teachings of the Dalai Lama, the head of Tibetan Buddhism. He is believed to be an avatar, or reincarnation, of the famous Bodhisattva, Avalokiteshvara. One of the most respected leaders in the world, the Dalai Lama preaches of the oneness of the human family, and of our universal need for compassion, love, and peace. He represents unitive religion in its most exquisite form.

The founder of Won Buddhism in Korea, Great Master Sotaesan said, "Enlightened people regard all religions as one family under one roof." The ecumenism of Won Buddhism embraces modern scientific thinking in its broad scope. Two other faiths that work for peace and ecumenicity are the Japanese Rissho Kosei-kai and the Italian Focolare.

The Kabala

The Jewish esoteric writing, the Kabala, lends itself well to unitive religion. Edward Hoffman points out its similarity to the other great mystical traditions, such as Tibetan Buddhism, Taoism, Sufism, and Christian mysticism. Kabalists were influenced by Sufis during the "Golden Age" in medieval Spain. A modern novel, *The Dance of Created Lights* by Jay Bremyer, captures the period's ecumenicity. In the novel, the Sufi Al-Kiran dances a spiritual dance with a Nubian Christian princess. They are taught by a Kabalist rabbi to transmute their erotic love into agape, thus gaining immortality. Their dance is the climax of the great celebration, The Festival of All Faiths.

Kabalist Abraham Abulafia was tolerant of many faiths; some of his best friends were Sufi and Christian mystics. Abulafia devised meditative techniques, similar to those used by Hindus and Sufis, to achieve spiritual ecstasy through musical chanting.

The Kabala describes three holy triads: Crown, Wisdom, Understanding; Beauty, Mercy, Judgment; and Foundation, Victory, Glory—these, plus the Shekhinah (Kingdom) constitute the ten Sephirot of vessels that contained God's Light and Glory at creation. Abulafia recognized a close relationship between the first triad and the three members of the Christian Holy Trinity.

To help understand how Jews could suffer such great persecution even as God's chosen people, the Kabala adopted the concept of reincarnation, or transmigration of souls. How many times does a soul need to be reborn? Kabalist Isaac Luria replied, "If some spark of a soul has not fulfilled even one aspect of these three—deed, speech, and thought—it must transmigrate until it fulfills all of them." This is very similar to Hindu and Buddhist teachings.

Kabalists say that, like the bodhisattva who postpones her/his eternal reward in order to help other people achieve theirs, so too "a handful of concealed sages in each generation are said to sustain all of humankind. Wherever they stand, they raise the fallen sparks of light back to their primal Source." Every person, by living according to her/his divine spark, plays a role in helping redeem the world.[55] Elie Wiesel say we need God and God needs us, if God's kingdom is to come on earth.

Hasidic Jews dance, twirling like the Sufi whirling dervishes. Both groups are expressing deep delight in God's creation, and dedicating themselves to honor and preserve creation's great beauty and glory. The Christian theologian Friedrich Schleiermacher wrote a hymn to "Saint Spinoza," a Jew.

Gotthold Lessing, a German Jewish dramatist, wrote a play *Nathan the Wise*, which depicts the interface among Judaism, Christianity, and Islam. In the play the Christian Templar wishes to wed the supposed daughter of the Jew Nathan. He has saved her life in a large fire. Nathan consents, knowing that his daughter was originally a Christian. But Nathan's superior wants Nathan killed as a traitor to their faith. The case is referred to the

Muslim Saladin for adjudication. Nathan assists Saladin by telling of three brothers who fought one another for possession of their father's precious ring. A wise judge says that instead of envying one another, each brother should act, out of love, as if his ring is the true one, and thus eliminate envy and jealousy. By this means the ring can become a symbol of love rather than of greed. As the *Encyclopedia Britannica* states, "the play proclaims the doctrine of the true religion of mankind, of love acting without prejudice in the service of mankind."

Islam

Islam traces its origin to the Torah. Ishmael, the first son of Abraham (by Hagar, Sarah's Egyptian maid), was cast out when 90-year old Sarah finally had her own son Isaac. The name Ishmael means "God hears," "because the Lord has given heed to Hagar's affliction" (Genesis 16:11). Then, in Genesis 17:20 God promises to greatly bless Ishmael and his descendants, just as God had previously promised to greatly bless Isaac and his descendants.

Muslims take very seriously Commandments #1 and #2: "Thou shall have no other gods before Me," and "Thou shall not make any graven image or likeness of any thing." The creed of Islam is "There is no God but God, and Mohammed is His prophet."

Mohammed married his wealthy employer Khadijah, who was fifteen years older than he. Their sons died in infancy, and of their four daughters only Fatima survived Mohammed. After Khadijah died, Mohammed had other wives, one of whom was Jewish and another of whom was black. Fatima married Mohammed's cousin Ali; Ali's followers are the Shiites.

Criticized in Mecca, Mohammed made an 8-day camel ride (the *hegira)* to Yathrib in 622 C.E. Yathrib was renamed Medina ("City of the Prophet") in honor of Mohammed. In Medina Mohammed built the first mosque. He led his forces to capture Mecca in 630, and cleared idols out of the Kaaba, making it Islam's holiest place.

Mohammed was no dictator. After taking power, he set up government in Mecca under a constitution. Before giving orders, he always consulted a council of advisers. There is egalitarianism in Islam—a black slave is eligible to become a caliph.

Slavery has been banned in all Muslim countries, and polygamy in most of them. Islam has permitted many rural people to maintain their original folk religions as a part of their faith. This tolerance of other religions, especially by the Sufis, has greatly assisted the spread of Islam, as it has of the Roman Catholic faith. Bektashi dervishes use bread and wine (like Christian communion elements) in their initiation rituals.

The Koran

The Koran ("reading aloud") has 114 *suras* or chapters, arranged in length from the longest to the shortest. It is about 4/5 the size of the New Testament.

There is some difference between the *suras* written in Mecca and those ascribed to the Medina period. The Mecca *suras* show a stronger influence of Judaism and Christianity than do the Medina *suras.* In general, there is greater tolerance of all other religions in the Mecca *suras.* There is even mention of Allah's three daughters in the Mecca *suras.* In the Medina *suras,* Allah resembles more the early Yahweh, an inscrutable tribal god who predestines human fate. Thus, as in all great scriptures, the Koran can be quoted as showing Allah as "the Compassionate, the Merciful" or as saying, "Woe upon those who forsake this religion—they will fear Allah!"

"Wealth should not be allowed to circulate among the rich only," says the Koran. Thus there are many kinds of taxes in Islam. The view of the Last Judgment is similar to that in Judaism and Christianity. The Koran states: "Let every people, on the way prescribed for it, press forward to good deeds. And let none laugh at any other men; perchance they may be better than themselves."[56] There is even a warning against religious disputes: the condemned are quoted as saying, "We were not those who prayed, not those who fed the poor, and we engaged in constant religious disputes."

Adultery is punished by 100 lashes to each unmarried person, and by death by stoning for married persons, following Deuteronomy 20:22. Modesty is becoming in all people, and "women should not make an exhibition of their beauty" (*sura* 24:31). As to food, Muslims are permitted to eat the food of the People of the Book (Jews and Christians).

Sufism

Traditional Islam sees humankind in three levels: first, believers (Muslims); second, People of the Book (Jews and Christians); and third, infidels (all other peoples). But Sufism, mystical Islam, regards all persons as children of one family, the family of Allah (God).

Various strains unite in Sufism. Syrian Muslims, influenced by Christian monks who wore a *suf* (woolen robe), became mendicant nomads, reciting endlessly the 100 names of God found in the Koran. The worldly renunciation found in Hinduism impressed these nomads, as did Neoplatonism with its stress upon the spiritual over the material. Their key scripture passage eventually became I John 4:16: "God is love, and those who abide in love abide in God and God abides in them."

Mystical Judaism and mystical Islam had very salutary influences upon each other. "Jewish sages regarded by Western scholars as following the Spanish Sufi schools include Juda Halevi of Toledo, Samuel ben Tibbon, Moses ben Ezra of Granada, Josef ben Zadiq of Cordoba, and Simtob ben Falaquera." One Sufi quotes this anecdote: Companion Omar was told by Mohammed, "To be a perfect Jew is better than to be an incomplete Muslim."[57] The Mogul king Dara Shikoh, a Sufi, made an effort to form an esoteric bridge among his Hindu, Muslim, and other subjects.

Mohammed's Night Trip to the Seven Heavens

The *Hadith* is a collection of sayings and teachings attributed to Mohammed. One *Hadith* describes Mohammed's *Mi'raj*, his night trip to the seven heavens for the purpose of receiving signs from Allah. It is significant that at each heaven, Mohammed is warmly greeted by persons found in the Book (the Bible). In order, the greeters are Adam, Jesus, Joseph, Enoch, Aaron, Moses, and Abraham. Muslims feel that Adam and Jesus are prophets, having received God's own breath or spirit. Joseph, it is believed, had been granted insight into the divine. Enoch allegedly went straight to heaven without dying. In 44 places in the Koran, it is stated that Moses talked to God. It is striking that the evidence of God's sign to Mohammed on this night trip are all couched in warm relationships with Judaic or Christian personages. The current bloodshed over Temple Mount (the assumed starting place for Mohammed's journey) might be alleviated if scholars and priests would tell their adherents whom Mohammed encountered on this famous night trip.

One of the first prominent Sufis was the freed slave, the woman Rabi'a. Asked when a servant of God is contented, Rabi'a replied, "When he is as thankful for tribulation as he is for bliss." To those who said that if we keep knocking at the door God will open it, she answered, "When did God ever close the door?" Men chided her that women never have been regarded as prophets or high religious figures. Her response was, "Everything you said is true. But egotism, self-worship, and 'I am your highest lord' have not welled up in any woman." Her most famous quote is this: "O Lord, if I worship you out of fear of hell, burn me in hell. If I worship you in the hope of paradise, forbid it to me. But if I worship you for your own sake, do not deprive me of your eternal beauty."[58]

The Rights of God

God too has rights, asserts Sufi al-Muhasibi in his *The Book on the Observance of the Rights of God*. Instead of listing these rights in tabular form, Muhasibi shows how God's rights are violated whenever we start worshipping ourselves. Signs of overdrawn egotism are found in boasting, competitiveness, conceit, envy, and vanity. In an effort to assert self-praise, the egotist forgets his own mortality, as well as neglects his reliance upon fellow humans and God. Muhasibi says that the worst form of slavery is that which we impose upon ourselves.

Ibrahim ben Adham was a Sufi greatly influenced by Buddhism. Abu Yazid al-Bistami had a deep reverence for the Hindu Upanishads. Bistami said that it was the wings of the Shekhinah which bore Enoch to heaven. Among Sufis Enoch was sometimes identified with Hermes Trismegistus (the Greek name for the Egyptian god Thoth). Bistami also described a *Mi'raj* he made to heaven, similar to that of Mohammed, and also like the Merkabah chariot of Jewish mysticism, as depicted in chapter 1 of the book of Ezekiel.

Al-Ghazali

Abu Hamid al-Ghazali (1058–1111) is considered to be the Thomas Aquinas of Islam because he successfully integrated Sufi mysticism into Islamic ritual and theology. He said that a human being is not truly human if he engages in covetousness, self-indulgence, temper, and attacks on other people. The core of religion, he stated, was not ritual and Islamic law but a humble soul. We should repent of our sins, purge our hearts of all but God, and practice the virtues, which he listed as patience, reliance on God, renunciation, repentance, spiritual poverty, and above all, love.

Like many Sufis, Suhrawardi (1153–1191) said that the inner core of all religions is the same. His readings led him to Egyptian Hermeticism and Zoroaster. He merged Islam with Zoroastrianism, describing God as the Light of Lights. He followed the Perennial Philosophy, which shows the oneness of all religious search. The Sufi writer 'Attar said that in Sufi unity, there are no distinctions such as man and woman.

Ibn 'Arabi

Ibn 'Arabi (1165–1240) synthesized Sufi thought with apophatic (so-called "negative") theology in other religious traditions: the Neoplatonism of Plotinus, the Kabala of Moses de Leon, and the Christian mysticism of Meister Eckhart. Ibn 'Arabi says the mystical union with the divine occurs only when one is in a constant state of self-transformation. This condition can be achieved in any faith. The basic religious error, he taught, was to try to limit God's infinity into any one's own finite outlook. Such narrow binding leads to idolatry, which is to worship oneself rather than God. Those who criticize God for creating sinners fail to understand how humans can be instruments of God's perpetual manifestation, demonstrating that God's love extends even to sinners. Through continual self-transformation, mystics participate fully in God's constant co-creation. Ibn 'Arabi said that wherever love is, in any religion, there God is also. Instead of merely tolerating other faiths while considering them to be inferior, one should rise to "complete immersion and acceptance of all manifestations of reality." It can be seen that Ibn 'Arabi is loved by those who prefer unitive religion but disliked by western positivists (who believe only in materialism) and also by religious so-called fundamentalists, who deny the validity of any religious approach other than their own.[59]

Modern Sufis

A Roman Catholic writer, Cyprian Rice, says that the future purpose of Sufism will be "to make possible a welding of religious thought between East and West." A modern Sufi, Hazrat Inayat Khan, states that Sufism believes in the God of the Bible. Sufism, he adds, serves a vital function in modern society, building bridges of understanding unifying philosophy, religion, and science.

Inayat Khan draws from Hinduism and Buddhism. He cites the Hindu term *Akasha*, meaning capacity or capability. Sufis urge us all to live up to our unique *Akasha*. Khan tells the story originally related by Gautama: A man, terrified, clung to a tree branch near a cliff in the dark. He spent the night in fear and prayer. When dawn came, he found he was one foot above the ground. We feel insecure, not knowing the assurance of divine protection.

Truth is one, Khan asserts. "One may look at it from the Christian, or the Buddhist, or the Hindu point of view, but in reality it is one point of view. It is a great joy to look at life from above, and from that position a Christian, a Jew, a Muslim, and a Buddhist will all see the same immensity."

"The Rasul (or *ishta-deva*)," says Khan, "is the soul through which God has attained the purpose of creation." We must not assert that "my Rasul is better than your Rasul!" If you say that, you disqualify your own Rasul. A spiritual student, in Khan's view, "makes a garland of the names by which different people have called their Rasul. He says, 'If there was any Buddha, it is you; if there was any Christ, it is you; if there was any Mohammed, it is you; in you I see him. If Moses came with a message, it was you (the Rasul) who came. I see you in Solomon, and in the wonders of Krishna as well as in the splendors of Shiva.'"[60]

A key Sufi concept is that there is a pre-eternal covenant between God and all human beings, a view that all humans revert to their pure selves as they existed before Adam's sin. There is a place called "Arafat" where we all stand at the Last Judgment and say "Here I am, Lord."

A modern Sufi, Idries Shah, describes how high-level unity of knowledge unites many thinkers. "This explains," Shah says, "why the Muslim Rumi has Christian, Zoroastrian, and other disciples; why the great 'invisible teacher' Khidr is said to be a Jew; why the Mogul Prince Dara Shikoh identified Sufi teachings in the Hindu Vedas; how Pythagoras and Solomon can be said to be Sufi teachers; why, indeed, Jesus is said to stand, in a sense, at the head of the Sufis."[61]

Hinduism's Openness to All Religions

The Hindu writer Paramahansa Yogananda says that humanity's goal is not mere physical pleasure but rather the Bliss of God. At some time in your life, he states, you have had, whether in prayer, worship, or meditation, the ineffable feeling of oneness with the Universe, a genuine unalloyed Peace. This is the Bliss of God. "This God-consciousness can pervade all our actions and moods, if we but let it. As God unites all religions, it is the realization of Him or Her as Bliss that unites the consciousness of the prophets of all religions."[62]

Professor Heinrich von Stietencron points out that the term "Hinduism" really refers to a great many religions. At present the largest groups worship either Vishnu or Shiva, and the next largest number of devotees are those who worship the goddess Shakti. "Vishnu is a cosmic God," according to Stietencron. "His incarnations are always for the good of the entire world, the salvation of its moral order, and the redemption of all humanity." Vishnuites say that if a person turns to another god, for whatever reason, "the grace of the highest God will not be taken from him," because "the highest God does not see other gods as rivals. They all exist only through Him. Any claim to absoluteness is alien to the great Hindu religions. This attitude has led the Hindus to develop an unusual capacity for assimilating other religions, while maintaining their own traditions."

"In Christianity," says Stietencron, "especially in the Sermon on the Mount, Indians rediscovered features of their own faith. The concept of God's incarnation on earth was familiar to them, and so they raised no objections to the claim of Jesus' divinity." Modern Hindus "share a universalist approach that sees the founders of foreign religions, such as Buddha and Rama, Jesus and Mohammed, as incarnations of the one godhead." Most of them look beyond the barrier of caste, trying to teach everyone to be tolerant and peaceful.[63]

Hans Küng reminds us that all mystics resemble one another in recommending three stages: purification, illumination, and union with the divine. "For example," he states, "amazing parallels can be noted between Patanjali's stages of inner contemplation and Teresa of Avila's stages of prayer. Ramanuja's critical insight is that Brahma is identical with the personal God." Christianity can live with this view, Küng feels. He believes that syncretism, far from being heretical, is a systematic blending of religious traditions, under the aegis of understanding, reconciliation, and peace.[64]

Buddhism as a Path to Inner Peace

Professor Heinz Bechert says Gautama warned adherents never to cling blindly to any doctrine, including his. "Under no circumstances was the teaching of the Buddha to be imposed upon anyone." Bloody sacrifices were banned, as a violation of the proscription against killing. "The first fundamental principle of moral behavior is not to injure any living thing. The goal of moral behavior is the mastery of the senses." The proper inner attitude leads to such mastery. That attitude is achieved by "four divine lingerings": kindness, serenity, sharing of joy, and sympathy. One can see that Buddhism possesses the kind of unitive religion that helps lead towards world peace.

A Buddhist is expected to show great kindness and compassion. Gautama's five rules of conduct are universals: do not lie, kill, or steal; avoid sexual excess; abstain from intoxicants.

Nirvana is not death, but extinction of that will that leads to greed, hatred, and illusion. One need not die to experience nirvana—it is the bliss that accompanies holiness, even in this life. "There is no room in Buddhism for religious persecutions, crusades, or an Inquisition," says Bechert, admitting reluctantly, however, that sometimes Buddhist monks have engaged in violence, as in modern Sri Lanka.[65]

Helena Blavatsky, founder of theosophy, taught a union of spirit and matter, since both stem ultimately from God. She stated that the moral duties of Buddhists are "to love each other, even our bitterest enemies; to offer our lives even for animals; to abstain from defensive arms; to practice all virtues, especially humility and mildness; to respect old age; to plant trees on the roads and to dig wells for the comfort of travelers."[66]

Sherry Chayat, an art teacher at Syracuse University, is one of the first American women to receive official "transmission" in the Rinzai Zen sect. Rinzai is a school of Zen formed in China through a fusion of Buddhism and Taoism, and now is most popular in Japan. Chayat encountered Buddhism after her father was killed in World War II. In her suffering she learned Zen meditation, and felt she had achieved deep inner peace. In her new role she is qualified to be an instructor, and thus "she has been accorded the highest honor in Buddhist religious life."[67]

Oriental Syncretism

Hyujong (1520–1604) was a Korean monk who practiced syncretism. He said, "Confucius planted the seed, Lao-tzu nurtured it, and Buddha harvested it." To him the three faiths complemented one another, providing a deeper understanding of human nature because of the multiple approach.

Thomas Merton said that the Ju philosophy of Confucius and his followers found that the noble-minded person had four virtues: compassionate love, responsibility, ritual correctness, and wisdom. Chuang Tzu added a Taoist concept, *wu-wei*, which involves a peaceful willingness to be absorbed into the mysterious Tao, a force of cosmic rhythm underlying all material things. Merton said that this belief showed something akin to St. Paul's deep faith in Christ. One abandons the "need to win," and humbly identifies with each part of nature, like St. Francis of Assisi. By not consciously seeking for specific happiness, Merton felt, one finds happiness everywhere. *Wu-wei* is thus more than inaction, for it is perfect action, which is submission to the will of Heaven. This is the way, says Merton, to discover the peace of God's heavenly kingdom abiding deep within oneself.

Belonging to the Universe

Thomas Matus, a Camaldolese monk, confesses that interreligious dialogue has intensified his personal commitment to truth. "In dialogue," he says, "I do not lose what is unique in my

Christian faith, which is really Christ himself." He adds that since he believes that the fullness of God dwelt bodily in Christ, as St. Paul said, "then I should turn to my Muslim brother or my Hindu sister or anyone and discover in their humanity the same divinity."

"Right!" responded Benedictine monk David Steindl-Rast. "We prove that we see God in Jesus Christ by seeing God in every human being we meet. Gandhi is recognized by many Christians as a Christlike figure. He did what Jesus most typically did, namely, empower others."

Physicist Fritjof Capra states that finally religion is laying the basis for peace. He cites the German Protestant Church, the Roman Catholics bishops in the United States, and the Dalai Lama. Matus adds that the "Holy See has been on the public record for decades as supporting a common world authority that would guarantee that war would no longer be waged among nations." How wonderful, concluded Steindl-Rast, that now Pope John Paul II and former communist leader Mikhail Gorbachev share the same goals.[68]

The Miracle Mile

A recent article in the *New York Times* describes a square mile in Flushing in Queens where there are forty houses of worship of every conceivable religious tradition. For example, half a block from a Hindu Temple is a Sikh *gurdwara* or shrine, which is across the street from a Chinese evangelical Christian church. In Flushing there are over 100 Korean Christian churches, one of which has 3500 members. The Muslim center of New York has a new $3.5 million mosque, as well as an elementary school. At the Hindu temple there are over 3000 worshippers every weekend. The Free Synagogue of Flushing rents out its worship hall to a Korean Presbyterian congregation on Sundays.

This neighborhood has been a haven for new immigrants, people who need comfort and orientation as they establish a new way of life in America. There has been remarkably little antagonism among the myriad faiths, except for an occasional squabble over parking space.

Lorraine Foltz, a hospital laboratory technologist, was asked whether the noise and traffic bothered her. She replied, "This is part of what New York is. There's been music. There's been chanting. It's been a lovely experience. To celebrate God is to celebrate God, no matter who it is."[69]

REFERENCES

[1] American Indian College Fund, postcard of Lakota staff.

[2] Robert S. Ellwood, ed., *Eastern Spirituality in America* (Paulist Press, 1987), p. 74.

[3] Aldous Huxley, in Ellwood, pp. 81, 82.

[4] Ibid., pp. 83, 84, 86.

[5] Marcus Bach, *The Unity Way* (Unity Books, 1982), pp. 99, 133, 137, 272, 324, 325, 361–364.

[6] Berger, pp. 54, 65, 150.

[7] Quoted in *Arizona Republic,* 27 December 1997, pp. R1, R4.

[8] Raimon Panikkar, *The Intra-Religious Dialogue* (Paulist Press, 1978), pp. xxii, 11, 68, 91.

[9] *New York Times*, 4 April 1999, 4:10.

[10] Matthew Fox, *Breakthrough: Meister Eckhart's Creation Spirituality in New Translation* (Doubleday, 1980), pp. 2, 3, 6, 10, 24, 28.

[11] Hans Küng, pp. 21, 30, 86, 93.

[12] Ibid., pp. 116, 117, 122, 123, 124.

[13] Mary C. Boys, *Has God Only One Blessing?* (Paulist Press, 2000), pp. 239, 244.

[14] Michael E. Lodahl, *Shekhinah/Spirit: Divine Presence in Jewish and Christian Religion* (Paulist Press, 1992), pp. 32, 33.

[15] Eugene J. Fisher, ed., *Visions of the Other* (Paulist Press, 1994), pp. 28, 29, 30, 36, 38–45.

[16] Boys, pp. 5, 6, 7.

[17] Ibid., pp. 7, 44.

[18] Quoted by Marvin Perry, in Perry and Frederick Schweitzer, eds., *Jewish-Christian Encounters over the Centuries* (Peter Lang, 1994), p. 242.

[19] Boys, pp. 43, 72

[20] Ibid., pp. 73, 74, 169, 170, 171.

[21] Ibid., pp. 211, 217.

[22] Ibid., pp. 284–287, 290–293.

[23] Ibid., p. 295.

[24] Ibid., pp. 210, 211.

25 Fisher, pp. 7, 10, 11, 14–19, 27, 46, 47, 50.

26 Ibid., pp. 69, 71, 79, 80.

27 Charles Meister, *Religion: Bane or Blessing?* (New Falcon Publications, 2000), p. 294.

28 *New York Times,* 10 September 2000, p. 23.

29 Ibid., 1 October 2000, 4:5.

30 Maria Jaoudi, *Christian and Islamic Spirituality* (Paulist Press, 1993), p. 35.

31 Ibid., pp. 47, 48, 60.

32 Küng, pp. 128, 130.

33 *St. Anthony Messenger,* February 1990, p. 35.

34 Ibid., December 1990, p. 8.

35 *Arizona Republic,* 2 January 1998, p. A13.

36 Küng, p. 240.

37 Raimon Panikkar, *A Dwelling Place for Wisdom* (Westminster/John Knox Press, 1993), p. 121.

38 Küng, p. 283.

39 Panikkar, *A Dwelling Place for Wisdom,* p. 142.

40 Ibid., p. 127.

41 Capra and Steindl-Rast, pp. 21, 26, 60, 107, 110.

42 Seiichi Yagi and Leonard Swidler, *A Bridge to Buddhist-Christian Dialogue* (Paulist Press, 1990), pp. 3, 5, 6, 65.

43 Marcus Borg, *Bible Review,* October 1999, pp. 25, 26, 27.

44 Ibid., pp. 26, 27.

45 Ray Riegert, *Bible Review,* October 1999, p. 22.

46 Borg, pp. 28, 29.

47 Yagi and Swidler, pp. 114, 116.

48 Ibid., p. 137.

49 Ibid., pp. 140, 144.

50 Ibid., p. 43.

51 Ellwood, p. 144.

52 Capra and Steindl-Rast, p. 5.

53 *The Catholic World,* May–June 1990, pp. 127, 128, 130, 131, 133, 143.

54 Ibid., p. 130.

55 Hoffman, pp. 201, 202, 203, 212.

56 Das, p. 522.

[57] Shah, pp. 37, 66.

[58] Michael A. Sells, ed., *Early Islamic Mysticism* (Paulist Press, 1996), pp. 163, 164, 166, 169.

[59] Ian P. McGreal, ed., *Great Thinkers of the Eastern World* (HarperCollins, 1995), pp. 476–78.

[60] Hazrat Inayat Khan, *The Sufi Message of Hazrat Inayat Khan* (International Headquarters of Sufi Movement, Geneva, 1979), pp. 18, 20, 164, 166, 167.

[61] Shah, p. 114.

[62] Ellwood, pp. 91, 92, 94.

[63] Küng, pp. 141, 143, 144, 146, 157, 158, 195.

[64] Ibid., pp. 173, 180, 203, 205.

[65] Heinz Bechert, in ibid., pp. 295, 296, 299, 300–303, 353.

[66] Ellwood, p. 221.

[67] William Kates, *Arizona Republic,* 24 October 1998, p. D5.

[68] Capra and Steindl-Rast, pp. 178, 179, 197, 202.

[69] Somini Sengupta, *New York Times,* 7 November 1999, p. 31.

CHAPTER IX

THE WAY

Jesus said, "I am the way, the truth, and the life. No one comes to the Father except by me" (John 14:6). Christ's way of coming to the Father was by absorption of his self into the Universal Self, that is, surrendering his private will into God's will for himself. Unless a person dies to his selfish self, he cannot live to his Real Self, that is, to God.

In Psalm 37:5 David admonished, "Commit thy way unto the Lord; trust also in Him, and He will bring it to pass." If we recognize a divine order in the universe, we automatically try to live in accordance with its laws.

There is surprising agreement on the good life, as seen by the major world religions. "The Only Way is no longer the Way that marks out one religion from all others," says William Hocking. "It is the Way already present in all. The several universal religions are already fused together at the top. The recognition of mystic by mystic is the essence of the religious world view— God is, and God is One."[1]

Confucius said that "when the Great Way was practiced, the world was shared by all alike. The worthy and the able were promoted to office, and men practiced good faith and lived in affection. People could leave their outer gates unbolted." According to Mercia Eliade, Confucius sought to eradicate four things: arbitrary judgments, a biased mind, egotism, and obstinacy. Asked about humanity, Confucius replied, "Love people.

To be able to practice five virtues anywhere in the world constitutes humanity: courtesy, diligence, good faith, kindness, and magnanimity."[2]

In Hinduism, the *Bhikkhu Silacara* says that the one who obeys the behests of morality, to whatever form of faith he belongs, is on the Path, whether he himself is aware of it or not. This is the *Dhamma*, the universal law or moral code. "It is," says Christmas Humphreys, "the Path of strict morality taught by Confucius and Zoroaster; it is the Way of Taoism and the teaching of the Upanishads. It is the clear commandment of Christ which Europe never heard. The Path is that which leads from selfishness to altruism, from the unreal to the Real."[3]

Living in harmony with the universe is what the Chinese call the Tao. The Tao is the way that everyone should live in imitation of the cosmic order. We must live within the Tao, said Christian writer C.S. Lewis. "Either we are rational spirit obliged forever to obey the absolute values of the Tao," Lewis declared, "or else we are mere nature to be kneaded and cut into new shapes for the pleasure of masters who must, by hypothesis, have no motive but their own 'natural' impulses. Only the Tao provides a common law of action which can overarch rulers and ruled alike."[4]

In his book *The Meaning of Life at the Edge of the Third Millennium*, Leonard Swidler summarizes the Way as seen in all major world religions: In Judaism, it is *Halacha* (rabbinical teachings); in Christianity, Christ is the Way; in Islam, it is found in the legal rules of the Sharia; in Hinduism it is *Moksha* (a combination of good deeds of karma, love of Shakti, and wisdom of jnana); in Buddhism it is *Magga*, the 8-fold path to virtue; in Taoism it is the Tao, harmony with the universe; the Confucian Way is T'ien, the Way of heaven; and in Shinto it is the Way of the gods.[5]

Beneath all religious mysticism lies the same common search. "Dionysius the Areopagite speaks of ascending hierarchies of angels to the God enthroned beyond time and space. St. Teresa describes exploring the Interior Castle for the indwelling God. The Kabala leads from the material world of Malkuth, via Beauty, Justice, and Mercy to the Supernal Crown. Each religious Way gives its characteristic flavor to the essentially same spiritual pilgrimage."[6]

One Islamic name for religion is *Mazhab*, which means "the Way to God." When conflicts of priests threatened to bring disaster to his country, Prince Regent Shotoku of Japan reconciled the competing factions by stating that "Shinto is the primal and root Way, Confucianism is the branch and middle Way, and Buddhism is the flower and final Way. Each new creed enlightens the old."[7]

Religious Trinities

Leonard Swidler elucidates the various trinities: Judaism has God as *Abinu* (Our Father), *Dabar* (God's Word), and *Ruach* (God's Spirit). Christianity has God the Father (Creator), God the Son (Savior), and God the Holy Spirit (Comforter). Hinduism's *Trimurti* is Brahma (Creator), Vishnu (Savior), and Shiva (Destroyer and Re-Creator). Mahayana Buddhism has the Trikaya, the 3-fold body of the Buddha: *Dharmakaya*, *Sambhogakaya*, and *Nirmanakaya*. Taoism has *T'ai I* (Grand Unity), *Ti I* (Earthly Unity), and *T'ien I* (Heavenly Unity).[8]

C.S. Lewis devoted an entire appendix of his book *The Abolition of Man* to show the universality of the cosmic law. He found it stated in these religious traditions: American Indian, Buddhist, Christian, Confucian, Egyptian, Greek, Hindu, Norse, Roman, and Taoist. Topics embraced by this universal law include family love, the Golden Rule, honesty, justice, magnanimity, and mercy.

Both Buddha and Christ, Arnold Toynbee said, show mankind the Way to live. Both conquered desire, and showed the power that comes from that conquest. Both chose suffering for fellow humans over a life free from pain and sorrow. Both demonstrated that God's nature is love, especially sacrificial love for one's fellow human beings.

The 8-fold path of the Buddha is a Middle Way between a life of sensuous living and a life of extreme mortification of the flesh. The eight components of this Way are:

1. Right action—do not kill, steal, or commit adultery.
2. Right balance—avoid undue desire and undue rejection.
3. Right concentration—elude pain and pleasure; achieve a pure mind and equanimity of soul.
4. Right effort—avoid bad thoughts and practice good thoughts.
5. Right intention—plan to never injure anyone.

6. Right livelihood—have an honest and worthwhile vocation.
7. Right speech—avoid lies, slander, and idle talk.
8. Right understanding—know pain, and how to avoid it.

Since the Judaic Way of life had gained wide acceptance, early Christians tended to follow it. In Acts 9:2 Saul the persecutor applied for letters authorizing him to arrest followers of the Way of Jesus. This Way was now an allegiance to Jesus as Lord: "a way of salvation, a way to the ultimate good for which man has been created, variously described as heaven, eternal life, the Kingdom of God, and the full realization of one's potential as a child of God."[9]

J.B. Phillips saw Christian humanism as humanity's best hope for survival. "Humanism without religion," he said, "lacks depth, purpose, and authority, but the humanism advocated by Christ seems peculiarly suited to our age. Even the least intelligent of men are beginning to see that unless they love and understand one another, they will most certainly destroy one another. Only in the Kingdom of God, which is the kingdom of love, is there hope, strength, and security. What matters ultimately is not religious exercises but the way in which we behave towards other people, our willingness or unwillingness to be involved in the vast purpose of love."[10]

The Sharia, or the Way, is the term for Islam's legal system. Islamic scholarship is devoted more to law than to theology. Codified are the laws of man's relationship to God and to other people. Islamic law enjoins followers to do good to others, and to deter fellow believers from improper action. Carrying out this law would cut down on terrorism and violence that has characterized the Middle East in recent years.

To the Jew, the Torah is a Way of conducting one's life. It prescribes ethical treatment of all persons, and mercy as a God-like attribute. The love and mercy of the Torah could go far in helping Palestinian Jews to be fair in their relations with displaced Palestinian Muslims.

The Good Life

The good life, said Bertrand Russell, is that which is inspired by love and guided by knowledge. Most major religions would agree with this definition, adding more details to both virtues. The *Rig-Veda* contains this prayer for release from sin:

> If we have wronged a brother, friend, or stranger,
> O Varuna, remove from us the trespass.
> If we cheat at play, have sinned unwittingly or on purpose,
> Cast these sins away, Varuna; let us be Thine own beloved.

The Hindu *Puranas* state that "he who lives pure in thought, free from malice, feeling tenderness for all creatures, speaking wisely and kindly, humble and sincere, has Vishnu ever present in his heart. The Eternal makes not his abode in the heart of that man who covets another's wealth, who speaks untruth, who is proud of his iniquity, and whose mind is evil."[11]

To the Hindu, *dharma,* or moral activity, implies rigorous justice and truthfulness. These traits lead to tolerance and non-violence, virtues highly regarded in India.

Asked what is religious, the Buddha replied, "Not by his shaven crown is one made religious who is intemperate and dishonorable. How can he be religious who is full of lust and greed? Not by lineage or caste is one a Brahmin. He is the Brahmin in whom are truth and purity and righteousness."[12]

Hinayana (small vessel) Buddhism lists as virtues benevolence, chastity, contentment, gratitude, humility, liberality, patience, purity, reverence, righteousness, self-restraint, temperance, toleration, and veracity. These qualities are very similar to the fruit of the Holy Spirit as listed by Paul in his epistle to the Galatians, 5:22. The six cardinal virtues of Mahayana (large vessel) Buddhism culminate in wisdom and love, reminiscent of Bertrand Russell's position.

Judaic laws as codified by Moses Maimonides show that they cover virtually every aspect of human experience. In a Midrashic text, Isaac asks God why He had said that all of creation was good except humans. God replies, "Because I have not yet perfected man, and because through the Torah man is to perfect himself and perfect the world."[13]

In Galatians 6:2 Paul advises his listeners to "bear one another's burdens and so fulfill the law of Christ." The Golden Rule is found in some form in most religions. Christ's version is stated affirmatively, and is a comprehensive summary of an entire law of conduct. Christ's teachings stand as statements of universal ethics, hammer blows against greed, lechery, moral mediocrity, vindictive rancor, and cowardice in serving the truth.

Christ's law is the law of love. People will know you are my disciples, he said, if you love one another. Love is the root of morality. Where there is little love there will be much avoidable evil, and little prospect for peace. Augustine's advice still holds: "Love, and do what you like."

The Bible states that our conduct shows who live like God's children. "The one who lives a consistently good life is a good person, as God is good. The one who does not lead a good life is no child of God, nor is the one who fails to love one's brother. The one who actively hates one's brother is a potential murderer, and the eternal life of God cannot live in the heart of a murderer" (I John 3:7, 8, 15).

For the believer, good can come out of bad. The Chinese philosopher Kung-chia Ta-shih believed that "those who speak ill of me are really my friends. When, being slandered, I cherish neither enmity nor preference, there grows within me the power of love and humility, which is born of the Unborn."[14]

"To those who love God, all things work together for the good" (Romans 8:28). Christians resent the killing of Jesus understandably, but a good person can only be harmed physically. There is nothing the Jews could have done to better immortalize Jesus. Instead of crowning Jesus king of Israel in his lifetime, the Jews unknowingly made him, in the Christian view, King of Kings forever.

When we know the truth, said Thomas à Kempis, it frees us from attempted evils, such as the harsh words of our critics, the assaults of evil doers, and the detractions of unjust people. Humility leads to exaltation, says Eckhart: "The more I abase myself, the higher God rises above me. The deeper I dig down into humility the more exalted God becomes, and the more gently and sweetly His divine influence pours into me."[15]

Passage to India

Walt Whitman saw the United States as the "passage to India" that Columbus had sought. And in his poem "Passage to India" Whitman speaks of the passage of his soul to India, a land of "budding bibles." The world was being united in his day, with the Atlantic cable laid in 1866, the Suez Canal opened in 1869, and the transcontinental railroad in America completed that same year. Thus, Whitman writes in his poem:

Passage, O soul, to India!
Lo, soul, seest thou not God's purpose from the first?
The earth to be spanned, connected by network;
The races, neighbors, to marry and be given in marriage;
The oceans to be crossed, the distant brought near,
The lands to be welded together.
Yet, not for trade and transportation only,
But in God's name, and for thy sake, O soul.

In his novel *A Passage to India*, E.M. Forster shows how hard it is for persons of one culture to understand and accept those from another culture. Yet the pragmatic English educator Fielding and the mystical Hindu Aziz have a friendship which can be the basis for building peace between their nations. And the melodramatic trial concerning the alleged rape of the English woman Adela has the unexpected result of building bridges of understanding between Indian Hindus and Muslims.

Building Bridges

Dominique Lapierre is a French writer who sponsors food and health aid projects to India. He and his wife have spent over $5 million on programs to help the lepers of Calcutta and the poor islanders in the Ganges delta, where old ferry boats have been converted into floating clinics. "The boats serve 900,000 inhabitants of islands not on the world map," Lapierre said. "In the eyes of the world, these people do not exist."[16]

As the year 2000 waned, there was even a tinge of optimism in troubled Kashmir, where the Muslim majority has been seeking for independence since the partition of India in 1947. India announced that it would extend its cease-fire, and Pakistan responded with a partial withdrawal of its troops. The journalist Michael Krepon said, "I've been pessimistic in recent years, but now, like the Kashmiris, I'm beginning to allow myself hope."[17]

Healing Humanity's Wounds

Born in the hectic 1960's, the French *Medicins Sans Frontieres* (Doctors Without Borders) has grown into "the largest—and some would argue the most efficient—medical relief organization in the world." It has a budget of $40 million annually, and sends 2000 volunteers into emergency areas every year. In a one-year period, it had emergency medical personnel in Bangladesh,

Jordan, Kurdistan, Liberia, Peru, Somalia, and Syria. Often their clinics operate within the sound of machine gun fire. From 1970 to 1990 this group has sent 20,000 volunteer medical personnel to 85 countries around the globe. Some have given their lives, others have been kidnapped and held hostage. With a bravery like the French Foreign Legion and a dedication similar to that of the International Red Cross, this organization knows no boundary to its loving service to suffering humanity. World peace will come when more of us have the determination to alleviate human pain and hardship as demonstrated by this remarkable group.[18]

At the age of 90, Dr. Kenneth Salyer, a craniofacial surgeon in Dallas, has helped reshape the faces and heads of 13,000 people, about 80% of whom were children. Little José was about to receive surgery when rain started to fall. "God is crying," said José. "Why?" he was asked. "Because He knows I'll have surgery tomorrow," replied José. But, said Michael Ryan, "if God were truly crying, these raindrops must have been tears of joy," because in a short time José's face was reshaped to give him the opportunity for a normal life.[19]

Dr. Gary Haas was one of America's leading pediatric cardiac surgeons when he was tragically killed in an automobile crash in 2000. Assisted by his nurse practitioner wife Heidi, Dr. Haas performed extraordinary heart surgery on newly born and other babies in the Tampa Children's Heart Center. "He often donated his services to children from Bosnia, Cuba, and other countries who were brought to Tampa by Rotary International." Hospital administrator Michael Aubin said that Dr. Haas was "the brain and inspiration" behind the center's work. "We've become one of the largest centers in the United States because of his inspiration and his hard work," Aubin said.[20]

La Crosse Adopts Dubna

The city of La Crosse, Wisconsin, knows how to help build the foundations of world peace. It has adopted the Russian city of Dubna, with its 67,000 people, located about 100 miles north of Moscow. Specifically, since La Crosse has an excellent healthcare system, it has sent people, materials, and techniques that have helped Dubna have one of the best health programs in Russia. The maternity hospital has been rebuilt; a kidney dialysis center has been installed as well as a diabetes education center.

There are "women's wellness clinics on both sides of the Volga River, and a rehabilitation center for disabled children and adults in a former kindergarten." The death rate has gone down, as has the abortion rate and the number of hospital admissions. Alcohol and tobacco education classes are conducted in all Dubna schools. Mayor Prokh of Dubna summarized the relationship: "We have a lot of friends in La Crosse."[21]

Gentleness

Wu-wei is the Taoist concept which recommends gentle response to opposition. Sometimes an assumed acquiescence is a more effective reaction than an overtly violent one. The Carmodys explain how this works. "Lao Tzu marvels at the *wu-wei* of water. Water benefits all living things, yet it does not shout about its benefactions. The Way is if anything less visible, less prominent than water. The sage wants to know how it all fits together. For the peace of his own soul, but also for the peace of his country, he wants to know heaven's purposes for all the times he must endure. We are as unjust and as bellicose as we are because our whole interaction is tilted, corroded, diseased. Lacking roots in Tao, our social relations are bound to wither and rot."[22]

Kofi Annan, Secretary General of the United Nations, has a quiet demeanor full of *wu-wei*. His gently modulated voice and his calm reassurance builds confidence in the justice of his decision making. It is virtually impossible to ever find him playing favorites. In one crisis after another, he seeks for peace, non-violence, justice, and fairness. His personal attributes qualify him as one of the great leaders in the modern world.

Annan quotes the five virtues of a Ghanian tribe that describe a good person: compassion, confidence, courage, dignity, and faith. Annan's wife Nane is the niece of the Swedish hero of World War II, Raoul Wallenberg. She has been a helpmate to him in his times of stress. What he believes, says Joshua Cooper Ramo, is that "the world needs to create a climate in which brutality is the exception rather than the rule. It means using other weapons—sanctions, for instance—to slow down killing. And it means giving nations trapped in cycles of violence the tools they need to join the world community. It means, in short, being compassionate."[23]

Satyagraha

The psychologist Erik Erikson holds that virtue is the chief goal of all action—we must try to create virtue in ourselves and others. The adult virtues of care, love, and wisdom, he says, build upon and help develop in the young the virtues of childhood and youth, such as fidelity, hope, love, and purpose, which precede the adult virtues. Violence such as that seen in school shootings can be avoided if young people develop a feeling for the sacredness of all life.

"Erikson," says Don Browning, "turns to Gandhi for the ultimate solution to the treatment of the 'other.' For Gandhi's philosophy of *satyagraha* is indeed a marvelous synthesis; it is the first great application of the Christian doctrine of love to political life. Erikson sees important parallels between Gandhi's *satyagraha*, the basic meaning of the Golden Rule, the ritual conflicts between animals, and the true essence of the psychoanalytic relationship."[24]

The search is always for worthwhile acts that enhance a mutuality among participants. Gandhi insisted that justice was achieved only when neither party to a dispute was harmed. William Hocking feels that *satyagraha* originated with Jesus, who insisted that facts be controlled by spiritual forces. In each case a determined effort is made not to violate the opponent's essence.

Browning lists the steps involved in *satyagraha*, which he calls "a ritual pattern for conflict in the name of truth:"

1. Study, define, and delimit the alleged injustice.
2. Propose arbitration.
3. Prepare both parties by announcing proposed non-cooperation.
4. Non-cooperative action, selected by a committee, is started with an ultimatum, but resistance and non-violent action never exceed that needed for the announced goal.
5. Crucial issues should help not only the disadvantaged but also the general public.
6. At all times the non-violent resister is willing to persuade and be persuaded.

Apparently assuming that political success must be built upon improper actions, Lord Acton said that all great men are evil. But what about Asoka, Lincoln, and Gandhi? It is more accurate to say that it is difficult for a great person to be good. Of course, it is far more important to be good than to be great, something the average person gets all wrong. How, then, can a great person also be good? Aldous Huxley provides two guidelines: Deny oneself all the personal advantages of power, and realize that having temporary political power in no way grants one spiritual authority.

Paul told the people of Corinth, "Though I be free from all men, yet have I made myself servant to all" (I Corinthians 9:19). Thus, he continues, by serving everyone, he becomes "all things to all people." Illustrating that the greatest among them would be their servant, Christ washed the feet of his disciples.

Maslow's Values

World War II influenced Abraham Maslow to devote the rest of his life to evolving a comprehensive theory of human behavior, a "psychology of the peace table," based on factual evidence that all the world could accept. He knew that people required values just as they need food and water. To a person lacking values, life is meaningless. Sigmund Freud found out about mental illness by studying the mentally ill. Since Maslow wanted to study mental health, he made special studies of mentally healthy people, whom he called self-actualizers.

Self-actualizers are achievers in life. Having harmonious personalities, they see the world in a unified way. They are at their best facing a creative challenge, a highly worthy goal, or a serious threat or emergency. These people should be in the forefront of leadership as the world community organizes itself to survive the nuclear threat.

Maslow found that self-actualizers, while developing their own best potential, at the same time help society to bring out its most productive capacities. These persons have little confusion between right and wrong, and surprisingly adhere to the same basic values no matter what culture they represent.

Anthropology, which had earlier made much of cultural relativism, was now pioneering in finding universals, Maslow asserted. Race and culture now seemed less essential in determining one's values than did the individual's personality and character, which often found parallels in persons of widely different cultural backgrounds.

Maslow drew up a hierarchy of needs that applied to all humans of whatsoever culture or historical period. Starting from the most basic, these needs were physiological, security, love, esteem, and growth needs. Growth needs, the attainment of which best characterized the self-actualizers, included such traits as goodness, individuality, justice, meaningfulness, order, playfulness, and truth. Maslow found that cooperation was as important as competition in the struggle for survival, and that aggression is not an instinct in human beings.

Maslow faced the future with optimism. He felt that the doctrine of deterrence might keep mankind from nuclear war. Moreover, since the entire human species has the same basic needs (and these needs are social, not antisocial, in nature), "the long-range prognosis for the human species is far more optimistic than that projected by Freud or Karl Marx. We can now reject, as a localism, the almost universal mistake that the interests of the individual and of society are mutually antagonistic, or that civilization is primarily a mechanism for policing human instinctual impulses. All these age-old maxims are swept away by the new possibility of defining the main function of a healthy culture as the fostering of universal self-actualization."[25]

The Good Society

The good society, said Maslow, is the one in which virtue pays. To achieve such a society, members need to elect their best persons to govern. Too many politicians know how to get elected rather than how to govern. In a fascinating exchange of letters between two former presidents, John Adams got Thomas Jefferson to change his original position—not everybody is fit to govern, so if a nation is to prosper, it must know how to select its most qualified leaders.

A healthy society, said Erich Fromm, furthers mutual agape love and creativity, and permits the individual his/her greatest productive powers. It would be one of high synergy, where what was considered good for the individual was what was good for the group. In this society people would be ends, not means, and there would be great limitation upon such factors as greed, possessiveness, and exploitation.

Over 2500 years ago the Chinese philosopher Mu-Ti expanded the Golden Rule to include all human groups: "Let one love another as oneself. Let a sovereign love his subjects as himself. Let a nation love another as its own."[26]

The Emperor Asoka not only worked for peace and inspired his people to practice the cardinal virtues of life, but he worked unceasingly for their welfare, building hospitals and stupas, digging wells and reservoirs, and providing an honest and efficient government. "By his kindliness to all men, his tolerance for all points of view, and his powerful exhortation to all people to live the Buddha-like life, he set an example which few, if any, rulers of history have even attempted to attain," said Christmas Humphreys.[27]

Buddhist ethics, says Richard Gard, stresses such values as production for social use rather than purely for profit, evaluating individuals in terms of wisdom and morality rather than their pecuniary worth, and weighing nations by their contributions to peace instead of their trade balances. Where the acquisition of wealth by any means, fair or foul, is the driving force of the society, Gard says, a high incidence of gambling, crime, and violence is to be expected.

When a nation tries to erect a government without a religious foundation, William Hocking warns, the effort fails. The areas which suffer most are those in which the government is expected to act, such as law and order, education, and social care. Without the help of the people, the state fails in these areas, Hocking states, because the state acting alone cannot civilize.

Global Values

In his book *A Study of Future Worlds*, Richard Falk describes four basic world values needed for human survival with dignity:

1. Minimize large-scale collective violence.
2. Maximize social and economic well-being.
3. Achieve political justice and fundamental human rights.
4. Rehabilitate and conserve the quality of the environment.

Chadwick Alger, former president of the International Studies Association, lists six basic international values: satisfaction of basic human needs; participatory government; national self-determination; international peace; international economic equity; and ecological care.

Professional groups have helped define the values worth preserving in the nuclear age. Physicians Against Nuclear War is an organization that speaks for humanity against irresponsible political leadership. Psychologists have banded together to demand responsible use of nuclear energy. Scientists and educators have been vocal in warning us of the dire results if we do not develop institutions to control wanton use of nuclear weapons.

In *Science and Human Values* Jacob Bronowski wrote that "the values by which we are to survive are not rules for just and unjust conduct but are those deeper illuminations in whose light justice and injustice, good and evil, means and ends, are seen in fearful sharpness of outline."[28] The Chinese civil law code of 1930 outlined juridical principles that are now becoming worldwide.

When a Soviet spokesman Georgi Arbatov attacked the United States in 1983 on twin grounds of being the last major country to eliminate slavery and the only country to use atomic bombs against people, most Americans would agree with the value assumptions underlying the attack, testifying that indeed a world conscience is being formulated.

Erich Fromm traced the development by Old Testament prophets of a code of justice applicable to all peoples, not just to the Jews. Don Browning finds validation of Fromm's universal ethos, saying that "the widely acclaimed generative linguistics of Noam Chomsky and the authoritative cross-cultural studies in moral development by Lawrence Kohlberg both suggest a universally shared common structure of the human mind that expresses itself in widely recognized common principles about the nature of the good and the true. It is Fromm's contention that these universal principles are implicit in the symbolism of the great world religions."[29]

Fromm felt that the dogmas, rituals, and orthodoxies in which most religions are wrapped are quite secondary to the inner ethical experience which the religions intend to convey. On the one hand, he says, we must affirm the common values clustered around love, reason, and truth. But in the context of modern pluralism, one must do more than merely affirm common values. One must be ready to accept the many differences, and understand how to find the universals that are imbedded in these differences.

Browning describes generative man as a person equally at home in the particulars or the universals. He shows that the merit of being grounded in the universals is that when changes come, as they must, one can retreat to the comfort of the universals. Change is thus considered to be merely external, and one's calm and peaceful interior is never ruffled.

To Give is the Way to Live

Philanthropists like Andrew Carnegie, Henry Ford, and John D. Rockefeller lived up to their title as "lovers of humanity." The foundations they established have given the human race incomparable benefits in education, libraries, medicine, research, and scholarship. They have shown us that "the way to give is the way to live."

Modern philanthropy is also impressive. Ted Turned donated one billion dollars to aid worthy international programs over a ten-year period. Recently Bill Gates matched Ted by making "the largest academic donation ever: $1 billion, to be distributed over the next twenty years to pay the full tab each year for about 1000 black, Hispanic, and Native American students seeking degrees in education, engineering, mathematics, and science." From 1997–2000, the Gates Foundation pledged $4 billion to various charitable causes. Other noteworthy donations include $92 million from the Lilly Endowment for Hispanic and Afro-American scholarships, $58 million from the W.K. Kellogg Foundation for Hispanic and Native American students, and $52 million from the Annenberg Foundation for the United Negro College Fund.

Celebrities Celebrate Life

Many celebrities have set up financial assistance programs to help those less fortunate than themselves. Here are a few examples. Andre Agassi has a foundation to assist low-income children. Pierce Brosnan has raised funds for cancer research and for ecological programs. Katie Couric has pioneered in both education and treatment for colorectal cancer. Rhonda Fleming established a center to combat ovarian cancer. Faith Hill is a national leader in supporting literacy programs. Derek Jeter's foundation focuses on substance abuse prevention. Susan Lucci campaigns for the March of Dimes and for a charity which provides foster care and adoption services for orphans. Dennis Quaid helps the International Hospital for Children, which furnishes medical services to needy children in many countries. Kristi Yamaguchi set up the Always Dream Foundation, which helps economically and socially disadvantaged children. These celebrities, and many more like them, have received much publicity, but their hearts are even larger than their fame.

World Unity

A most encouraging signpost for survival of our species is this voluntary sharing of resources from the more affluent to the more deprived. This is the philosophy of unitive religion at work. Another encouraging sign is the common core of cultural values outlined in this chapter. Our common world has produced the nuclear threat to survival, says Jonathan Schell, and only world peace can save us from this threat. "Only because there is a common world," Schell feels, "in which knowledge of the physical world accumulates over the generations, can there be a threat to the common world. And only because there is a common world can we hope, by concerting our actions, to save ourselves and the earth."[30]

Edmund Burke spoke of "the partnership of the generations." We have an implied contract, Burke believed, with those of the past and those of the future. It extends into every area of our lives, he said, and we dare not let posterity down by our poor stewardship. Rabbi Abraham Isaac Kook says that our sacred responsibility now is to embrace all spiritual paths and integrate them into a full harmony.

Teilhard found an amazing inherent oneness in the human species. "Under conditions of distribution," he said, "which in any other initial phylum would have led long ago into the break up into different species, the human verticil as it spreads out remains entire." Instead of shattering into many subspecies, we find "a movement of convergence in which races, people, and nations consolidate one another and complete one another by mutual fecundation."[31]

In 1954 Yasaki Tagaki published a book *Toward International Understanding* in which he stated that the only way to save Japanese civilization was for it to engraft itself into the tree of Western civilization based on the Judeo-Christian concept of human personality, which he felt was the major trunk of universal human society.

The Hindu Radhakrishnan believed that once Christian churches freed themselves from ethnocentricity, Jesus would be the universal figure uniting humanity. Radhakrishnan said that "the practice of the principles of Jesus will mean a society for all mankind, a society in which we bear one another's burdens and sympathize with each other in joy and in sorrow. Such a society will be free from national rivalries and industrial competition. The *national* churches of Christianity constitute an open revolt against the gospel of Jesus."[32]

Ruth Nanda Anshen wrote widely on the topic of world perspectives. She concluded that "mankind can finally place its trust not in a proletarian authoritarianism, not in a secularized humanism, both of which have betrayed the spiritual property right of history, but in a sacramental brotherhood and in the unity of knowledge. Clear the way for thc foundation of a genuine world history not in terms of a nation or race or culture, but in terms of man in relation to God, to himself, his fellow man, and the universe. The meaning of the World Age consists in respecting man's hopes and dreams which lead to a deeper understanding of the basic values of all peoples. Today in the East and in the West men are discovering that they are bound together, beyond any divisiveness, by a more fundamental unity than any mere agreement in thought and doctrine."[33]

References

1   William E. Hocking, *The Coming World Civilization* (Harper, 1956), p. 149.

2   Eliade, *From Primitives to Zen*, pp. 566, 568.

3   Christmas Humphreys, *Buddhism* (Penguin, 1954), pp. 92, 93.

4   C.S. Lewis, *The Abolition of Man* (Collier, 1962), p. 84.

5   Leonard Swidler, *The Meaning of Life at the Edge of the Third Millennium* (Paulist Press, 1992), pp. 8, 9.

6   Meister, p. 158.

7   Das, p. 71.

8   Swidler, *The Meaning of Life*, pp. 108, 109.

9 John Hick, *God and the Universe of Faiths*, rev. ed., (Collins, 1977), p. 109.

10 J.B. Phillips, *God Our Contemporary* (Hodder & Stoughton, 1960), p. 181.

11 Louis Renou, ed., *Hinduism* (Braziller, 1962), pp. 69, 171, 172.

12 Eliade, *From Primitives to Zen*, p. 583.

13 Progoff, pp. 250, 251.

14 Aldous Huxley, *The Perennial Philosophy* (Harper, 1945), p. 84.

15 Blakney, p. 234.

16 *New York Times*, 22 August 1999, p. 10.

17 Ibid., 24 December 2000, p. 4.

18 Kathleen Hunt, *New York Times Magazine*, 28 July 1991, pp. 30, 50.

19 *Parade Magazine*, 22 December 1996, p. 4.

20 Susan Leonard, *Lubbock Avalanche-Journal*, 17 August 2000, pp. A1, A13.

21 Michael Wines, *New York Times*, 31 December 2000, pp. 1, 10.

22 Denise and John Carmody, pp. 100, 101, 119, 120.

23 Joshua Cooper Ramo, *Time*, 4 September 2000, pp. 35–42.

24 Browning, p. 212.

25 Frank Goble, *The Third Force* (Pocket Books, 1971), p. 110.

26 Oliver L. Reiser, *Cosmic Humanism and World Unity* (Gordon & Breach, 1975), p. 3.

27 Humphreys, p. 47.

28 Roger A. Coate, *Global Issue Regimes* (Prager, 1982), p. 187.

29 Browning, pp. 132, 133.

30 Jonathan Schell, *The Fate of the Earth* (Avon Books, 1982), pp. 120, 121.

31 Teilhard de Chardin, pp. 241, 242.

32 Sarvepalli Radhakrishnan, *East and West in Religion* (Allen & Unwin, 1967), pp. 66, 67.

33 Erich Fromm, *The Art of Loving* (Bantam, 1963), pp. 114, 115.

CHAPTER X

THE MIDDLE EAST:
PROMISES AND PORTENTS

The young man was deeply distressed. His clan, the Hashemites, was once again embroiled in warfare. There would be the usual killings, slaughter which had been going on for centuries. By now one would think that the Ommayads would realize that their gods were inferior to those of the Hashemites. Must it be proved again, and in the traditional way? How many innocent young men must die to prove that their gods are the superior ones?

The young Mohammed believed that there must be a better way to find God's will than to kill people. Thus he began a deep and systematic study of the scriptures. In the Torah he discovered that there is but one God—the God of Abraham. In the New Testament he found out that Jesus was sent by God to reveal His Word to humanity.

As a boy, Mohammed had been impressed by the piety of the Jews in Jerusalem. In Syria he admired the way the Christians cared for the poor. He was convinced that Allah, the God of Abraham, spoke through both of these religions. But why did Jews and Christians often kill one another? And why were Nestorian Christians outcasts from the great church at Rome?

The *suras* of the Koran written in Mecca are largely unitive. Allah is depicted as having great compassion, and there is a tolerant acceptance of the other People of the Book: Jews and

Christians. There is an emphasis upon free will and individual responsibility for one's conduct. A great hero of the Koran and later Islamic literature is the Jew Joseph, who resisted the advances of Potiphar's beautiful wife Zuleika, because of his dedication to God.

Later, in Medina, Mohammed found little acceptance from Jews and Christians. The *suras* written here show Islam as the one true faith—all other believers are infidels. Allah is an inscrutable tribal God, who predestines human life and fate. This is largely divisive religion.

The tragedy of the Middle East is that far too often Muslim countries have followed the divisive, rather than the unitive, teachings of the Koran. Stubborn ayatollahs and imams, purporting to have a monopoly on Allah's mind, have recommended pathways leading to discrimination, hatred, terrorism, and warfare. The unitive Sufi doctrine, that love is the surest route to God, has too frequently been neglected. Before long, Muslims are once again killing so-called infidels and sometimes even fellow Muslims whose views differ somewhat from their own.

After Mohammed's death in 632, Islam spread like a sirocco. By 640 Khalid had conquered Iraq, Syria, and Palestine. Persia and Egypt fell by 1652. Four-fifths of all booty could be retained by Muslim soldiers—wealth begat military success. To die in battle ensured immediate entrance into a paradise with green oases and almond-eyed houris.

The Great Schism

Since Mohammed left no living sons, succession to the caliphate was contentious. Upon Othman's death in 656, two men had followers as his successor. Mohammed's son-in-law (and cousin) Ali lived in Iraq, and the Ommayad chieftain Mu'awiyah resided in Syria. Ali's superior army was silenced when Mu'awiyah's soldiers attacked with copies of the Koran tied to their lances.

Ali's willingness to substitute dialogue for swordplay so enraged the Kharijites ("seceders") that one of them killed Ali in 661. Since then Islam has been a divided faith. Ali's followers were further incensed when Ali's son Hussein was killed by Ommayads in 680 and his head was sent to Yasid, Mu'awiyah's son, the caliph of Damascus. Henceforth the Sunni, the majority of the faith, opposed the Shiites, who were the followers of Ali's line. Many other rifts occurred in the faith, especially among the Shiites.

In 750 Abu-al-Abbas, a descendant of Mohammed's uncle, captured Damascus and inaugurated the long and illustrious reign of the Abbasids. While Europe was in the Dark Ages, Muslim culture flourished. Friend to Charlemagne, Caliph Harun al-Raschid encouraged scholarship and made Baghdad, with its white mosques and teeming markets, a rival to Byzantine Constantinople.

The Crusades, initiated as an effort to return Jerusalem to Christian control, was a main divisive factor between the two great religions. Christian armies often slaughtered Jews in Europe before leaving to fight the "pagan" Muslims. The height of absurdity occurred in the Fourth Crusade when western Christians and eastern Christians killed each other over control of Constantinople. Eventually the Christians were repulsed by Muslim armies, and Islam resumed control of the Holy Land.

The Sufi Spiritual Revolution

Like all religious peoples, the Muslims felt that God was on their side. Six hundred years of virtually unbroken conquest seemed to lend credence to this belief. But the myth was shattered in 1258, when the Mongolian Golden Horde destroyed Baghdad. Other conquests by the Mongols shook Islamic pride, and caused a spiritual revolution.

If Islam was not to win the world through military power, reasoned the Sufis, maybe it was because Allah was to use Islam as a religion of love. The Sufis interpreted the *jihad* as a holy war waged within each person's soul, with the forces of good seeking Allah's help in reducing the evil aspects of one's own nature. If there were to be any killing, it would not be physical but instead overcoming one's adversary through kindness.

The Sufi revolution provided balm when the lame Tamerlane, himself a Muslim, sacked Baghdad in 1401. As the Sufis insisted, Islam had to be careful lest its divisive tendencies lead to civil war and mutual destruction.

Located at the crossroads of the Middle East, Baghdad has been easy prey to conquerors. Iraq was ruled by Mongols, Turkomans, and Persians until the Ottoman Sultan, Suleiman the

Magnificent, captured Baghdad in 1543. The country remained a land of divided loyalties. It owed political allegiance to Turkey but its heart lay in its faith: pro-Arabian Sunni in the north and pro-Persian Shiite in the south. The present boundary between Iran and Iraq was set in 1639.

Origins of Zionism

After the destruction of Jerusalem by Hadrian in 70 C.E., Jews were prohibited from living in their former capital. The Diaspora took place, with Jews seeking peaceful enclaves in whatever countries seemed hospitable. Largely because of the presence of the Muslim Moors in Spain and Portugal, Jews received their best treatment there. Many Jews were employed as court physicians, treasurers, and scholars. In fact, Cecil Roth said that here "the most important section of Jewry became Arabized. They flaunted Arab names, spoke Arabic only among themselves, and adopted Muslim intellectual fashions and standards."[1]

During the Middle Ages Jews were convenient scapegoats for Christians who encountered disaster. Such diverse things as fires, inclement weather, economic depression, and the bubonic plague were all blamed on the Jews! The Jews paid one-fourth of the levy to support Richard I's Crusade, even though anti-Semitism was a feature of that crusade.

When Ferdinand and Isabella expelled the Jews from Spain in 1492, Islamic Turkey offered the Jews a haven. Sultan Bazajet said, "Call ye this Ferdinand 'wise'? He who depopulates his own dominions in order to enrich mine?" Bazajet encouraged Jewish immigration and soon Turkey had many skilled artisans, merchants, and scholars.

Jews who refused to leave Spain or convert to Christianity were condemned to death. Sedate Christians brought picnic lunches on a Sunday afternoon to watch the auto-da-fés in which the Spanish Inquisition burned Jews in the market place. Later, some Catholics blamed Jews for the Protestant revolt!

Deprived in most European countries of both religious and civil rights, Jews longed for a sanctuary from persecution. Love of the Torah bred in them a deep desire to return to their Biblical homeland.

Shocked by French anti-Semitism during the Dreyfus affair, Theodor Herzl, a Hungarian journalist, wrote a pamphlet in 1896 asserting that the Jews should have their own state. Herzl predicted that the Muslims would welcome the Jews back to Palestine, as had happened earlier in Turkey. The Arab population in Palestine resented this intrusion from the start, and at first were joined by the British in opposing Zionism. Palestine, which had formerly been governed by Syria and was now a part of the Ottoman Empire, had been under Islamic control ever since Saladin had defeated the Latin Kingdom of Jerusalem in 1187.

The Jewish theologian Martin Buber, who had helped transform Hasidism into one of the world's great mystical movements, was an outstanding proponent of Jewish-Arab cooperation. However, he early expressed deep reservations about Zionism as a possible solution to the Jewish problem. Begun as a desperate effort to find a haven for the constantly persecuted Jews, Zionism developed into a form of Jewish nationalism that bred its own type of persecution.

British Interests in the Middle East

For centuries the British East India Company used Middle Eastern ports and cities as way stations for commerce with the Orient. From India Britain dominated most of the southern and eastern fringes of Arabia and the Persian Gulf, even though they were a part of the Ottoman Empire. Britain had trade agreements with many small Arab states, such as Aden, Bahrain, Kuwait, Muscat, and Oman. Practically of these small kingdoms lie at the door of Iraq. Also, even before the Suez Canal was built, Britain used the Red Sea as a trade route, for a railroad connected the Mediterranean with the Red Sea.

Around the year 1900 Zionists, led by Herzl, made little progress getting British support for their cause. But Britain disliked the growing Jewish immigration into England, feeling it would undermine British labor. Colonial Secretary Joseph Chamberlain (father of Neville) suggested Uganda as a possible Jewish homeland. In 1909 Tel Aviv (the Hill of Spring) was founded on land north of Jaffa. By 1914 there were 43 Jewish agricultural communities in Palestine, with a total population of 12,000.

During World War I a British soldier of fortune, T.E. Lawrence, collaborated with Husain, Sharif of Mecca, in revolting against the authority of the Ottoman Empire, then an ally of

Germany. The revolt cost the British government $50 million. Three of the Arab leaders later served as prime ministers of Iraq. The Arabs said that they were guaranteed autonomy in the liberated territory, including Palestine. The revolt was successful, and the Ottoman Empire collapsed as a result of the war. When the Russians surrendered to the German army in 1916, Germany was able to shift more troops to the French front. Needing reinforcements, the British army was forced to leave Palestine to the rule of the Arabs.

Out of this background came the Balfour Declaration in November 1917. Lord Balfour issued a letter to Lord Rothschild, leader of the Jewish community in Britain, pledging support for a Jewish national home in Palestine. Although the declaration stated that "nothing shall be done which may prejudice the civil and religious rights of existing non-Jewish communities in Palestine," T.E. Lawrence and others felt that the British government had reneged on its promise to the Arab leaders.

Balfour himself saw the contradiction, especially when President Woodrow Wilson's Fourteen Points included self-determination of nations. Palestine at the time was 90% Muslim. Nevertheless, Balfour said that "the four Great Powers are committed to Zionism. And Zionism, be it right or wrong, good or bad, is rooted in age-long tradition, in present needs, in future hopes, of far profounder import than the desires and prejudices of the 700,000 Arabs who now inhabit that ancient land. Zionism will not hurt the Arabs." Richard Allen commented that "1918 was the year of skillful prevarication by the Allies to counter a variety of protests, and to mask the contradictions between the promises they had made."[2]

Britain not only wanted to get the United States into the Allied war effort, but also sought support for its Zionist position. Leading American Zionists were Supreme Court Justice Louis Brandeis and future Justice Felix Frankfurter. President Wilson appointed Henry King and Charles Crane to study the problems of the Middle East, and recommend a course of action for the United States. The King-Crane Commission said that Syria, Lebanon, and Palestine should be ruled by King Faisal, under a British or American mandate. They not only reported strong anti-Zionist emotions among the Arabs, but quoted a number of British officers who predicted that the Zionist plan could be implemented only by force of arms. Despite all the dire warnings, the European powers ignored the recommendations of the King-Crane Commission.

British Mandates in the Middle East

With the collapse of the Ottoman Empire, Britain took over the mandates of Iraq, Transjordan, and Palestine. British historian Hugh Seton-Watson said that these nations were given "extremely artificial frontiers." "All of the Eastern Mediterranean states are 20th century creations. Kuwait exists because of an agreement between a British agent and an Arab chieftain at the end of the 19th century—a time when British policy was driven by a concern of defending lines of imperial communications. The Sabah abu Abdullah family wanted protection against the exactions of Ottoman imperial authorities."[3]

A British White Paper, issued by Winston Churchill in 1922, said that the Balfour Declaration never intended that Palestine should be only the Jewish national home, but that it should also be the national home of the Palestinians. Britain, said Churchill, expected that Jewish immigration would not exceed the economic capacity of the region to absorb Jews, and that there should be no emigration or subordination of the native Palestinians to the Jews.

As Colonial Secretary, Churchill made an effort to fulfill British pledges to the Arab nations. He found Iraq engaged in a bloody and costly revolt against the British mandate. So Britain authorized a plebiscite in Iraq, and King Faisal and his family ruled Iraq from 1921 until 1958. The British mandate in Iraq was lifted in 1922. King Faisal's older brother Abdullah became the ruler of Transjordan. Iraq joined the League of Nations in 1932.

In 1922 Britain lifted its protectorate in Egypt, giving Egypt autonomy. The Sultan was declared to be King Faud I. Britain retained control of the Suez Canal, the Sudan, the defense of Egypt, and protection of foreign interests in the land.

In 1939 a British White Paper provided for the creation of an independent binational Palestinian state within ten years. By treaty, Britain would guarantee protection of the holy places, of foreign interests, and of British strategic needs. Further Jewish immigration would be subject to Arab agreement. Arabs and Jews would be represented on the British High Commissioner's

Executive Council. The Arabs accepted these recommendations, but the Jews did not.

European Interests in the Middle East

Since France had been the chief country sponsoring the Crusades, it kept an interest in the Christians in the Ottoman Empire. France assumed a guardianship for Christians in Lebanon and Syria, for French Crusaders had used those countries as their base of operations. Under the League of Nations, the French exercised a mandate over Syria and Lebanon until the close of World War II. As a rival of the Hapsburg Empire, France had allied herself in 1535 with Suleiman the Magnificent. This gave France an entry into Turkish ports, as well as custodianship over Christian holy places in the Ottoman Empire.

As a colonial power, France had the goal of absorption of the Arabs into French civilization, and she was thus far slower than Britain to grant autonomy to Arab nations. Also, France feared that if she lifted the mandate over Syria and Lebanon, her other mandates in North Africa (Algeria, Morocco, and Tunis) would want similar independence. Under the French protectorate, Lebanon was doubled in size at the expense of Syria. Small wonder that later Syria demanded that the lost territory be returned. By its maneuvering, France managed to deny Syria access to the Mediterranean coast.

Germany's interest in the region was centered chiefly on Turkey. In 1898 Kaiser Wilhelm II visited Syria, Turkey, and Palestine, meanwhile proclaiming his friendship with all Muslim peoples. From 1901 to 1908 Germany built the 900-mile Hejaz Railroad from Damascus to Medina. These interests, coupled with common strategic concerns, led the Ottoman Empire to ally itself with Germany during World War I.

As the leading Orthodox Christian country, Czarist Russia felt responsible for protecting the Orthodox faith in such places as Iraq, Syria, and Turkey. Russia felt itself to be the Third Rome (successor to Constantinople as the Second Rome). As the Ottoman Empire weakened, Russian influence in the Middle East grew stronger. In 1907 Persia was divided into British and Russian areas of interest. As Iran, Persia regained its autonomy at the end of World War II.

The New Israeli State

The Soviet Union cordially welcomed the new Israeli state in 1948, but as the Cold War warmed up, the Soviet Union took a predictably hostile attitude towards Israel, feeling that it was a puppet ally of the United States. Iraq, like most Arab nations, sent troops to fight the Israeli army in 1948. Iraq also closed its oil pipeline to Israel. Of its 150,000 Jews, Iraq saw all but 25,000 leave for Israel.

In the 1948 military skirmishes, the Jews defeated the troops of the Arab coalition. By the end of the year, 300,000 Palestinians had left Palestine, leaving only 167,000 in the new Jewish nation proclaimed in May 1949 by David Ben-Gurion. The United States quickly recognized the new nation, and soon many other countries did too.

Suez Crisis and North Africa

In 1956 Gamal Nasser of Egypt announced the nationalization of the Suez Canal, so that Egypt could use canal revenues to build the Aswan Dam on the Nile. In October 1956 Israel attacked Egypt. British and French planes bombed Egyptian airfields and destroyed most of the Egyptian air force. Israel seized control of the Sinai Peninsula and the Gaza Strip. Although Nasser lost the war, he gained prestige in the Arab world for having stood up against the western powers. Egypt also found that it had obtained a new ally in the Soviet Union.

During the Casablanca Conference in 1943, President Franklin Roosevelt promised Sultan Mohammed V that the United States would support Moroccan independence after the war, thereby angering France. In 1956 France reluctantly granted Morocco self-government, and immediately withdrew its financial and technical support. The United States began to furnish this aid to Morocco. Morocco's constitution states that "Islam is the religion of the state, which guarantees the liberty of sects." But the League of Moroccan Ulama stated as one of its prime goals, "to oppose all Christian missionary efforts in Morocco." A Moroccan newspaper said that Christian missionaries do not work for peace and tolerance, as Christ did, but instead sow sedition in the hearts of Muslim youth. Newspapers in Morocco frequently attack Jews, Christians, and Baha'is. A Morocco law provides for up to three years in prison for anyone trying to convert a Muslim to another religion, "either by exploiting his weakness or his needs, using institutions of education, health, asylums, or orphanages."[4]

France granted independence to Algeria in 1962. Algeria promised to guarantee "the liberty of the Catholic, Protestant, and Jewish religions." Algeria has always made a distinction between its Jewish population and the Zionist state in Palestine. Islam played a large part in the independence movement, assuming that the Christian imperialists must be driven out. Premier Ahmed ben Bella, however, thanked the Abbé Berenger and other Christians for their help during the liberation struggle, saying that they understood that "Algeria is trying to restore dignity to the poor."[5]

A number of Sufi orders tried to maintain peace between the French and the revolutionary leaders. These included the Sanusiya, the Rahmaniya, and the Taibiya. Once independence came, these orders suffered from Algeria's secularism, which was fed by Marxist propaganda from China and the Soviet Union.

Arab-Israeli Wars

In modern times there has never been tranquility between Jews and Muslims in Palestine. From 1965 to 1967 Yasir Arafat led a series of guerrilla raids against Israel's borders. Ships carrying cargo for Israel were seized in the Suez Canal. All members of the Arab League agreed on one thing: the Palestinians should regain control of their country. Israel accused Syria of harboring terrorists who were attacking Israel. Egypt blocked the port of Aqaba from carrying Israeli goods.

When the war started in 1967, thirteen Arab states vowed to help fight Israel. Actually, little help came to the border states of Egypt, Jordan, and Syria. Within six days Israeli aircraft had carried the day. Israel gained the Sinai Peninsula from Egypt, the West Bank from Jordan, and the Golan Heights from Syria. Israel was now four times as large as it was before the war.

The modern state of Israel was now larger than the Biblical one. For only 80 years, under David and Solomon, had the Jews dominated all of Palestine. For most of the Biblical period the Jews shared Palestine with other kingdoms, and had often been vassals of more powerful neighbors. "The new Israel covered the ancient lands of the Philistines and some parts of the Biblical kingdom of Israel that has disappeared around 700 B.C.E."[6] To lay claim to all of Palestine based on its short period of Biblical sovereignty would be like England claiming much of France, the French lands owned by England in the Middle Ages. In effect, six million Jews have held over 150 million Muslims at bay, thanks largely to American assistance.

The year 1973 was fraught with tension in the eastern Mediterranean. In January the Israelis had border clashes with Syrian troops. Israel shot down a civilian Libyan plane in February, resulting in 113 deaths. In March the PLO bombed several sites in Israel. In retaliation, Israeli troops raided Beirut in April, killing a number of PLO leaders. Anwar Sadat of Egypt announced that, in preparing for combat, his goal was to enforce U.N. Security Council Resolution #242 of 1967, which called for Israel to withdraw from occupied territories.

Egypt and Syria attacked Israel on Yom Kippur with 3000 tanks. Libya refused to join its Federation partners. Jordan and Iraq provided 1300 tanks and 160,000 soldiers. Saudi Arabia, Iraq, and Kuwait temporarily cut off oil shipments to the United States and Netherlands, because of their support for Israel. To counteract American support, the Soviet Union gave military aid to the Arab coalition.

Using its forces wisely, Israel first defeated Syria and then swung south to drive back the Egyptians. When the fighting ended, Israelis troops were within thirty miles of Damascus and fifty miles of Cairo. Again Israel's army had proved to be too powerful for its Arab opponents.

Muslim Rifts

Pan-Islamic unity has been a will-of-the-wisp ever since the Great Schism of 661 C.E. Extreme Muslim individualism goes back to the early nomadic tribes, each of which insisted on self-government. European imperialism in Muslim lands has caused shame and embarrassment to a once proud and independent people. Today we are witnessing an effort by Arab countries to regain their full independence. But unifying the Islamic movement has always been impossible.

In World War I the Ottoman Empire expected all of its components to support Germany. But Arabia took advantage of the situation and broke free from Ottoman rule.

To protect tiny Kuwait from attacks by Saudi Arabia, a neutral zone was set up around Kuwait in 1921. As soon as Britain granted Kuwait its complete freedom in 1961, Iraq immediately claimed Kuwait as a province. As Kuwait's oil wells made it very affluent (in 1974 Kuwait had the highest per capita GNP in the world), Arab neighbors became envious of their wealthy sister. Half of Kuwait's population consists of foreign nationals, most of whom work in the oil industry. In 1976 Kuwait nationalized Gulf Oil Corporation and the British Petroleum Company. To placate neighbors, Kuwait has contributed generously to the PLO, the two Yemens, and to any opponent of Israel.

Iraq has had constant friction with its neighbors. In 1973, when Iraq occupied a police post in Kuwait, tension mounted. That same year Iraq accused Iran of supplying arms to Kurds in northeast Iraq. The Kurds said that Iraq had reneged on a 1970 pact with them. Iraq often accuses Syria of diverting too much Euphrates water. Syria sometimes responds by closing Iraq's oil pipeline across Syria.

Efforts at Muslim Unity

In 1944 the Protocol of Alexandria created the Arab League, consisting of Egypt, Iraq, Lebanon, Palestine, Saudi Arabia, Transjordan, and Yemen. The federation was weak, since League decisions were not binding on member states.

Egypt and Iraq have longed battled over territory between them, now chiefly Jordan and Syria. In 1955 Iraq, fearful of Soviet expansion, drew up an alliance with the United States, Iran, Britain, Pakistan, and Turkey. President Nasser of Egypt opposed this Baghdad Pact, and stirred up opposition to it. In 1958 King Faisal II of Iraq and Iraqi Minister Nuri es-Said were assassinated, and Iraq withdrew from the pact, followed by Jordan and Syria. The Soviet Union sent military supplies and equipment to Egypt, as part of the Cold War.

In 1958 Egypt and Syria combined to form the United Arab Republic. When Yemen joined them the new coalition was called the United Arab States. This union was dissolved in 1961 when an army coup overthrew the Syrian government.

To offset the United Arab Republic, Iraq and Jordan in 1958 formed a union called the Arab Federation. The head of state was King Faisal II of Iraq, and his deputy was his cousin, King Hussein of Jordan. Within five months the federation was destroyed by the revolution that cost the lives of Faisal and his son, the Crown Prince.

In 1971 Egypt, Libya, and Syria announced a new union called the Triple Federation. Unity of the group was unstable, largely due to the mercurial Muammar Quaddafi of Libya. Under pressure from Quaddafi, Anwar Sadat ordered the immediate withdrawal of Soviet military advisors and pilots from Egypt.

In July 1973 the United States vetoed a U.N. Security Council resolution calling for Israel to observe Resolution #242, which required Israel to return their territories to Egypt, Jordan, and Syria. The Organization of Arab Petroleum Exporting Countries (called OAPEC and later OPEC) drew up a plan to restrict oil production progressively by 5% each month, until Israel had withdrawn to its pre-1967 boundaries, and the legal rights of the Palestinians had been restored. Oil prices rose sharply. Saudi Arabia, formerly friendly to the West, became an OAPEC leader.

Because of its oil resources, the Middle East will always be crucial to the interests of the industrial world. Persian Gulf countries have 60% of the world's proven oil reserves, with Saudi Arabia alone having 24%. Moreover, the cost of oil production in the region is very low. For example, "fewer well have been drilled in all six countries than have been drilled in the continental United States alone."[7]

The Israeli-Palestinian Conflict

Bernard Avishai, an Israeli writer, feels that modern Israel is guilty of a twofold betrayal of the cause of Zionism. For one thing, the conquest of adjacent territory, such as the West Bank and the Gaza Strip, has resulted in the Muslims becoming almost as numerous as the Jews in many parts of Israel. This vitiates the goal of a unified Jewish nation.

Avishai feels that the second betrayal of Zionism occurred when its founders, including Ben-Gurion, accepted the Halakha (the Jewish religious law) as the law of the land. Although their goal was a secular Zionist democracy, the leaders felt that they had to accept the religious law in order to escape the challenge of socialism. But now civil and political rights are subordinate to rulings of rabbinical leaders who have little use for democracy. Had the unitive influences of Kabalism and Hasidism been allowed to prevail, religion could be a factor helping ease tensions with the Palestinians. But the Middle East preference for divisive religion had once again led to discord in the Holy Land.

A more serious charge threatens Israel. A nation nurtured on scriptures advocating justice, mercy, and righteousness cannot long play the role of a hypocrite. Either it must treat its resident Palestinians more humanely, or openly disavow its own great spiritual tradition.

"During the past ten years," says Amos Elon, "two out of every five Palestinians over the age of 15 in occupied territories have been imprisoned for political reasons. Hardly a day passes without complaints of savage behavior by Israeli troops. The number of soldiers now on duty on the West Bank is said to be more than three times the number needed to conquer it during the Six-Day War. General Ephraim Snah says that in the *intifada* uprising the Palestinians have discovered the power of their weakness and the Israelis the weakness of their power."[8]

During the first year of the protest 318 Palestinians were killed and over 20,000 were wounded. Abraham Yehoshua, a leading Israeli novelist, says that he now understands how Germans could say that they never heard of concentration camps, when he sees the Jewish complacency over their own troops' atrocities. Some of the dead are children under ten and men over eighty. Pregnant women have aborted, and babies have died as a result of tear gas grenades being detonated in closed rooms.

Divisive religion continues to bear its unholy fruit. Almost every day Jerusalem sees violence. "After each incident, municipal cleaning machines, marked 'CITY OF PEACE' in 3 languages, come out to wash blood from the streets in time for the next group of pious pilgrims to pass by, fingering their rosaries and muttering solemn prayers."[9]

Efforts at Reconciliation

Rabbi Bruce Cohen runs a project called Interns for Peace. He recruits Jews and Muslims in their early 20's, teaches them each other's language, and sets up joint Muslim-Jewish education, construction, and recreation projects. Besides interschool visitation, there are joint athletic programs and summer camps. Cohen's interns find that elementary students cooperate freely with one another, but by the secondary level some hardening of attitude has already set in.

Women in Black is an organization of 400 Israeli women who protest the way Palestinians are treated. Each Friday they demonstrate in busy Tsarfat Square in Jerusalem. Clad in black, they carry signs saying, "Stop the occupation." One woman said, "I'm embarrassed as a human being by what's going on." Another remarked, "We're becoming a country of masters and second-class citizens."[10]

Founded in 1988, Physicians for Human Rights/Israel is a group of 400 Jewish doctors who go out of their way to provide medical services to Palestinians. They circumvent Israeli army roadblocks and travel on dirt roads to Palestinian villages. They bring with them nurses, a pharmacist, and prescription drugs which they distribute free to their patients. "This is my way of dealing with the Israeli-Palestinian problem," says Dr. Ayelet Shauer. "As a professional I want to send a message of peace, so that Palestinians will see that not every Israeli is a soldier at a roadblock." Dr. Daphna Shefet agrees, saying she is trying to "promote peace at the most basic personal level." Dr. Meir Liron and his colleagues sometimes refer Palestinian patients to Israeli hospitals, working with Israeli officials to procure the necessary permits.[11]

Portents for the Future

King Hussein worked hard to prevent the Persian Gulf War. He believes that Saddam Hussein would have pulled out of Kuwait, if non-Muslim nations had not entered the controversy. King Hussein visited President George H. Bush in Maine, and Saddam Hussein in Baghdad. He also tried to build Muslim coalitions, especially in North Africa, that would act to mediate the dispute, in an effort to avert war. He felt that Bush blocked his every effort for peace.

"You Americans are inconsistent," said one Jordanian leader. "You told us that in dealing with Israel we had to learn to compromise, so we did. But now you reject compromise. You told us to accept the principle of a negotiated settlement, but now you want to solve your problem with Iraq by ultimatum. You told us that we need to accept more democracy and human rights, and now you are supporting this spendthrift reactionary family that rules Kuwait. In Saudi Arabia and Kuwait, America is tying itself to the ugliest image of non-democracy in the world."[12] A majority of the exiled Palestinians are in Jordan, a country with few natural resources. It has no oil, and only 6% of its land is arable. Its only significant industry involves processing phosphates and potash from the Dead Sea. Arab states have promised to pay annual subsidies to Jordan but few have done so. One-third of Jordan's annual income comes from the 300,000 Palestinians who work in Gulf states, and send money home to their families in Jordan.

Many Palestinians earn good wages in Kuwait but feel unwelcome there. A majority in Jordan, they have helped turn Amman into a clean, well-governed city. But Sheikh Abdul Weheidi, director of a Jordanese refugee camp, says that the refugees are ready to fight against Americans. "Kuwait is an ally of Israel," he said. "Kuwait sends its money to the West, and then the Americans send it to Israel. We are not against the American people. The Americans are good people. But we are hostile to American policy."[13]

Most Arab nations are anti-Western. They feel that they have suffered under European colonialism, and had their rights denied by American, British, and French imperialism .To them the Seven Sisters (Western oil conglomerates) have been more evident than have Christian compassion and justice. They are determined to regain lost pride, at whatever the cost. One-sided application of principles can never build a new world order, they say. Why does Iraq have to obey United Nations resolutions, but not Israel?

So Much Faith, So Little Peace

Billy Graham once said that some people have such heavenly thoughts that they are no earthly good. He was not especially referring to the Holy Land. Mordecai Richler, in *This Year in Jerusalem*, describes three weekly Sabbaths wrought with tension and ill will. On Friday morning, as the muezzin calls to prayer, "fervent Hamas youngsters are sharpening their daggers in praise of Allah." Shortly before sunset, "God-crazed settlers wearing prayer shawls and with Uzis protruding from their belts, invoke Jehovah's name in their call for vengeance." On Sunday church bells summon worshippers to ask for peace. "Alas, this overwhelming religious presence has not made for Isaiah's dream of a peaceable kingdom."[14]

Chaim Herzog, president of Israel from 1983 until 1993, used the Camp David Accords between Egypt and Israel as an example of how mutual trust and sacrifice can gain peaceful goals. He stated that not a single Egyptian or Israeli soldier has been killed on the Egyptian-Israeli border since the 1979 treaty. Rather, there is an open border carrying tourists and commerce back and forth the way one would expect between friendly nations. Herzog admits that with the Palestinians there is the added problem of two groups claiming sovereignty over the same land, but he asks for more mutual trust and sacrifice from both sides.[15]

Some Israeli officials are seeking that trust and sacrifice. Carmi Gillon, director of Israel's secret service from 1994 to 1996, says that words, not bullets, must be the currency of dialogue. He states that "enduring security dialogue cannot happen without political dialogue. If there is to be a crackdown on Palestinian terrorists, Mr. Arafat must be able to demonstrate that some benefits will accrue to those not in the camp of Hamas and Islamic Jihad. The only benefits he can offer are economic progress and a peace process that is not continually side-tracked."[16]

Shimon Peres points out that it is in Israel's interest to help the Palestinians secure an effective economy. "A border cannot protect us from economic flows," he states, "because the economy is now global. Markets are more important than states. Borders can no longer stop an armed attack since they make no impression on either missiles or terrorism. Hotels on borders could be a better guarantee of peace than military bases."[17]

Like Yitzhak Rabin, recent former Israeli prime minister Ehud Barak is a victorious general who became a hard worker for peace. Deborah Sontag says that in his speeches, "Barak went out of his way to express compassion for Palestinian suffering, and to try to make Israelis see things through their eyes. He made good on the deal he signed at Sharm el-Sheik. He returned land, released prisoners, and opened a safe passage between the West Bank and Gaza. Despite his feeling of deep connection to the

Jewish people's Biblical roots in the West Bank, he sees a diplomatic imperative to return land to the Palestinians."[18]

By pulling Israeli troops out of southern Lebanon, Barak put pressure on Syria to also withdraw its forces from Lebanon. To answer Israeli critics that Barak was thereby risking Israeli security, he replied that now if there is anti-Jewish terrorism coming from Lebanon, Israel is justified in making a strong military response against the terrorists.

A strange byproduct of Barak's brave move might be an upheaval in some Muslim nations. Up to now, these states justified huge military expenditures, pointing to Israel's presence in Lebanon. With less justification for military expenses, the Arab nations may have to try to catch up with the rest of the world on a number of modern issues, such as free trade, democracy, women's rights, economic growth, and responsible citizenship in the global village. This will be a fascinating process to watch for the next several decades.

Israel as a Moral Conscience

A somewhat similar process is at work within Israel. Zionism had always assumed that Israel would be a Jewish state. But now with many non-Jews within its borders, the Jewish conscience is saying that *all* citizens of Israel, not just Jews, have civil rights and economic needs that must be addressed in a democratic nation. A change in viewpoint is inevitable. Judaism will once more be seen not merely as a survival mechanism, but as a moral conscience for the entire world community. This will enable all people to see how Judaism has the God-given authority to serve as the moral and spiritual foundation of the world's two largest spiritual communities, the Christian and the Muslim.

Unitive Religion at Work

President Jimmy Carter tells of a statement agreed to by both Menachem Begin and Anwar Sadat during the Camp David discussions. This kind of agreement, Carter feels, might be the basis for solving the thorny question of sovereignty over sacred places like Temple Mount in Jerusalem. Not made public at the time, this agreement contains a message of peace and tolerance still greatly needed. It acknowledged Jerusalem "to be holy to Islam, Judaism, and Christianity; guaranteed free access to all parts of it; permitted the holy places to be under control of their own religious representatives; and approved a municipal council with balanced representation of the inhabitants to supervise all community functions and to guarantee the integrity of the various cultural and educational institutions."[19]

Karen Armstrong relates that "Muslims have lived and worshipped in Jerusalem as long as Anglo-Saxons have been in Britain, and that it is only since 1967 that Israel has claimed exclusive control over the whole city. When the Muslims captured Jerusalem in 638, they invited the Jews to return to the holy city, and left Christian shrines and residences undisturbed. Until the Crusades, the city had a huge Christian majority, and the three religions coexisted in relative harmony. Today, Rome is the capital of two sovereign states, which live together in peace. Could this be a model for a future Jerusalem?"[20]

Like his father King Hussein, King Abdullah II of Jordan is a gifted peace negotiator. He is always fair, and he seems to genuinely like, and thus be respected by, all of the current leaders of Middle Eastern countries. Although Jordan is at present the guardian of the Muslim holy sites in Jerusalem, in a recent interview Abdullah said that "the holy sites need to be run by the three religions." Asked about Ehud Barak, Abdullah replied, "I'm very impressed by him. I have a close personal friendship with him. He's very direct, honest, and courageous." Speaking of Israel's withdrawal from southern Lebanon, Abdullah called it "a tremendous move that showed the seriousness of Israel's attitude toward the future prospects for peace." Of Syrian President Bashar Assad, Abdullah stated, "Bashar is a bright man and I have a lot of respect for him, He's been educated in the West and is very open-minded." President Clinton was viewed as a peace maker. In Abdullah's words, "The parties involved all enjoyed great confidence in Clinton, who should use his good credit to push the Palestinian and Syrian tracks along."[21]

Divisive Religion at Work

When the peace process got derailed by Yasir Arafat in 2000 and the *intifada* resumed, two nations rejoiced. Both Iran and Iraq are strongly anti-Israel, and both support terrorism to embarrass and harm Israel. Pictures of Israeli soldiers shooting young Palestinians fan the flame of Muslim hatred and vengeance.

Especially Saddam Hussein gains increasing support for keeping United Nations inspectors out of Iraq, and for lifting economic sanctions. "Syria and Iraq plan to re-open their cross-border oil pipeline, in defiance of sanctions, and Turkey has recently become the first NATO country to upgrade relations with Baghdad to ambassadorial level. Saddam Hussein has made a series of startling belligerent speeches, as he did before the invasion of Kuwait in 1990. At a recent emergency Arab summit in Cairo, Iraqi officials criticized their Arab brothers for not waging holy war against Israel." "He's trying to prove to his own population and to the Arab street that he's the only Arab standing up to the West," said Judith Yaphe, a research professor at the Israeli National Defense University.[22]

Perfecting Terrorism

Prosecutors involved in the law suit against Muslim terrorists who bombed the American embassies in Kenya and Tanzania in 1998 discovered a terrorist training manual linked to the attacks. The manual, called "Military Studies in the Jihad Against the Tyrants," has 180 pages of advice on gathering research, planning, and executing a successful terrorist mission. There are 18 lessons on a wide range of subjects, "from forgery and surveillance to advice on how to beat hostages, and detailed instructions for various assassination techniques."

Violence is recommended in order to achieve "the overthrow of the godless regimes and their replacement with an Islamic regime." The ideal follower is "one willing to undergo martyrdom for the purpose of establishing the religion of majestic Allah on earth." Hence, kidnapping and killing of opponents is encouraged, as well as blasting bridges, economic centers, and foreign embassies. Booby traps are a preferred method of killing, since they make survival of the terrorists more likely.[23]

Strangely, the United States government provides assistance to terrorists. William J. Broad states that "months into an expanded war on bioterrorism, the government is still making available to the public hundreds of formerly secret documents that tell how to turn dangerous germs into deadly weapons. For $15, anyone can buy 'Selection of Process for Freeze-Drying, Particle Size Reduction and Filling of Selected Biological Warfare Agents.' The 57-page report includes plans for a pilot factory that could produce dried germs in powder form, designed to lodge in human lungs." Another report shows how to manufacture military anthrax, and still another, 'The Stability of Botulinum Toxin,' deals with a "germ-derived substance that is the most poisonous known to science." Federal agencies routinely sell such documents over the Internet or telephone, or through the mail under the Freedom of Information Act.[24]

Suicide Bombers

Sheik Ahmed Yassin, spiritual leader of Hamas, the Islamic Resistance Movement, says that the future will be determined by suicide bombers. Scholars wonder what will happen when Muslim "martyrs" master the use of deadlier weapons, such as those employing biological, chemical, or even nuclear technology. Long decades of frustration have led Palestinian zealots to be desperate in their struggle for a homeland.

Muslim warriors are promised rich rewards if they die a martyr's death. "In some versions the delights include the sweetest of wines and unlimited sex with 72 virgins, lovely as rubies, with complexions like diamonds and pearls." Little mention is made of the fact that with each use of violence, Israel responds by electing more conservative leaders, like Ariel Sharon, those who are adamant against granting lands or rights to Palestinians.[25]

What of the Future?

The Middle East continues to be filled with promises and portents. There is probably no other spot on the globe where religion, which could do so much for world peace, actually accomplishes so little. It is a textbook area for demonstrating the difference between divisive and unitive religion. Divisive religion says, "I will hold onto my own narrow concept of God, no matter how many people will be killed as a result." Unitive religion says, "You have as much right to your concept of God as I have to mine. If we both love each other, despite having differing religious beliefs, maybe that's what God had in mind for us all along." If we are ever to have a just and lasting world peace, it is obvious that unitive religion will have to replace divisive religion in most places in the world, and especially in stifling volcanoes of religious intolerance, hatred, and terrorism like the Middle East.

Olive Trees for Peace

Hope is a survival emotion for our species. A group of over 400 rabbis and other Jewish spiritual leaders recently issued a call for the replanting of olive trees in a number of Palestinian towns. They recall the words of the Torah: "Even if you are at war with a city, you must not destroy its trees" (Deuteronomy 20:19–20). Some of the destroyed trees were hundreds of years old, having provided a livelihood for the residents. "Each one of them paid the cost of year after year of schooling for a child, or a dowry for a girl about to be married." Additionally, the statement said, "Anyone who cares about Israeli lives should demand the end of the dangerous settlement of Israelis within the West Bank and the Gaza Strip, for they put Israeli soldiers at totally unnecessary risk. The Jewish settlers should be given the compassionate and honorable choice either to come home to Israel, or to live as citizens of Palestine under Palestinian law. And Palestinians living in East Jerusalem should be given the right to elect their own leaders." The closing message from the Torah described Israel as "A Tree of Life she is, for those who hold her close—a Tree of Life, for Shalom."[26]

REFERENCES

[1] Quoted in Richard Allen, *Imperialism and Nationalism in the Fertile Crescent* (Oxford University Press, 1974), p. 89.

[2] Ibid., pp. 245, 246.

[3] William Pfaff, *New Yorker*, 28 January 1991, p. 88.

[4] John K. Cooley, *Baal, Christ, and Mohammed* (Holt, Rinehart, & Winston), 1965), p. 333.

[5] Ibid., p. 314.

[6] Allen, p. 420.

[7] Marvin Zonis, *University of Chicago Magazine*, Fall 1986, p. 29.

[8] Amos Elon, *New Yorker*, 13 February 1989, pp. 76–78.

[9] Ibid., 24 December 1990, p. 81.

[10] Martha McGaw, *St. Anthony Messenger*, May 1990, p. 24.

[11] Joel Greenberg, *New York Times*, 20 January 2002, p. 4.

[12] Milton Viorst, *New Yorker*, 7 January 1991, pp. 45, 46.

[13] Ibid., p. 36.

[14] *New York Times Book Review*, 13 November 1994, p. 64.

[15] *New York Times*, 12 September 1993, 4:19.

[16] Ibid., 17 August 1997, 4:15.

[17] *World Press Review*, July 1998, p. 47.

[18] *New York Times Magazine*, 19 December 1999, p. 86.

[19] *New York Times*, 6 August 2000, 4:15.

[20] Ibid., 16 July 2000, 4:15.

[21] Lally Weymouth, *Newsweek*, 12 June 2000, p. 45.

[22] Elaine Sciolino, *New York Times*, 5 November 2000, p. 3.

[23] Benjamin Weiser, ibid., 8 April 2001, 4:7.

[24] William J. Broad., *New York Times*, 13 January 2002, pp. 1. 13.

[25] John F. Burns, ibid., 1 April 2001, 4:5.

[26] *New York Times*, 8 April 2001, p. 16.

Chapter XI

The Divine Feminine

Many people believe that women will continue to be regarded as second-class citizens worldwide as long as almost all existing deity images are conceived of as masculine. It is divisive religion to assume that God would prefer one half of God's creation over the other half.

In Genesis human beings are said to be created, male and female, in God's image. Our species worshipped the Great Goddess, in a remarkably peaceful era, at least five times as long as we have worshipped the male deities.

"Outside mainstream Western culture and the Islamic world, female deities are still worshipped about everywhere," says Elinor Gadon. "Some, like the Hindu Devi, are believed to be the godhead itself."[1] Gadon believes that the death blow to Goddess culture in the western world and Islam came when monotheism, governed by an all-powerful male deity, was reputed to rule both the heavens and the earth.

In a letter to the editor of the *New York Times* on 31 December 2000, Carolyn Nash, executive director of Sanctuary for Families, said, "The practices of female infanticide in China, genital mutilation in Africa, and kerosene burning and honor killing in India are each essentially about the control of women in all aspects of their lives. Such criminal acts may indeed have deep cultural roots, but are perpetuated today by a lack of government intervention. Sadly, the same elements of control and domination play major roles in the often lethal incidents of domestic violence inflicted on countless women in the United States."

Every human being is born of a woman. As men's nipples testify, at conception all human embryos are designed to become feminine. "Without testosterone," says Andrew Sullivan, "humans will always revert to the default sex, which is female." Despite the Genesis story saying that Eve came from Adam's rib, "it isn't women who are made out of men. It is men who are made out of women."

"Without testosterone we would all be female," writes Derek Bickerton. "A trigger gene on the Y chromosome produces the hormone, causing gonads that would otherwise be ovaries to turn into testes." Both sexes have testosterone, but males have more. "Testosterone may have more influence on aggression and the drive for dominance. Higher testosterone levels are statistically linked to 'rambunctious' behavior: any activity, from careless smoking to mayhem or murder, that defies social norms. The ill effects of excessive testosterone can be reduced by loving families, good schools, and stable communities."[2]

Monica Sjöö and Barbara Mor state that "the female X chromosome is three to four times longer than the male Y chromosome. It carries the overwhelming preponderance of critical genetic information unrelated to sex needed to create a human being."

"In recent years," says Christine Downing, "many women have discovered how much we need the goddess in a culture that tears us from women, from ourselves. To be fed only male images of the divine is to be badly malnourished. We are starved for images that recognize the sacredness of the feminine and the complexity, richness, and nurturing power of female energy. We hunger for images of human creativity and love inspired by the capacity of female bodies to give birth and nourish."[3]

Sandra Schneiders states that an inadequate self-image distorts a person. Carl Jung said that all males have a female principle (called the anima) and all women have a male principle (called the animus). A balanced personality is one in which the two principles, far from being at war, instead complement each other to produce an aware and self-reliant person.

Men need to reject unbridled patriarchy, and avoid the language and deeds of male chauvinism. Women, in return, need to accept men as equals. Women should be willing to reject all assumptions of inferiority or superiority with regard to men. As in a successful family, woman and man should be loving and cooperating members of a team of equals.

Because of women's long-term treatment as inferior to men, says Diane Tennis, it is necessary to restore the divine feminine. "The image of the female God makes women fully human, which in turn promotes the equality of the sexes," Tennis feels. "The presence of feminine divinity in the tradition helps legitimate that tradition as credible religion."[4]

Rosemary Radford Ruether also insists on the full humanity of women. "Whatever diminishes or denies the full humanity of women must be presumed not to reflect the divine. Patriarchy itself must fall under the Biblical denunciations of idolatry and blasphemy, the idolizing the male as representative of divinity. It is 'idolatrous' to make males more 'like God' than females." This kind of reconsideration is nothing new, asserts Ruether. For example, although the Torah is considered to be scripture by many Christians, hardly any of them practice the rituals described in Deuteronomy. Likewise, texts in both testaments that supported slavery are no longer considered to be scriptural by most Christians and Jews. Ruether says that "feminism claims that *women too* are among the oppressed whom God comes to vindicate and liberate."[5]

Karen Armstrong casts light on the concept of the feminine divine. She states that in Arabia the name of the divine essence of God, *al Dhat*, is feminine. In the trinity proposed by Plotinus, the One is impersonal, the Mind is male, and the Soul is feminine. She quotes the Kabalist Isaac Luria as stating that the mating of God's male and female aspects would restore order to the universe. Both Kabalists and mystical Muslim Sufis, she says, have long tried to introduce a feminine element into the divine.

Edward Hoffman cites the Kabalist *Zohar* as recommending that each person, in order to be an integrated personality, should permit equal stress from that person's masculine and feminine components. Each Sabbath morning, says Hoffman, Luria and his followers would dress in white garments, waiting to receive the spirit of the Shekhinah, the "Sabbath Queen."

Many women, not to mention some men, want to be able to pray to God the Mother, says Denise Carmody. "The way that we pray is the most crucial index of our actual religious beliefs. Thus, religious feminists should urge women to seize the fullest freedom in their prayer, and to take the greatest responsibility." What would a feminist prayer be like? Carmody answers that it would be like the expression of emotion of a child who feels beloved by a splendid parent.[6]

The Plague of Patriarchy

There can be no world peace without justice. When half of the world's people are considered to be inferior, peace is a delusion. The size of one's biceps is a wholly inadequate measure of human worth. Male chauvinism is an atavistic survival of the crude assumption that might makes right. It is hard to conceive of a God who would want one half of human creation (either half) to be considered inferior to the other half. Equality of the sexes, especially in the spiritual dimension, is an obvious necessity. Since men wrote the original scriptures, they took the liberty of asserting that all deity images are masculine. Jean Jacques Rousseau, the famous champion of liberty, told woman how to fulfill her nature: "She should early learn to submit to injustice, and suffer the wrongs inflicted on her by her husband without complaint."

United Nations Secretary General Kurt Waldheim, in his Official Report to the U.N. Commission on the Status of Women in 1982, said: "While women represent 1/2 of the global population and 1/3 of the labor force, they receive only 1/10 of the world income and own less than 1% of the world's property, despite producing 2/3 of all the working hours on earth." In *The Anatomy of Freedom*, Robin Freeman says that over 90% of refugees are women and children.

In her book *Sex and Power* Susan Estrich points out that 497 of the Fortune 500 chief executives are men, and that there are only 63 women among America's top 2500 executives. Obviously the current system is not working and will have to be modified. This book provides guidelines on how to make giant strides towards a world of equality, justice, and peace.

Early Patriarchy

Nancy Schuster Barnes finds evidence of patriarchy in early Buddhism. Some Buddhist texts say that a woman cannot be a Buddha or a bodhisattva. Some even allege that a woman is a man whose poor karma led to this type of punishment in his reincarnation! Other texts assert that the only chance for a woman to be a Buddha would be for her to change her sex.

"Sumer began as a Goddess-oriented agricultural village," state Sjöö and Mor, but it ended as a triumph for patriarchal gods. "Tribes of Amazons in Syria, Thrace, Africa, and Macedonia fought to preserve their matriarchal religion and culture," but their defeat marked the start of a long male God reign.[7]

William Irwin Thompson says that Mesolithic society saw the domestication of animals, Neolithic society the domestication of plants, "but what the age after the Neolithic sees is the domestication of women by men."

In Akkadia, "in the period of the first Semitic kings, about 2500 B.C.E., the older Neolithic and Bronze Age mythologies of the Goddess Mother of the universe, in whom all things have their being, gods and men, plants, animals, and inanimate objects, and whose cosmic body itself is the enclosing sphere of space-time, were suppressed, and set aside in favor of the male-oriented patriarchal mythologies of thunder-hurling warrior gods. By the time 1000 years had passed, about 1500 B.C.E., they had become the dominant deities of the Near East."[8]

"As the Iron Age began, the first implements constructed by the male metallurgists were war weapons. As Margaret Mead and others have shown, the more warlike and authoritarian a society is, the stronger is its menstrual taboo. Warlike male societies are in rivalry with women over which sex sheds the most sacred blood. War is men's response to women's ability to give birth and to menstruate; all three are bloodshedding rituals. Women's blood rites, however, give life, while men's bloody rituals give only death. To compensate for this, authoritarian societies culturally repress women's blood functions, while elevating murderous war to a holy act."[9]

Early women were gatherers and gardeners, while men were herders and hunters. "It is possible that the social origins of male monotheism lie in nomadic herding societies. These cultures lacked the female gardening role, and tended to image God as the Sky-Father." As male monotheism developed, men were seen as God's "sons," and women as men's servants. In the New Testament, Paul says that "a man ought not to cover his head, since he is the image and glory of God, but the woman is the glory of man" (I Cor. 11:7). Here man is depicted as God's superior spiritual vessel, and woman as the inferior material vessel.[10]

"The few can rule the many only with the help of punitive religious ideologies. And so this new male God must be enforced on the people by the guilt-projecting ideologies of a privileged priesthood." Thus we get the Original Sin doctrine, with Eve as the villain. "Now the primary relation is not that we share the same divine substance, but that we share the same material corruption. Matter is now the stupid female. In Muslim and Christian doctrine, matter has become inert, demonized, and hostile to spirit. It is the female world, as opposed to the divine spirit heaven, that males are born to inherit."[11]

Hebrew Patriarchy

Capitalism came from Latin *caput* (head, of cattle). Men were cattle herders, and the more cattle, the more wealth. Cattle stealing was the first organized warfare. In warfare, men prayed to a male war god for victory—and soon women became war booty!

In Numbers 31:15 Moses bawls out his military commanders for having spared the lives of the captured Midianite women. He tells them: "Kill all the male children. Kill also the women who have slept with a man. Spare only the lives of the young girls who have not slept with a man, and save them for yourselves" (verse 17). Then, "the spoils, the remainder of the booty captured by the soldiers, included sheep, cattle, donkeys, and 32,000 women who had never slept with a man" (verses 32–34).

In Deuteronomy Yahweh gives permission for Israelite soldiers to marry beautiful captive women (21:11). "Then, if you have no delight in her, let her go where she will. Do not sell her for money, since you have humiliated her" (21:14). In Exodus 19:15 Jewish men about to receive the covenant are warned not to touch a woman, lest they be defiled. If a married Jewish city woman was raped, she was killed (Deut. 22:23–24). Merlin Stone suggests that Jewish circumcision may have been a test to ensure that Yahweh had qualified male priests, and not eunuchs who had once served the goddess. Often Yahweh, through prophets, calls Israel a whore or a harlot, but never an immoral man. Criticizing Israelites, Yahweh states: "To me, their conduct was as unclean as a woman's menstruation" (Ez. 36:17).

Mary Dale concludes that as men's property, Jewish women had no rights. The assumption seemed to be, "If God is male, then male is God." Sandra Schneiders says the emerging masculine image of the deity in the Torah helped solidify patriarchy: As God the Father, Yahweh seemed to prefer men to women. Obviously a parent who prefers some children over others will ultimately lose the respect of all the children, especially as the deity image. It should be pointed out that, as the Torah evolved, the Father image showed many desirable "feminine" traits.

Muslim Patriarchy

"In Arabia of the seventh century Mohammed brought an end to the national worship of the Sun Goddess, Al Lat, and the Goddess known as Al Uzza. In the Koran, *sura* 4:31 states that 'men have authority over women because God has made the one superior to the other, and because they spend their wealth to maintain them.' Mohammed said, 'When Eve was created, Satan rejoiced.'"[12]

Christian Patriarchy

Nicholas King says that women have suffered, sometimes gravely, because of patriarchal passages in the New Testament. He cites the books of Colossians, Ephesians, Timothy, and Titus as containing especially derogatory statements about women.

"The figure of Divine Wisdom in Proverbs 8 and in The Wisdom of Solomon," says Ruether, "is theologically identical to what the New Testament describes as the *Logos* or 'Son of God.'" But Christianity, she says, "chooses the male symbol for this idea," rather than the female Divine Wisdom. "Males project onto women their own rejection of their 'lower selves,'" Ruether states, adding that "Augustine declared that women bear God's image only when they are joined to men, but men bear it apart from women."[13] Denise Carmody sees Church Fathers like Augustine, Chrysostom, Jerome, and Tertullian as clearly misogynistic. Aquinas, she says, follows Aristotle in considering a woman as a "misbegotten male."

"Every woman should be overwhelmed with shame at the very thought she is a woman," declared St. Clement. "The Ecumenical Council at Macon in 900 decided by only a one vote margin that women had souls."[14] St. Bernard of Clairvaux warned his monks that "to live with a woman without incurring danger is more difficult than to resuscitate the dead." Among the Church Fathers there were suggestions that "in the resurrection of the dead, the female body will be transformed into that of a male."[15]

Medieval Patriarchy

In medieval Europe the Roman Catholic Church ruled it a crime against God for a woman to have a miscarriage, even after a fall or an accident. In some cases the woman was put to death for such a "crime."[16]

The witch hunts were a continuation of the suppression of the ancient Goddess religion. The chief charge against witches was insubordination. Ann Hibbens was executed as a witch for protesting a carpentry contract. Joan of Arc's judges said, "Though Joan had recanted and been received into the Church, the moment she put on male attire she was doomed on that account only." "She was killed in the most horrible way—burned alive—whereas her lieutenant Gilles de Rais, was granted the mercy of strangulation before burning."[17]

The Reformation

By no means did the Reformation liberate women. As nation states arose, women almost universally were not given citizenship rights, such as the right to vote. Martin Luther said that woman started out originally as man's equal, but through Eve's fall into sin, woman is now subordinate to man: "The rule remains with the husband, and the wife is compelled to obey him by God's command. The woman is like a nail driven into the wall. The wife should stay home and look after household affairs, as one who has been deprived of the ability to administer those affairs that are outside and concern the state. In this way Eve is punished."[18] Luther added, "If a woman grows weary and at last dies from childbearing, it matters not. Let her die from bearing, she is there to do it."[19]

John Calvin said that to keep down sin, men should rule their wives. The Puritans agreed that women should be docile helpmates to their husbands. William Perkins found women to blame in *The Damned Art of Witchcraft*, published in 1596. When the Roman Catholic Church burned persons (chiefly women) as witches, the church acquired the alleged witch's property. Similarly, in the suttee custom in Hinduism, when the woman was burned on her husband's funeral pyre, the Brahmin priesthood inherited all of the couple's worldly goods.

Women's Rights

As women struggled to get the right to vote, fundamentalists quoted Bible passages declaring women to be defective. Women still cannot be ordained as full clergy in at least five prominent religious groups: The Church of Jesus Christ of Latter-Day Saints, Orthodox Christianity, Orthodox Judaism, the Roman Catholic Church, and the Southern Baptist Convention. If women are men's spiritual equals, they deserve full ordination. "The broader the pool of talent, experience, insight, and gifts of the Spirit, the better the churches are likely to fare. For too long in their history most Christian churches limped along on the talent of only half their members."[20] Some churches further limit that talent pool by saying only celibate men can be priests.

Recent Violence Against Women

In 1999 Secretary of State Madeleine Albright convened a meeting of ten foreign ministers, all women, to draw up a protest against mistreatment of women. Their letter, addressed to the United Nations, said: "It is unacceptable that human beings around the world are sold into situations such as sexual exploitation, domestic servitude, and debt bondage that are little different from slavery." They asked the United Nations to add a prohibition of human trafficking to the list of forbidden actions drawn up by a convention on international organized crime control.

In 1996 an informal group of Muslim women worldwide published a manual *Claiming Our Rights: A Manual for Women's Human Rights Education in Muslim Societies*. The goal is to facilitate discussion on how Muslim women can protect their human rights. This is indeed a problem area. "In Egypt today under the law a man may take four wives. A girl may be married off by her father without her consent. No woman may petition for divorce. A man may obtain a divorce by the simple act of repudiation. A woman has no right of custody of her children. A husband need not pay alimony or child support if his wife has withheld herself sexually. A husband has the right to forbid a wife to work or travel or even to move freely in her own environment. A husband has the right to have his wife returned to his home if she has left it without his consent."[21]

Zazi Sadou, a veteran journalist in Algiers, describes "the murderous rampages in the name of God" that have occurred in Algiers since the military government voided elections in 1992. "The violence has been so barbaric that it is taking the shape of genocide. These are crimes against humanity," committed by an Islamic terrorist group, the Armed Islamic Group, Sadou said. Girls whose skirts are considered too short have their legs burned with acid. "In these attacks 150 terrorists might divide up their tasks. One group would do the killing, the beheading. Another would choose the most beautiful women to take with them. And a third group would make sure no one would flee from the village. Women are seen as devils. We are the permanent enemies," Sadou stated. It is estimated that 60,000 persons, many of them women and children, have been killed in violent clashes between 1992 and 1997.[22]

"In a drive to restore 12th century Islamic fundamentalism, the Taliban has launched the greatest assault on womanhood in a millennium," writes Maggie O'Kane, who calls this the "ethnic cleansing" of an entire gender within Afghanistan. Ten million women have been denied education, work, and hospital care. A couple found in adultery was punished. "What do you prove by burying a man and a woman in the ground up to their necks and then crushing their skulls with stones?" the military commander was asked. "Nothing special," he replied. "It is the law of God." A man and his wife were riding a bicycle. A Taliban commander said that her ankles were exposed. "I will deal with this shameless woman," he said. He then shot the husband in the foot and the woman straight in the heart.[23]

One Afghan woman, under the alias of Saba, explains how the RAWA (Revolutionary Association of the Women of Afghanistan) try to achieve human rights for all Afghans, but only under threat of death. "If the Taliban caught me inside Afghanistan,"

Saba said, "they would definitely torture and kill me, stoning me as an alleged prostitute. The punishment has already been decreed. But I'm ready—it will be a prouder death than from some natural cause."[24]

Second-Class Citizens

It is not only in Islam where women are considered to be second-class citizens. The Fourth U.N. Conference on Women in 1995 found that "family violence is epidemic in most societies around the world. It is clear that one of the most dangerous places for a woman is in her own home." Men commit 89% of all violent crimes. Neil Jacobson, author of a book on why men batter women, says, "I'm absolutely convinced that if we didn't have a legacy of patriarchy, there wouldn't be domestic violence." Kathleen Fischer adds that "patriarchy is founded on the conviction that this system of dominance and subordination was ordained by God as the order of creation. We must ask, 'Who is Eve?'"[25]

Patriarchy's Effect Upon Religion

What is the effect of the patriarchal approach to religion? First, it has clearly resulted in gross mistreatment of women, even inventing unjust theologies to perpetuate the dangerous dogma that might makes right. Second, our whole human race has suffered by being deprived of much of the creativity, knowledge, wisdom, and goodness of half of the human population. Finally, by propagating a hidden agenda that male is good and female is bad, it manufactures tidal waves of ignorance, injustice, cruelty, and war that moves us ever farther away from our most treasured goals of peace, love, tolerance, and respect for the sacred dignity of every single person on our planet.

A word of caution is timely. Radical feminists like Mary Daly postulate a matriarchy which would have many of the evils of the current patriarchy, except with reversed roles. This is no solution to the present problem. Loss of worship of the Great Goddess occurred partly because too many persons suffered unjust cruelty or death. Feminist extremists today often speak in absolutist terms that harbor hatred and warlike overtones. For example, such people fail to compliment the countless millions of men who are kind and loving to their wives, children, and other persons. They ignore the divine gentleness of Jesus Christ. They neglect to show how the compassionate Gautama Buddha has brought great mercy to millions of human beings. They do not acknowledge that while the Jewish people were refining their concept of Yahweh from a tribal war god to a universal deity of justice and righteousness, they were contributing importantly to the establishment of a world of peace and international understanding. They look past the fact that each *sura* of the Koran is addressed in the name of God, "the Merciful, the Compassionate."

Humanity needs not to eliminate the masculine element of divinity but to remarry it to the feminine element of divinity. When the Shekhinah returns from her exile and once more consorts with the masculine Crown, as the Kabala describes it, then indeed we will be prepared for the coming of God's kingdom of peace, of love, of light.

Early Goddess Concepts

As a prelude to suggestions for restoring the Divine Feminine in world theology, let us examine some of the early goddess concepts.

The Great Goddess in Hinduism could, like Vishnu and Shiva, be seen as a supreme deity who creates, preserves, destroys, and battles demons to defend *dharma,* the body of cosmic principles by which all things exist. In some regions, such as Bengal, the Goddess even dominated. Hinduism also had many independent women, including Tantras, bhakti saints, and devidasis, women who sing and dance for God. Nevertheless, despite the fact that the 1947 constitution gave women equal rights, Hindu women still encounter much discrimination, and still are in general not allowed to become Hindu priests.

In China women were treated better than in India. Confucianism, although somewhat patriarchal, offered a spiritual basis for human rights by asserting that *all* life is precious, that human beings should see themselves as part of a greater whole (the family), and that cosmic order can be achieved only through family order. In China some Buddhist nuns became great scholars, and others have become Zen masters. A bodhisattva is someone who has achieved enlightenment but postpones going to nirvana in order to help others achieve enlightenment. Female bodhisattvas and goddesses are very popular in Tibet and in other parts of east Asia. Kwan-yin, the Buddhist Goddess of mercy, is still worshipped in China.

Unlike most world religions, Taoism has always shown great respect for the divine feminine. Taoists speak of The Mysterious Female as a symbol of cosmic power, and they say that the Great Mother is a symbol of the Tao (the Way). Taoists believe that the proper way for all humans to live is the female submissive way. Taoists advocate *wu-wei* (let it be) as a universal principle. Forget resistance—remember that water wears down mountains.

A balanced life shows equal force from the Yin (female) and Yang (male) components. Women can be Tao masters, and many male Tao leaders have been influenced by women shamans. The Jade Mother of Divine Mystery, they say, gave birth to Lao Tzu, who created the world. Since "pregnancy is a basic Taoist model for attaining immortality, males must become females, at least metaphorically, to achieve their goal of deathlessness."[26]

Some of the many early Chinese goddesses were creators. Others were nature deities affiliated with heavenly bodies or natural events like rain and lightning. It is said that the Empress of Heaven promises special protection to sailors, and the Sacred Mother gives special care to women and children.

Christianity will be discussed later in connection with Jesus and Mary. Here it can be recognized that some of the early Christian "heresies" treated men and women alike. Montanism allowed women to be not only ministers but also prophets. Some forms of Gnosticism gave women privileged relationship to the divine Sophia. In the 18th and 19th centuries certain Utopian societies, like the Shakers, asserted the androgyny of God. They felt that "the Messiah must appear in female form as well as male. The messianic community must also reflect this parity of male and female in its organizational structure."[27]

Creation Stories

"The oldest cosmogonies, like the oldest worship of concretely represented deities, typically start with a primal goddess, out of whose body the earth was born."[28] "We can speak of the root human image of the divine as the Primal Matrix, the great womb within which all things, Gods and humans, sky and earth, and nonhuman beings, are generated. It survives in the metaphor of the divine as Ground of Being."[29]

Sumer and Babylon

In early Sumer and Babylon, male and female deities shared powers. In one widespread myth, the dying and rising God/king is rescued by and married to the Goddess. Thus the female supremacy continues from the early Great Goddess period. A second myth is the defeat of the old Goddess (now representing Chaos) by the younger warrior God—for example, the defeat of Tiamat by Marduk. "Tiamat is the primal womb impregnated by Apsu, her consort, out of which emerged all beings, Gods and humans." Having defeated Tiamat, Marduk "fashioned the cosmos out of the body of Tiamat," and created humans to be servants to the Gods. Strangely, both myths were used together, one showing the female deity triumphant, and the other indicating the male as winner. Each victor is allegedly restoring order out of chaos, thus explaining relief from problems like drought or defeat by an enemy.[30]

"Babylon was built above the 'Gate of Apsu,' the serpent waters before creation, Apsu being the other half of Tiamat. Everywhere this mythic rite of building the holy male city on the conquered body of the Mother-Serpent is enacted as the origin of patriarchy. In Hebrew Genesis, the serpent is doomed by the war God Yahweh to be forever the enemy of the human race."[31]

"Patriarchy's inaugural epics and myths, from the Mahabarata of Vedic India to the Greek Iliad to the Heroic Age epics of the Hebrews, Teutonic, and Celtic peoples are all the same: an endless glorification of war. Everywhere they settled, the Indo-Europeans established themselves as a priestly, intellectual, and warrior elite. The conquered did the work." Racist theories, equating women with darkness and sin, espoused the Aryans as male masters of the former Goddess worshippers.[32]

Hindu Creation Myths

One Hindu creation myth tells of the Aryan Sky God Indra decapitating the Goddess Danu and her son Vrta, thus starting the act of the creation of the universe. Heinrich Zimmer provides a poetic description of the Hindu concept of creation. He says: "Maya-Shakti is personified as the world-protecting, feminine, maternal side of the Ultimate Being, and as such, stands for the spontaneous, loving acceptance of life's tangible reality. She is the creative joy of life. She is Eve, The Eternal Feminine, *das Ewig-Weibliche.* Having mothered the universe, Maya then immediately muffles consciousness within the wrappings of her perishable production.

This mother of the world was actually supreme in India long before the arrival of the conquerors of the north." When they came, they replaced her with their patriarchal gods. "Nevertheless, in the hearts of the native population she gradually returned to her position of honor. She is visible everywhere in the monuments of early Buddhist art, and in the works of the classical period she stands triumphant on every side. Today she is the greatest person in the Orient." Her sign is the lotus. Often even male deities copy her poses. "In India she appears as *Padmapani* ("lotus in hand"), the greatest of the bodhisattvas. In China she is called Kwan-yin and in Japan Kwannon. She is the most spiritual feminine symbol in Eastern iconographies. She is the very meaning, the very truth, of Buddhist law. Also, she is the Buddhist version of Sophia, the mother of enlightening knowledge. All of us are brought forth from the divine creative essence, as virtually parts of the Highest Being. This concept is insisted upon in later Hinduism and Buddhism."[33]

Divine Father and Mother

In some forms of Hinduism Shiva and his consort Goddess Shakti are envisioned as the original Divine Couple. "Their Sacred Marriage is variously figured in many traditions of world mythology. They are the Archetypal Parents, Father and Mother of the world. Under the form of Father Heaven and Mother Earth they were known to the Greeks as Zeus and Hera, or Uranos and Gaia, and to the Chinese as T'ien and Ti, Yang and Yin. The God and Goddess are the first self-revelation of the Absolute, the male being the personification of the passive aspect which we know as Eternity, the female of the activating energy Shakti, the dynamism of Time. Though apparently opposites, they are in essence one. They represent the polar aspects of the one essence and thus cannot be at variance."[34]

Divine Play

Some Hindu creation myths see the origin of the universe as the result of *lila*, the play of the Gods. "The Nobel prize winner for Biology Manfred Eigen and Ruthild Winkler in their book *The Game* (1975) point to the variables that govern the course of natural and human history, as they show that humans did not invent play. Play is a phenomenon of nature that has guided the evolution of the world from the very beginning." Christian theologians like Hugo Rahner and Jurgen Moltmann use this symbolism also. "Humans are seen, not as God's toys, but as God's free partners in the great game of creation."[35] Hasidic mystics describe a rabbi's grandson disconsolate because no one sought him when he hid. "Now," says the rabbi, "I finally understand the search for God. Let's play hide and seek, and have some fun." A Sufi saying is:

> To play at Love the better with Himself
> He put on separate masks of man and wife.

In the Upanishads we read:

> Lonely He felt, and all unsatisfied;
> So into Two He did divide Himself,
> To have a Playmate; Man and Wife He was,
> All wishes of each other they fulfill.

Thomas Matus says that "we work to achieve a purpose, but we play to arrive at meaning." A Muslim statement attributed to Allah states, "I was a hidden treasure, and so in order to be found, I created a world." Fritjof Capra finds a spiritual truth in scientific theories. He says that Geoffrey Chew's bootstrap theory shows that nature cannot be analyzed down to any primary physical entities. Matus concludes that religion and science concur that objective reality is illusory, and thus one now says, "I belong to the whole universe, a vital part of the living cosmos."[36]

Celtic Creation Story

"In West Munster, the life spark was believed to be governed by the Goddess Aine. She has been identified with Anu, the Great Mother ancestor of the Danann gods. Among herbalists and faith healers, Aine was responsible for the vital spark of life which they felt traversed the entire body every 24 hours. Anu is the Source-Mother of the gods, a figure so ancient that she is the womb of life, the high One herself." Her name means "pleasure" or "melody," and it is through her that we find life's meaning.[37]

Japanese Creation Myths

"The central myth is solar, built around the Sun Goddess, who was the tutelary deity of the Yamato clan which first unified the Japanese islands. The early primacy of the Yamato clan meant that throughout Japanese history the Sun Goddess is the head of the gods." A brother and sister pair of gods, male Izanagi and female Izanami, created the first land. "Izanami produced deities, including the eight islands of Japan and the divinities of the earth, sea, seasons, wind, trees, mountains, and moors." Then Izanagi produced many deities. "From his left eye was born the Sun Goddess Amaterasu (Heaven Shining), who ruled over the plain of High Heaven." One of her descendants was Jimmu, the legendary founder of Japan.[38]

Philo

Philo was a first century C.E. Hellenistic Jewish philosopher. This is how he describes creation: "The Architect who made this universe was at the same time the father of what was born, while its mother was the Knowledge possessed by its Maker. With His Knowledge God had union, not as men have it, and begot created things. And Knowledge, having received the divine seed, when her travail was consummated, bore the only beloved son who is apprehended by the senses, the world which we see. Wisdom said, 'God obtained me first of all his works and founded me before the ages' (Proverbs 8:22). True, for it was necessary that all that came to the birth of creation should be younger than the mother and nurse of all." In the words of Raphael Patai, "God has thus two aspects: God the Father (the Creator, full of Reason and Goodness) and God the Mother (the Bearer and Nurturer, full of Wisdom and Sovereignty)."[39]

The Kabala Cosmogony

Like many cosmogonies, the Kabala's states that sexual union between Father-God and Mother-Goddess created the births of Heaven and Earth, also called Son (King) and Daughter

(Matronit). Son and Daughter married (on high there is no incest), but their marriage was a stormy one. When Israel sinned, the Matronit (or Shekhinah) went into exile, leaving the King powerless without her. The Jewish people are so family minded that they could not imagine an aloof single God—hence, the divine tetrad. A Jewish son is expected to marry and have a son and a daughter, imitating the divine family. Moses de Leon, who wrote the kabalistic *Zohar*, may have been influenced by Hebrew family-god beliefs.[40]

Early Goddess Figures

"God was female for at least the first 200,000 years of human life. This is a conservative estimate," say Sjöö and Mor. "In the world's oldest creation myths, the female god creates the world out of her own body. The Great Mother everywhere was the autonomous creatrix of the world." In India natives called Mount Everest the "Mother Mountain of the Universe."[41]

The earliest human societal progress, in such areas as agriculture, law, medicine, wisdom, and writing, occurred under the Great Goddess, who was supreme in, among other places, Arabia, Crete, Egypt, India, Mesopotamia, Micronesia, Sumer, Turkey, and Hittite lands.

In the Late Paleolithic Age, the Goddess was "ultimately one supreme reality. In the Neolithic Age the religion of the Goddess flowered. It was earth-centered, body-affirming, and holistic. The Goddess was immanent, within every human being, not transcendent. The religious quest was above all for regeneration of life, and the Goddess was the life force." Only when the patriarchal Aryans overthrew the Goddess culture and replaced Her with their sky-gods, was she fractured into many goddesses, "each with an all-too-human personality."[42]

William Irwin Thompson says that "woman was the first to notice a correspondence between an internal process she was going through and an external process in nature. Women were the first observers of the periodicity of nature, upon which scientific research is made." Sjöö and Mor state that "the mystery of earthly life has its origins in water. Before a child is born, water flows out of the womb-ocean within the mother." The cave, home of early humans, was a symbol of the vulva. So was the labyrinth, a design found throughout early religion. Part of the midwife's job was to predict the date of the baby's birth. Lunar calendars and lunar sticks were also used. "Priests and shamans must always dress as women to take on women's original magic."[43]

"Ritual dances, such as those performed by the Hopis, the Hasidim, and the dervishes, are efforts to introject or pull down the Godhead to the human sphere. The serpent was a symbol of eternal life, for it would shed its skin each year, and appear to be reborn. In another context, the serpent came to symbolize the phallus. We can learn from some modern cultures, such as the Native American and the Hindu Indian, clues to the earlier veneration of the feminine. The word 'ritual' comes from *rtu*, Sanskrit for menses. Menses, literally month, is from the Latin. The earliest rituals were connected to the women's monthly bleeding."[44] Mircea Eliade speaks of a "primary intuition of the earth as a 'religious' form." To all primal people the earth was considered to be "the source of nourishment, protection, and mystery of cyclic recurrence."[45]

Archeological Evidence

"Nearly 200 female figures have been found at dwelling sites all across Eurasia from the Pyrenees to Lake Baikal." The Earth Mother of Willendorf, Austria, dates from 30,000–25,000 B.C.E. "Nowhere in Neolithic Goddess culture is there any sign of warfare. There is no evidence of fortifications, invasion, conquest, or violent death."[46]

Catal Huyuk, in Anatolia, is the most important site in the Near East. Large images of the Goddess celebrate her powers as life giver and life taker. She is "the fountainhead of regeneration." She is seen as a Triple Goddess: young maiden, birthgiving mother, and wise old crone. Barbara Walker states that "because it was believed that women became very wise when they no longer shed the lunar wise blood, the Crone was usually a Goddess of Wisdom. There is also a complementarity of female and male principles. The Goddess is alongside a horned bull, which might symbolize the fallopian tubes and the uterus, or the male principle. Later the bull was used as an animal form of male gods like the Greek Zeus and the Hindu Shiva."[47]

Archeologist Marija Gimbutas says that the earliest European civilization was Old Europe, about 6500–3500 B.C.E. After its destruction by patriarchal Aryan invaders, Goddess worship continued long among the rural people. By 1974 archeologists had unearthed 30,000 miniature female sculptures, as well as a great many vessels, altars, temples, and religious paintings. Knowing folklore, Gimbutas could explain the meanings of much of this religious art.

Gimbutas says that the Old European culture was woman-centered and matrilineal, with descent through the mother. It was not, however, necessarily matriarchal. "Although female images greatly predominate, male and female principals were manifest side by side. The male divinity in the shape of a young man or a male animal appears to affirm and strengthen the forces of the creative female. Neither is subordinate to the other; by complementing each other, their power is doubled."

Malta was a healing center, with over 30 temples built with a floor plan in the shape of the body of the Goddess (about 3500 2500 B.C.E.). "To enter the temple was to be within the body of the Goddess, and to be in touch with the elemental force that creates and maintains life." "The cave extending into the earth was the womb of the Goddess, the original place of the emergence of life." Entering the temple one passed through a labyrinth of stone portals, suggesting passing out of a material world and into a spiritual world. Large piles of earth were at the entrance of the temple, enhancing the feeling of entering the womb of the Earth Mother. "The kiva, the ceremonial chamber of the Hopi Indians, is the womb of the Earth Mother." Christians built their churches in a cruciform design, to give the feeling of entering the body of Christ.

"In the third millennium B.C.E. the life story of the Goddess was celebrated at Avebury in a seasonal round of festivals. The major events in her life—puberty, marriage, childbirth, and death—were the themes. The land was the Great Mother. The hills were her breasts (like the Grand Tetons in Wyoming), and her womb was the great cavity in the large hill at Silbury."[48]

Crete

"The Great Goddess kept her supremacy throughout the Mediterranean, the Aegean, Turkey and the Near East, northwest Africa, and Europe through Neolithic times, until the very end, the Bronze Age. Robert Graves speculates that Crete was the legendary Atlantis. The only other peoples we know of with such a long peace record (such as those of the Indus Valley and of southern India) were also Mother Goddess cultures."[49]

Minoan culture was the first great civilization of Europe. "The apogee of Goddess culture was Minoan Crete (3000–1500 B.C.E.), a free joyous society, where people lived in peace and harmony with nature. The whole of life was pervaded by an ardent faith in the Goddess, which reinforced a woman-centered society." The Greek poet Hesiod sang of Crete: "In peaceful ease they kept their lands with good abundance, and did not worship the gods of war." The dove was a symbol of the Goddess.

"Christians later adopted the dove as a sign of the Holy Ghost, but originally the bird stood for Sophia, God's female soul." The bull was used as a symbol of male potency. "The complementarity of male and female principles continued to evolve as a fundamental aspect of Goddess religion." "Europa is the manifestation of the Great Goddess as the mother of an entire continent. Her name means 'full moon.' Her rape by Zeus symbolizes the triumph of patriarchal Aryan gods over feminine nature goddesses."[50]

Mesopotamia

In Mesopotamia, "the earth was a woman. She gave birth each year to the new vegetation. Nin-tu, as Mother Earth, is the incarnation of all reproductive forces in the universe, the mother of the gods and also the mother and creator of mankind, responsible for the perpetuation of the human race."[51] The Goddess was worshipped in Mesopotamia from about 3500 to 500 B.C.E. She had many names: Inanna (the goddess of Sumer), and also Asherah, Astarte, and Ishtar. In Sumer she was also Goddess of Love, and was the most powerful deity. She ruled over all three worlds: Sky, Earth, and Underworld.

Origin of Monotheism

Elizabeth Gould Davis, in *The First Sex* (1971), says that "monotheism, once thought to be the invention of Moses or Akhnaton, was worldwide in the prehistoric and early historic world." For example, the Goddess Inanna was an all-powerful deity in Sumer. Later Yahweh appeared beside her, as "in the time of Jereboam, the Goddess shared the temple with Jehovah."[52]

Egypt

"To the Egyptians, the heavens signified the mystery of the divine mother through whom man was reborn. Like Isis, the sky-goddess Nut was a loving mother-goddess. Heaven is depicted as a woman bending over the earth with outstretched arms while the good Shu (god of the air) supports her. Nut is the mother of Osiris, and also the mother who gives birth each evening to the stars, each morning to the sun. The earth was considered to be male. The gods themselves lived within a cosmic order, and thus humans had absolutely nothing to fear."[53]

Other Goddess Figures

The female-energy figure symbolism used in Tantrism can be traced back to the Paleolithic cave culture of 30,000 B.C.E. "The Threefold Goddess of Arabia, Magna Dea, was enshrined in the sacred black stone, the Kaaba, at Mecca. The male priests who serve her today are called Beni Shaybah, which means 'the sons of the Old Woman (the moon).'" Tlazolteotl was the Aztec Great Mother, goddess of matter, and mother of the gods. She lived in the *sipapu*, the hole in the earth from which all human life emerged, according to Indian lore.

"All the great culture heroes of the past, mythic or historic, were said to be born of virgin mothers: Buddha, Osiris, Diony-sus, Gilgamesh, Marduk, Jesus, Genghis Khan—they were all affirmed as sons of the Great Mother."[54] The Great Goddess was not only the source of all life, but, as Mother Earth, the one to whom we returned at death. Thus a woman-goddess controlled both human life and human death.

Classical Goddess Figures

"All Greek religious ritual and mythology was of Cretan-Mycenaean origin. Greek mythology involved breaking down the one original Great Goddess into her many aspects: Aphrodite (Love), Athena (Wisdom), Demeter (Mother), Persephone (Daughter), and so forth. In these partial forms, the 'goddesses' were often at war with one another. Under the original Great Mother religion, this fragmentation could not happen, for each different face of the Goddess was recognized as an aspect of the one being."[55]

Gaia is Mother Earth. "In Greek tradition, Gaia stretched out at the beginning of time, becoming the earth's land. In this form, she continues to give life and sustenance to all things that dwell on the planet."[56] She is a fertility goddess with the gift of prophecy.

"The maiden form of the earth-goddess is Pandora, giver of all gifts." Her song is "I bring you wisdom, and justice with mercy. I bring you caring and communal bonds. I bring you courage, strength, and endurance. I bring you loving kindness for all beings. I bring you the seeds of peace."[57] This form of unitive religion is badly needed in our modern war torn world.

"Themis is another of the earth-mother's incarnations. Themis is the force that binds people together, the collective conscience. She became the personification of justice and righteousness." For millennia Greece prospered under her guidance. But barbarians captured Greece, held Themis captive, and established their new God Zeus. In the new order children had to be named after their father, and power was worshipped. Themis protested, "You dare not crush the primal Order." When the new gods assemble on Mount Olympus, she said, "I alone will have the right to convoke them. I will not die."[58]

Athena

Athena was originally a Cretan goddess who protected each family and town. Not born of a woman (she sprang from Zeus's head), she at first was considered to be too masculine to understand women's feelings. Without renouncing feminine traits, she showed that such qualities as courage and creativity can also be considered feminine virtues. Hesiod and Ovid say that in creation, Prometheus molded humans after the image of the gods, but it was Athena who breathed their souls into men and women. "Athena is not a virgin in order to be alone, but in order to be with others without entanglement. She is the goddess most identified with the work of civilization, the work that makes us human."[59]

Athena is the patron of arts, skills, and wisdom, and is especially protective of architects, potters, sculptors, spinners, and weavers. "As the mortals moved forward, Athena guided the impulse of the arts. She knew they would never flourish in an air of strife, so She protected households from divisive forces, and guarded towns against aggression. So invincible was the aura of Her protection that the Minoans lived in unfortified coastal towns. Their shipping trade prospered and they enjoyed a peace that spanned a thousand years."[60] Later, mainlanders conquered Crete, carried her away to Athens, and tried to turn her into a war goddess. Her previous military role had been that of solely a defender.

Aphrodite

Born of the ocean foam, Aphrodite was goddess of beauty and love. Akin to Ishtar and Astarte, she was a fertility goddess, "the primal mother of all ongoing creation. She alone understands the love that begets life. At Paphos she was attended by Her Graces: Beauty, Flowering, Growth, Joy, and Radiance."[61] Christine Downing addresses her: "All Greek goddesses are beautiful, but your beauty is divine—it has a special kind of energy, a goldenness, a warmth, a charisma. Warmth and truth conjoined, that is your magic, which enhances natural beauty. What distinguishes love in your realm is its celebration as a self-validating cosmic power. Yours is the love that begets life, a creative energy that far transcends human sexuality. You are the mediator between earth and sky and sea."[62]

All beauty comes from God, or if you wish, this Goddess. The highest beauty is spiritual beauty, which Aphrodite epitomizes. A mortal person has no right to be vain about beauty, since some comes from the corner drugstore, and the natural beauty beneath is a gift from Aphrodite or God. The Kabala postulates Beauty as a Sefira, a manifestation of divinity from the Godhead.

The Eleusian Mysteries

The mystery religions centered at Eleusis were the final outgrowth of the pre-Aryan Great Mother religions. "Originally these mysteries were all fertility rites, and the Great Mother is the embodiment of the forever resurgent, all-generating force of nature." Through the use of glaring light and sound effects, like a Neil Diamond concert, a mystical spiritual ambience was created. "The Godhead is thus brought much closer to believers.

Everything compels an inner concentration for which the bustle of life otherwise leaves no room."[63]

Christianity, after borrowing amply from these mysteries, labeled the residue as "pagan." "Pagan" comes from the Latin *paganus* (country dweller), so paganism was spitefully called the religion of country people, those who continued to worship the Goddess. "The enigma of the Eleusian Mysteries and the extent of their appeal indicates the power the Goddess still had over the Hellenistic world and the Roman Empire (3rd century B.C.E. to 5th century C.E.)." These rites were open to all, "Greek and foreign, women and slaves; the only requirements for initiation were knowledge of the Greek language, and hands free from blood—that is, from having taken a human life." Two former rituals were preserved: puberty rites, a young girl's initiation into womanhood, and the universal rite honoring the Great Mother as the giver of grain, the staff of life."[64]

Roman Goddesses

"The worship of the Phrygian Mother of the Gods was adopted by the Romans in 204 B.C.E." It was felt that she would help the Romans drive Hannibal from Rome, and indeed Hannibal was defeated. "The worship of the Great Mother of the Gods and her lover or son was very popular under the Roman Empire." Her worship extended to far-flung parts of the Empire, such as Africa, Bulgaria, France, Germany, Portugal, and Spain. Even after Constantine adopted Christianity, the festival of the Great Mother continued to be enacted. Even in the days of Augustine (about 400 C.E.), priests paraded in her honor in Carthage.[65]

The Hebrew Goddess

"Down to the end of the Hebrew monarchy, the worship of old Canaanite gods was an integral part of the religion of the Hebrews," says Jewish archeologist Raphael Patai. "No doubt that the goddess to whom the Hebrews clung with such tenacity was no foreign seductress, but a Hebrew goddess, the best divine mother the people had had to that time. To this day, in every Jewish temple or synagogue she is welcomed in the Friday evening prayers with the words, 'Come, O bride!'"[66]

Oxford Professor S.H. Langdon states that "the Mother-Goddess of the West Semitic races held even a greater place in their religion than the local gods of their most important cults."[67] Archeologist William F. Albright excavated the Biblical town Devir, and found that the most prevalent objects from the period 21st to 13th centuries B.C.E. to be clay plaques of Astarte. Other nude female statuettes are found in the Israelite layers of the excavation, dating from the 12th to the 6th centuries B.C.E. Patai found that the three goddesses worshipped by the ancient Hebrews down to the Babylonian exile were Asherah, Astarte, and Anath, the Queen of Heaven.

Asherah

"Asherah was the earliest female deity known to have been worshipped by the Children of Israel," says Patai. From the time they arrived in Canaan until the destruction of Jerusalem by Nebuchadnezzar in 586 B.C.E., "the Hebrews worshipped Asherah (and next to her also other originally Canaanite gods and goddesses) in most places and times." Gradually this ceased in response to the demands of the various prophets. Biblical accounts are not contemporaneous with the events they describe. Thus, editorial revisions occurred, and anything opposing male monotheism suffered in the written account. Many female statuettes have been found, but it is hard to know whether they were used in Canaanite or in Hebrew worship rituals.

Asherah was the wife of the chief god El. "She was also referred to as Elath or Goddess. She was the 'Progenitress of the Gods'; all other seventy gods were her children." She and her daughter Anath suckled the gods, and she suckled even human princes. Several recent archeological finds in Israel have inscriptions reading "May you be blessed by Yahweh and his Asherah."

Intermarriage between Israelites and Canaanites occurred. We are told in Judges 3:5–7 that "the Children of Israel served the Baals and the Asherahs." When Solomon married a foreign princess, she was allowed to keep worshipping her god. He had wives from Egypt and from Syrian Hittites, as well as daughters of his Moabite, Ammonite, and Edomite vassals. Solomon apparently at times worshipped Asherah, "Goddess of the Sidonians."

Under Jezebel's influence, King Ahab built an altar to Baal and made an Asherah image. When Elijah destroyed the Baal symbols, he apparently did not attack the Asherah images. In II Kings 13:6 it says that King Joahaz left the Asherah remain standing in Samaria. King Jehu destroyed the Baal temple but not the Asherah figures. The Israelites were still worshipping Asherah when the Assyrians conquered them in 722 B.C.E.

In Judah, Solomon's daughter Maacah introduced Asherah worship into the Temple itself and it lasted until the reforms of King Asa. Asa's son, King Jehosafat, removed all the Asherah images from the land. Under King Joash, an image of Asherah was reintroduced into the Temple, where it remained for a century until removed by King Hezekiah. But Hezekiah's son Manasseh restored the Asherah.

King Josiah, the reformer, wished to abolish Asherah worship forever, so "he brought out the image of Asherah herself from the Temple, had it burned in the Kidron Valley, ground it up into powder, and cast the dust over the graves of those who had worshipped her. Finally, he cut down the Asherahs wherever they were found."

Still, a few years later, Jeremiah found it necessary to once again attack Asherah worship. In summary, "during the 370 years during which the Solomonic Temple stood in Jerusalem, for 236 years the statue of Asherah was present in the Temple, and her worship was a part of the legitimate religion approved and led by the king, the court, and the priesthood, and opposed only by a few prophetic voices."[68]

Rosemary Radford Ruether says that "most of the polemics against Canaanite religion in the Old Testament are against Baal, not Anath or Asherah. Yahweh does not do warfare primarily against the Goddess. Rather, it is Baal, her male escort, who must be replaced. The Goddess is not so much eliminated as absorbed, and put into a new relationship with Yahweh as her Lord. In addition to the transformation of the Sacred Marriage from a Goddess-king relation to a patriarchal God-servant wife, Yahwism appropriates female images for God at certain points."[69]

Isaiah shows this assimilation: "The Lord goes forth like a mighty man, like a man of war he stirs up his fury. For a long time I have kept still and restrained myself. Now I will cry out like a woman in travail. I will gasp and pant. These things I will do and I will not forsake them" (Is. 42:13–14, 16).

Origin of Semitic Mythology

Sjöö and Mor state that the major myths of the Torah were not original with the Hebrews but came from their Babylonian captivity: The Garden story, the Flood story, and the struggle between "ancient agricultural Goddess people and the new Bronze Age war God elites. Levite priests," they say, "were originally serpent priests of the Great Mother. 'Levi' is related to 'Leviathan,' the World Dragon of the Goddess." In Leviticus female blood (which had been sacred under the Goddess), for example, menstrual and childbirth blood, is now considered unclean, a cause for shame. The new covenant is made with male blood, from the foreskins of circumcised male infants."

Sjöö and Mor call the Torah the first scripture advocating holy war: kill people if they oppose your idea of God. Nevertheless not only Judaism but also its offspring Christianity and Islam recognize the Torah as a sacred text. Sjöö and Mor conclude that "a most unholy trinity dominates the patriarchal tradition: rape, genocide, and war."[70]

Anath (Astarte)

Another goddess revered by the Israelites was Anath, the daughter of Asherah and El. She was often also called Astarte, or in the singular Ashtoreth and in the plural form Ashtaroth.

Semitic poetry often uses parallels: the same idea rephrased in different words. In naming gods, therefore, often two names are used, and Anath and Astarte are names frequently used in pairs Anath was the most important Canaanite goddess, the goddess of love and war. She seems to be the heiress of the Sumerian Inanna and the Akkadian Ishtar, since she shares many of their qualities. Patai points out that the original meaning of "Astarte" was "womb," indicating that she was a fertility goddess. The Christian term "Easter" derives from the Anglo-Saxon Eostre, a northern form of Astarte.

Anath and Baal

Anath's chief lover was her brother Baal. Anath was often called "mistress of the gods." Like Athena, however, she was sometimes labeled a war goddess.

"The most important theological symbol of the feminine in the Christian tradition," says Ruether, "is that of the Church as the 'Bride of Christ' and 'Mother of Christians.' This symbol is rooted in the Old Testament motif of Israel as God's wife. The Song of Songs probably has its roots in Canaanite psalms of love between Anath and Baal. The Canaanite conception of this divine love made the lovers equal." The Song of Songs retains this equality of the lovers. "In antiquity, divine love was the prototype of human love."

But the author of Ephesians, in chapter 5, changes this. This author, "by making the husband analogous to Christ in relation to his wife, even suggests that a wife should consider her husband representative of Christ or God! Her husband is her Lord, as Christ is Lord of the Church. She is his body, as the Church is the body of Christ."[71]

The Shekhina(h)

"'Shekhinah' is the frequently used Talmudic term designating the visible and audible manifestation of God's presence on earth," says Patai. In late Midrash literature, she is an independent feminine deity who, because of her deep compassion, argues with God in defense of humanity. She thus seems to be "a direct heir to such ancient Hebrew goddesses as Asherah and Anath."

"In actual usage, the term Shekhinah, when it first appears, means that aspect of the deity which can be apprehended by the senses. The term comes from the Hebrew *shakan*, "the act of dwelling." The Talmud states that "both the desert sanctuary and the Solomonic Temple were the earthy abode of the Shekhinah." Human sin sent the Shekhinah into exile, and only good acts can return her. But when the Israelites went into foreign bondage, the Shekhinah accompanied them. "Good deeds, even if performed by idolaters, attract the Shekhinah. When the prophets of Baal practiced hospitality, the Shekhinah descended and rested upon them."[72]

"The radiance of the Shekhinah is so great that the angels must cover their faces with their wings so as not to see her. The ministering angels are removed from the Shekhinah by myriads of parasangs, and the body of the Shekhinah herself measures millions of miles." Thus, like the Holy Spirit, the Shekhinah can be anywhere and everywhere at the same time. In the Talmud, the terms Shekhinah and Holy Spirit are used interchangeably. To show she is separate from Yahweh, she argues with Him to forgive sinning humans. The great Kabalist scholar Gershom Scholem concluded that her constant defense of humans, even in sin, showed the Jewish people's deep-seated religious need for a feminist aspect of the divine.[73]

To show that the Shekhinah was indeed feminine, Patai analyzes the Hebrew phrase for "the Shekhinah rose up and said." The "a" ending of the noun shows femininity, as does also the feminine form of both verbs, "rose up" and "said."

"That the Shekhinah is the love aspect of God is clearly stated in a parable which compares the Temple to Solomon's palanquin; just as the latter was inlaid with love, so did the Shekhinah fill the sanctuary. But again like the Holy Spirit (which the New Testament says 'convicts us of sin'), the Shekhinah represents the divine punitive power."

The Talmud said that there were six people so meritorious that the Angel of Death could not overcome them. These six (Abraham, Isaac, Jacob, Moses, Aaron, and Miriam) died only from a kiss from the Shekhinah.[74]

Kathleen Fischer states that "we all need faith that the universe will catch us and hold us. We need word of the Shekhinah, the divine presence that meets us in unexpected ways in a broken world. She is the divine compassion active in tragic situations. Wherever the Israelites wandered, Shekhinah was with them, in all the hostile places and rough times."[75]

The New Testament describes the Holy Spirit as the *paraclete*, one who walks beside you to comfort you. Ruether says that many early Christian texts, especially in the Apocrypha, speak of the Holy Spirit as feminine. The Gospel of the Hebrews refers to "my mother, the Holy Spirit." The Gospel of Philip describes the Holy Spirit as feminine. "Clement of Alexandria and the Syriac father Aphraates did too, as did the 3rd century Church order the Didascalia." Thus calling the Holy Spirit feminine need not be heretical, but rather a return to an early Christian usage.[76]

Matronit

Matronit (matron) is a name used in the Kabala for the Shekhinah (or Daughter). "She is the central link between the Above and the Below, the person through whom one can most easily grasp the ineffable mystery of the deity, and unquestionably the most poignant and most Jewish expression of the idea of a goddess," in Patai's view. To Kabalists, Matronit became like the Virgin Mary to Roman Catholic Christians, "the Mother of God."

Matronit was thought of as a virgin, even though she is said to have had many lovers: Jacob, Moses, and then finally the King (her brother), when Solomon completed the building of the Temple. It is assumed that when a Jewish couple have sex, especially on the Sabbath, it is an imitation of the divine union between the Shekhinah and the King. When the people of Israel sin, this gives Satan (in the form of a serpent) the chance to rape the Shekhinah. The King then deserts her until the Day of Atonement, when a scapegoat is hurled off a cliff, and the King returns to his Shekhinah. But the destruction of the Temple (their bedroom) separated them again. While separated, the King had sex with one of her handmaids, Lilith, causing the King to lose respect. In exile, the Shekhinah was violated by other gods, against her will.

The Shekhinah, says Patai, is a mother figure, "the woman who bears, suckles, rears, and protects both gods and men." Originally this trait belonged to the Mother Goddess (her mother) but it was transferred to the Shekhinah, who suckled even heathens as well as the Israelites. As the war goddess, she led the army in the exodus from the Egyptians, and in their long sojourn in the desert. But when Israel sins, her power recedes.

The Hindu influence of Kali may be seen in this warlike stance of the Shekhinah. She is even sometimes depicted in black, like Kali. Another parallel is with the Virgin Mary, who, like Athena, was a war goddess to the Byzantine armies. Mary was regarded as "the empress of the universe, the ruler of the world, the queen of heaven and earth." Mechthild of Magdeburg even called Mary "goddess." "Like the Matronit, Mary too was considered the spouse of God, the intermediary between God and men, the best and easiest way to God."

Gershom Scholem saw the Matronit as a mythological figure, subordinate to the masculine monotheism of mainline Judaism. But Patai honors the central myth of the Kabala: the supernal King and Queen. In Patai's view, Adam's mistake was to confuse Sefira #10 (Malkuth-Kingdom-Shekhinah) with the totality of the Godhead, thus causing a split between the King (Sefira #1, Crown) and his Queen. The world will not be right until the Royal Couple is reunited, and this cannot happen until humans quit sinning.

"Only the coming of the Messiah will put an end to the suffering caused by this situation to Israel, and to their divine parents, God and the Shekhinah." In this perspective, Judaism has a crucial role to play in saving the modern world. "Nothing else could have endowed the Jew in exile with a firmer conviction, a greater self-assurance concerning his own religious value and his crucial spiritual role in the world." The exile of the Diaspora has been painful, but it prepares Israel to show the world the path to God.[77]

The Shekhinah Returns from Exile

The Kabala recommends several types of prayers to assist in the reconciliation of the Shekhinah with God. The *Zohar* even said that Adam was the offspring of God and His Shekhinah. Isaac Luria taught that whenever one performed any mitzvah (religious commandment), one needed to concentrate on its secret mystical purpose, that is, to bring about the unification of God and Shekhinah. Luria believed that one should stress the unity of the Yatl (God) with the Wetl (Shekhinah), thus showing that God is really one.

The exile of the Shekhinah meant that one part (or aspect) of God was separated from another part (or aspect) of God. The leading Jewish prayers, the Eighteen Benedictions, are given to help unite God and Shekhinah. These benedictions are called "Amida." Amida is the name of the Buddhist God of the Pure Land Sect. To repeat Amida's name prayerfully is to gain access to the Pure Land, or Buddhist heaven.

Moses Cordovero was a Kabalist who gave instructions on how to put on the *tallith* (prayer shawl) and the *teffilin* (phylacteries). Before performing these rites, Cordovero said, one must recite a prayer showing the symbolism of the wedding between God and the Shekhinah. Cordovero also said that a complete person unites his/her male and female attributes, in something like the manner prescribed by psychologist Carl Jung.

Others who spoke of this union of God and Shekhinah included Hayyim Vital, Elijahu de Vidas, and Nathan of Hannover. "In Kabalistic teaching, the divine name Yahweh has a masculine and the name Adonay a feminine connotation." One prayer asks the person to make himself a chariot for the Shekhinah. One Kabalist teacher said that "the Shekhinah is the source of all souls." For Hayyim Azulai the entire Seder ritual is aimed at unifying the Shekhinah with God. The *maggid* (sayer) was a channeler, one who brought messages from God to common people. The Kabalist master Joseph Caro said that his *maggid* was the Shekhinah. Some Hasidic Jews report having had visions of the Shekhinah.

The Sabbath

"The Sabbath is a unique example of a day of the week having been developed into a female numen and endowed with the character of virgin, bride, queen, and goddess." In the Talmud, Rabbi Hanina said, "Let us go to receive Sabbath the Queen," and Rabbi Yannai put on festive clothes and said, "Come, O bride!" "The Talmud shows the Sabbath as the bride of Israel and a queen." Philo depicts the Sabbath as the virgin daughter of God. Isaac Luria spoke of God the King and His bride, the Sabbath-Shekhinah."[78]

The Shekhinah and Moses

Moses is an Egyptian name. A mural from an excavation site of Dura Europa in Syria depicts a woman rescuing the infant Moses from the Nile. Patai believes that the woman was the Shekhinah. The Midrash showed a close connection between Moses and the Shekhinah. It also states that the Shekhinah, along with the two Tablets of the Law, dwelled in the Ark of the Covenant.[79]

The Shekhinah Today

"Rabbi Leah Novick reinterprets the Shekhinah in the light of contemporary Gaia consciousness. She draws on traditional Jewish teaching that nothing in nature can exist without the

Shekhinah, who sustains and nourishes all life on the planet." Novick looks to the next generation to fully embrace the Jewish goddess.[80]

"The religion of the Hebrews and the Jews was never without at least a hint of the feminine in its God-concept. In the Biblical and again in the Kabalistic eras, it occupied an important place in popular theology, occasionally even to the extent of overshadowing the male deity or the male component of the Godhead. Among the Sephardim, the Oriental Jews, and the Hasidic Ashkenazim, the mystical-mythical doctrine of God and the Shekhinah has retained its hold."[81]

Celtic Faith

Celtic religion has two contributions to make to world religion: reverence for all of nature as a part of God's creation, and a reverence for the divine feminine.

The Celts originated around 1900 B.C.E. in southwestern Germany and the Strassburg area. They may have migrated from India. Alwyn and Brinley Rees show interesting parallels between the Bhagavad-Gita and Celtic myths. They say, "The Celts found divinity in nature all around them—in the sky, mountains, trees, lakes, and the sea. Mother goddesses and feminine deities played a large role in their faith."

"Buddhism has always had its goddesses and deep connections with nature," says Elinor Gadon. "Tara, the Mother of Mercy, and Kwan-yin, the Bodhisattva of Compassion, have traditionally been sources of comfort and salvation."[82] Tantra and Taoism also respected feminine aspects of divinity.

The Celtic tradition is grounded in faith in Mother Earth and Her spiritual power. The early Irish knew Mother Earth as the Goddess of Sovereignty. Eventually the Celts were conquered by the Milesians. The wives of the seven Milesian chiefs gave their names to various places in Ireland, except for Scota, daughter of the Pharaoh Nectanebus, after whom Scotland was named. The leading shaman of the Milesians, Amairgin Whiteknee, made a deal with the three major goddesses of Ireland to use their names as a name for the island, but Banba and Fotla were ignored in favor of Eriu (Eire). Her name signifies "one who is elevated."

Although Aryan, the Celts were unusual in their respect for women. Celtic women owned their own property and were free to choose their own mates. Legal contracts were made by the wife independently of her mate. Celtic heroes were named after their mothers. The Celts did not own slaves or believe in capital punishment. Their tribal councils were often presided over by women, and their kingship and inheritance of property were matrilineal. "The women enjoyed greater economic, social, and sexual autonomy than women in present-day Britain, France, and America."[83] In the Celtic Catholic Church, women distributed the wine and male priests the wafers in the communion ritual.

Two of the main charges made by Augustine and Jerome against the Celtic Christian Pelagius were his associating with women and admitting that he had learned a lot from them. The Celts have a long tradition of male/female monasteries, many of which were presided over by women. Compare this with the official Roman Catholic Church's attitude towards women today.

The Celtic union of God with nature is seen later in St. Francis of Assisi, who liked to speak to Brother Sun and Sister Moon. Meister Eckhart was also deeply rooted in the Celtic Christian tradition. His *joie de vivre* is captured in many Celtic celebrations of nature's beauty. In the words of Noragh Jones, "Christ's birth was seen as the coming of a great light to benighted earth."[84]

Gaia Consciousness

"The birth of Gaia consciousness can be traced to that incredible moment when the astronauts first landed on the moon in 1969." Then we humans saw ourselves as others see us—a beautiful blue orb, a part of the heavens. "Gaia consciousness means peace, not war. Painter Helena Aylon works full-time for peace. She joined Arab and Jewish women who worked together to fill sacks with stones as a sign of their wish to end enmity." Vijali Hamilton carves monuments to Gaia out of rock. "Her goal is to promote peace and the relation of all of earth's peoples to one another and to earth."

Edward Whitmont believes that as old values are breaking down, we seek new ways of understanding our existence. "Yet paradoxically these new ways require a retrieval of old discarded and repressed modes of functioning. The magical, mythological, and feminine ways of dealing with existence left behind thousands of years ago must now be reclaimed by us." Elinor Gadon adds: "The Goddess has reappeared in our midst as a symbol of the healing that is necessary for our survival. The emerging consciousness is pluralistic. The promised healing is that in honoring all that lives, we will no longer need to oppress, despoil our planet, or make war."[85]

Ecofeminism

Gadon also says that "ecofeminism is a new political philosophy bringing together ecology and feminism, founded on the belief of the oneness of all forms of life. The devaluation of nature is at the root of our ecological crisis. Deep ecologists see all of humanity, both men and women, as situated in and ultimately connected to nature." So-called "pagans" felt trees were sacred. What would they say about modern clear-cut tree harvesting, and the loss of rain forests to make cardboard boxes and toothpicks?

Men wanted ever larger herds of cattle. But when the cattle ate off the grass, the topsoil eroded, and once productive land became a desert. "It takes 20 million tons of grain-protein to feed cattle, which in turn give back only 2 million tons of meat-protein. The land used to feed cattle is used inefficiently. This is a major cause of world famine today."[86] In the words of Ruether, "an ecological-feminist theology of nature must rethink the whole Western theological tradition. It must challenge the right of the human to treat the nonhuman as private property and as material wealth to be exploited."

Soul Loss

Caitlin and John Matthews state that "war is one of the major causes of collective soul loss. As the social dislocation of returned war veterans today testifies to their shock at the atrocities witnessed, so we find similar instances of Celtic battle shock." Celtic peoples felt that one's soul wanders when subjected to shock, illness, or distress. They said a human soul has three components: psyche, heart, and mind. Trauma can dislocate the trinity, causing anomie or even insanity. Mental healing involves overcoming this fragmentation by restoring the missing segment.

The Spiritual Strength of Indigenous People

Caitlin and John Matthews feel that the modern world needs what the Celtic way of life has to offer. "A great number of indigenous people worldwide have become fully integrated into Western society yet have rediscovered the spiritual path of their ancestors and have returned to simpler ways of life. Many such people have become teachers, bridge-builders between disparate traditions, able to interpret one culture to the other and so defuse conflict. We need these people." A straight white piece of wood was given to Irish kings at their coronation. "It was straight to typify justice, white to signify peace—bloodshed was not to be needlessly caused."[87]

Mary MacLeod of Gairloch recited a Celtic prayer for peace in all relationships:

> Peace between neighbors, peace between kindred,
> Peace between lovers, in love of the King of life.
> Peace between person and person, peace between wife and
>   husband,
> Peace between women and children, the peace of Christ above
>   all peace.

Noragh Jones declares that "one of the offerings of the ancient Celtic church today is the greater balance between the feminine and the masculine, as well as its celebration of the interweaving of matter and spirit, and its affirmation of the goodness of creation and the human body. St. Brigid, for instance, in her leadership of double monasteries of men and women, stands for us as a model of equality between the sexes."[88]

Native Americans

In 1852 Chief Seattle said that "the earth does not belong to man, man belongs to the earth. All things are connected like the blood which unites one family. Whatever befalls the earth befalls the sons of earth." Ruether ruefully remarks that "the white race remains a spiritual stranger to the land which it has stolen."

Many American Indian tribes have sacred land sites, where the Great Spirit blessed the Earth. The Indian drum is round, symbolic of the universe. Its steady beat is to the rhythm of the human heart—it depicts the heart throb of the universe, the voice of the Great Spirit. A charming Navajo ritual is the puberty rite for the young maiden, called "Walking into Beauty."

The Hopi tribe in Arizona offers a striking example of how a deeply religious people can achieve peace and good will. Violence is almost unknown to Hopi culture. Not only have the Hopis sought peace with other Indian tribes and their own white conquerors, but they have also practiced a way of life that could teach others how to live within their own groups. In their own way, the Hopis show a Celtic respect for nature, a Buddhist passion for self-control, a Judaic sense of justice, and a Christian love of all humanity. It would be utter folly to seek for foundations of world peace and international understanding without seeking out the treasure to be found in the faiths of many of Mother Earth's indigenous people.

Women Sages and Mystics

St. Jerome said that Marcella (325–410) was the authority on scripture in Rome. Paula (347–404) worked closely with and inspired Jerome. Together they founded monasteries, some for women and some for men. Macrina the Younger (330–379) was the sister and spiritual teacher of three brothers who were saints: Basil the Great, Gregory of Nyssa, and Peter. Hilda (614–680) was so great an abbess that the famous Synod of Whitby was held at her abbey.

The Beguines were a medieval order of laywomen of great importance in Europe. "In 1317 there were over 200,000 Beguines in Germany." One of them, Mechthild of Magneburg, was a significant influence on German mysticism in general and Meister Eckhart in particular. Her book *The Flowing Light of the Godhead* used images similar to those employed by Eckhart. "Among them are the images of dancing, of God's delight, of awakening, of growth, of letting go, and of God as a flowing stream. If much of Eckhart's spiritual vision is profoundly feminist—and it is—that is because he listened to and read what women had to say about the spiritual journey."[89] Juliana of Norwich (1342–1417) showed mystical joy in her embrace of Christianity. In her *Revelations of Divine Love* she called God "our Father, Mother, and True Spouse."

St. Catherine of Siena (1347–1380) helped resolve the tangled papacy problems at Avignon. St. Catherine of Genoa (1447–

1510) resembled the Sufi mystic Rabi'a of Basra. She forgave her husband's infidelity and provided funds for his child born out of wedlock. The husband and his mistress was so impressed by this Christlike agape that they reformed their lives and spent their lives, as Catherine did, helping the sick and the poor. St. Teresa of Avila (1515–1582) founded 21 monasteries and greatly influenced the Counter-Reformation. Jean Frances de Chantel (1572–1641) was a co-worker with the great Francis de Sales. Together they established over 60 monasteries in France, Italy, and Sicily.

Jacob Boehme stated that Adam was originally androgynous. The Shakers believed that God was androgynous. The Quakers gave women full equality in their church. Margaret Fuller (1810–1850) pioneered for equal rights for women, based upon their equal position with men as children of God. Helena Blavatsky (1831–1891) founded theosophy as a worldwide spiritual movement accepting all persons as equals under God. Mother Teresa (1910–1997) was considered by many to be the most saintly person of the 20th century, for her work with the poor, the dying, and the lepers of Calcutta. Finally, in 1956 Methodists and Presbyterians began the ordination of women as ministers, something many churches still refuse to do.

American Goddesses

In 2000 the New York Historical Society gave a program on American goddess symbols. The earliest was the Indian Princess, used during Colonial times as an icon of native bravery, beauty, and innocence. During the Revolutionary period, Americans responded to iconography of the Goddess of Liberty, holding a liberty pole and wearing a Phrygian cap, symbol of freed Roman slaves. "The goddess-like Columbia, with her shield and starred tiara, signified American strength after the Revolution." The Statue of Liberty, Frederic-Auguste Bartholdi's gift to the United States, symbolized "the Enlightenment ideas that our founding fathers borrowed from French philosophers—about political freedom for all mankind, and human rights for all people."[90] Thus, America's iconography of lofty political and social idealism is carried out mainly through feminine rather than masculine images.

Jesus and Women

Pilate's wife told Pilate that Jesus was innocent of the charges against him. During his trial and crucifixion, Jesus was deserted by most of his apostles but attended to by his faithful female followers. In two parables, Jesus shows God working like a woman with yeast, and like a housewife who finds a lost coin. Speaking to Jerusalem, Jesus said, "I wanted to gather your children as a bird gathers her brood" (Matt. 23:39). When Jesus was called "a glutton and drunkard, a friend of tax collectors and sinners," Matthew responds, "Yet wisdom is justified by her deeds" (Matt. 11:19). Comforting his apostles at his coming death, Jesus describes their sorrow as that of a woman in child-birth, with the pain ultimately replaced by joy (John 16:20–22).

"Jesus was utterly unbounded in his vision of God's design for the human family. Nowhere was this more evident than in his dealings with women, whom he trusted as not only equal to men but as his intimate friends and disciples. Nothing in Jesus' preaching was meant for men only. He raised the daughter of Jairus, as well as the son of the widow of Nain, recognizing that a girl child is no less precious than a boy, despite society's unequal valuation of them. Jesus accepted women's ministry to himself, and defended them from the law applied unequally to women. To a woman he entrusted the evangelization of the Samaritans, and it was to women that he entrusted the Easter proclamation."[91]

Gregory of Nazianus said that the terms Father and Son to describe aspects of God were metaphors—not terms of gender but of relationship, since God was pure Spirit (John 4:24). The maleness of Jesus, in the view of Sandra Schneiders, is not essential but accidental. Medieval mystics, she says, consistently show the feminine aspects of Jesus' nature. Among Montanists Jesus sometimes appeared in visions in the form of a woman. Some of the followers of Joachim of Fiore believed that a new Third Age, that of the Holy Spirit, was coming, in which the Holy Spirit would appear in the form of a woman. Some modern Christians adhere to this view.

Jesus and Sophia

Denis Edwards feels that "Jesus knew God not only as Abba but also in and through the feminine image of Holy Wisdom." In her book *In Memory of Her* Elisabeth Schussler-Fiorenza develops the idea of Jesus' relationship with God as Sophia. Sally McFugue, in her *Models of God*, describes the world as God's body. She discusses models of God as Mother, Lover, and Friend. Karl Rahner concurs, stating "Christ is already at the heart and center of all poor things of this earth, which we cannot do without because the earth is our mother."[92]

Recent Biblical scholarship often presents Jesus as "the incarnation of the feminine Old Testament hypostasis of God, Holy Wisdom or Sophia." This is true especially in the prologue of John's Gospel, "in which Jesus appears as the Word made flesh. This Word, who is in the bosom of God from all eternity and through whom all things are made, is Holy Wisdom, for whom Solomon, equating Word and Wisdom, prayed: 'O God, who hast made all things by Thy Word, and by Thy Wisdom has formed humanity, give me the Wisdom that sits by Thy throne' (Wisdom 9:1–4)." In her carefully researched book *The Feminine Dimension of the Divine,* Joan Engelsman elaborates that "Jesus of the New Testament is predominantly Holy Wisdom incarnate." The Apostle Paul in several places calls Jesus "the wisdom of God," and "in Matthew's Gospel Jesus is clearly portrayed as Sophia."[93] Ruether states that "Jesus rejected kingly and chauvinistic understandings of the Messiah" but "interpreted the Messiah as Suffering Servant. He opposed human suffering wherever he found it, and like Buddha, taught people how to live a peaceful and a more abundant life."

Jesus as Liberator

Ruether conceives of Jesus as a revolutionary liberator. "Once the mythology about Jesus as Messiah or divine *Logos*, with its traditional masculine imagery, is stripped off, the Jesus of the synoptic Gospels can be recognized as a figure remarkably compatible with feminism. Jesus speaks on behalf of the marginalized and the despised, saying the last shall be first, and the first last. He says that the religious leaders are blind guides and hypocrites. Relations to God means that we are to call no man

'Father, Teacher, or Master' (Matt. 23:1–12). Relations to God makes us all brothers-sisters of each other. Women play an important role in this Gospel vision of the vindication of the lowly in God's new order." He even has an ear for the oppressed prostitutes.

"Jesus as a liberator calls for a renunciation of the status relationships which define privilege and privation. Theologically speaking, the maleness of Jesus has no ultimate significance. Jesus, the homeless Jewish prophet, and the marginalized women and men who respond to him, represent the overthrow of the present world system and the sign of a dawning new age in which God's will is done on earth. In the language of early Christian prophetism, we can encounter Christ in the form of *our sister*. Christ is not confined to a static perfection of one person 2000 years ago. Rather, redemptive humanity goes ahead of us, calling us to yet incompleted dimensions of human liberation."[94]

Sandra Schneiders states that "Jesus' ultimate allegiance was not to his race, or religion, or gender, or class. It was to the Reign of God. He was a revolutionary who never carried a gun, and never permitted a fight. He was a revolutionary because he said (and practiced) 'Love your enemies.' He is the model of both nonviolent pacifism and justifiable spiritual revolution."[95]

God the Mother: Sophia

"In the Bible, cities, nations, the people of Israel, and later, the universal Church, are represented in the image of a female individuality, and this is not a simple metaphor."[96] The Christian Church is symbolized by feminine figures in a number of Biblical books, such as Song of Solomon, Ephesians, and Revelation. The New Testament states that "wisdom is justified by her deeds (Matt. 11:19) and by her children" (Luke 7:35).

Upon their return from Babylonian exile, around 540 B.C.E., the Jews discovered "various personages and personified attributes" who seemed to act as a "chief agent" for God. "Such figures offered a treasury of images for the early Christian community to draw upon in its following of Jesus. Most striking among these images is Lady Wisdom—Sophia—whom God brought forth from the beginning of the earth; like a 'master worker, she accompanied God in the act of creation' (Prov. 8:22–31). She is a 'breath of the power of God,' a 'pure emanation of the glory of the Almighty, a reflection of eternal light, a spotless mirror of the working of God, and an image of his goodness'" (Wisdom 7:25–26).[97]

Other scripture passages attesting to Sophia's presence with God at creation are Proverbs 3:19, Psalm 104:24, and Job 28:27. In the *Wisdom of Solomon* Sophia is described as being God's wife. The first nine chapters of the book of Proverbs focus on the need for Wisdom, and the rewards she gives. Prov. 3:17 says "her ways are pleasantness, and all her paths are peace."

Vladimir Solovyov, Russian mystic and philosopher, describes three visions he had of Sophia. He was sure that She was returning to earth soon. He said:

> Let it be known: today the Eternal Feminine
> In an incorruptible body is descending to Earth.
> In the unfading light of the new Goddess
> Heaven has become one with the depths.

Orthodox Christianity gave its blessing to the concept of Sophia as the Mother of God, just as the Roman Catholic Church was embracing the veneration of the Virgin Mary. Influenced by Solovyov, Daniel Andreev wrote of "The Divine Feminine": "No one is questioning the oneness of God. In manifesting Himself externally, the One God reveals His inherent inner polarity. These two principles, eternally united in creative love, bring forth the third principle, the Son, the *Logos*. That is why we call Divine Femininity the Mother of the *Logos*, and through Him, Mother of the entire Universe. But the eternal union between the Mother and the Father does not change Her timeless essence. For that reason we call the Mother of Worlds the Virgin Mother.

God does not love Himself (such a claim would be blasphemy) but each of the Transcendencies within Him directs His love onto the Other, and in that love a Third is born: the Foundation of the Universe. Thus, we have the Father, the Virgin Mother, and the Son."[98]

Robert A. Powell recalls Philo's account of creation: God created Sophia, and then created the cosmos by Sophia. Thus, God is the Father, Sophia is the Mother, and the cosmos (the *Logos*) is the Son. St. Augustine called Sophia "Our Mother, the Bride of Zion, Heavenly Jerusalem. She is the highest creation, the most blessed, the greatest of all created beings."

Hildegard of Bingen had many visions of Sophia. Some show her as co-worker at creation, the Mother of the World. Others show her as Mary-Sophia, the Mother of the Church. Jacob Boehme is called "the father of Sophiology" in the Western world. He said that Sophia appeared to him, comforting him and turning his sorrow into joy. She was also reputed to have appeared to Solomon, who said that Wisdom built her house upon seven pillars (Proverbs 9:1).

Vladimir Solovyov influenced the Russian Orthodox priests Pavel Florensky and Sergei Bulgakov to embrace Sophia. Florensky called Sophia the pinnacle of creation. "As the first created being, she is the link between the Trinity and creation. She is 'eternally created by the Father through the Son, and crowned in the Holy Spirit.' Sophia participates in the life of the Godhead. From the point of view of the Father, Sophia is the ideal substance, the foundation of creation. From that of the Son, she is the reason of creation, its meaning. From that of the Holy Spirit, She is the spirituality of creation, that is, its holiness, purity, and beauty."[99]

The Most Holy Trinosophia

Robert Powell envisions a female Holy Trinity, encompassed in Sophia, with a female counterpart of each of the male persons in the traditional Christian Holy Trinity. He explains his concept: "The Most Holy Trinosophia comprises the Mother, the Daughter, and the Holy Soul." At his first Coming, Christ revealed the way to the Father. Now, in the second Coming, he is revealing the path to the Mother. At mankind's Fall, the relationship between Father and Mother (Nature) was severed, as well as the relationship between humanity and Mother Nature.

But Christ's descent into hell after Golgotha reestablished the connection between Son and Mother. Our own descent into hell came with the use of the A-bomb in 1945. But just as Christ taught us the 'Our Father' prayer in His first Coming, in His second coming He will teach us the 'Our Mother' prayer, which will restore the Divine Unity of Father and Mother: 'through the deed of the Son the immeasurable pain of the Father will be stilled.' Jews have reason to believe that humanity's descent into hell came with the Holocaust.

Powell says that in Revelation 12:1 John describes his vision of Sophia: "I saw a great sign in heaven—a woman clothed with the Sun, with the Moon under her feet, and on her head a crown of twelve stars." Thus John describes the Cosmic Virgin, known by that name to Egyptian Hermeticists. "This was the same being who spoke through Solomon and inspired the people of Israel." The love of the people of Israel for Sophia prepared some of them later to welcome Mary and Jesus. Jewish mothers had that love of babies found in the Mother Mary.

Just as A-bombs disrupt Mother Earth's energy frequencies, so did the Holocaust disrupt humanity's spiritual stability. John's Woman was about to bear a Child, but Satan stood poised to devour the Child. The Child found safety at the throne of God; the Woman found safety in the desert. Many people, including some non-Christians, feel that what will save the human race in the present crisis is "Christ consciousness," a rebirth of the Messiah that will atone for the various descents into hell in the 20th century.

Just as the Last Supper embodied the *Logos* mystery, says Powell, so did the appearance of the Holy Spirit at Pentecost embody the Sophia mystery. "Just as Christ incarnated in Jesus, so Sophia united with Mary." Whereas Easter showed the resurrection of the body, Pentecost showed the resurrection of the soul. Sophia incarnated into Mary to strengthen her so that she could bear the *Logos*.

Pavel Florensky said, "Sophia is personified virginity, the force which makes the human being whole." Just as Jesus had twelve apostles at the Last Supper, so Mary-Sophia has a crown of twelve stars, which to believers in the Cosmic Virgin could be the signs of the Zodiac. To the Jews they could stand for the twelve sons of Jacob.[100]

Rudolf Steiner said that the reappearance of the Divine Feminine in our time is that of the resurrected Divine Sophia, "who helps us to find Christ in spiritual form, in his second Coming." Philosophy means "love of Sophia," so every true philosopher is Her friend. Theosophy means "God's Sophia," and its founder, Helena Blavatsky, wrote *Isis Unveiled* to show the unity between Sophia and Isis. Steiner called his work "anthroposophy" meaning "human Sophia." "Through the help of archangel Michael and Sophia," said Robert Powell, "anthroposophy arose in the name of Christ on his path of descent from cosmic heights to the Earth, on the downward path leading ultimately to the Mother."

Powell states that in pre-Christian times the Jewish people knew the Holy Soul as the Shekhinah. She brought peace and harmony to all people. "The Holy Soul or Shekhinah is the feminine counterpart of the Holy Spirit," says Powell. She relates to Sophia (Divine Wisdom) as the Holy Spirit relates to Christ.

"With the creation," says Powell, "the androgynous Godhead polarized into the eternal Father and the eternal Mother." The Father is in heaven, and the Mother is in the earth. She is called Maya (illusion), since she seems to be apart from the Father. Sergei Bulgakov said that "the most holy Mother of God is the created Sophia. This is Wisdom, Queen of Heaven and Earth." Powell adds that "Christ is the *Logos,* the creative Word, and Sophia is the Wisdom underlying the Word."[101]

The New Revelation of the Divine Feminine

Robert Powell feels that Christ's second Coming is imminent, and that he will return in his feminine form as Sophia. Powell states that "Christ, in his ethereal form as the *Parousia* (Greek for "Presence"), is the guiding power of the New Age, and is behind the new revelation of the Divine Feminine." Powell explains that we all live in polarity, with a male physical body and a female ethereal body. One sign of the return of the Divine Mother is the ecological movement, a tender concern for the welfare of Mother Earth, "a direct consequence of the activity of the Etheric Christ." The spreading Goddess consciousness is an "outpouring of Divine Love, signifying a new phase of Christ's work to redeem the Mother and all the beings of nature."[102]

The Value of Sophiology

Sergei Bulgakov, a Russian Orthodox priest, explains the value of Sophiology:

1. It restores the Divine Feminine.
2. It returns to a consideration of creation as a theophany or a divine manifestation.
3. It restores Nature as a bridge of humans to God.
4. It reiterates divine love, as seen in John's Epistle, "God is Love."

To Bulgakov, Sophia is the great Unifier, uniting humans with Nature and with God, and also uniting the male and female genders. "We must discover how we can overcome the secularizing forces of the Reformation and the Renaissance in a positive way—through love for the world. Divine Wisdom is God's nature revealing itself. The Wisdom of God itself is spread like a canopy over our sinful but still hallowed world. Sophia unites God with the world as the one common principle, the divine ground of creaturely existence."[103]

There are many St. Sophia churches throughout Orthodox Christianity. St. Sophia Cathedral in Istanbul has a heavenly dome, portraying heaven bending down to embrace the earth; meanwhile, immense light pours in from the heavens above.

The hymn "O Come Emmanuel" has a stanza asking:

> O come, thou Wisdom from on high, and order all things far
> and nigh;
> To us the path of knowledge show, and cause us in her ways to
> go.

Kathleen Fischer describes the spiritual love existing between Ruth and her mother-in-law Naomi. Ruth loves Naomi so much that she will even accept Naomi's God. "They stand as witnesses to a God of inclusiveness who wants all to flourish. They come to know Sophia, the God especially concerned with the poor, the suffering, the outcast. Of them we might say, 'You are truly daughters of Wisdom, alive with the breath of God's power, acting with the strength She deploys from one end of the earth to the other' (Wisdom 7:25, 8:34)."

Fischer invites us to "join with women everywhere in a chorus of blessing and hope:

> Praise to you, Spirit-Sophia, source of all transformation.
> Healing torn places, you give birth to change.
> In you we create, find joy, make new beginnings.
> Hidden but moving, your signs are fire, wind, and water.
> Sister, mother, grandmother, lover, and friend,
> You keep us singing, hoping, believing, fiercely steadfast.
> Praise to you!"[104]

God the Mother

Phyllis Trible cites numerous maternal images of God in the Torah. "Metaphors such as God the pregnant woman (Isa. 42:14), the mother (Isa. 66:13), the midwife (Ps. 22:9), and the mistress (Ps. 123:2) are diverse and partial expressions of the female image of God."

Trible says that "God conceives in the womb, fashions in the womb, judges in the womb, destines in the womb, brings forth from the womb, receives out of the womb, and carries one from the womb to gray hairs. In Biblical traditions an organ unique to the female becomes a vehicle pointing to the compassion of God. The maternal metaphor *rahum* witnesses to God as compassionate, merciful, and loving."

In Jeremiah 31:15–22 Rachel is weeping over the loss of her sons Joseph and Benjamin. Yahweh comforts her and accepts the confession of Ephraim: "I will truly show motherly compassion upon him." Strophe four is the voice of Yahweh the mother. As Rachel mourns the loss of the fruit of her womb, so Yahweh, from the divine womb, mourns the same children. But there is a difference. "The human mother refuses consolation; the divine mother changes grief into grace." Jeremiah draws a striking conclusion: "Yahweh has created a new thing in the land—a female encompasses a man." But, adds Trible, "to encompass is to surpass."

Likewise, Isaiah shows that God will not forget Her people in exile: "Can a woman forget her sucking baby, that she should have no compassion on the child of her womb? Even these may forget, yet I will not forget you" (Isa. 49:15). In the Torah, says Trible, "the language has enfolded new dimensions of the image of God male *and* female."

In Numbers, chapter 11, Moses appeals to God when the Israelites complain about lack of food: "Did I conceive all this people? Did I bring them forth that thou shouldst say to me, 'Carry them in your bosom, as a nurse carries the sucking child?'" Trible concludes that in various Torah passages, "God conceives, is pregnant, writhes in labor pains, brings forth a child, and nurses it. Such language expands and deepens our understanding of the Biblical God."[105]

Mother and Child in Religion

Carl Jung speaks of the mother-baby relationship as an archetype deeply imbedded in the human psyche. "The worship of the ideal Mother and Babe is not only common to all religions but is their purest and most ennobling part. So necessary is it for the human heart that Buddhism in China has found a Kwan-yin, a female Buddha with a divine babe to worship. And Fatima and Hasan-Husein are as prominent in Islam as Madonna and the Babe in Christianity, or Yashoda and Krishna, and Kausaly and Rama, in Hinduism."[106]

Mary and Isis

Isis was originally an Egyptian goddess of the harvest. As Rome declined, "the serene figure of Isis with her spiritual calm, her gracious promise of immortality, appeared to many like a star in a stormy sea, and aroused in their breasts a rapture of devotion not unlike that paid in the Middle Ages to the Virgin Mary. Indeed, her stately ritual, with its shaven and tonsured priests, its matins and vespers, its tinkling music, its baptisms and aspersions of holy water, its solemn processions, its jewelled images of the Mother of God, presented many points of similarity to the ceremonies of Catholicism."[107]

Joseph Campbell describes a cylinder seal of about 300 C.E. which shows a crucified person as a redeemer. He says, "The Goddess Mother of the Universe, whose womb is the apriority of space and time, it is she who is symbolized by the Cross. It is into and through her that the god-substance pours into this field of space and time in a continuous act of selfgiving."[108]

In Mithraism there was a belief that a Virgin Goddess brought forth a son on December 25, the supposed day of the winter solstice. "This Virgin was the great Oriental goddess whom the Semites called the Heavenly Goddess. In Semitic lands she was a form of Astarte."[109] In *The Golden Ass* by Apuleius, a work praising her many virtues, "she claims to be the universal Goddess, incorporating the attributes of all others. She tells Apuleius that she is Nature, the Universal Mother, sovereign of all things spiritual. Many Roman emperors regarded her (Magna Mater) as the supreme deity of the empire."

Mary as Queen of Heaven

At the Council of Ephesus in 431, the Virgin Mary was proclaimed to be *Theotokos*, the Mother of God. Jesus had previously been declared to be the Son of God. For centuries Christians wondered whether they were to think of Mary as a goddess, and thus worship her. Through the Dark Ages in Europe, she grew greatly in esteem, especially among the common people.

By the Middle Ages there was a huge Mary cult. Almost all of the great Gothic cathedrals were built on sites sacred to Mary.[110] Notre Dame (Our Lady) is known all over Europe not for famous football teams but for the veneration and at times worship of the Virgin Mary. "In the single century 1170–1270 the French built 80 cathedrals and nearly 500 churches of the cathedral class." Most of these structures, not only in France but all over Europe, were dedicated to Our Lady. In his great study of medieval Christianity, *Mont-Saint-Michel and Chartres*, Henry Adams, the American historian, showed the courageous balance achieved between masculine and feminine energies in the Christian church. The semi-island fortress Mont-Saint-Michel, honoring the archangel Michael, portrays the masculine spirit, and Chartres Cathedral, with its marvelous rose windows, depicts the feminine energy.

"The proper study of mankind is woman," declared Adams, "and by common consent it is the most complex." Ernest Samuels relates how Adams described Mary: "In his daring imagery the Virgin Mary symbolized the popular rebellion against the artificial male-centered theology of the early Church. In the 12th century Mary emerged as the last and greatest of the Mother Goddesses, the goddesses of fertility known to all early religions. Her portrayal as the Virgin of Majesty in the sculpture and iconography of Chartres reflected the harmony of appearance and reality, of the graceful submission of man to woman."[111]

Adams said that "Our Lady of Chartres was known to be peculiarly gracious and gentle." As Queen of Heaven, Mary is fused with her Son in many statues. "At Chartres, Christ is identified with His Mother, the spirit of love and grace." Mary, with a crown on her head and her Son in her lap, sits enthroned as an empress. She receives prince and peasant alike, endowed with a humanity which, as a mortal, understands sin and thus forgives it. The Queen of Heaven was far more familiar to most French medieval Christians than was their own queen.

"In all Europe at that time," said Adams, "there was no power able to enforce justice or to maintain order, and no symbol of such power except Christ and His Mother. But the worship of the Virgin was never strictly orthodox. The bishop was much more afraid of Mary than he was of any Church Council ever held." Chartres Cathedral was huge: it could easily hold 10,000 people, and when crowded 15,000 persons. The rose windows are the most glorious ones in the world. The rose was the flower that symbolized Mary. The Bible said, "Wisdom has built herself a house, and has sculptured seven columns." Here Mary is depicted alongside seven pillars, which represent the seven liberal arts.

King Henry III and his wife Queen Louise walked fifty miles from Paris to Chartres in the middle of winter to ask the Virgin Mary for children, and then walked back to Paris. They did this year after year until the death of Henry III in 1589.

The Virgin Mary, it was said, went out of her way to help the poor, people like beggars and tramps. One day a banker and a destitute old woman died. The priest went to the banker's funeral, the Virgin went to that of the aged lady. Peasants saw the Holy Trinity as Father, Son, and Mother, with the Mother (as the Holy Spirit) focusing on applying maternal love and charity.

The adoration of Mary was particularly pronounced in the Eastern (Byzantine) Church. She became the patron saint of Constantinople at a time when that city was the center of Christendom, Rome having fallen to the German hordes. Countless miracles were attributed to her in both the Eastern and Western Christian Churches.[112]

Since the Hebrew language has no neuter gender, it is understandable that when writers of scripture needed personal pronouns for God, they used masculine pronouns. "This is not to deny in any way," says John Boswell, "that adherents of such traditions consequently project masculinity onto the deity so designated, or that this has disadvantaged women spiritually and often socially. Even so, many of these 'male' traditions center on female figures that are necessary for the spiritual life of men as well as women. The 'spirit' (*ha-rach*) of God was feminine in

Hebrew, neuter in Greek, and ultimately masculine in Latin and western Romance languages.

But that loss was not without compensatory gain. In addition to Mary, the only sinless person other than Jesus in the Christian cosmos—whose cults as the co-redeemer of the human race, dispenser of all graces, and Queen of Heaven attracted as many men as women—the church (*ecclesia*) was also a female figure, to whom priests were married. And the entire drama of Christian life focuses on the anima, the 'soul' or 'life force' conceptualized as feminine by nearly all ancient peoples. The name Eve (Hebrew *chavva*) is related in a direct way to 'life.'[113] The Italian cardinal St. Bonaventure called Mary 'the spouse of the Eternal Father.'"

Pope Pius IX proclaimed the doctrine of the Immaculate Conception in 1854. This meant that Mary was the only sinless person other than Jesus. The proclamation stated that "God had elected her his beloved daughter from the beginning of time and predestined her to be the mother of his only begotten son." In 1950 Pope Pius XII announced the doctrine of the Assumption of Mary, meaning that she never died but was bodily raised to heaven. "The sequel to the Assumption is *The Coronation of the Virgin*, in which Mary is crowned Queen of Heaven and united with the totality of the Godhead." Magnificent altarpieces in a number of cathedrals showed God the Father and God the Son together placing a crown on Mary's head. "The Catholic Church came dangerously close to declaring Mary Co-Redemptrix with Christ at Vatican II."[114]

Carl Jung welcomed the new status granted to Mary as a sign of a more complete paradigm of God. "The new dogma," he declared, "affirms that Mary as the Bride is united with the Son in the heavenly bridal chamber, and as Sophia (Wisdom) she is united with the Godhead. Thus the feminine principle is brought into immediate proximity with the masculine Trinity." Jung reminded us that in the Kabala, the two Sefirot Malkuth and Tifereth "represent the female and the male principles within the Godhead." Jung believed that images reflecting "the archetype of the self and those embodying the archetype of the divine are functionally indistinguishable. In the womblike cave, divinity would appear in the form of a child. The rediscovery of a child still alive in us may be regarded as the beginning of all *depth* psychology."[115]

The Compassion of Mother Mary

"Spiritual mothering needs to be done by both women and men," says Noragh Jones, "for it is the way we express our solidarity with other human beings and with the rest of creation. If mothering is confined to the domestic and private, the whole cosmos suffers. Mary therefore is being given a new focal place in Christianity by liberation theologians, because in her, mothering becomes universal rather than particular, and yet she is Everywoman, struggling with the ordinary everyday things that women do in all times and places."

Celtic people, Jones adds, have great affection and respect for Mary as "Mother of God and the model of divine compassion," but still think of her as "one of us," with great understanding of human frailty. Like a good mother, Mary cares for you when you are sick, so you pray to her for healing, Jones states.

"There are beautiful litanies emphasizing Mary's universal mothering. Her role as mother of the cosmos does not give her the remoteness that the all-powerful Father God sometimes connotes, for she still remains the good mother, close and compassionate:

> Be you my safeguarding by night, be you my safeguarding by
> day,
> Be you my safeguarding both night and day, you bright and
> kindly Queen of Heaven."[116]

Sufis point out that the Divine Names of God include the Compassionate and the Merciful, from the root word *rahim* (matrix), akin to the word maternal. Ruether states that the "Magnificat" in Luke 1:46–56 has become a key text for the spiritual journey of many Latin American women. "Its depiction of God exalting the humble inspires the struggle for justice. For contemporary Mexican American women, Our Lady of Guadalupe is a model of strength, competence, enduring presence, and fresh possibilities."[117] Ruether adds that Luke's Magnificat (and Mariology) suggests "a real co-creatorship between God and humanity, or in this case, woman." A Protestant woman from Indonesia, Marianne Katoppo, envisions Mary as "the model of humanity, truly liberated, truly human, compassionate and free."

Someone has said that we humans create God in our own image. The Bible tells us relatively little about what sort of person Mary was. The continually growing respect for Mary is an indication of how badly the modern world needs images of the divine feminine. What Germans call the *Weltgeist*, or World Soul, demands that women be treated as fairly as men, even in the divine prototypes.

In a recent sermon at Washington National Cathedral, the Reverend Caroline Fairless declared that "Advent is more than a wait. It's a time of shouting out what you know, of making bold statements in word and deed. Like Mary the Mother of God who says, 'My soul proclaims the greatness of the Lord,' you speak not only of what you know, here in this moment, but of what you believe is to come."

Divine Mates

God is infinite. God's infinity encompasses female and male nature and the supernatural, all of time and space. All we finite creatures do is concentrate on those limited aspects of God's being that are familiar to us, or seem most useful to us. Many of humanity's problems grow out of our denial of our neighbor's path-construct to God. If we want our neighbor to respect our path-construct, we must in all fairness respect his/hers.

The Torah shows the Divine Pair at work in creation (Proverbs 8:23–35). But the heavenly balance has been lost. Robert Powell says that we humans pride ourselves as being at the peak of worldly achievement. "Yet, to the yogis, the mystics, the saints who know God, we are unenlightened, ill, at war, separated, unable to create a world of hope and joy for all people."[118]

"English therapist John Rowan believes that every man in Western culture needs this connection to the vital female principle in nature and urges men to turn to the Goddess" to help restore the balance. "Perhaps this is how it was in prehistoric times, when men and women existed peacefully under the hegemony of the Goddess."[119]

"For those eager to know and love the Christ in a more holistic way, Sophia introduces feminine insight to yoke with the Christ as loving Master. Christ-love and Sophia-wisdom become one. The son and daughter of the trinosophia are acknowledged. One modern term for such love-wisdom is Christ consciousness. Sophia brings us to a greater understanding of the universe, of ourselves, and of the Plan. The primary work of the divine feminine is to call us to a conscious awareness of our soul purpose and our collective Oneness."[120]

"The cult of the Virgin, of the divine feminine, of the divine maternity, helps us complete the personalization of God by constituting Him a family." God has been conceived of as a father, a judge of His family. "To counterbalance this, the Mother element was required, the Mother who always forgives, the Mother whose arms are always open to the child who flies from the angry father." To complete a wholly caring family, we have recourse to providing the male God with a feminine mate. "We have placed by the side of the God-Father the Goddess-Mother, she who always forgives because, seeing the cause of the fault, knows the only justice is forgiveness."[121]

The common mind has trouble conceiving of a Father and a Son without a Mother. In Sumer, when both women and men wrote the scriptures, the deities were both female and male. Also, the Bhagavad-Gita gives this description of God:

> I am the Father-Mother of this world.
> Spouse, Master, Ruler, Judge, Witness, Nurse, Friend;
> I am the deathless seed of all the world.

Reaffirmation and Reconciliation: The Kingdom of God

"To date, no archeological or historical evidence has been found for any widespread female dominant cultures in which males were oppressed." Does this mean we should return to matriarchy? Of course not. "Man is not the enemy. He too is caught up in a culture that denies expression of the feminine. The Goddess is the means by which we know the universe is sacred. We have to live our lives so that they come into harmony with the sacred."

Dominican priest Matthew Fox asks, "What would it mean to live in a nurturing society, one where even men nurtured self, one another, and others? From a theological point of view, it would mean a recovery of the tradition of God as Mother." The wisdom and compassion of the Mother would "revitalize Western religion and civilization, forge new links with non-Western traditions, create gentler relationships to earth, to body, to pleasure, to work, to the artist within and among us."[122] There would be no terrorism in such a world.

Christine Downing adds that we know the Great Mother from our unconscious. For all of us, from life in the womb, our mother was our universe. Knowing ourselves means becoming conscious of our beginning, reawakening our phylogenetic memory, and thus recovering the key to the storehouse of species memories. This could bring us in touch with what Jung called 'the collective unconscious,' and help us to know that there is more to us than the personal and historical."[123] Jungians say that the Mother Goddess archetype exists in "the collective unconscious of both men and women, to be mined for psychological wholeness."

"Feminist spirituality today," says Ruether, "is re-assessing pre-Christian religion. By applying prophetic faith to sexism we reveal in new fullness its revolutionary meaning." She bases her approach on pre-Christian religions suppressed by Judaism and Christianity, as well as on Biblical prophetism, Christian theology, and the historical cultures of Western thought. Thus she sees us creating the ideological conditions necessary for a world community constituting the Kingdom of God. "In God's Kingdom," she says, "the corrupting principles of domination and subjugation will be overcome. People will no longer model relationships, even those to God, after power that reduces others to servility. Rather, they will discover a new kind of power, a power exercised through service. This critique of power relationships is central to Jesus' radical interpretation of the prophetic-messianic tradition. When Christianity became an imperial religion, no element in the Gospels was so totally deformed to conceal its original meaning. The Church then uses this spiritual understanding of the Kingdom anti-Jewishly to claim that Christians alone have the higher spiritual view of the Kingdom.

The Church suppresses the social justice dimension fundamental to the entire Biblical prophetic tradition of messianic hope. The continuity between the Jewish understanding of the Messiah and the Christian use of the term 'Christ' is lost. Christianity can then claim a new Christian imperialism over not only the Jews but the rest of the world.

Feminist theology is not asserting unprecedented ideas; rather it is rediscovering the prophetic context as norm." In effect, feminism is another liberation theology. It shows mistreatment of women as another prophetic denunciation of an unjust social hierarchy. Women who support patriarchy often become oppressors. Their visions of liberation need to be confronted by "voices of women from oppressed classes, races, and non-Christian religions."[124]

Anna Cooper, a 19th century African-American activist, gave a succinct statement of human goals: "We need to take our stand on the solidarity of humanity, the oneness of life, and the injustice of all special favoritism, whether of sex, race, country, or condition."

Ruether says that "sexism is gender privilege of males over females. The dehumanization of the other ultimately dehumanizes oneself. Men need to overcome their fear of loss of male status. At this point men are able to recognize that the struggle against sexism is basically a struggle to humanize the world, to humanize ourselves, to salvage the planet. And to be in right relation to God/ess. On this, men and women can really join hands in a common struggle."[125]

The Godhead

The Godhead is the source of all supernatural power in creation. Manifestations of the Godhead are seen in the starry heavens, in majestic mountains and swirling seas, in gardens of flowers, in forests of trees, and certainly in all living creatures, including humans.

But the precise nature of the Godhead is unknowable, as if a drop of water could comprehend an ocean, or an oxygen molecule understand the Grand Canyon.

Karen Armstrong explains the paradox. "The *hypostases* Father, Son, and Spirit should not be identified with God himself, because, as Gregory of Nyssa explained, 'the divine nature is unnameable and unspeakable.' The three *hypostases* are only incomplete glimpses of the Divine Nature itself, which lies far beyond such imagery. The Trinity, therefore, should not be seen as a literal fact but as a paradigm that corresponds to real facts in the hidden life of God."[126]

Islam knows the Godhead. Mohammed said Allah is the Beneficent, the Nourisher, the Forgiver—and who give the child more of these qualities than the mother? Bhagavan Das quotes the Koran: "Where the mother-heart is, there is Godhead; where Godhead is, there is heaven." And from the *Hadith* (sayings of Mohammed): "The Being of Godhead rests amidst the Pairs, maintaining even justice over all."[127]

Sufis believe in the Rasul, who like the *ishtadeva*, is one who represents God's perfection overcoming human limitations. Religious seekers follow the Rasul familiar to them, but at the higher levels all Rasuls merge in their approach to the Godhead.

Kabalists can also explain something about the Godhead. By merging Gnostic ideas with Neoplatonism, early Kabalists in Spain evolved the doctrine of the Godhead as a dynamic complex of Sefirot ("potencies") emanating from the inaccessible God.

The Orient knows of the Godhead. Some Taoists speak of the Godhead, as proclaimed by Confucius, Christ, and especially Lao-Tse, "and in the deepest sense by all the religions of the earth as 'Seat of the supreme True Lord and originating master of all religions.'" Ramakrishna said that Mother God warns us that only a fool would say, "My religion is the only true one." Ramakrishna described the Godhead as consisting of the union of the male Brahma (the shoreless ocean) with the female Shakti (the infinite waves).

Heinz Bechert states that Shaktist Tantrism personifies divine forces as female deities. He says that Shakti ("force") refers to the Highest Being as feminine. Hans Küng believes that like Shaktist Tantrism, modern Christianity must recognize the female archetype: "The starting point of all Christian theology today must be that 'God' is not subsumed under masculinity, but that 'he' at once embraces and transcends, sublimating masculinity and femininity in a kind of 'coincidence of opposites.'" Modern Christians can use the term God the Father only "in a sense that includes motherliness. Küng quotes Ruether as saying, "God is not male. God is Spirit."[128]

The medieval mystic John Ruysbroeck in his *Seven Degrees of Love* says that in the eternal Now "we can speak no more of Father, Son, and Holy Spirit or of any other creature, but only of one Being, which is the very substance of the Divine Persons.

There we all are before our creation. There the Godhead is, the superessence of all created things."[129]

The Primal Matrix, the Great Womb, and the Ground of Being are terms that have been used to refer to the Godhead. In the Celtic creation myth, Anu is the Source-Mother of the Gods. Above all, the Godhead is Ultimate Reality. Christianity expresses this as Deitas; Judaism in the Kabala calls Ein Sof the Infinite. Islam describes Al Haqq as the Ground beyond Allah. In Hinduism the ultimate essence is Brahman. In Taoism the eternal Tao is the Mother of everything.

Meister Eckhart on the Godhead

Eckhart calls the Godhead the very love with which God loves God's own nature. The divine spark in us is our link with the Godhead. Thus, says Eckhart, we have a part of divinity within us. Let us live up to our royal ancestry!

Other Christians, like Clement of Alexandria and Origen, had similar views. What distinguishes Eckhart's approach is that he considers our divine spark to be the birth of God within us. He says, "As long as you love another person less than you love yourself, you do not love yourself rightly," for love is giving, not getting. The Hindus have the proper greeting when they say, "*Namaste!*" It means, "I bow to the Spirit of God within you!"

Matthew Fox, editing an edition of Eckhart's "creation spirituality," calls the book *Breakthrough*, meaning being born again, this time in the Spirit. As he summarized Eckhart's concept of the Godhead, Fox cites illustrative examples for clarification. He says that many theologians before Eckhart made the distinction between God and the Godhead, including Pseudo-Dionysus, Thomas Aquinas, and Gilbert of Porreta. Some said that God operates on earth, but the Godhead remains in heaven. Godhead is an effort to go beyond the all-male God. Godhead is the God beyond God, the transcendent ineffable Deity. The Godhead is the deep Ground out of which the Trinity flows. If given a sexual identity, the Godhead is feminine: Deitas in Latin and Gottheit in German are both feminine terms. Eckhart recalled Jesus' words that his disciples would do greater acts than he did (John 14:12), and that perfect love brings unity (John 17:23). There, says Fox, "all barriers will break down, and in the unity of our origins in God, joy will not cease."[130]

Tetrads

Many religions conceive of the Godhead as having four dimensions. These include the Sumerians, Hittites, Canaanites, Greeks, Romans, Hindus, and the Japanese. Raphael Patai gives an explanation of the Biblical Tetragrammaton, Yahweh (YHWH), as listed by the Kabalists: "The four elements are *Hochma* (Wisdom), *Bina* (Understanding), *Tiferet* (Beauty), and *Malkhut* (Kingship). Here Wisdom is identified with the Father, Understanding with the Mother, Beauty with the Son, and Kingship with the Daughter. Patai also tells how Yahweh appeared to Abraham in the form of three men (Gen. 18:1–33). This three-in-one Deity, says Patai, is masterfully presented in a narrative which switches constantly between the plural and the singular.[131]

The Unified Godhead

Most religions have some version of a triune Godhead. Unfortunately, almost all of these trinities consist of solely male deity manifestations. Consistent with the evidence given in this chapter, a symbolization of a Godhead uniting equal female and male components is hereby presented. Several words of precaution are needed.

Anglo-Saxons, those speaking the English language, want God to be called "God," because that is the term used from their childhood. But most Christians do not use the term "God." Not in France, Germany, Greece, Italy, Latin America, Portugal, Russia, Spain, or the Scandinavian countries is God called "God." Also, God is not called "God" by most Christians in Africa and Asia. Every nation has its own term for God, and so does every religion. It is provincial for Americans to assume that everyone who uses his/her native term for the God concept is an infidel. Had I been born a Hopi, I would call God "Massau'u" (Great Spirit), and I am sure that the Godhead would know whom I was addressing. Let us not let language get in our way in addressing the Absolute.

Let us honestly remind ourselves that we finite beings cannot fully comprehend the Godhead's infinity. But we know love when we experience it, and like God, the Godhead is Love.

No one is expected to surrender her/his belief system as presently constituted. Generally speaking, one's own *ishtadeva* (that aspect of the Deity that has appeared to you) will always be your own best approach to the Godhead. The point at which you are sincerely requested to consider any modification in your approach is when you observe that your approach is harming someone for racial, religious, class, nationality, or gender reasons. It is profane to worship a God who either hates creation or hates humanity, or some part of it.

Like the mind, the human spirit grows by expansion. Countless people have experienced the liberating feeling of getting rid of prejudice, of expanding their consciousness to include all of humanity, indeed all of creation. As this group grows in number, we can expect to see the real foundations laid for world peace, and the erection of a Kingdom of God fitting to be called God's world.

Why Our Images of God Should Include the Feminine

Virginia Ann Froehle, a Religious Sister of Mercy, offers "six reasons why all of us, both women and men, should enlarge our images of God to include the feminine:

1. To know God better and to relate to God with a fuller sense of who God is.
2. To help recognize that feminine qualities are as necessary as masculine for guiding the world.
3. To help men and women reach wholeness by making it easier for them to embrace their feminine sides.
4. To help women experience themselves as identified with God as daughters.
5. To provide an alternative for those who have difficulty relating to God as father.
6. To provide a feminine image of healing for those who have had inadequate mothering."

Sister Virginia Ann says, "I believe we live closer to the truth of God as we are able to live and pray comfortably with both masculine and feminine images of God."[132]

Men's Liberation

Most readers will regard this chapter as a fervent plea for women's liberation. There is of course some truth in that view. But far more it is an argument for *men's* liberation. For five thousand years men have been slaves to their own worst selves: ego domination, brute force, projection of evil, and simple dishonesty concerning the limitations of their own gender and the merits of the other gender. *All* men need to "come out of the closet"—to openly confess that the trampling of feminine civil, economic, human, political, and religious rights is a disgrace to the wonderful excellence that men are capable of, and also a sacrilegious disregard for God's love, fairness, justice, and truth.

The family of *Homo sapiens* is really the family of God. In such a family there is no room for special favoritism, a "good old boy" network, or a desecration of God's nature through allegations of trumped-up superiority of either sex over the other. God is good. We will never know how good He is until we let Her light shine through our everyday thoughts, prayers, and deeds.

The Unified Godhead

As you contemplate this diagram of the Godhead, substitute your own *ishtadeva* for any of the indicated components. A list of possible substitutions, drawn from the major world religions, is provided beneath the diagram.

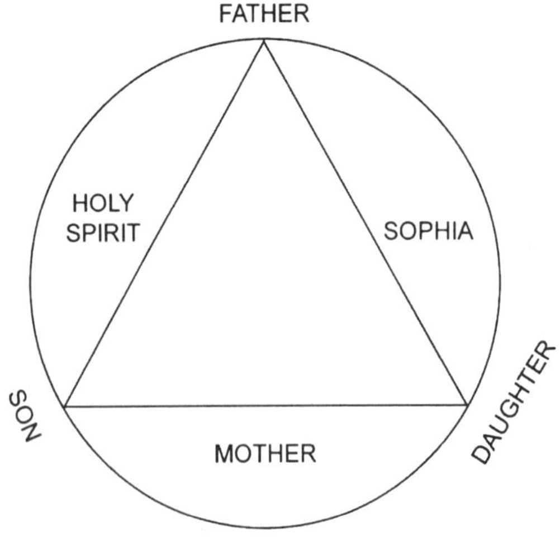

1. Alternate names for God the Father: Allah, Brahma, Great Spirit, Hokhma, Yahweh, and others.

2. Alternate names for God the Mother: Gaia, Great Goddess, Ground, Mary, Maya, Mother Earth, Mother Nature, Shakti, Tao, and others.

3. Alternate names for God the Son: Buddha, Christ, Jesus, Krishna, *Logos*, Rama, Vishnu, and others.

4. Alternate names for God the Daughter: Asherah, Holy Soul, Malkhut, Matronit, Shekhinah, and others.

5. Alternate names for the Holy Spirit: Comforter, Counselor, *Paraclete*, Presence, Truth, Unifier, Universal Wave Function, and others.

6. Alternate names for Sophia: Athena, Ishtar, Kwan-yin, Lakshmi, Mercy, Wisdom, and others.

Dynamics of the Configuration

1. The Godhead is One. The circle is the perfect geometrical figure. St. Bonaventure said that the Godhead is "a sphere whose center is everywhere and whose circumference is nowhere." Ken Wilber states that "who sees not God everywhere sees God truly nowhere."

2. The circle can also symbolize the Void or Nirvana (see Chapter 7).

3. The Unified Godhead resembles the Taoist Yin/Yang circle, which represents the necessary complementarity of male and female forces at all levels of the Cosmos, even the Divine.

4. I John 4:16 says, "God is love, and those who abide in love abide in God, and God abides in them." Of the four forces in nature (electromagnetism, gravity, radioactivity, and the strong force), strongest of all is the force binding the nucleus of the atom together. So too with Divine Love. Unless the Father and the Mother love each other, the Cosmos is shattered. Similar tragedy occurs when there is no love between the Daughter and the Holy Spirit (or alternates), or between the Son and Sophia (or their alternates).

5. Father-Mother God created us out of Love, saved us by Love, and desires for us to live in the Spirit of Love. Each time we obey a unitive Scripture teaching, the Cosmos is strengthened. Each time we follow a divisive Scripture passage, the entire Cosmos is weakened.

6. The Talmud says that "to redeem one person is to redeem the world." Each person is a child of God. We reverence God

when we revere all of God's creation. "Each life is like a whole world, and the spiritual obligation of a Jew is commitment to *tikkun olam*, the restoration and healing of a world ruptured from God," says Tanya Luhrmann.

7. For a discussion of the similarities between Jesus and Buddha, see Chapter 8.

8. A traditional Christian still has the male Holy Trinity (the left side of the Unified Godhead), but ignoring the Divine Feminine has borne ill fruit through the centuries, and stands in the way of world peace and justice.

9. A radical feminist has a female Holy Trinity (the right side of the Unified Godhead) but to forego union with the Divine Masculine is to deny the reunion of the Shekhinah with the Crown, and bodes ill for the prospect of a world of peace and justice.

10. Ultimately what is at stake is the survival of our species on planet Earth. Never before has humanity had such threats (atomic, biological, chemical, ecological, military, and terrorist) to our continued existence. But never before has humanity had such powerful means (agricultural, economic, energetic, medical, and religious) of continuing our existence. The solution to our survival is simple: we can live if we can love.

The Ultimate Outcome

Thank God for God's universe! We humans did not create it, nor have we proved to be good stewards of that portion of creation that we inhabit. If we continue to practice divisive religion, we will bring incomprehensible disaster to this globe and all of its inhabitants.

But we can never escape from the Godhead. We can continue to ignore unitive religion, and thereby harm our fellow humans. We can continue to erect barriers that try to impede the Godhead's access to us. But ultimately our strength is incredibly weak compared to that of the Godhead. The Godhead is Love, and eventually Divine Love will prevail.

St. Paul tells us that someday the Godhead, not only God, will rule the Cosmos. In I Corinthians 15:28 Paul writes that evil will eventually lose, and then "God will be God in all."

1 Elinor W. Gadon, *The Once and Future Goddess: A Symbol for Our Time* (HarperSanFrancisco, 1989), p. xiii.

2 Derek Bickerton, *New York Times Book Review,* 8 October 2000, p. 27.

3 Christine Downing, *Goddess: Mythological Images of the Feminine* (Crossroad, 1981), p. 4.

4 Quoted in Sandra M. Schneiders, *Women and the Word* (Paulist Press, 1986), pp. 17, 68–71.

5 Rosemary Radford Ruether, *Sexism and God-Talk* (Beacon Press, 1993), pp. 19, 23, 24.

6 Denise L. Carmody, *Responses to 101 Questions about Feminism* (Paulist Press, 1993), pp. 42, 43, 110.

7 Monica Sjöö and Barbara Mor, *The Great Cosmic Mother: Rediscovering the Religion of the Earth* (HarperSanFrancisco, 1991), p. 244.

8 Joseph Campbell, *The Masks of God: Creative Mythology* (Penguin, 1976), p. 626.

9 Sjöö and Mor, p. 193.

10 Ruether, pp. 53–54.

11 Sjöö and Mor, pp. 231, 233.

12 Merlin Stone, *When God Was a Woman* (Dorset Press, 1990), pp. 195, 224.

13 Ruether, pp. 94, 95, 117.

14 Sjöö and Mor, p. 292.

15 Gadon, pp. 219, 220.

16 Sjöö and Mor, p. 206.

17 Mary Daly, *Beyond God the Father* (Beacon Press, 1985), pp. 148, 149.

18 Ruether, p. 97.

19 Sjöö and Mor, p. 205.

20 Carmody, *Responses,* p. 41.

21 Vivian Gornick, *New York Times Book Review*, 14 March 1982, p. 33.

22 Bob Herbert, *New York Times*, 9 November 1997, 4:15.

23 Maggie O'Kane, *Arizona Republic*, 21 December 1997, p. A16.

24 Katha Pollitt, *New York Times Magazine*, 14 May 2000, p. 23.

25 Kathleen Fischer, *Transforming Fire: Women Using Anger Creatively* (Paulist Press, 1999), pp. 132, 133.

[26] Barbara E. Reed, in Sharma, pp. 161–163, 165, 167, 173.

[27] Ruether, pp. 34, 35, 36.

[28] Raphael Patai, *The Hebrew Goddess* (Wayne State University Press, 1990), p. 24.

[29] Ruether, pp. 48, 49.

[30] Ibid., pp. 49–52.

[31] Sjöö and Mor, p. 251.

[32] Ibid., pp. 253, 257, 258.

[33] Heinrich Zimmer, *Myths and Symbols in Indian Art and Civilization*, ed. by Joseph Campbell (Harper Torchbooks, 1962), pp. 25, 26, 90, 92, 96–102.

[34] Ibid., pp. 127, 128, 139, 199, 202, 203, 207, 208.

[35] Küng, pp. 210, 211.

[36] Capra and Steindl-Rast, pp. 138, 139, 140, 160, 161.

[37] Caitlin and John Matthews, *The Encyclopedia of Celtic Wisdom* (Element Books, 1994), pp. 283, 284.

[38] *Encyclopedia Britannica*, 1971, vol. 12, pp. 958, 958A.

[39] Patai, pp. 77, 78.

[40] Ibid., pp. 126, 129, 130, 131, 133.

[41] Sjöö and Mor, p. 49.

[42] Gadon, p. xii.

[43] Sjöö and Mor, pp. 59, 73, 74, 145.

[44] Gadon, p. xv.

[45] Sjöö and Mor, pp. 42, 47.

[46] Gadon, pp. 6, 24.

[47] Ibid., pp. 25, 29, 30, 31.

[48] Ibid., pp. 37, 40, 41, 44, 55, 57, 59, 61, 62, 66, 69, 79, 80.

[49] Sjöö and Mor, pp. 213, 217.

[50] Gadon, pp. 87–90, 94, 99, 106.

[51] Thorkild Jacobsen, in Henri Frankfort et al, *Before Philosophy* (Pelican, 1954), pp. 147,158.

[52] Sjöö and Mor, p. 266.

[53] Henri and Mrs. H.A. Frankfort, in Frankfort, pp. 26–28, 237–240.

[54] Sjöö and Mor, pp. 156, 158.

[55] Ibid., p. 212.

[56] Patrica Telesco, *365 Goddesses: A Daily Guide* (HarperSanFrancisco, 1998), October 15.

57 Charlene Spretnak, *Lost Goddesses of Early Greece* (Moon Books, 1978), pp. 38, 42.

58 Ibid., pp. 47, 49, 50.

59 Downing, pp. 118, 119.

60 Spretnak, pp. 90, 94.

61 Ibid., pp. 54, 58.

62 Downing, pp. 194, 195, 199, 215.

63 Hugo Rahner, "The Christian Mystery and the Pagan Mysteries," in *The Mysteries*, ed. by Joseph Campbell (Pantheon Books, 1955), pp. 347, 349, 351.

64 Gadon, pp. 143, 144, 146, 150.

65 Fraser, pp. 404, 413, 414.

66 Patai, pp. 31, 32, 33.

67 Campbell, *Creative Mythology*, p. 628.

68 Patai, pp. 35–38, 41–44, 47–50.

69 Ruether, p. 56.

70 Sjöö and Mor, pp. 267, 268, 270, 271, 291.

71 Ruether, pp. 140, 141.

72 Patai, pp. 96–101, 103.

73 Ibid., pp. 104, 105, 114.

74 Ibid., pp. 107, 109.

75 Fischer, p. 50.

76 Ruether, p. 59.

77 Patai, pp. 141–45, 147–53, 158–62, 166–73, 175, 203, 211–220.

78 Ibid., pp. 255, 259, 260, 268, 272.

79 Ibid., pp. 283, 287, 288, 289.

80 Gadon, pp. 244, 245.

81 Patai, p. 279.

82 Gadon, pp. 248, 249.

83 Sjöö and Mor, p. 259.

84 Noragh Jones, *Power of Raven, Wisdom of Serpent: Celtic Women's Spirituality* (Lindisfarne Press, 1995), pp. 97, 99.

85 Gadon, pp. 290, 341, 358, 359, 360, 364, 375, 376.

86 Sjöö and Mor, pp. 162–164.

87 Matthews, pp. 301, 314, 316, 433.

88 Jones, pp. 59, 106, 226.

89 Fox, in Eckhart, pp. 35, 39.

[90] Sarah Bayliss, *New York Times*, 2 July 2000, 2:31.

[91] Sandra M. Schneiders, *With Oil in Their Lamps* (Paulist Press, 2000), pp. 102, 103.

[92] Denis Edwards, *Jesus and the Cosmos* (Paulist Press, 1991), pp. 10, 45, 60, 101.

[93] Schneiders, *Women and the Word*, pp. 51, 52.

[94] Ruether, pp. 135–138.

[95] Schneiders, *With Oil in Their Lamps*, pp. 104, 105.

[96] Vladimir Solovyov, *The Meaning of Love* (Lindisfarne Press, 1985), p. 114.

[97] Boys, pp. 163, 164.

[98] Daniel Andreev, in Robert A. Powell, *The Most Holy Trinosophia and the New Revelation of the Divine Feminine* (Anthroposophic Press, 2000), pp. 26, 27.

[99] Powell, pp. 32, 35, 36, 37, 38.

[100] Ibid., pp. 40–47.

[101] Ibid., pp. 48, 50, 51, 60, 61, 71–74.

[102] Ibid., pp. 86, 87, 97, 98.

[103] Sergei Bulgakov, *Sophia and the Wisdom of God* (Lindisfarne Press, 1993), pp. xviii, 1, 20, 21, 74, 88.

[104] Fischer, pp. 184, 185.

[105] Phyllis Trible, *God and the Rhetoric of Sexuality* (Fortress Press, 1978), pp. 22, 38–40, 45, 47, 48, 52, 56, 63, 65, 67, 69.

[106] Das, pp. 455, 456.

[107] Fraser, pp. 444, 445.

[108] Campbell, *Creative Mythology*, pp. 24, 25.

[109] Fraser, p. 416.

[110] Gadon, pp. 189, 190, 195, 196, 197.

[111] Henry Adams, *Mont-Saint-Michel and Chartres* (New American Library, 1961), p. vii.

[112] Ibid., pp. 78, 80, 85, 95, 97, 179, 249, 273, 299.

[113] *New York Times Book Review*, 15 July 1984, p. 7.

[114] Gadon, pp. 204, 205, 206.

[115] Carl Jung, *Memories, Dreams, Reflections* (Random House, 1965), pp. 202, 294. Also, Downing, pp. 219, 221.

[116] Jones, pp. 91, 94, 95.

[117] Fischer, pp. 70, 71.

[118] Powell, p. 17.

[119] Gadon, p. 290.

[120] Powell, pp. 15, 16.

[121] Miguel de Unamuno, *Tragic Sense of Life* (Dover Publications, 1954), p. 173.

[122] Gadon, pp. 239, 294, 300, 303, 304.

[123] Downing, p. 6.

[124] Ruether, pp. 30–33, 39, 45.

[125] Ibid., pp. 165, 191, 192, 231.

[126] Karen Armstrong, *A History of God* (Knopf, 1994), p. 116.

[127] Das, p. 40.

[128] Küng, pp. 366, 416.

[129] Quoted in F.C. Happold, *Mysticism*, rev. ed. (Penguin, 1970), p. 66.

[130] Fox, in Eckhart, pp. 77, 78, 79, 82, 225, 287, 289, 290, 320, 472, 474.

[131] Patai, pp. 111, 116, 117.

[132] Virginia Ann Froehle, "Feminine Images of God Can Enhance Your Prayer and Change Your Life," *St. Anthony Messenger*, May 1989, p. 27.

Chapter XII

The Family of God

God's family is the human race. All human life is sacred by the act of divine creation. To demand preferential status in the eyes of our Creator is to evade God's will that we should be loving members of a common family. The basic root of the political goals of freedom, equality, and comradeship is our joint origin and destiny as children of God. Political goals not built upon a sound spiritual base are worthless, for they can readily become selfish grasps for power.

Further, political or social goals built upon an ethnocentric religious base have led to enormous suffering for humanity. The only worthy religious base is one which respects *all* of God's creation as sacred, not merely that part preferred by any one person or group.

Christianity, nearly mortally wounded through internal division, has been reuniting itself in the face of the twofold challenge of communism and secularism. In the process it has become reacquainted with some of its historic roots as the incipient Kingdom of God. Thomas Torrance points out that the continual modern violence over race, religion, and nationality has challenged all Christian churches "to mobilize their resources in the cause of peace and reconciliation, to seek for a solution in which the search for ecumenicity in the world church becomes part of a wider search for the emerging world community of the human race."[1]

Vatican II Council of the Roman Catholic Church issued a Dogmatic Constitution on the Church, a decree which sets aside church history and traditional structure in favor of Jesus Christ and the Bible. To Torrance, this change is momentous. He says that "this reorientation of the Catholic Church upon Christ Himself had the effect of opening the Roman Church in a new way both to the other churches and to the world beyond the Church, for now the Church comes to be regarded as a sign of intimate union with God, and of all mankind in Christ."[2]

Torrance perceives a new understanding of the Incarnation, now seen as the coming of God into human nature, in order to restore the unity and harmony of all of life. Thus the Church is called upon to thrust itself into world affairs, "in fulfillment of the divine purpose for the reconciliation and unification of the world, through which it looks for the emerging world community in which the redeemed life of the people of God and the life of all mankind will be one and the same." Torrance also sees the World Council of Churches as earnestly seeking "not only to find ways of eliminating the divisions between churches but ways of making real in the modern world the ancient vision of the catholicity and universality of the Church."[3]

Finally many Christian churches are now trying to practice what they preach. Aldous Huxley had bemoaned the practice of church leaders putting haloes on the heads of warmongering leaders and then wondering why the world could not find its way to peace.

Divisive religion can declare its own bankruptcy. Not long ago evangelist James Robison confessed using unchristian methods during his 21-year ministry, and asked forgiveness: "That which I believed to be God-given conviction often came across as personal attack, or prejudice, casting many unnecessarily into the same pot and possibly damaging the very body of Jesus." He regretted that his statements "often caused unnecessary division and strife, thereby hindering the work of grace so badly needed in the church."[4]

The Family of God

The Confucian mystic Chang Tsai (1022–1077) said that "since Heaven is my father, all people are my brothers and sisters, and all things are my companion." Charles Kraft states that

God's protective covenant with Noah extends to the whole human family. Kraft quotes Paul in Acts 17:26 saying "God created every race of humans from one stock."

The Founding Fathers

On July 4, 1788, a great parade was held in Philadelphia, celebrating the ratification of the U.S. Constitution. Then, toasts were drunk, first "to the people of the United States," ending 13 rounds later with a toast "to the whole family of mankind." Benjamin Franklin was recognized throughout Europe as a citizen of the world, and other delegates also had this perception. Gouverneur Morris reminded the Constitutional Convention that delegates were "representatives of the whole human race." Delegate James Wilson said that civilized nations were finally realizing that all mankind are brothers. Law and order would reign in the family of mankind, he said, as soon as a peacekeeping authority was established through the worldwide community.

Later Ralph Waldo Emerson built his whole philosophy upon human dignity. He advocated self-reliance, but pointed out that each soul is a part of the Over-Soul or God. Thus, to harm your neighbor is to harm yourself, and to help her is to help oneself.

Mysticism culminates in togetherness or unity. Since this unity is founded in God, it is stronger than the ties of family, race, religion, or nation. By calling God "Father," Jesus united humanity in a divinely ordained family. Mystics know that God is the God of their enemies as well as of their friends, and that by loving God, the Universal Parent, enemies can become friends.

Eliminating Boundaries

"Wherever there is a boundary," says Ken Wilber, "there is a potential war. The aim of the mystics is to deliver man and women from their battles by eliminating boundaries. The discovery of the ultimate Whole is the only cure for unfreedom. When the self sense dies, all that dissolves is a boundary that was never real."[5]

"Ken Wilber detects many signs of an emerging worldwide wisdom culture. These signs include the fact that people are beginning to see beyond color to recognize the family of humanity. Other signs are the revolt of the younger generation against purely pecuniary values, and the growing merger of science and religion. Also encouraging is the nascent acceptance of the transcendent unity of all major religions, rejecting any system that insists that it is the only true path to God. The time might come when voters will demand that candidates be mentally and spiritually mature in order to hold public office. The ultimate goal is the expansion of consciousness to where every person is seen to be an equal member of the mystical body of Christ/Krishna/Buddha."[6]

Unifying Concepts

Friedrich Heiler finds that although the major religions have important differences, these are overarched by an ultimate unity found in the following areas:

1. The immanence of the Divine Reality in human hearts.
2. The identification of this Reality with humanity's highest good.
3. The way of God to humans as ultimate Love.
4. The way of humans to God as sacrifice and prayer.
5. The way of Love uniting person to person.
6. The way of Love as a human being's superior way to God.[7]

Aurobindo Ghose believes that "a spiritual religion of humanity is the hope of the future. It means a growing realization that there is a divine Reality in which we are all one, that the human race is the means by which it will progressively reveal Itself here. It implies a growing attempt to bring about a kingdom of this divine Spirit upon earth. Only when His race knows God and lives in the Divine will the ideal sense of Her strivings begin to unfold itself and the kingdom be founded."[8]

Only once, says Teilhard, has this planet been able to envelop itself with life. And only once has life here succeeded in crossing the threshold of reflection. Too much is at stake to have this precious heritage lost due to political bunglers.

The Search for Meaning

Frank A. Wilson declares that hatred, crime, and violence are found in large numbers in prosperous industrial societies in which the universe is regarded as meaningless and humanly irrelevant. Yet modern science proclaims a deep meaning to the universe, Wilson feels. The new field theories of quantum mechanics postulate a transcendental field in which quarks, the ultimate constituents of matter, are considered as both localized in a particular atom and at the same time having a universal reference. "The universe is a unity," Wilson says, "with its contents spaced out with astounding regularity, and only a sustaining field influence, working through gravity, can possibly ensure this. The non-material aspect of the universe—one can call it the universal field—possesses inherent timeless organizational potentialities."[9]

So exquisite is the balance among its parts that even a minor variation in its atoms would have ruled out the possibility of the universe creating stars or planets. Even a slight change in the bonding powers of carbon and other life-giving elements would have prevented the formation of molecules, on which life depends. The universe, Wilson avers, is geared to support life in a very purposive meaningful way.

"Many of the claims of the great religions," Wilson believes, "can be interpreted in the light of the field paradigm, and so be fitted into an emerging self-consistent view of human responsibility in a cosmos. The unifying bonding power of love is a property of immense importance, for it is the means whereby the pooling of mind-events into groups of ever-increasing power is sustained."

Wilson sees the collective unconscious, as described by Jung, to be a unifying force, "the field involvement of human minds, a sort of automatic universal pooling." All human psyches are united in Theos, he feels, and thus "Theos (God) is the means whereby the disunity of the creation is resolved in a culminating fulfilling love."[10]

As pointed out in Chapter 5 above, mathematical physicist Frank J. Tipler professes to having found proofs for both the existence of God and for human immortality. Tipler states that he arrived at these proofs "in exactly the same way physicists calculate the properties of the electron."

Miguel de Unamuno says that "if you believe in God, God believes in you, and believing in you God creates you continually. For in your essence you are nothing but the idea that God possesses of you. We must needs believe in the afterlife, in order that we may live this life, and endure it, and give it meaning and finality."[11]

Peace with Justice

Frustration leads to aggression. Muslim nations naturally resent Western favoritism towards Israel, and sometimes strike back in blind fury. The United Nations must ensure fairness in areas of deep controversy, such as the Holy Land, Kashmir, and Ireland. Respected peace makers like Jimmy Carter, George Mitchell, and the Dalai Lama should be used to help work out equitable compromises.

No group of people has ever experienced such persecution as have the Jews. They were forced out of their original homeland, and then treated with discrimination and prejudice in virtually every land in which they dwelled. It is remarkable that they have been nonviolent for so long. They, more than any other people, have borne the brunt of divisive religion. The Holocaust should make all of us who were alive in World War II ashamed of ourselves, for not having done more to prevent such obscene human behavior. I apologize for being a human being, when humanity sinks to such depths. Today each of us, as children of God, should make a pledge to never again permit such an attempted dehumanization of fellow children made in God's image.

Ten Commandments for the Coming of God's Kingdom

Robert Powell lists things to avoid if we want to help God's Kingdom come on earth:[12]

1. Turning away from God.
2. Substituting abstract conceptions for the reality of God.
3. Pursuing one's own ends, but disguising them as pursuing God's cause.
4. Living so as to exclude the Divine from consciousness.
5. Spurning the past and all of its rich gifts.
6. Destruction of all positive and living things.
7. Infidelity to that which one has vowed to be faithful.
8. Taking for oneself what belongs to others.
9. Criticizing or passing judgment on others.
10. Coveting that which belongs to others.

Meditation for Peace

Kathleen Fischer quotes a 2500-year-old Buddhist meditation to seek for peace:

> May I be filled with loving-kindness, may I be well.
> May I be peaceful and at ease, may I be happy.

She then suggests that we try this form of prayer for someone who has hurt us:

> May you be filled with loving-kindness, may you be well.
> May you be peaceful and at ease, may you be happy.[13]

East-West Dialogue

Religious dialogue between East and West is gathering pace. Peter Berger reports that both the Vatican, through its Secretariat for the Non-Christian Churches, and the World Council of Churches, have been having discussions with representatives from Asian religions. Robert Bellah, Harvey Cox, and Robert Ellwood have studied the effects of Asian religions in the United States. John Hick and Raimon Panikkar have worked hard to reformulate aspects of Christian doctrine by confronting them with elements from Buddhism and Hinduism. William Hocking says that the Society of Friends is showing its universality by finding common ground with mystical tendencies of Buddhism in Japan and Hinduism in India. William Johnston, professor of religious studies at Sophia University in Japan, shows in his book *The Mirror Mind* how there can be profitable dialogue between Christianity and Eastern religions. He recommends, for example, that Buddhists and Christians meditate and search for truth together, in an open attitude of responsibility. "The greatest asset," said Joseph Grassi in reviewing Johnston's book, "is to be a mystic, for it is the mystic who reaches to the heart of meaning."[14]

U Thant, when he was U.N. Secretary General, said that "we have seen how the great religions of the world, after lamentable periods of bigotry and violence, have accommodated to each other, without losing their spiritual independence, by a mutual respect for and understanding of the spiritual and moral aims which are common to all of them. We must try to extend that process of accommodation to the economic, political, and racial alignments of the world."[15]

International Organizations

Article 2 of the Charter of the United Nations states that "all members shall settle their international disputes by peaceful means, and refrain from the threat or use of force against the territorial integrity or political independence of any state." In case of a dispute, non-violent conflict management involves the use of a neutral third party, often a United Nations agency, to work for reconciliation. Normally the mediator searches for common ground in a larger group identification involving both parties. For example, since both Catholics and Protestants in Ireland are Christians, they should be expected to show some Christian love towards each other. Likewise, since both Jews and Muslims build their religions upon the God of Abraham, they should be expected to behave toward each other like God-respecting cousins. Our one ultimate large group identification is in the entire human family, the family of God.

In *Confronting War*, Ronald Glossop lists covenants achieved by U.N. sponsorship:

1. Universal Declaration of Human Rights (1948).
2. Covenant on Economic, Social, and Cultural Rights (1966).
3. Covenant on Civil and Political Rights (1966).
4. Declaration on the Elimination of All Forms of Intolerance and Discrimination Based on Religion or Belief (1981).

There are also United Nations treaties against genocide and slavery, and protecting women's rights, refugees, and homeless persons. Many humanitarian activities are sponsored by such U.N. agencies as UNESCO, UNICEF, WHO, World Food Council, and the U.N. Environmental Programme.[16]

In seeing the numerous humanitarian achievements of the United Nations, we can say that the world is starting to behave like a caring and loving community. Now we must take the next step, and make sure we have a coalition of peaceful states unified in outlawing terrorism, aggressive warfare, and uncontrolled nuclear explosions in earth's atmosphere.

The World Citizen

Epictetus said that when asked one's country, one should reply as Socrates did, "I am a citizen of the universe." Marcus

Aurelius said, "As Aurelius, I am a citizen of Rome, but as a man, I am a citizen of the world." As he was signing the Declaration of Independence, Benjamin Franklin told John Hancock, "We must all hang together, or we shall certainly hang separately." The lesson is clear: the way to survive is to unite.

"There was a time," said *The New Yorker* in 1973, "when the notion of a world order was thought to be a utopian vision. We can see now that it is a vital necessity. As for man's old dream of the world becoming one, that, whether we like it or not, occurred years ago."[17]

Women's Rights

In 1979 the United Nations adopted a Convention on the Elimination of All Forms of Discrimination Against Women. It has been ratified so far by 163 countries, not including Saudi Arabia and the United States. "The convention guarantees women's rights across many fields, including education, employment, health care, marriage and divorce, nationality, voting, and equality before the law. Although President Jimmy Carter signed the convention, the Senate never ratified it. But the city of San Francisco recently did so, and Los Angeles has promised to follow suit. Many Muslim countries have ratified the convention, including Jordan, Morocco, Pakistan, and Tunisia."[18]

Bill of Spiritual Rights

Finally the world has a long-needed Bill of Spiritual Rights, to go along with the various bills of rights dealing with economic, political, and social rights. Here are some of its main provisions:

> Since you are a child of God, you are entitled to be free from physical, mental, and spiritual intimidation and violence.
> You are entitled to the sanctity of your own personality.
> The right to express religious opinions, hold religious offices, and secure religious respect will not be curtailed because of your gender, race, nationality, or religion.
> Since the terror of nuclear destruction frightens and threatens the entire human family, all people have a right to expect that their governments will work to abolish this threat by achieving world peace and justice under God's law.

> Since no right exists without a corresponding responsibility, other persons have the right to expect that you will observe their spiritual and other rights as described herein.[19]

Implications of World Community

What are the implications of the fact that we now live in a global village? First of all, we must recognize and accept this fact. Einstein said that if we were going to split the atom, we must unite the world. Wendell Willkie put it succinctly: One world or none."

Next, we should all be good citizens of the world community. Since law and justice are the cement that holds together a community, we must codify those laws necessary to accomplish the limited but vital important purposes of that community. Senator Robert Taft, a conservative, felt that the United Nations Charter did not go far enough in giving the Security Council the authority to outlaw war. There needs to be an international security force designed to keep order in the world community. Offenders must be restrained from terrorism and lawbreaking, as in any orderly community.

The only security humanity can now have is a common security. Stockpiles of atomic weapons will not provide security, as we learned on 9/11/2001. On the contrary, they provide ever greater tension, ever greater stockpiles, and ever greater insecurity. What constitutes security to one nation, constitutes insecurity to its neighbors.

The new world coalition can learn both positive and negative lessons from federative experiences of various countries. The British Commonwealth furnishes examples of both types of lessons. So too with insights to be gained from the American federative experience. In the United States the federal government promotes its social support by serving the people in myriads of ways—protecting rights and safety, enhancing welfare, facilitating mobility, improving communication, and providing recreation. These services build more patriotism than provision of a standing army. Thus, the international community may be enhanced not so much by instruments of coercion as by international service agencies, such as United Nations auxiliary organizations.

The federative principle works well in America for several reasons. For one thing, there are so many overlapping memberships in this pluralistic society that no clear-cut divisions of loyalty and interest can be found. Often an American's loyalty is to the larger rather than the smaller entity. In the words of Inis Claude, "Texas cannot revolt against the United States because its people are more fundamentally Americans than they are Texans. These are the basic conditions which make the maintenance of order possible in the United States, and which must be reproduced in the international community if stable world order is to become a reality."[20]

A deep sense of justice in Americans bodes well for the future. This sense of justice makes it increasingly harder for Americans to say that they believe in a world court only as long as it never overrules an American standpoint. No court of justice can be founded on such a principle.

Some opposition to even a limited world federation of nations concerns the question of national sovereignty. Before 1800, international affairs were conducted by sovereign heads of states. The flaw here was that the international law which was to control sovereigns was itself controlled by them. Little wonder that its chief fruit was to protect the concept of national sovereignty, even as wars grew larger and more frequent. Last century witnessed the growth of international agencies created to help preserve peace among the world community of nations.

Certainly great care must be given before a sovereignty should be limited or relinquished. But science, weapons technology, the rise of terrorism, and the course of world affairs have stripped all nations of a part of their sovereignty. Right now the United States has no sovereignty over much nuclear experimentation, including that which could harm us. The challenge is to create a sovereignty to outlaw use of nuclear and other disastrous weapons. Again, we cannot believe in one principle of law for us, and another principle for others. The world quickly sees through hypocrisy. Without justice, there will be no law and order in the international community.

Since it is American policy never to start a nuclear war, what sovereignty is lost by outlawing aggressive warfare? Only the aggressor stands to lose, just as it is the thief who loses when a community takes a stand against robbery. Since the former fully sovereign nation can no longer play its historic role of guaranteeing the lives, values, and property of its citizens, a sufficient sovereignty will have to be created to do these things.

Leaders Speak for Peace

In 1998 the University of Virginia sponsored an academic conference for peace, led by seven winners of the Nobel Peace Prize. The leaders "preached forgiveness and a shared responsibility for ending suffering around the world." Archbishop Desmond Tutu of South Africa asked for support in realizing his dream of "a world that is more caring and more compassionate, a world where people matter more than profits." Jody Williams, an American who shared the 1997 prize for her fight to get rid of land mines, attacked student apathy. "Don't sit back and cry, or wait for the other guy to do it," she said. "Join in and make yourself better." "Caring about others," said the Dalai Lama, "is a great benefit for the self."[21]

The Washington National Cathedral

Entering the year 2000, The Washington National Cathedral sponsored services welcoming in the new millennium. At the first Sunday in 2000, President Bill Clinton took part in a program of reconciliation. "Following references to the New Testament, Talmud, and Koran, the president prayed this prayer: 'Help us accept, at long last, the enduring truth that the most important fact of life is not wealth or power or beauty or scientific advance, but our kinship as brothers and sisters and our oneness as children of God.'"

The Cathedral's vigil for the new millennium included members of the Baha'i, Episcopal, Hindu, Jewish, Latter-Day Saints, Muslim, Roman Catholic, and Sikh faiths.

A prayer by Judy Chicago was read:

> And then all that has divided us will merge,
> And then all will live in harmony with each other and the
>   Earth,
> And then everywhere will be called Eden once again.

Archbishop Tutu gave a New Year's Eve meditation. He said, "Religion, the different faiths, have often fueled and exacerbated sectarian strife and spawned extremisms that have given religion a bad name. But most frequently these days they seem to work together for peace and for a different ordering of society. In the new millennium, let us discover that we are family."[22]

In his sermon on 2 January 2000, Dean of the Cathedral Nathan D. Baxter declared that "Martin Luther King, Jr., said that 'Either we will learn to live together as brothers and sisters, or perish together as fools.'" Baxter added: "To know this truth, we need only look at the effect of religious intolerance in this past millennium, specifically the latter half of last century. We will be judged by our commitment to justice and peace, not our dogma, ritual, and rhetoric. If there is to be hope for world peace, if we are to address the problems of violence, poverty, and bigotry in our communities, there must be respect for the gifts we all offer. Only together can we stand against the abuses of religion. Only together can we find a global ethic against poverty, illiteracy, and depletion of the earth. Only together will we find a spiritual basis that can contribute to the ever so fragile task of peace. We must honor our religious differences but not allow them to get in the way of God's dream for the world. Indeed, those who work for the vision of peace will be called 'children of God,' whether they name God Adonai, Allah, Great Spirit, Abba, Father, or Jehovah."[23]

Rabbis for Peace

The Central Rabbinical Congress of the U.S.A. and Canada, a worldwide organization representing over 150 Orthodox Jewish communities, issued a recent statement asking for an end to violence in the Holy Land. Although they may be unacceptable to many Jews because they oppose Zionism as a legitimate answer to the age-long Jewish longing to return to a homeland, some of their position can perhaps be considered in the search for peace in the Holy Land. Their statement said: "Two thousand years ago, at the time of the Temple's destruction, the Jewish people were forbidden by the Creator (Kesubos 111a) to exercise sovereignty over the Holy Land prior to the Messianic era. They were further forbidden to wage any form of war against other nations during their exile. Rather, the paradigm of Jewish existence in the diaspora is to behave in a civil, honest, and grateful manner towards their hosts throughout the world.

The goal of Torah Jewry is to live in quiet piety and dwell peacefully with all nations and peoples. Those following this Divine agenda are not linked to any wars that are falsely depicted as Jewish wars but are, in reality, Zionist wars. We conclude with a prayer that the Creator Himself will soon send his Messiah to redeem the Earth and all mankind will forever join together in worship of Him."[24]

Citizens of the Global Village

In summary, we must all recognize our citizenship roles in the world community. Those who would deny its existence must first destroy the factors creating it: multinational corporations; the Internet; a revolution in transportation and communication; religious terrorism; nuclear stockpiles of frightening destructive power; and extreme inequality in the distribution of the world's economic goods. Failing to destroy these factors, we must be good citizens in each of our communities, but especially in the global village, the only arena in which global problems can be solved.

God did not create a world full of bountiful blessings, and endow the flower of that world with the crown of reason, for the purpose of having us misapply our knowledge and blow one another to smithereens. Common sense dictates that from now on, the chief requisite of our leaders must be that they be architects of the new world order of peace and justice. Surely it is not too much to expect that they possess something of the charismatic charm and communicative ability shown by the remarkable Samantha Smith, the 12-year-old girl from Maine who shattered the iron curtain through love. The true conservative wishes to conserve the whole human family, not merely that part of it known to him or residing in her district. The divine principle of agape revealed by Christ, the power of non-violence as demonstrated by Gandhi, can inspire the human family to love its way out of its current impasse. The world must become a loving community if our species is to endure.

REFERENCES

1   Torrance, p. 48.

2   Ibid., p. 60.

3   Ibid., p. 77.

4   *Arizona Republic*, 5 March 1983, p. F4.

5   Ken Wilber, *Up From Eden* (Shambhala, 1983), pp. 334, 337.

6   Meister, pp. 325, 326.

7   Robert L. Slater, *World Religions and the World Community* (Columbia University Press, 1963), p. 38.

8   Ghose, pp. 554, 595.

9   Frank A. Wilson, *The Work of Creation* (Coventure, 1985), pp. 11, 12, 114.

10 Ibid., pp. 27, 63, 76, 92, 115.

11 Unamuno, pp. 180, 258.

12 Powell, p. 114.

13 Fischer, pp. 162, 163.

14 *St. Anthony Messenger*, September 1981, p. 52.

15 *On the World Community* (Center for the Study of Democratic Institutions, 1965), pp. 20, 21.

16 Ronald J. Glossop, *Confronting War* (McFarland, 1983), pp. 54, 146–48, 206.

17 *New Yorker*, 10 December 1973, p. 38.

18 Paul Lewis, *New York Times*, 21 March 1999, p. 11.

19 Meister, pp. 283–88.

20 Inis Claude, *Swords into Ploughshares* (Random House, 1961), p. 443.

21 Ian Zack, *New York Times*, 8 November 1998, p. 14.

22 *Cathedral Age* (Washington National Cathedral, Spring 2000), pp. 5, 11.

23 Ibid., p. 21.

24 *New York Times*, 11 February 2001, p. 16.

Chapter XIII

We Can Live If We Can Love

"You can pay me now, or pay me later," says the auto mechanic holding up an oil filter in a television commercial. The filter costs several dollars, he explains, but repairs to the car with a faulty filter can cost many hundreds of dollars.

So, too, the human race. We can do it right—unite now to outlaw terrorism and aggressive war, or do it wrong—unite later, after the unspeakable horrors of a nuclear war. Then the grim lesson will be so devastatingly tragic that survivors will wonder why the clear necessity for outlawing terrorism and nuclear war seemed so unattainable.

Dr. Karl Menninger posed the recent predicament vividly: "Here are two populous and intelligent but poorly communicating masses of people, living far from each other, and really having nothing tangible to quarrel about, who are poised ready to attack each other. In past wars, only pieces of the world have been sacrificed in a sort of massive self-mutilation. Any future wars may bring not just world sacrifice but world suicide as well."[1]

A study called *The Long-Term Consequences of Nuclear War* describes "a world that will be so cold, dark, and radioactive that no one can survive." Two of the authors, Dr. Paul Ehrlich of Stanford University and Dr. Carl Sagan of Cornell University, said that "those who survived the initial shock would be breathing in toxic gases and the baleful fumes of fires that could rage everywhere. They would be subject to the sun's ultraviolet rays." "You would have an unprecedented biological disaster," said Ehrlich. "You can kiss the Northern Hemisphere goodbye. We could not preclude the extinction of Homo sapiens."[2]

Patricia Mische points out the suicidal effect of using nuclear weapons. "The weapons we have invented to protect ourselves," she says, "will now destroy those they were intended to protect, as well as those aimed at. They will irradiate food and water supplies, and cause flooding and tidal waves through a global thermal effect. They will deplete the protective ozone layer around the earth, cause genetic mutations, and render the earth uninhabitable for present and future generations."[3]

During the Cold War between the United States and the Soviet Union, in one 18-month period, "the U.S. warning system produced 147 false warnings of Soviet missile attacks."[4] Scientists at the Australian National University announced that in 1998 and 1999, while trying to create a virus to make mice infertile, they accidentally made a virus that kills them. "And humans have the same gene that paralyzed the mouse immune system. The scientists say that their discovery shows that nations need to strengthen a global treaty banning germ warfare."[5]

In the nuclear age, says Paul Warnke, a former U.S. arms negotiator, security means common security. It is either co-existence or no existence. Can it be that we humans are so stupid that we will ignore George Orwell's satiric warning in *1984*, and dig our collective graves beneath the rubble piles of nuclear debris?

Loving: Our Way to World Peace

"We can live if we can love," said Karl Menninger. "Love is the medicine for the sickness of the world. Love transforms the impulse to fight into the impulse to work or play. When we have accorded love the pre-eminence it deserves in our scale of values, we shall have re-aligned our faith in God to include more faith in human beings, and extended our identifications to include more brothers, sisters, sons, and daughters in a vastly wider family concept."[6]

"God is love," said the Apostle John, "and those who dwell in love dwell in God, and God dwells in them" (I John 4:16). Teilhard describes love as the strongest, most universal, and most mysterious of all cosmic forces. Basically, he says, it is the attraction of each element of the universe by Omega, the universal evolutionary force. At its most elementary level it is the same as molecular energy. At a higher stage of evolution it is the reproductive drive. In humanity, love enters the realm of the spiritual, of reflexive consciousness, of God.

People are to be loved for God's sake, says Aldous Huxley, because they are temples of the Holy Spirit. Love, Huxley added, shows a steady will to conform to the divine Tao or *Logos*. Humble love brings peace. If we truly desire the peace that passes understanding, we must start with such understandable peace as concord with our mate, our children, our friends, and even our enemies. Peace is not a magical emanation from outside us. It comes, as earned and practiced, from within. If we want the reward, we must be willing to pay the price.

Marriage sanctifies love, says Jonathan Schell, by laying the foundation for a stable world built to house future generations. Thus we can say, in Schell's opinion, that "love creates the world. But every generation that holds the earth hostage to nuclear destruction holds a gun to the head of its own children." Love, says Schell, "is a spiritual energy that the human heart can pit against the physical energy released from the heart of matter; it can create, cherish, and safeguard what extinction would destroy."[7]

"Love alone," said Teilhard, "is capable of uniting living beings in such a way as to complete and fulfill them, for it alone joins them by what is deepest in themselves. And if that is what it can achieve on a small scale, why not repeat this one day on worldwide dimensions?"

The summation of our love of all human beings is the love of their creator, God. "A universal love," Teilhard felt, "is not only psychologically possible; it is the complete and final way in which we are able to love. We should accept the responsibility of some source and object of love at the summit of the world above our heads."[8] When you realize that your neighbor's and even your enemy's God is as valid as your own, there can be no hatred, terrorism, or war, but only understanding, forgiveness, love, and peace. But, on the other hand, "to define human beings as exploitable means rather than as sacred ends is to create a perpetual state of war."[9]

Leonard Swidler recalls the loving attitude of Jesus toward those who were not of his faith. The Good Samaritan (a non-Jew) was seen as preferable to the priest and the Levite. Jesus said of the Roman centurion, "Never have I seen faith like his" (Matt. 8:10). When the Canaanite woman persisted in asking for healing, Jesus soon granted it. From the cross Jesus said, "Father, forgive them."[10]

Love surpasses legal codes, say both Jesus and Tagore. In Mahayana Buddhism, the Lord of Mercy, Avalokiteshvara, is praised above all bodhisattvas because, overcome by all of the suffering in the world, he does not even think of becoming a Buddha until he has done all he can to relieve human suffering. In the Bible we are told to be perfect, even as God is perfect. Love leads towards perfection. St. Teresa said it is much easier to impose harsh penalties upon oneself than it is to patiently and lovingly bear the ordinary crosses of everyday family life. How, then, can one master the art of loving? St. Francois de Sales replies, "Just as you learn to speak by speaking, so you learn to love God by loving. Begin as a mere apprentice, and the very power of love will lead you on to become a master in the art."[11]

"The main condition for the achievement of love," said Erich Fromm, "is the overcoming of one's narcissism." This state of mind results in assuming that everything outside oneself is unreal, and might be a threat to us. "For the insane person the only reality that exists is within him, his fears and his desires." The religious terrorist is mentally ill. He deludes himself into thinking that because there is injustice in the world, things will improve if he adds to that injustice. The healthy person learns that giving is getting. Love is reciprocal. The more you give away, the more you have. "In thus giving of his life," says Fromm, "the lover enriches the other person; he enhances the other's sense of aliveness by enhancing his own. Giving means receiving. The teacher is taught by his students, the actress is stimulated by her audience, the psychoanalyst is cured by his patient—provided they do not treat each other as objects, but are related to each other through love."

Frank Laubach: Literacy Through Love

The Christian missionary Frank Laubach was the greatest teacher of literacy in world history. When he tried to make converts in undeveloped nations, he found countless people who could not read or write, even in their own tongues. Rather than expecting them to learn English, he would learn their languages, and translate parts of the New Testament into their dialects. He mastered over 80 languages, and his teaching method has been used in more than 200 languages

His method was called "each one, teach one." Through this technique, more than 100 million people learned to read and write their own languages. In New Guinea, Laubach found that the natives had eaten their last Christian missionary! But Laubach was patient and loving towards them. Finally one chief confessed: "We used to eat our enemies. Now teach us how to love them." The Dani tribe experienced a remarkable decline in violence, homicide, and warfare. Although Laubach was not pushing his faith, tribe members wanted to learn more about Jesus and his love. Laubach said, "I could write a book called *2000 Places Where Love Alone Won.*"

Despite the Muslim opposition to all non-Muslim missionaries, Laubach was invited into every Muslim country in the world. He studied the Koran assiduously. When he learned that the Biblical Joseph was also a great Muslim hero, he wrote many stories about Joseph in Maranaw, the native tongue of the Moros. One Afghan teacher said, "Never have I seen so kind a man as he."

Laubach said, "The world is full of hatred and crime, and yet it is afraid to trust love. The way to stop hatred is to build a backfire of love. I would rather make good Muslims than bad Christians. Let us stop being God's problem and start being God's answer."[12]

The United Nations for Peace

The foundation for peace is respect for human dignity. A low point in this regard was achieved in the 19th century Chicago "unsightly beggar ordinances, which barred from public view 'any person who is diseased, maimed, mutilated, or in any way deformed so as to be an unsightly or disgusting object.'"[13]

At the opposite extreme is the vision of the goal of the United Nations for the present millennium, as expressed by Secretary-General Kofi Annan. In September 2000 Annan "reiterated his advocacy of environmental protection, military interventions to stop genocide and mass murder, and curbs on nuclear proliferation." He also has an ambitious program to fight poverty by bringing Internet access to undeveloped nations, including an online healthcare network to areas lacking medical facilities. He wants to reduce H.I.V. infection rates, particularly in Africa.[14]

The United Nations sponsors an ongoing World Conference on Religion and Peace. In August 2000 the U.N. also set up a Millennium Summit of Religious and Spiritual Leaders "that produced a document signed by several hundred religious leaders pledging them to work for world peace, against poverty, and for the protection of the environment." Chief Rabbi Jonathan Sacks of Great Britain said that religion goes beyond mere political power. "Politicians sign peace agreements," said Sacks, "but it is our people, out there, on the ground, who will determine whether peace is real, or just a breathing space between wars."[15]

"So long as power is maintained by violence," observes Richard Falk, "it will be challenged by violence."[16] In other words, those who live by the bomb die by the bomb. To endure, we need to perfect nonviolent attitudes and techniques. There will always be aggressors. To restrain them, we may need to develop non-lethal weapons to temporarily incapacitate them.

Thy Kingdom Come

"Thy Kingdom come" automatically means "our kingdom go." All of us have multiple citizenship—in our country, in the human family, and in the Kingdom of God. What happens when there is a conflict among our citizenships?

The higher level must naturally be given the priority, but a word of caution is needed. Since allegedly in the name of God every manner of atrocity has been committed in human history, the Bill of Spiritual Rights must be conscientiously enforced, lest man's love for God be perverted into man's hate for man. The daily news report tells of supposedly religious persons killing other human beings, in God's name. Divisive religion will destroy unitive religion, if we permit it. This type of hypocrisy must cease. Killing, even when clothed in nationalistic disguise, is murder, perhaps the gravest violation of God's law. If someone is determined to violate God's law, the conscience of humankind must require that person to cease doing it in God's name, and cease doing it all.

P.W. Martin explains that withdrawal into one's innermost being for renewal with the Holy Spirit is for the ultimate purpose of engaging in building God's Kingdom. A part of God's Kingdom dwells within every one of us. If we are to have peace, we must free and nurture that element of goodness so that it can resist the temptation to hate the outsider. A chaplain I met in World War II was the essence of peace. He quoted Isaiah 26:3: "Thou will keep him in perfect peace whose mind is stayed on Thee, because he trusts in Thee."

Erich Fromm believed that the modern world has evolved into the Torah vision of messianic time, as we recognize that without peace, we have nothing. For humanity to endure, Fromm said that freedom, responsibility, and love would have to be nurtured so as to develop a structure of peace and harmony between person and person, person and nature, and person and God.

Religious Cooperation

Prince Hassan, uncle to King Abdullah II of Jordan, constantly works for peacemaking dialogue among the three Abrahamic faiths. Episcopal Bishop Richard Grein of New York City applauded the award of one million dollars by the New York City Council to rehabilitate the Eldridge Street Synagogue, stating that this action "recognizes not only the wide range of community services that religious buildings house, but also the buildings' importance as a part of our cultural and historical patrimony."[17]

St. Mary's United Methodist Church in St. Marys, Georgia, turned its back on a $60 million bequest from a telephone magnate, Warren Bailey, in order to donate the money to charitable causes. Forty million dollars will go into a foundation that will award grants to nonprofit groups. Sixteen million dollars will be given to other churches and ministries. The church will keep $2.8 million in an endowment fund named for Mr. Bailey, to be spent not on operating funds but on service projects.[18] This is the kind of love that leads towards world peace.

The Lessons of Chernobyl

Dr. Robert Peter Gale, U.S. chairman of the advisory committee of the International Bone Marrow Transplant Registry, flew over Pripyat, the workers' village at Chernobyl, the site of the nuclear reactor meltdown in the Ukraine in 1986. The town of 40,000 was completely deserted. "This is what we've been afraid all these years: a city devoid of human life because of radiation. We did not learn all we could from Hiroshima and Nagasaki," Gale said. "We have not controlled the proliferation of nuclear weapons. Yet we have to learn. I hope Chernobyl will be the final lesson."[19]

Mikhail Gorbachev recognized the problem. "Ensuring reliable and safe nuclear power development," he said, "must become a universal international obligation of all nations."[20]

The U.N. International Atomic Energy Agency (IAEA) has drawn up regulations calling for early and full communication concerning nuclear accidents and for coordination of emergency assistance. The world has more than 400 operating nuclear power plants, with another 300 in various stages of construction. Worse accidents than the Chernobyl incident could arise in countries like Cuba, Egypt, Pakistan, or the Philippines, where nuclear experience has been limited.

The IAEA was set up in the wake of President Eisenhower's Atoms For Peace program. It has become very effective in spreading the knowledge of beneficial uses of nuclear science, not only in energy but also in agriculture, health, and medicine. Nuclear isotopes are being used, for example, to control both the Mediterranean fruit fly and the tsetse fly.

Russia has permitted a team of Western scientists to monitor its main underground nuclear test site. Dr. Thomas Cochran, senior scientist for the U.S. private group, the National Resources Defense Council, feels that new technology makes verification of nuclear testing feasible. Nuclear tragedy, like that at Chernobyl, can awaken us to the necessity for more adequate safeguards concerning all aspects of nuclear engineering.

Meanwhile the sensitized conscience of humanity continues to call for a reduction in nuclear weapons. The council of bishops of the U.S. United Methodist Church issued a pastoral letter in 1986 calling the arms race an issue of social justice. Deploring the squandering of wealth, the letter states that "U.S. arms are now being purchased with food stamps, welfare checks, Medicaid payments, and nutrition supplements for poor mothers and their children."[21]

Albert Einstein realized the vast political implications of modern science and technology. He said, "The real cause of international conflicts is the existence of competing sovereign nations. At the present high level of industrialization and economic interdependence, it is unthinkable that we can achieve peace without a genuine supranational organization to govern international relations. Our defense is not in armaments, nor in science, nor in going underground. Our defense is in law and order. Is it naiveté to suggest that those in power decide that future conflicts must be settled by constitutional means rather than by the senseless sacrifice of great numbers of human lives?"[22]

World leaders are coming to realize that religious liberty is essential to the cause of world peace. In his World Peace Day message in 1988, Pope John Paul II urged worldwide protection for all religious believers. "Every violation of religious freedom, whether hidden or open, does fundamental damage to the cause of peace, as does subtle discrimination."[23]

The Peace Paradigm

In World War I there were twenty servicemen killed for each civilian killed. By the Vietnam War the figures were reversed: twenty civilians killed for each serviceman. Had nuclear weapons been used, an even greater ratio of civilians would have been killed. World peace is now everybody's business. We are dramatically relearning the old spiritual truth that the only proper way to live is God's way, the way of love.

This book outlines the paradigm of a peace ethos. Great stress has been placed upon the spiritual aspects of that paradigm, for unless religion serves as a part of the solution (an aspect called unitive religion in this book), it shall continue to be a part of the problem, causing divisiveness, discrimination, and terrorism. The world is ready for religion to serve at its best.

In summary, here are the main features of the peace paradigm. Modern science has rediscovered and reaffirmed what religious mystics always knew: the universe is one, it has an exquisite pattern, it bears the hand of its Maker, and it seems to show a benevolent preference for human existence. Evolution, especially at the spiritual level, provides human beings with meaning, responsibility, and organic linkage with God.

Peace requires oneness with God's purpose for humanity. To achieve mystical oneness with God, one must first die to oneself (abandon one's selfish self), learn to know oneself, and with the help of the inner Holy Spirit, concentrate upon union with the Divine.

Through one's *ishtadeva* (that aspect of the deity that has been revealed to oneself), a person can achieve the spiritual ecstasy of union with God. One does not lose one's individuality—rather, one finally recognizes one's true identity as a child of God. Then all things fall into place, for the divine pattern is revealed. All of life is a celebration of God. There is a wholeness within oneself, between oneself and others, and between oneself and God.

Now an inner serenity is attained, for one lives each day as a moment of eternity. A sign of possession by the Holy Spirit is a deep love for all of God's creation, particularly one's fellow humans. In Galatians 5:22 Paul lists the fruit of the Holy Spirit as faithfulness, gentleness, goodness, joy, kindness, love, patience, peace, and self-control. To a person living in this condition, violence, terrorism, and war become unthinkable.

Religion, being a personal experience, differs from person to person. Thus there will always be many valid approaches to God. To deny others their approach to God raises questions about how universal one's own God concept can be. Although ritual and dogma seem to be necessary in a religion, they should always be checked to make sure that they are employed in a unitive, rather than in a divisive, way. Otherwise they defeat their own purpose.

When world religions interface, the opposite of Gresham's Law takes place: good belief drives out bad. Good belief is unitive, celebrating the love of God through the love of humans. As John says in his Epistle, he who says he loves God but hates his neighbor is a liar. The world religions are in substantial agreement on their most important ethical principles. In the current Age of Survival, each faith needs to reconceive itself, validating its own principles in such a way as to permit other faiths to validate theirs.

Human Dignity

Human dignity is a consequence of all persons being the children of God. No one has the right to transcend this God-given dignity. Road rage, school shootings, and religious terrorism are all violations of God's law. Political goals and individual religious views are no excuse for denying God's sovereignty and will over God's creation. It is an insult to God to say that God prefers one part of His creation over another, some of Her children over others. This would be a sign of an unjust God, a contradiction in terms. The Bill of Spiritual Rights codifies relationships that exist among all members of the human family, and protects individuals from having the sacredness of their personalities violated.

There is surprising agreement among the major world religions as to what constitutes the good life. Invariably a great religious teacher places righteousness ahead of ritualism. As religions age, adherents lose sight of the original intent of the founder, and soon divisive religion is replacing unitive religion, with much bloodshed and suffering.

If we can learn to love one another, and we must in order to survive, God's Kingdom can virtually come on earth. Never before have the stakes been so high between love and hate, between unitive and divisive religion. The former Soviet republics and the Islamic world can be important contributing members of the world community, Agape love must become the ruling passion of humankind. Because we love ourselves we must also love others, for eternity which cannot be shared with others is no eternity at all.

Can Jews and Muslims live together in peace? Of course, if they follow the unitive teachings in the Torah and the Koran that say we must love our neighbor. Divisive elements in each faith dishonor their own scriptures by neglecting the many unitive teachings in those scriptures. In this Age of Survival, we can no longer afford the luxury of intolerance.

The Divine Feminine

There can be no peace without justice. The human species flourished for many centuries when it worshipped the Great Goddess. About five thousand years ago, masculine deity images replaced images of the Great Goddess throughout most of the world. The patriarchal approach to religion has not only denigrated women into second-class citizenship, but has also instigated mammoth and suicidal wars. With the development of sophisticated and proficient ways to destroy ourselves, we must now reject patriarchy, and create a wholly balanced approach to all of the world's problems and conditions.

Might makes right is obsolete. Now might, when undisciplined by love, law, and order, makes the future of our species precarious. Not only in the name of justice and fairness but also in the name of survival, we need to return to adoration of the Divine Feminine, as explained in Chapter 11. Patriarchy in religion and life is more than obsolete. In the modern world, with our fantastic skills of destruction, it is obscene. Let us love one another as we restore an equitable balance in the delineations of our Divine Heritage.

Your Role in Bringing about Peace

You and I have important roles to play, if we are to have world peace. Remember, in case of conflict, the higher citizenship role prevails. So compare the secular patriot with the spiritual one:

Secular Patriot	Spiritual Patriot
Willing to die for his country.	Willing to live for God.
Defends country against all enemies.	Through love, turns enemies into friends.
Will sacrifice for his country.	Sacrifices oneself as a Kingdom investment.
Tries to extend country's realm.	Wishes God's Kingdom to prevail everywhere.
Heroes are generals and politicians.	Heroes are Jesus, Moses, Buddha, & Mohammed.
Takes part in elections.	Casts vote once and all for God.
Cherishes freedom highly.	Knows that only freedom under God lasts.
Prefers his country over all others.	Sees his country as a part of God's Kingdom.
Opposes absolute kings.	Makes God the Absolute King of his life.

Studies forms of government.	Studies to make oneself acceptable to God.
Looks upon other cultures as rivals.	Looks upon all persons as God's children.

Promise for the Future

In a recent edition of Dante's *Divine Comedy*, Thomas Berry rediscovers the healing virtues of nature. He describes the symbolic significance of Dante's meeting with his beloved Beatrice in Paradise. "In that meeting, Dante is describing not only a personal experience, but the experience of the entire human community at the moment of reconciliation with the Divine after a long period of alienation and human wandering away from the true center."[24]

James Lincoln Collier asks us to put selfishness aside in favor of the common good. "We must come to see that this America is our community," Collier said, "and that, as members of it, we are going to be damaged one way or another if we do not from time to time put the interests of the whole above our own concerns. A people who will not sacrifice for the common good cannot expect to have any common good."[25]

The inaugural address of President George W. Bush in 2001 gives great hope for a large step towards compassion and world peace. The grandest of our ideals, Bush said, is "an unfolding American promise that everyone belongs, that everyone deserves a chance, that no insignificant person was ever born. This is my solemn pledge: I will work to build a single nation of justice and opportunity. I know this is within our reach, because we are guided by a power larger than ourselves, who creates us equal in his image.

A civil society demands from each of us good will and respect, fair dealing and forgiveness. We must show courage in a time of blessing, by confronting problems rather than by passing them on to future generations. Persistent poverty is unworthy of our nation's promise. Abandonment and abuse are not acts of God, they are failures of love. All of us are diminished whenever any are hopeless. Church and charity, synagogue and mosque, lend our communities their humanity, and they will have an honored place in our plans and laws. When we see that wounded traveler on the road to Jericho, we will not pass to the other side.

I will speak for greater justice and compassion. What you do is as important as anything government does. I ask you to serve a common good beyond your comfort, to defend needed reforms against easy attacks, to serve your nation, beginning with your neighbor. We renew our purpose today: to make our country more just and generous, to affirm the dignity of every life."[26]

Summit meetings between American and Russian leaders suggest that perhaps the two major nuclear powers are finally coming to their senses. Ridiculous overkill capacity, bought at the expense of economic chaos and irresponsible indebtedness, is no sane way to build a safe future for any nation. The scaling down of huge military budgets will permit growing expenditures for such socially desirable investments as education, health, the arts, and the environment, as well as care for the needy. God's will will yet be done on earth.

We Shall Survive

Living is an art. We should devote the same careful attention to life's details as the painter gives to her canvas or the poet to his sonnet. "To affect the quality of the day," said Henry Thoreau, "that is the highest of the arts." We shall not have a satisfactory society until we stress the GNQ (Gross National Quality) above that of the GNP (Gross National Product).

Many places in the Bible and other sacred books we are told that we will be judged according to our works. Never before has this seemed more obvious than in this Age of Survival. You and I have the responsibility to guarantee the existence of all future generations. This stirring challenge should arouse us to new heights of bravery and altruism.

In his final paragraph of his essay on "Nature," Ralph Waldo Emerson reminded us of the infinite potential within each of us. "All that Adam had, all that Caesar could, you have and can do. Build therefore your own world." Each of us must ask ourselves daily: "What have I done today to help bring God's Kingdom to earth, the Kingdom of love and peace? Also, what have I done today to hasten, or retard, the spread of terrorism and the likelihood of nuclear war? If you think that yours is an insignificant vote, remember what happened in Florida in the 2000 election.

Ask, what stand did I take today for world peace? Too much is at stake for us to dare to be neutral just to avoid unpopularity.

Here are a few guidelines. Never assume that you have a monopoly on ways to God. When in doubt, test a faith by its fruitfulness in building love of God and humanity. Differentiate between a person and the person's actions. You may hate his actions but as a fellow human being you are obliged to love that person and respect his/her human dignity. Distinguish between the many compromisable and the few uncompromisable issues. Always question your own infallibility as well as everyone else's. Never lose faith in human beings. This is a corollary of its companion: never lose faith in your Creator.

Humanity of course will survive. We have come too far to give up the ghost completely. But let us survive with dignity, love, intelligence, and a faith in God and in our species.

"By the very fact that we have measured the truly cosmic gravity of the sickness that disquiets us," said Teilhard, "we are put in possession of the remedy that can cure it. Either nature is closed to our demands for futurity, in which case thought is stifled, or else an opening exists—that of the Supersoul above our souls.

To bring us into existence, the world has from the beginning juggled miraculously with too many improbabilities for there to be any risk whatever in committing ourselves further and following it right to the end. If it undertook the task, it is because it can finish it, following the same methods and with the same infallibility with which it began. The best guarantee that a thing should happen is that it appears to us as vitally necessary. Life, by its very structure, having once been lifted to its stage of thought, cannot go on at all without requiring to ascend even higher."[27]

REFERENCES

[1] *New York Times*, 30 October 1983, p. 24.
[2] *Arizona Republic*, 6 November 1983, p. C5.
[3] *St. Anthony Messenger*, October 1983, p. 26.
[4] Glossop, p. 33.
[5] *New York Times*, 28 January 2001, 4:2.

6 *Presbyterian Life*, 15 July 1959, pp. 10, 36.

7 Schell, pp. 157, 158, 225.

8 Teilhard, pp. 265, 267.

9 Sjöö and Mor, p. 394.

10 Swidler, p. 111.

11 Huxley, p. 90.

12 Frank Laubach, *Forty Years with the Silent Billion* (Fleming Revell, 1970), pp. 391, 392, 421, 480.

13 *New York Times*, 20 August 2000, 4:3.

14 Ibid., 9 April 2000, 4:16.

15 Ibid., 17 September 2000, 4:6.

16 Richard A. Falk, *A Study of Future Worlds* (Free Press, 1975), p. 155.

17 *New York Times*, 29 October 2000, 4:16.

18 Ibid., 17 December 2000, p. 31.

19 *New York Times Magazine*, 13 July 1986, pp. 22, 46.

20 *New York Times*, 29 June 1986, 4:23.

21 *St. Anthony Messenger*, July 1986, p. 7.

22 *New Yorker*, 2 January 1984, p. 50.

23 *St. Anthony Messenger*, February 1988, p. 6.

24 *New York Times*, 17 November 1991, p. 39.

25 Ibid.

26 Ibid., 21 January 2001, p. 13.

27 Teilhard, pp. 232–234.

BIBLIOGRAPHY

Adams, Henry. *Mont-Saint-Michel and Chartres.* New American Library, 1961.

Allen, Richard. *Imperialism and Nationalism in the Fertile Crescent.* Oxford University Press, 1974.

Armstrong, Karen. *A History of God.* Knopf, 1994.

Aronson, Martin, ed. *Jesus and Lao-tzu: The Parallel Sayings.* Seastone, 2000.

Bach, Marcus. *The Unity Way.* Unity Books, 1982.

Barrow, John D. and Frank J. Tipler. *The Anthropic Cosmological Principle.* Oxford University Press, 1996.

Berger, Peter L. *The Heretical Imperative.* Anchor, 1979.

Blakney, Raymond. *Meister Eckhart.* Harper, 1941.

Boys, Mary C. *Has God Only One Blessing?* Paulist Press, 2000.

Browning, Don S. *Generative Man.* Westminster, 1973.

Bulgakov, Sergei. *Sophia: The Wisdom of God.* Lindisfarne Press, 1993.

Campbell, Joseph. *The Masks of God: Creative Mythology.* Penguin, 1976.

——— ed. *The Mysteries.* Pantheon Books, 1955.

——— ed. *Spiritual Disciplines.* Princeton University Press, 1985.

Capra, Fritjof. *The Tao of Physics.* Bantam, 1977.

——— and David Steindl-Rast. *Belonging to the Universe.* HarperSanFrancisco, 1991.

Carmody, Denise L. *Responses to 101 Questions about Feminism.* Paulist Press, 1993.

—— and John T. Carmody. *Peace and Justice in the Scriptures of the World Religions*. Paulist Press, 1988.

Claude, Inis. *Swords into Ploughshares*. 2nd ed. Random House, 1961.

Coate, Roger A. *Global Issue Regimes*. Prager, 1982.

Cooley, John K. *Baal, Christ, and Mohammed*. Holt, Rinehart, and Winston, 1965.

Cragg, Kenneth. *The Wisdom of the Sufis*. New Directions, 1976.

Daly, Mary. *Beyond God the Father*. Beacon Press, 1985.

Das, Bhagavan. *The Essential Unity of All Religions*. The Theosophical Press, 1966.

Davies, Paul. *God and the New Physics*. Simon & Schuster, 1983.

—— *The Cosmic Blueprint*. Simon & Schuster, 1989.

Downing, Christine. *Goddess: Mythological Images of the Feminine*. Crossroad, 1981.

Durant, Will. *The Reformation*. Simon & Schuster, 1957.

Eckhart, Meister. *Breakthrough: Meister Eckhart's Creation Spirituality in New Translation*. Matthew Fox, ed. Doubleday, 1980.

Edwards, Denis. *Jesus and the Cosmos*. Paulist Press, 1991.

Eliade, Mircea. *From Primitives to Zen*. Harper & Row, 1967.

Ellwood, Robert S., ed. *Eastern Spirituality in America*. Paulist Press, 1987.

Esslemont, J.E. *Baha-u-llah and the New Era*. Baha'i Publishing Committee, 1948.

Faricy, Robert. *The Spirituality of Teilhard de Chardin*. Winston, 1981.

Ferguson, Marilyn. *The Aquarian Conspiracy*. Tarcher, 1980.

Fischer, Kathleen. *Transforming Fire: Women Using Anger Creatively*. Paulist Press, 1999.

Fisher, Eugene J., ed. *Visions of the Other: Jewish and Christian Theologians Assess the Dialogue*. Paulist Press, 1994.

Foster, David. *The Philosophical Scientists*. Dorset Press, 1985.

Frankfort, Henri et al. *Before Philosophy*. Pelican, 1954.

Fraser, James. *The Golden Bough*. Macmillan, 1951.

Fromm, Erich. *The Art of Loving*. Bantam, 1963.

—— *The Sane Society*. Fawcett, 1967.

Gadon, Elinor W. *The Once and Future Goddess: A Symbol for Our Time*. HarperSanFrancisco, 1989.

Ghose, Aurobindo. *The Human Cycle; The Ideal of Human Unity; War and Self-Determination*. Sri Aurobindo Ashram, 1971.

Glossop, Ronald. *Confronting War*. McFarland, 1983.

Goble, Frank. *The Third Force*. Pocket Books, 1971.

Gorbachev, Mikhail. *Perestroika*. Harper & Row, 1987.

Granfield, David. *Heightened Consciousness: The Mystical Difference*. Paulist Press, 1991.

Hennesey, James. *American Catholics*. Oxford University Press, 1981.

Hick, John. *God and the Universe of Faith*. Rev. ed. Collins, 1977.

Himelick, Raymond, ed. & tr. *Erasmus and the Seamless Coat of Jesus*. Purdue University Studies, 1971.

Hocking, William E. *The Coming World Civilization*. Harper, 1956.

Hoffman, Edward. *The Way of Splendor*. Shambhala, 1981.

Humphreys, Christmas. *Buddhism*. Penguin, 1954.

Huxley, Aldous. *The Perennial Philosophy*. Harper & Brothers, 1945.

Jantsch, Erich. *The Self-Organizing Universe*. Pergamon, 1980.

Jaoudi, Maria. *Christian and Islamic Spirituality*. Paulist Press, 1993.

Jones. Noragh. *Power of Raven, Wisdom of Serpent: Celtic Women's Spirituality*. Lindisfarne Press, 1995.

Jung, Carl. *Memories, Dreams, Reflections*. Random House, 1965.

Juergensmeyer, Mark. *Terror in the Mind of God: The Global Rise of Religious Violence*. University of California Press, 2001.

Kennedy, Eugene. *The Now and Future Church*. Doubleday, 1984.

Khan, Hazrat Inayat. *The Sufi Message of Hazrat Inayat Khan.* International Headquarters of the Sufi Movement (Geneva), 1979.

Küng, Hans et al. *Christianity and the World Religions.* Doubleday, 1986.

Laubach, Frank. *Forty Years with the Silent Billion.* Fleming Revell, 1970.

Lewis, C.S. *The Abolition of Man.* Collier, 1962.

Lodahl, Michael E. *Shekhinah/Spirit: Divine Presence in Jewish and Christian Religion.* Paulist Press, 1992.

Martin, P.W. *Experiment in Depth.* Pantheon, 1955.

Matthews, Caitlin and John. *The Encyclopedia of Celtic Wisdom.* Element Books, 1994.

McGreal, Ian P., ed. *Great Thinkers of the Eastern World.* HarperCollins, 1995.

Meister, Charles W. *Religion: Bane or Blessing?* New Falcon Publications, 2000.

Miller, Perry, ed. *The American Puritans.* Doubleday, 1956.

Muhaiyaddeen, M.R. Bawa. *Islam and World Peace: Explanations of a Sufi.* Fellowship Press, 1987.

Nicholas of Cusa: Selected Spiritual Writings. H. Lawrence Bond, tr. Paulist Press, 1997.

Niebuhr, Reinhold. *The Self and the Dramas of History.* Scribners, 1955.

Olin, John C, ed. *Christian Humanism and the Reformation.* Fordham University Press, 1975.

Panikkar, Raimon. *A Dwelling Place for Wisdom.* Westminster/John Knox Press, 1993.

—— *The Intra-Religious Dialogue.* Paulist Press, 1978.

Parrington, Vernon L. *Main Currents in American Thought.* Harcourt Brace, 1930.

Patai, Raphael. *The Hebrew Goddess.* 3rd ed. Wayne State University Press, 1990.

Perry, Marvin and Frederick Schweitzer, eds. *Jewish-Christian Encounters Over the Centuries.* Peter Lang, 1994.

Phillips, J.B. *God Our Contemporary.* Hodder & Stoughton, 1960.

Powell, Robert A. *The Most Holy Trinosophia and the New Revelation of the Divine Feminine*. Anthroposophic Press, 2000.

Progoff, Ira. *Depth Psychology and Modern Man*. McGraw-Hill, 1973.

Radhakrishnan, Sarvepalli. *East and West in Religion*. Allen and Unwin, 1967.

Reiser, Oliver L. *Cosmic Humanism and World Unity*. Gordon and Breach, 1975.

Renou, Louis, ed. *Hinduism*. Braziller, 1962.

Ruether, Rosemary Radford. *Sexism and God-Talk: Toward a Feminist Theology*. Beacon Press, 1986.

Schell, Jonathan. *The Fate of the Earth*. Avon Books, 1982.

Schneiders, Sandra M. *With Oil in Their Lamps: Faith, Feminism, and the Future*. Paulist Press, 2000.

—— *Women and the Word*. Paulist Press, 1986.

Sells, Michael A., ed. *Early Islamic Mysticism*. Paulist Press, 1996.

Shah, Idries. *The Way of the Sufi*. Dutton, 1970.

Shannon, Thomas A. *What Are They Saying About Peace and War?* Paulist Press, 1983.

Sharma, Arvind, ed. *Women in World Religions*. State University of New York Press, 1987.

Sjöö, Monica and Barbara Mor. *The Great Cosmic Mother: Rediscovering the Religion of the Earth*. HarperSanFrancisco, 1991.

Slater, Robert L. *World Religions and World Community*. Columbia University Press, 1963.

Smoot, George and Keay Davidson. *Wrinkles in Time*. William Morrow, 1993.

Solovyov, Vladimir. *The Meaning of Love*. Lindisfarne Press, 1985.

Spretnak, Charlene. *Lost Goddesses of Early Greece*. Moon Books, 1978.

Stone, Merlin. *When God Was A Woman*. Dorset Press, 1990.

Swidler, Leonard. *The Meaning of Life at the Edge of the Third Millennium*. Paulist Press, 1992.

Tagore, Rabindranath. *Gitanjali*. Macmillan, 1970.

Talbot, Michael. *The Holographic Universe*. HarperPerennial, 1992.

Teilhard de Chardin, Pierre. *The Phenomenon of Man*. Harper & Row, 1965.

Telesco, Patricia. *365 Goddesses: A Daily Guide*. HarperSanFrancisco, 1998.

Tillich, Paul. *A History of Christian Thought*. Simon & Schuster, 1972.

Tipler, Frank J. *The Physics of Immortality*. Doubleday, 1994.

Torrance, Thomas F. *Theology in Reconciliation*. Eerdmans, 1976.

Toynbee, Arnold. *A Study of History*. Oxford University Press, 1957. Abridgment of volumes 7–10 by D.C. Somervell.

Trible, Phyllis. *God and the Rhetoric of Sexuality*. Fortress Press, 1978.

Unamuno, Miguel de. *Tragic Sense of Life*. Dover Publications, 1954.

Wilber, Ken. *Eye to Eye*. Anchor, 1983.

—— *The Spectrum of Consciousness*. Theosophical Publishing House, 1985.

—— *Up From Eden*. Shambhala, 1983.

Wilson, Frank A. *The Work of Creation*. Coventure, 1985.

Witteveen, H.J. *Universal Sufism*. Element Books, 1997.

Yagi, Seiichi and Leonard Swidler. *A Bridge to Buddhist-Christian Dialogue*. Paulist Press, 1990.

Zimmer, Heinrich. *Myths and Symbols in Indian Art and Civilization*. Harper, 1962.

Zukav, Gary. *The Dancing Wu Li Masters*. Bantam, 1980.

The paradox of religion is that it is at once responsible for both the highest achievements and the cruelest inhumanity in human history. How can we understand this enigma? *Divisive* religion separates person from person, and sometimes people from God. On the other hand, *unitive* religion has produced unparalleled heights of love, compassion, and forgiveness. This book is dedicated to encouraging and advancing dialogue among people of diverse and sometimes seemingly incompatible belief systems. If we can do this, we can improve the lives of *all* people and bring greater peace to the planet.

ISBN 1-56184-141-2

New Falcon Publications

Invites You to Visit Our Website:
http://www.newfalcon.com

At the Falcon website you can:

- Browse the online catalog of all of our great titles
- Find out what's available and what's out of stock
- Get special discounts
- Order our titles through our secure online server
- Find products not available anywhere else including:
    - One of a kind and limited availability products
    - Special packages
    - Special pricing
- Get free gifts
- Join our email list for advance notice of New Releases and Special Offers
- Find out about book signings and author events
- Send email to our authors (including the elusive Dr. Christopher Hyatt!)
- Read excerpts of many of our titles
- Find links to our author's websites
- Discover links to other weird and wonderful sites
- And much, much more

Get online today at http://www.newfalcon.com